'Making her debut, Schwartz offers a novel created with the discipline of a seasoned pro ... The author endows Jenny and her circle with attributes that make them linger in one's memory'

Publishers Weekly

'I enjoyed the movie,' he said afterwards, 'but you gave it stiff competition.'

I asked him what he meant.

'Your face,' he said, 'everything that played on the screen – every emotion – played on your face. After a while I didn't know which I should watch, your face or the film, so I divided my time equally. But if I had just watched you and listened to the sound track, I wouldn't have missed a thing.'

I became flustered. 'I didn't realize,' I started to say.

Nat interrupted me. 'Don't be self-conscious. This ability you have, this exquisite responsiveness, is a gift. I wish I had it.'

Realities

MARIAN SCHWARTZ

SPHERE BOOKS LIMITED
30-32 Gray's Inn Road, London WC1X 8JL

To my children

*If you don't have the ability to begin
again, you don't have grace*

Martha Graham

My children are gambling. They are sitting in front of the television set screaming for horse number seven in the second race. It is my daughter's turn to hold the ticket, color coded and included with the week's groceries. Cereal, milk and racing tickets: staples of life. She is waving it in her six-year-old hand, screaming at horse number seven to run faster. Her cheeks are pink with excitement; they still haven't lost their baby roundness, yet she urges that horse on like a seasoned pro at the track.

Groceries and racing tickets. Why not? Nothing is in bad taste anymore; everything that exists can be promoted. I try to imagine the ad man who dreamed up a night at the races with Ringer's Supermarkets. Does he have children? Does he care about his children if he has them? No matter. He cares more about his baby, 'Saturday Night at the Races with Ringer's Supermarkets.' A winner for every race. A commercial between every race. Five races and five commercials. The commercials run longer than the races, a sponsor's dream.

The ad man has his job for another year. He is almost safe.

I let the children watch and scream for horses that will finish last, but I won't let it happen again. Next week I'll shop at another chain, one with a promotion for dishes or washcloths. Tonight I didn't have a choice. When I told them they couldn't watch the races, they argued: 'Daddy would let us. He wouldn't care.' I relented, fearing another round of questions. The questions are becoming frequent. Is our daddy really dead? How did he die? Why did he die?

I have gone back to that night, studied the seconds of every minute like a jeweler examining the facets in a gemstone, and found nothing, not a clue.

It was a Thursday like any Thursday. You came home at six thirty. We had dinner with the children – roast beef, baked potato, salad, and ice cream. After dinner, they watched television. You went upstairs to your study. I gave the children their baths and put them to bed. You went to their rooms to say good night, looking preoccupied. It was not unusual. You generally wore that look when you came out of your study. We had no social plans for the evening, no meetings or parties. You went back to your study. I took a bath. You were still in your study. I put on a robe, checked my calendar for Friday, and went downstairs. It was ten o'clock. I picked up some needlepoint and turned on the television. A commercial for trash bags was on the air. I remembered that you hadn't taken out the garbage. I went back upstairs and knocked on the door of your study. You didn't ask me to come in. Again, nothing unusual. 'Tomorrow is garbage day,' I said, trying to speak loud enough to penetrate the door without waking the children. 'The garbage in the kitchen needs emptying, too.' I heard your chair swivel. 'I'll take care of it,' you said. I returned to the family room. You came down an hour later with some papers in your hand. The eleven o'clock news was just beginning. You picked up the trash container in the kitchen, which was the only unusual thing about that evening. You generally emptied the garbage after dinner. Garbage in the house offended you.

'I'm going to bed now,' I said, turning the television off.

'I'll take care of the garbage,' you replied.

You took the garbage into the garage. I knew it would be a while before you were finished. You always put the garbage into plastic bags and carried them to the street. You took care of the garbage the same way you took care of everything else; our garbage was lined up each week in

2

a straight, neat row at the curb. Each bag was perfectly balanced.

I went upstairs, checked on the children, brushed my teeth, and set the alarm. I was in bed with the light out at eleven fifteen. You were still in the garage.

I must have fallen asleep immediately. I rolled over at one o'clock and realized you weren't there. You had been having difficulty sleeping, so your absence wasn't unexpected. Some nights you would go to bed, lie still at first, then toss for a while, moving your legs as though they were painfully cramped, and finally get up. You had always been a heavy sleeper, able to block out the children's cries at night, thunderstorms, even my first attempts to awaken you when my labor pains were coming eight minutes apart with Catherine. The insomnia came suddenly, like a bad cold, a few years before your death. We had argued about it. I wanted you to go to Barney Leadman for a checkup. You refused. I insisted. You said it was your insomnia, not mine, and you had no intention of discussing it with Barney. I didn't understand, then. It was another argument to add to the neat stack we were accumulating like a pile of canceled checks. Today I understand the insomnia, if nothing else.

I couldn't fall back to sleep. I wish I could say it was intuition, or some kind of premonition, but that wouldn't be true. I was trying to decide upon an outfit to wear to the Foxes' cocktail party Friday night. I had narrowed it down to the blue or the black. Your life had already been extinguished, and I was lying in bed debating the relative merits of dresses versus pants.

By two o'clock, I had mentally cleaned my closet without making a decision. The blue and the black no longer appealed to me. I got out of bed and checked on the children. When I looked in your study and you weren't there, I went downstairs. There was a hum, the noise of a running engine. It was coming from the garage. I opened the door and found you. You had taken care of the garbage first.

I have gone back over that evening and found nothing, not a clue. You knew you were going to do it. When I forced myself to enter your study the next day, the sum of our life together was neatly arranged on the desk: the insurance policies, the deed to the house, the key to the safety deposit box. Your last act before emptying the garbage was to show us how to obtain the rudiment of our existence, the money to survive. Nothing was missing; everything was there but you.

The funeral was fast and private. I was numb. There were words spoken, but I cannot remember what was said. By the time you were lowered into the ground, I could no longer see. I just stood in place like a mannequin until someone steered me into the waiting limousine.

I didn't cry until almost a year later. You know that the women in our family don't cry, at least not in public. If one must cry, it is done in the privacy of one's room. With the door closed. I didn't sleep in our room – my room – after you died, so I couldn't cry. I slept in the spare room like a guest in my own house and never closed the door.

That was the one thing about me you always admired: I wasn't a crier. I didn't use tears to get what I wanted or hit you with them when we fought. I was fair, you always said. You should have thanked my mother for that.

I believe I should curse her for it.

The tears came when I went to visit your grave. I started to drive to the cemetery a number of times but always turned back until that day. It was easier for me to accept your death as a permanently extended absence than to see the reality of it, the neat plot and the headstone with your name and dates carved in polished granite.

RICHARD WEAVER
1942–1975

The stone is in good taste, Richard. You would have approved.

I had difficulty finding you. A sense of direction has

4

never been one of my strong points, which is why I could never protest when you told people I could get lost in my own backyard. 'Jenny has problems finding her way to the bathroom,' you used to say. You weren't always kind.

In case you are interested, you are buried on the extreme right side of Section 9 in Forest Heights Cemetery. By the time I spotted your stone, I must have walked better than half a mile on soggy grass looking at strange names on headstones. My shoes were soaked and muddy. I was tired and aggravated, ready for a fight. I stood at the foot of your grave, unbuttoned my coat, and threw it open. 'Look at me, Richard,' I said. 'Look at me. I'm five feet five and weigh one hundred twelve pounds. I'm svelte, as thin as you always wanted me to be. I've lost twenty pounds since you died.'

Quoting figures to a dead husband on the first belated visit to his grave, the last visit before leaving permanently. I was still your wife, a statistic-spouting wife of a CPA, although until that time I hadn't realized it. Did I quote figures when you were alive?

I am beginning to discover things about myself, about the way I was when you were alive. Discoveries aren't always pleasant. That is one of the things I have discovered.

I don't know what I expected, speaking to you as though you would rise out of the grass, sit on the headstone with your legs crossed, and congratulate me for my weight loss.

You didn't materialize. I was ready for a fight, expecting you to sit there and take credit for my figure. I could almost hear you saying, 'My death did it.' I had the perfect rebuttal. I was going to tell you the weight loss was mine because you weren't there, forever counting the calories I consumed without subtracting one for chewing. It would have made a great argument.

When you didn't appear, I buttoned my coat. Your death was no longer an extended absence. It was a fact.

Even after I had sold the house, given your clothes to

the Salvation Army, and packed for California, your death wasn't real. It was a nightmare, but nightmares are never real. They aren't supposed to be real. You wake up and they are gone. I woke up when I buttoned my coat. The nightmare was still there.

'Why, Richard?' I cried to the headstone. 'Why?'

The waste of your death stood before me mute, hands extended, palms up and empty.

I sobbed until I was reduced to watery hiccups. The hiccups lasted for hours. I still get them occasionally, especially at night after the children are in bed. They start suddenly and for no apparent reason. None of the remedies I've tried has helped, so I alternately hold my breath and hiccup until I fall asleep, exhausted.

When I meet people and they inquire politely about my husband, I say, 'I am a widow,' and lower my eyes. The sign language of facial expression generally works. Most people understand lowered eyelids. They say, 'Oh, I'm sorry,' and change the subject or stand awkwardly until I do it for them, much to their relief and mine. I have become quite adept at changing the subject.

Others aren't put off that easily. If they pursue the circumstances of my widowhood, the when, how, or why, I close my eyes completely and whisper, 'It was recent.' Few people dare trespass over closed eyelids. For the inquisitive few who do, I give my finest performance. When they ask, 'How did he die?', I hesitate, choke, clear my throat slightly, and manage to croak three words: 'in a car.' If I am standing, I turn and look for a chair. If I am sitting, I stand and excuse myself, barely managing to get the words out. Bernhardt couldn't do it any better. But then, she didn't have as much time to rehearse and polish a single act.

I don't know how much is an act and how much is real. I do choke sometimes when I think of your death. Or I hiccup. My throat muscles constrict and the saliva in my mouth evaporates. And I do lower my eyes, as if to shut the world or the memory out. It doesn't work, though. I see you silhouetted against my eyelids, sharp and clear, slumped in the seat of your Mercedes in the oak-paneled garage.

Matthew and Catherine are entitled to more than the evasions I use with strangers, but your choice of death hasn't made it easy. Oh, I could tell them the basic facts. I could start out by saying, 'Your daddy killed himself.' That's basic. But where do I go from there? I want to give them something more than a daddy who killed himself because he couldn't face what he had done or the people he had done it to. I want to give them – I hesitate to use the word – I want to give them an honorable death. A death with honor. Immaculate. Pure and honest. A death they can attach healthy memories to. And I don't know how to do it.

At dinner tonight, Catherine asked, 'How old would Daddy be?'

'Why?' I asked, dreading another round of how-and-why-did-Daddy-die questions.

'Lisa's daddy is forty and he's bald,' she said. 'Was our daddy bald?'

'No,' I answered, 'Daddy wasn't bald.'

'Well, how old was Daddy when he died?' she persisted.

'Daddy was thirty-three,' I said, firmly but nonchalantly in an effort to end the conversation.

'Would he be bald if he were here now?'

'Do you think he would be bald?'

'No, I wouldn't want Daddy to be bald,' she said. 'Does dying make you stop getting bald?'

'What do you think?' I asked. 'And what do you think about chocolate cupcakes for dessert?'

The diversionary tactics worked. I fed our daughter sweets and answered her questions. It isn't always as easy as it was this time. How long can a dam built with cupcakes last?

We have lived in California for over a year, and it still doesn't seem real to me. It could be because of my choice of site, Sherwood Village, a residential complex of apartments and townhouses that out-Tudors anything we saw in England. Tudor with palm trees under perpetual sun – an unresearched movie set. I wake up in the morning and don't know where I am.

I don't know why I picked Sherwood Village. It could have been for practical reasons. It was new and clean and had recreational facilities for the children: a swimming pool, a playground, bicycle paths, tennis courts. But other places had the same things.

I could have picked it because it had palm trees instead of chimneys, because it tried so hard to be what it was not.

I could have picked it because it reminded me for a moment of our trip to England, the last happy vacation we took together. Everything in our lives was perfect. You had made a lot of money in the stock market, and I was pregnant with Catherine. Six months later we moved into our house in Eagles' Landing. Nothing was the same after that.

I don't know why I am writing this down, either, why I am writing to you, Richard Weaver, deceased. Old ladies talk to dead husbands. I am thirty-two, hardly old, more approaching the middle I would say. But I should be exact. The widow of a CPA should be precise with figures. I am thirty-two and approaching middle age. If my life meets the latest expectations of the actuarial tables, barring a fatal illness or accident, I should be entering middle age in four years. A comforting thought: the tables give me four more years of relative youth.

I work at a place called Briarhill Retirement Home. Yes, Richard, I am working. And getting paid. There is something to be said for getting paid for one's labor. I worked harder as a volunteer when we lived in Eagles' Landing than I do now, and it didn't mean as much. But the motivation behind it was different: volunteering was the thing to do in Eagles' Landing. Work hard to be accepted on the right Junior Board of the right hospital. Work for the art gallery but not for the zoo. I remember how pleased you were when I was nominated to be on the committee to nominate a nominating committee for the Philharmonic. Our stock rose twenty social points.

There are no social points for working at Briarhill. To be honest, I took the job because I couldn't find one anywhere else where I could work part-time. It's hard to find a job in California, any job, unless you're well connected. Your wife and children no longer belong to that select group, so I had to accept the best of a poor selection.

Actually, it isn't too bad, and it's close to where we live, another rarity in these parts. People in California think nothing of driving over an hour, one way, to get to work. They are probably the same ones who complained if they lived more than thirty minutes from their jobs when they lived in the East, or South, or wherever they came from. California is a state of transplanted people, and their momentum doesn't seem to decrease after they arrive. They just keep moving. Cars are important here. More than important. Cars are a necessity of life, and sometimes they tell more about a man than his clothes.

Briarhill is not exactly a nursing home, or at least it didn't start out that way. The man who built it, Simon Gentile, was sharp. When he was in his mid-fifties, running hard to catch his final dreams, he had a heart attack. Mortality and the process of getting there became real to him, and when his wife died quickly of cancer a year later, he became temporarily disconnected.

Simon was a neat man. He wanted his meals on time, his laundry done, and his room immaculate without marrying again. It was too great a risk. When he couldn't find a residential hotel that would give him the service he wanted, he looked around him. One overwhelmingly clear fact presented itself: his generation was going to die within the next two decades. Simon decided to gamble his final fortune on it. He would build a residential home to anticipate his contemporaries' needs and meet his own at the same time.

Simon built Briarhill in the late fifties. As long as he was going to live there, he had to be selective about the people who lived with him without overtly discriminating. He decided upon a lump-sum deposit of fifty thousand dollars to be paid as a kind of entrance fee, much like a country club initiation fee. The residents would pay a monthly bill to cover the cost of their share of running the home. The original Briarhill looked like a country club. It was a sprawling brick southern-style building on one level. The rooms were all private, elegantly furnished, and had their own baths. Each wing had a separate living room and game room.

It was a terrific idea, and Simon promoted it with finesse. He got the people he wanted by charging a stiff entrance fee, made an enormous profit, and had his place to live. I understand that all the rooms in the original building were filled before construction was completed, with applicants who were active people, either retired or semiretired. Couples lived there, also.

When Medicare came through, Simon literally raised the roof. He added a second floor and then a third. Again, his timing was perfect. Some of the original residents were running out of money; others had become ill. Today the active aged are on the first floor, those who need custodial care are on the second floor, and the seriously ill are on the third floor. Briarhill residents lower their voices to whispers when they mention the third floor. They say, 'He [or she] was taken to the third floor.' Then their voices fade and their eyes seem to go temporarily out of focus.

I have never visited the third floor.

Simon told me the story of Briarhill on one of his better days. He is in his late seventies now, crippled with arthritis, and he has been having anginal attacks. Simon seems to view his physical limitations as a minor inconvenience. He whips down the halls in his wheelchair like

10

a teenager playing with a toy, his sharp brown eyes darting everywhere at once behind steel-rimmed glasses. Nothing escapes him. His vigor is so much a part of his presence that I sometimes forget he is old and bald and round-shouldered. Simon will never arrive on the third floor. He would successfully will himself dead before he would allow that to happen.

There is an elderly man at Briarhill named John Gallisdorf. He is seventy-nine and paralysed on his left side as the result of a stroke. He has a thin gray mustache that he trims carefully every day with his right hand. He was left-handed, and the effort this must take astounds me; the mustache is always impeccably clipped.

There is a gentle quality about the man, a courtliness and simple dignity that draws me to him. I cannot show favoritism as the recreation director, but it is difficult to hide my fondness for Mr Gallisdorf, and I find myself seeking him out before leaving if I don't see him during the day. Lately, I haven't had to do that. He seems to find me, either by coincidence or deliberately, before I leave. It isn't easy for him to get around, which flatters me. He maneuvers his wheelchair with his good arm and never complains.

Perhaps that is what originally attracted me to Mr Gallisdorf: he never complains. I know there are times when he is in pain, but he bears it silently, without anger or whimpering. He sits in his wheelchair as straight as he can, his mustache crisp and even, always wearing a spotless white shirt, and exchanges daily pleasantries with the staff and residents.

When he is around, a perceptible change takes place in the residents, particularly those who need a certain amount of custodial care. I don't think they like him. He seems to embarrass the ones who are mentally alert. They don't complain about their aches and pains within his hearing, and the residents who have grown careless about their physical appearance rub their beards or adjust their dresses in his presence. Even I put my bitterness in my pocket

11

when I am with him. My problems don't disappear, but the rancor seems to subside.

He spends most of his time reading, mainly history, a subject I could never stand because it just repeated with different men in different battles. Besides his reading, he participates occasionally in the bridge tournaments and attends the lighter movies.

Mr Gallisdorf has told me only a few things about himself, and those out of politeness in response to my questions. He was married for forty-two years and is a widower. There were no children. He volunteers nothing more, and it is clear that one does not ask.

I have told him little about myself. He knows I am a widow with two children. He inquires about the children but doesn't mention my husband, as if sensing that the subject isn't welcome, although I have said nothing to deter him from asking.

Perhaps I have by volunteering nothing.

Simon's son, James, runs Briarhill now. Jim Gentile was a physical education teacher until he saw how well Briarhill was succeeding. He took some courses in hospital administration and presented himself at Simon's door. One of the oldest ambulatory residents told me Jim had a hard time persuading Simon to let him in. I can see why. Jim Gentile is an ass in a polyester leisure suit.

I have never met anyone like Jim Gentile. He is fortyish, a faded-blond ex-jock with pale, almost colorless blue eyes. His face and body are growing paunchy at an equally fast rate, and he has funny skin, the kind that blotches rather than tans. His perception of himself, however, is what is most astounding about the man. Jim Gentile thinks he is irresistible: suave, bright, macho. He is a living caricature of himself.

Jim has been pursuing me since I started working at Briarhill. He's married and has children, but that hasn't deterred him. He constantly refers to my widowhood as my 'unfortunate condition,' making it sound like a debilitating disease, and has told me a number of times that what I really need is a 'full life.' What he means, of course, is a sex life, and he has offered his services in blatant innuendoes that I have found not only offensive, but insulting. He seems to feel that I should be grateful for his attention, if for no other reason than that he is a man. I am not grateful. Unfortunately, he hasn't noticed.

When Jim isn't chasing me, he is shifting his work to my desk. He hired me at slightly above minimum wage to plan and supervise recreation ('Planning fun and games doesn't require skill,' he said), but lately I have had to take care of some of his correspondence and handle difficult relatives of the residents, as well as run errands and place small orders to suppliers. A raise in pay has not been mentioned. Jim's salary is outrageous, and I am helping him earn it.

Although Jim is the administrator of Briarhill, Simon still sets the basic policies. No one is admitted without paying the fee, which has risen to one hundred thousand dollars. There is a long waiting list, and the people who are called are the biggest potential profit makers. Money, however, is not a guarantee of admission. Simon personally screens the applicants, and like a host compiling a guest list, he makes his selections carefully.

The first person I met when I went for my interview at Briarhill was Ellen Cooledge, Jim Gentile's secretary. I was taken aback when I saw her, because she looks like Aunt Maggie. I would guess that Ellen is in her early fifties. She is taller than Maggie and her hair is dyed blond, but she has the same facial structure – the fine patrician nose, the deep-set eyes, the quick broad smile. I must have stared at her stupidly, for she asked me if something was wrong. 'You remind me of someone,' I said. If Jim Gentile hadn't come out of his office, I would have excused myself and left.

After I started working at Briarhill, I became aware of Ellen's special position. She is officially Jim's secretary, but she has lunch with Simon several times a week in his private quarters. They are long lunches. I am positive Ellen reports everything that goes on in Jim's office to Simon, but the length of their lunches and passing remarks made by the nursing staff have led me to believe that their relationship is more than business.

Ellen is as crisp and efficient as the tailored clothes she wears. In the beginning, she helped me schedule activities and tactfully offered suggestions in a casual manner that I later realized were vital to the success of my job. Although I am grateful, I still find it difficult to look at her. Instead of Ellen, I see Maggie. Then I remember Florida and Maggie's death. I avoid Ellen whenever possible and keep the past at a safe distance.

I don't know why I told you the history of Briarhill.

That is wrong. I do know why. My nights are lonely after the children go to bed. I have no one to talk to. There have been moments when I've caught myself speaking to you as if you were alive. Once Catherine overheard me and came downstairs. 'Where's our company?' she asked when she saw there were no guests in our living room.

I was mortified. 'Oh, it was just Mommy singing,' I said. Then I hummed a few bars of a song I had heard on the radio that afternoon to convince her.

I think she was satisfied with my lie, but I was shaken. The children cannot have doubts about me. There is a mutual dependency between us that didn't exist before. Matthew, Catherine, and I are like a tripod: we must stand together to stand at all. That is why I must find a way to tell them the truth. We are so delicately balanced, the slightest wind shift could topple us.

In the beginning, after your death I mean, I wasn't bitter. The bitterness came later. It took root in the shallow remains of my life and grew there, a common weed, until it became the primary growth, the dominating emotion. I did not cry, of course, but neither did I laugh, except with the children. I had not realized how much of life is anticipation, how much is hope, how precious are the rare moments of joy. It is an insidious thing, this wild growth

14

of bitterness, for it kills long before the victim is aware of loss. I have suffered losses, Richard. Even survivors don't come out whole.

Fortunately, the children escaped bitterness. They both remember you, Matthew more than Catherine, only they speak of you with a kind of detachment that must be special to childhood. You are something they had once that is gone, like an afternoon at a puppet show. They haven't seen you for almost two years, and although I have not asked, I'm fairly sure they would have difficulty describing you. I believe you have become a part of the patchwork in their quilt of dreams.

It is at once a relief and disquieting, this resiliency our children have. They have adapted well to California, much better than their mother. I hide here; they live here. When Eagles' Landing is mentioned, which isn't often, they say, 'Oh, where we used to live' as if it were a town they had once passed through and stopped in for lunch.

The memories Matthew clipped to save in his scrapbook of childhood are the ones I wish he would forget. His most vivid memory of Eagles' Landing is of Adam Lynch. For this, I can't fault him. Who could forget Adam Lynch, little Adam with a streak of black cruelty running from his sticklike ankles to the roots of his carrot hair? Matthew talks about the time Adam picked up a baseball bat and whacked him on the head with it, over and over again, because he didn't like the game they were playing. I can still hear Matthew's screams. Sylvia Lynch was outside when it happened, and when I ran out to see why Matthew was screaming, she grabbed Adam and comforted him.

'Adam didn't mean it,' she said, burying his head between her breasts as if she were afraid I would decapitate him. 'You didn't mean it, Adam, did you sweetheart?'

Adam shoved his face into her left breast.

'See, Matthew. Adam didn't mean it. Come home with Mommy, Adam. We'll have a Popsicle.'

As I think back, Matthew couldn't have been more than four or five at the time. He had three raised lumps on his

15

head, the one on his forehead enormous and discolored. When you came home and I told you what had happened, I asked you what you were going to do about it, if you were going to say anything to Bruce or Sylvia about Adam.

'Did you say anything to Sylvia when it happened?' you asked.

'No,' I replied, 'I was too upset, and then she whisked Adam away. Matthew was screaming. We were both frightened. I was afraid he had a concussion.'

'It's too late now to say anything.'

'You have to talk to the Lynches. This isn't the first time he's gone after Matthew, and it will happen again. Adam is a monster.'

'We'll tell Matthew to stay away from Adam until he learns to fight back. He has to be able to defend himself,' you said with a shrug.

'Are you afraid of offending Bruce Lynch? Is that it?' I asked, furious at your indifference.

'Don't be ridiculous,' you said, walking away. 'Adults shouldn't get involved in their children's fights.'

'Matthew wasn't fighting,' I replied after you were already out of the room. You always did that. You left the room when a disagreement started getting tacky. Your final lines were always delivered with your back to me; I couldn't argue with your shoulder blades.

I knew why you walked away that time. By avoiding me, you could avoid offending Bruce Lynch. Bruce had money, his father's old money, and the bank the money came from. When we were discussing building a home in Eagles' Landing, you hesitated until the developer showed you Bruce Lynch's lot. That clinched it. You bought our lot because of its proximity to the Lynches'. You cultivated Bruce like a prize rosebush, and I had to be nice to Sylvia, whose primary challenges in life were displaying her cleavage and decorating her house. When I think of the deadly evenings we endured listening to Bruce talk about his gun collection while Sylvia posed with her breasts resting on the tablecloth, as if they were ample reward for being in her presence, I feel sick. But at the time those evenings were important to us. We were living in the right place and dining with the right people.

I remember when we first saw Eagles' Landing, how impressed we were with the entrance, the brick archway that had 'Eagles' Landing Estates' affixed in large gothic letters. We were so mesmerized by the expensive homes with their three-car garages, the gaslight lampposts, and the long, winding driveways, that we didn't notice the mosquitoes or the lots that were partially filled with water. The developer had bought a parcel of swampland, called it a restricted subdivision, and promoted it in a style worthy of Simon Gentile to make a fortune.

Richard, I wasn't aware of what he had done until this moment. I had to move three thousand miles away to understand.

And I remember how it was after we moved in. The neighbors' snubs made it clear to me within weeks that we were undesirables. 'Who in the hell do they think they are?' I exploded, angry and hurt after a month of being ignored. 'I want out.'

'No, you don't,' you replied firmly. 'Be patient. It will take a little longer than I had planned to break into Eagles' Landing, but we'll belong.'

'You knew?' I asked, shocked. 'Why didn't you warn me? We could have built a house where the people are civil.'

'I wasn't sure,' you hedged. 'I didn't know which way it would go. Besides, the Lynches and the Foxes live here.'

You did know, Richard. I was almost sure when you avoided my eyes and positive when you mentioned the Lynches.

You waited until I was calm. Then you talked about the importance of the people in Eagle's Landing, of the affluent newcomers and the others, the ones like the Lynches with inherited names and wealth, and you explained how their influence could help you. 'Their acceptance will put us in the big leagues,' you said in that convincing way you had. 'It's simple – success by association. Once we're accepted, I'll be able to open my own accounting firm. Our Eagles' Landing connections will practically guarantee blue chip clients. But I can't do it alone, Jenny. Unfortunately, you'll have to do most of the groundwork. It will be through your efforts that we gain acceptance. After that . . .' Your voice trailed off; it was caught on a dream.

And so it began. I volunteered at the Philharmonic and the Art Gallery and inched my way into the Junior League. There was also the seasonal work of the United Way, not to mention the fund raising drives for the new theater. I smiled at women I detested and quickly learned to spot and grab the jobs that would earn me the greatest publicity. Mrs Richard Weaver became a familiar name on the society pages of the newspapers, and within two years my face, in stilted photographs with other Eagles' Landing wives, accompanied my name.

I worked harder than I had ever worked in my life. I made a career out of Eagles' Landing. There were morning meetings and afternoon meetings. There were benefit luncheons, social luncheons, and cocktail parties. In the evenings, there were dinner parties and nights at the country club. Our bedroom reminded me of a hotel room, a place for a quick shower and change of clothes. By the end of our first year in Eagles' Landing, we were on almost everyone's guest list. Midway through our second year, we were a favored couple.

All of that work, Richard. For what? So that I could spend a year as a prisoner in my own house? I know it sounds ridiculous, but I wish you could have been there to see how the Lynches behaved after you died. They were solicitous in the beginning. Then, as the reason for your death became clear, they were the first to turn their backs on me and the children. They led the pack. Your wife and children were outcasts; the Lynches decreed it, and the decree held.

18

Bruce felt your death where it hurt him most. Whenever I saw him, he looked at me as though I were unclean, his thin lips curled in disgust. I knew his schedule and stayed in the house when he left in the morning and returned at night. It was the first time in my life that I was grateful for human rigidity. Nothing varied in Bruce's schedule. I believe he urinated at the same time every day.

There were pleasant evenings when I wanted to go outside. I could never go for a walk. I stayed in the backyard with Catherine and tried to keep Matthew with us, too. I didn't want to stand in front of the house to call him home. From evenings of enduring the Lynches, I went to evenings of imprisonment by having to avoid them.

Matthew's days were curtailed as well as his nights. He wouldn't go out to play if Adam was already out, and he would come home if Adam decided to join the children he was playing with. I think Bruce would have given Adam one of his guns to finish Matthew off with if he thought he could get away with it.

I wonder if Matthew sensed that I was thinking about him. I just came back from his room; he was moaning in his sleep, probably having a bad dream. I was going to wake him up but hesitated when I heard him speak, softly and rather unintelligibly, the tone earnest, almost placating. He wasn't stuttering. Poor Matthew. His bad dreams let his tongue relax while his daily life keeps it twisted in knots, imprisoning sounds in his throat until I want to scream, weep, or shake him, anything to get the words out.

Matthew started to stutter approximately one month after you died. It wasn't too noticeable at first, just a little more hesitation than usual. The speech therapist I take him to says everyone hesitates when they speak. We are all nonfluent. Pauses like uh, ah, I mean, you know – they are acceptable nonfluencies people rely upon when they talk to fill the spaces between thoughts. Matthew's stutter is a secondary nonfluency, differing from what she calls a normal primary nonfluency. She doesn't like the word stutter either, preferring the term secondary nonfluency. Whatever it is called, it is a problem.

Matthew's speech was at its worst the last six months before we left Eagles' Landing and the first few months in California. He would start to say something, then gag trying to get a word out. His face would become red with either effort, frustration, or rage, or a combination of all three, and I would wait in agony, unable to do anything to help him. I tried supplying words, but it only made him angrier. Sometimes he would just look at me, his face flushed, tears running down his cheeks, his mouth open, his jaw locked on a blocked sound, and nothing would come out. Nothing. A piercing scream isn't as intense or as devastating.

Catherine started to speak for him. She seemed to do it naturally, in a casual, offhand manner, and Matthew accepted her help with the same spirit in which an inarticulate younger child relies upon an older sibling for speech. Matthew translated her wants into words when she was a baby. Now it was as if she were repaying the debt, compensating for his lack of speech with her own quick tongue. He wouldn't allow me the same privilege. Only his sister.

The speech therapist wants Catherine to stop supplying words for Matthew. We have talked to her about it and she promises to stop, but she still substitutes for him. I feel it would be damaging to reprimand her in front of Matthew, but when I mention it later, she either plays innocent or looks hurt and says, 'But Mommy, I only help when Matthew gets stuck.' I remind her that the teacher says Matthew must get himself unstuck. She sighs, tells me that she won't do it again, then continues to supply words for him. Catherine doesn't let go easily.

It is getting better. Matthew is becoming more articulate and is blocking less frequently. When he does block, he no longer chokes or gags, and the rage seems to have subsided from his eyes, although I can still see it there at times. I don't know how much of the improvement is due to the therapy and how much can be attributed to our move to California. I do know that the change in environment has helped. But California cannot be credited completely. Any move away from Eagles' Landing, far, far away, would have worked as well.

Sometimes when I look at our son, at his gray eyes fringed with thick black lashes so like yours, I catch my breath. But when his eyes meet mine, they are solemn, as if they have seen more than they can absorb. The expression in your eyes was never quite like that. Before we were married and after, almost until the end, the flecks of brown in your eyes were alternately full of mischief, laughter, and warmth, and the tiny bits of green pigment flashed your displeasure. I could look into your eyes and get an emotional reading. I wonder if Matthew's eyes will ever lose their solemnity, if someday a woman will be able to read love or tricks in them as I once did in yours.

Our son looks at me with the eyes of one who has borne witness.

It is starting to become a ritual, this nocturnal writing to you, a nightcap of sorts. I wait until the children are bathed and in bed. Then I read the paper, pour myself a glass of wine, and write. After two years of filling empty evenings with television and needlepoint or novels, I have a new interest: my late husband. We didn't spend as much time together when you were alive as I spend with you now.

My weeks are basically the same, one following the other as if they have been stamped from the same pattern. I feed the children breakfast and get them off to school. They are bussed, and I can see them board from the living room window. When the bus door closes, I put the dishes into the dishwasher, make the beds, shower, and leave for Briarhill. Mondays, Tuesdays, Thursdays, and Fridays never vary: I arrive at Briarhill a few minutes before nine o'clock and leave at two, in time to meet the children when they get home from school. Wednesdays are catch-all days reserved for shopping, errands, haircuts, cleaning, laundry – the necessary mechanics of daily life. I am able to spend entire Wednesdays without thinking.

Weekends have become as repetitious as weekdays. I take the children to the ocean, to amusement parks, on simple picnics, to the movies on rainy afternoons, and to anything special that comes around for them. Although I have the suspicion that I'm doing the children an injustice, I can't seem to escape the weekend-to-weekend cycle.

I wasn't aware of how easily people's lives form patterns until you died, how the daily business of living dictates our schedules. These past months have taught me that life rarely comes to a climax. Birth, marriage, death, the purchase of a house – life's climaxes – are infrequent. Perhaps that is what was wrong with our marriage: instead of living for each day, we stockpiled dreams. When we were first married, I would have been content to share the trivia of my days with you and listen to your office anecdotes during dinner, but you weren't interested. Your impatience made it clear to me that talking about the present was a waste of time unless it could be usefully applied to the future, the time when we would finally arrive. The birth of the children and the house in Eagles' Landing were important to us, but arriving was to be the big event, the one overwhelming climax.

Richard, it's just occurred to me that I never knew exactly what arriving meant. There was a lot more wrong with our marriage than I thought there was.

Aside from the loneliness, which I still haven't overcome, the biggest adjustment I had to make after you died was being a parent alone with two children. In Eagles' Landing, everything from golf clubs to families belonged in matched sets. Now that we live in California, I no longer feel quite so strange. Parents are alone here more often than not. The only thing that may be different in my case is that I am a female rather than a male alone with children on the weekends. Solo daddies greatly outnumber mommies in amusement parks, if one does not count married couples

who take their children for an occasional outing. I have noticed that single parents feel obligated to amuse their children, to 'show them a good time,' while couples do not seem to feel pushed in that direction. They can stay home on the weekend without guilt or excuses and water the lawn. But they do not have visiting days or feel obligated to be two parents in one.

It is an impossibility, this crazy notion of being two parents in one, a super androgynous being who can be both a mother and a father to a set of children. In the beginning, I tried. I was concerned, particularly about Matthew and the absence of an adult male in his life. There was no one to serve as a strong, companionable male image, not even a grandfather.

Your father had a heart attack three months after you died. He's a cardiac cripple now, counting the cholesterol in each mouthful of food he eats, and he wears a pedometer on his leg to make sure he gets the proper amount of daily exercise. The man is unswervingly compulsive. He hangs on to each day like a jailer to his set of keys, counting calories and steps to confirm his existence and to ensure another day of counting. Your mother spends her days helping your father count. Their life is joyless, filled with fear and consumed with counting. They can think of nothing else.

My father wasn't interested in giving Matthew male companionship. Being the man in a little boy's life, even if the little boy happened to be his grandson and in need, appealed to him as much as an early retirement. I tried to encourage a relationship between them, but it was impossible. I bought tickets to sports events – basketball games, football and baseball games – and my father suffered, audibly and at length. 'You know I'm not interested in sports,' he said. 'I never had the time when I was young. I worked. From the time I was ten, I worked. I'm still working. I can't relax by watching grown men chase a ball. Besides, I don't like beer.'

Matthew heard him. I wish my father had learned to

lower his voice in the course of his ongoing affair with work. Nothing has modified him. To his family he says what he thinks in a hundred-decibel voice and is hurt when someone tries to shut him up, so he raises the volume to make himself clear. I know you wouldn't be displeased that Matthew and my father didn't develop a close relationship – my father was not one of your favorite people – but Matthew was hurt. He felt that he had failed somehow without knowing why, for his grandpa took no more interest in him than he did in a traffic signal. He stopped for attendance to his family the same way he did for a red light: he paused for the necessary amount of time and continued, mildly resenting the interruption.

I do not honor my parents. I love them, but I do not honor them. Again, the word honor plagues me. The Commandment says 'Honor thy father and thy mother.' I take it to mean respect, veneration of age, a form of devotional gratitude to the bestowers of one's life. I do not believe that an act of procreation, whether by desire or by accident, entitles one to automatic honor.

I feel as though I have blasphemed in denying my mother and father honor. But I have seen them, not as they want to be seen, but as they are. They have left me no room. I am not unlike a sexually aware child who stumbles upon the fully disrobed parent of the opposite sex. There is an astonishing moment of revelation, immediately followed by acute embarrassment. It is too late to divert one's eyes; the image is forever fixed.

I was eleven when I saw my father naked. Until that time my knowledge of males was limited to fat cherubs in Renaissance paintings, a small replica of Michelangelo's David on a high shelf in the library, and a modest ink drawing in a sex-education pamphlet the Girl Scout leader had given each member of the troop after a film on menstruation. My mother read the pamphlet after I did, and I recall her saying something in a between-us-girls voice about how lucky I was to have such an informative booklet. The film on menstruation and the booklet on

basic reproduction (it alluded in one brief sentence to a penis mysteriously finding its way into a vagina, then leaped ahead to sperm and eggs) were more than she had as a girl. She was sure, she added, that the pamphlet would answer any questions I might have. Later, I overheard her tell my father that we had had a *meaningful talk*, and wasn't it marvelous to have *that business* over with so painlessly. She talked about how wonderful the modern way of handling these things was, so effortless she said, not at all tacky as it had been when she was a girl. She had fulfilled her duty, and it hadn't hurt a bit. The day's unqualified success was deserving of a second martini, which my father happily poured.

It was after dawn when I saw him. I had awakened with nausea and stomach cramps and went to my parents' bedroom. My mother was sleeping, and as I started to walk over to the bed, my father came out of their bathroom. Surrounded by a ring of black hair, his penis and testicles looked huge, purplish and rubbery in the dull morning light. He tried to turn his back casually and said something to me, probably asked me what I wanted, but I couldn't hear his words. My eyes wouldn't blink. I stood there trying to suppress my nausea, alternately fascinated and repelled, seeing only the large veined penis in its nest of black hair. The nausea finally won, and I ran from their bedroom to the hall bathroom dry heaving. For a long time afterward, I was uncomfortable in his presence. No matter where we were or what we were doing, at dinnertime or reading the paper in the living room, the moment would come when I would look at him and feel myself flush with embarrassment. There were times when I believe he sensed it, when his discomfiture matched mine.

I digress. I write about what was rather than what is. Contrary to what the modern gods of psychiatry preach, I find that the far past is safer than the near past; each year is another brick added to the firewall. (I considered seeing a psychiatrist several times but decided against it. My past is no one's business. Besides, why should I pay a stranger to listen to my life story when I can write to you? Not only is this economical, but I have unlimited time and a guarantee against interruption.)

I know that my parents have remained essentially the same, but I didn't know as much when I was eleven as I know now. The knowledge hurts. They have unwittingly revealed themselves to me and are unaware of their exposure. The embarrassment is mine alone.

I would never have been able to make this kind of admission when you were alive. It was impossible to acknowledge any weakness in my parents; you wouldn't let me relax. It seemed that you looked for their soft spots each time we were with them and after, when we were alone, you would press hard with a sarcastic crack. The remark was usually funny, but the underlying animosity was always there, most of it directed toward my father. He made you uncomfortable. I remember how he irritated you after we moved to Eagles' Landing with his pointed questions about your business affairs and the wisdom of opening your own accounting firm. 'I never asked to see his tax return,' you seethed. 'What right does he have to pry into mine?'

My father didn't have the right, and I was wrong to defend him. But with all of his faults, he wouldn't have killed himself. He believes that nothing is worth dying for, that no problem, however impossible, is worthy of the expenditure of one's life. I agree. If I didn't, I would have joined you. It hasn't been easy.

I couldn't fall asleep after I wrote to you last night. I kept thinking about the Commandment 'Honor thy father and thy mother.' I was positive there was more to it but couldn't remember the rest, so I went to Briarhill's library today to look for a Bible. I found one on the highest shelf in the reading room, clearly out of reach for residents in wheelchairs, and it was dusty. At first I thought Simon had bought it. He had purchased several hundred books when

Briarhill was completed and speaks of the books with great pride, as if they put Briarhill on a plane above other nursing homes. When I flipped back the cover, I saw that a rectangle that had held someone's name had been cut out of the cover page. The Bible had probably been part of a deceased resident's estate that relatives weren't interested in claiming; Briarhill's library has grown substantially with such books.

It took a bit of searching to find the Ten Commandments. I know it is absurd, but I was uneasy standing in Briarhill's library flipping through a Bible. I walked to a far corner of the room and turned a chair around so I could sit with my back to the door.

I found what I was looking for in Exodus. The man who wrote that section was thorough – you would have trusted him to prepare your tax statement. Not only are the Commandments fully listed, but laws pertaining to each one are enumerated. The laws, it seems, are for those who break the primary laws, which are the Commandments. Nothing has changed in five thousand years: men are still making new laws to enforce old laws, fully expecting the original laws to be broken.

The Commandment unsettled me. It says: 'Honor thy father and thy mother: that thy days may be long upon the land which the Lord thy God giveth thee.' What land can I relate to, an acre in Eagles' Landing that we owned together and I sold, or a rented townhouse in Sherwood Village? Neither seems to fit. I wasn't given an entire country, like the ancient Israelites.

I sat for a while and thought about the Commandment, trying to relate to it, when I heard a voice behind me. 'Mrs Weaver,' it said softly. I jumped out of the chair and turned, hiding the Bible behind my back as if it were a piece of hard-core pornography.

The voice belonged to Miss Manfred. Miss Manfred is a tiny, compactly built and corseted woman of about seventy. Her blued hair matches her eyes. She can't be more than five feet tall, and she totters around on the highest heels I have ever seen; some of them look like authentic antiques. No one can persuade her to wear lower heels, not even a visiting orthopedic surgeon who talked to her about the danger of falling and breaking a hip. 'My heels and I are inseparable,' she said to him. 'I have walked this way for over fifty years, young man [the doctor was in his forties], and I'm not about to change.' She put him down with the absolute authority of an old schoolteacher, and he walked away sheepishly.

Miss Manfred said she hoped she hadn't startled me.

'No,' I lied, 'I was just taking a quiet break. It has been a hectic morning trying to get everything ready for the fashion show.'

'Oh, yes,' she said, beaming, 'the fashion show. To think, I shall model! It's so exciting.' She clapped her hands together with the enthusiasm of a little girl.

'I'm hoping it will be as successful as the last show,' I said. 'Now tell me, can I help you or were you just coming in to browse?'

Miss Manfred seemed to hesitate. 'Actually, I was kind of hoping I would find Mr Gallisdorf here. I thought he could recommend a history book for me to read – light reading, nothing too heavy. Do you know where he might be?' The rouge spots on her cheeks flamed.

'Why don't you try the solarium?' I suggested. 'Mr Gallisdorf enjoys sitting in there on sunny days.'

She thanked me and tottered off on her fantastic heels in the direction of the solarium. As soon as she was gone, I replaced the Bible on the shelf, put the chair back, and left the library.

Miss Manfred's interest in Mr Gallisdorf, which had always tickled me, turned into something to be grateful for. It was easy to send her off in hot pursuit of a man I knew was unavailable. She must have known it, too, but she was still making the attempt. I used to think it was amusing: a maiden lady, as my grandmother would have called her, chasing a half-paralysed man whose interest in females doesn't extend beyond the pages of his history books. Now I'm not sure; her pursuit keeps Miss Manfred active.

There is something I have become aware of after these months at Briarhill: some of the elderly women here who have never married or borne children seem to be in better shape than the women who are alone after spending their lives caring for husbands and families. I don't mean the physical aspects of female aging, the incompetent bladders of elderly women who have given birth, pelvic disorders, post-menopausal complaints, and that sort of thing. It is a mental and emotional, rather than a physical difference. The unmarried women appear to be more self-sufficient. Perhaps they care for themselves because they have always had to care for themselves. The widows, women who have spent their lives caring for others, don't seem to realize that they have lives of their own. They wander aimlessly down the halls, some of them unkempt if an aide hasn't groomed them, talking about their late husbands and the accomplishments of their children to anyone who will listen.

When I first started working at Briarhill, a tall, emaciated woman named Mrs Fry would greet me at the door each morning. I was flattered. By the end of the second week, I was coming in through a different entrance every day to avoid her. Mrs Fry would follow me up and down the corridors, plucking at her thinning gray hair while she talked incessantly about her sons. There were times when she spoke of them as if they were Matthew's age. One of them is in his early sixties, the other is in his late fifties. She used to say, 'We understand things; don't we, Jenny? We are both mothers.' I wanted to scream and run. Instead, I nodded and she continued her monologue.

Mrs Fry's sons come to visit her once a month, sometimes less, and never together. They take turns. Mrs Fry is fairly stable for the first week or two after a visit. Then she begins to deteriorate. When she starts losing control of her bladder, the office has instructions to call her sons on an alternate basis. One of them receives a call, promises a definite visiting date, and Mrs Fry is told to expect him. She starts using the toilet again, gets her hair done, tells everyone her son is coming, and tries on all of her dresses, struggling to remember which son has seen which dress last.

I have seen her sons on their visits. The eldest, a balding, distinguished-looking man, gives her his arm and they walk for a while, Mrs Fry clinging to him as if he were her lover. She insists upon introducing him to everyone. He smiles uncomfortably and reminds her that he has come to see her many times, so he doesn't need to be introduced each time. She ignores his protests and continues her introductions.

When she is sure she has not missed anyone, they go to her room. Mrs Fry has just enough energy left to recount each slight and indignity she has had to endure since his last visit. Her imagination is extraordinary. She tells him that the cooks have instructions to spit in the meatloaf, that they give her soiled underpants to wear, that she can drink only half a cup of coffee because the grounds are poisoned, and if she has played cards and lost, that the women cheat by hiding aces in their girdles. She weeps with each tale, exhausting herself until she falls asleep. Her son tiptoes out of the room, then races down the halls and out of the building, his face pale under a cold sweat.

Mrs Fry's younger son, a stocky man who has the fiercest eyebrows I have ever seen, is brusque and impatient. Once I saw her try to take his arm. He snapped it away as if her hands were unclean, grabbed her by the elbow, and steered her out to a remote corner of the terrace. I have noticed that the staff makes a little extra effort on Mrs Fry's behalf after her younger son's visits. What disturbs me is that she always seems more grateful for his visits than those of his older, more considerate brother. There may be some truth in the lines from a poem I once read: 'Every woman adores a Fascist/The boot in the face . . .' Not for me. For Mrs Fry.

Incredible as it may seem, nurses on the staff have told

me that Mrs Fry was an elegant lady when she checked into Briarhill with her husband five years ago. The Frys used Briarhill as a home base while they traveled for three years until it was discovered that Mr Fry had cancer. He died within a month. According to the third floor staff, Mrs Fry cared for him almost single-handedly. They marveled at her stamina and efficiency. She started to deteriorate after he died.

Oh, Richard, it took her less than two years to become what she is.

Mrs Fry has really gotten to me. If I looked at my job as Recreation Director objectively, or if I didn't need to fill my days, I would probably quit. Most of the time I feel that I am nothing more than a perpetual hostess with inevitable failures. It is impossible to make people who are sure they won't have a good time, have a good time. At least in Eagles' Landing I could serve liquor. Yet there are compensations: the flush of excitement on the face of a bingo winner, the quiet pride of residents who model in fashion shows I have arranged through a local store, and the measured anticipation residents have expressed for the duplicate bridge tournaments.

There are those on the staff who say elderly people aren't enthusiastic for anything but enemas. I don't agree. The residents of Briarhill are capable of enthusiasm, but many of them seem to hold it in check. It is as if they are afraid to show enthusiasm for fear of having the focus of their excitement taken away.

Or is it the realization that death may come before the good time?

I am not different from the residents of Briarhill. If anything, I may be in worse shape. Those like Miss Manfred do anticipate and show enthusiasm. Even Mrs Fry manages to pull herself together for her sons' visits. I cannot remember the last time I was enthusiastic about anything, nor can I recall the sweet taste of anticipation.

There are moments, Richard, when I believe we are both dead.

Except I am breathing.

My parents called tonight as I was putting the children to bed. Actually, I don't 'put' them to bed anymore; I supervise. It was easier to put them to bed bodily when they were infants than it is to supervise them now that they are older. They always have just one more thing to do: a television show to finish, a last commercial to watch after the show, brushing each one of their teeth two hundred times (on each side), combing their hair when they don't bother combing it all day. The bedtime stalls are endless. Some nights I feel like standing in the middle of the hall and screaming. But it would only work for one night.

My parents' call surprised me; it wasn't for a special occasion, and they remembered the time difference. Usually they ignore it. The last time they called it was to wish Matthew a happy birthday, and he was in school. My father was irritated. 'Why is he still in school?' he asked. 'Is he having problems?'

'No,' I replied, 'school is in session until two thirty, and it's two twenty-five here.'

'Oh, the damned time difference. I had forgotten. We're leaving for the club now. Entertaining some people from out of town. They deal in scrap aluminum. We'll try to call back and catch Matthew before he goes to bed. If we get tied up, wish him our best.'

They didn't call back. It must have been a profitable dinner. I had enough sense not to tell Matthew that they called. At least I have learned something from the past, even if it is only that my parents are unreliable. They have disappointed him so many times, yet Matthew remains vulnerable, a sweet turtle with his head out and his belly exposed. They did send him a gift, though, an expensive remote-control car that had arrived the day before. There was no point in tarnishing either their gift or his day by telling him.

I didn't say much to my parents tonight. It was polite stranger conversation – inquiries about their health, the weather, the scrap metal business. The children did most of the talking, and they didn't say too much, either. They simply repeated their latest activities aloud, but I could see that they were pleased, happy that their grandparents had called. Although it was difficult, I pretended to share their pleasure.

It is ironic, Richard. When you were alive, I felt obligated to defend my parents, to honor them because you didn't. And I did honor them. Now that you are dead and I no longer honor them or even like them, I must feign love and respect for the sake of the children. My life is like a rope that is twisted and knotted, and I don't know how it happened.

But I do know how it happened. Your death changed things. After the fact of your absence and the adjustment to bearing the sole responsibility for the children, the biggest change in my life (as if that weren't enough) was in my relationship with my parents, and it had everything to do with you.

When your death was a fresh incision in our lives, my parents were supportive. And I needed them. Your parents fueled my need. Your father glared at me as if I had murdered you with my bare hands, and your mother wailed in minor chords, going up and down the scale, singing the song of her grief. If anyone offered me sympathy within earshot of your mother, she would begin her awful wail and continue until that person and anyone else within hearing range would rush to her side. I don't know if people went to her moved by embarrassment or a desire to shut her up.

Your mother made her loss clear. The untimely death of an adored only son is more than a woman can bear, worthy of the longest of laments and deserving of the deepest of sympathies. But she was always like that where you were concerned, a self-appointed life guardian for her precious son. I never took her dislike of me personally; she would have disliked any woman you married. In fact, she began grieving for you long before you died. I still shudder when I think of her telephone calls after we moved to Eagles'

Landing. 'We never see Richard anymore,' she whined whenever she managed to catch me at home. Then I had to listen to her threats of operations that would require intensive care in our guest room, your father's diverticulitis problems and his latest, special diet. She always concluded her conversation with the same cute remark: 'Wait until Matthew grows up,' she said. 'Then you'll know what it is to lose a son.'

When I invited your parents for dinner, she was impossible. Each time she went through the house on an inspection tour that would have left an army sergeant breathless, calculating the money we spent and begrudging me every penny. 'Such lovely things,' she commented, looking straight at me, 'but are they really necessary?' I noticed that she was never concerned about the money we spent on her Christmas gifts. She opened her presents with enthusiasm and gushed her thanks to you as if you were her suitor, not her son. 'You always had such wonderful taste, Richie,' she crooned, calling you by your childhood name. You hadn't been 'Richie' since you entered adolescence. Then your eyes would seek mine, defying me to tell her that I was the one who had chosen her gifts. I didn't utter a word, although I was sorely tempted to ask whether your good taste included picking me for a wife.

Richard, I have never been able to do this before: attack your parents without fielding a counterattack on my parents. It isn't fair, but it feels good. It feels better than good. It feels terrific. Healthy. It would feel even better if you were here. But that would be asking for the impossible. If you were here, I would have to lower the attack to flesh wounds and steel myself for their return. Then I wouldn't feel terrific.

I must be fair. If this is a quest for truth, a search for answers so that I can give Matthew and Catherine answers, then I must unmask my parents.

It wasn't the business with Matthew and my father that

precipitated my feelings toward them. My father's lack of interest wasn't unexpected. He has made a life manifesto of living on his terms, and since the role of doting grandfather was one he did not choose to play, had never chosen to play, I could not foist it upon him. If he had acquiesced, Matthew would have sensed it and the failure would have been the same.

My relationship with my parents changed when the reason you took your life surfaced. Your death could not have been called accidental by the bravest of imaginations, but it could have been blamed on depression, insomnia, or an early male climacteric when it first happened. Although my parents weren't happy about it, they felt it could be excused and, in time, forgotten. Naturally they were unhappy that their daughter was left a widow with two small children, but they accepted it without undue strain. They knew I had been left financially cushioned, and I suppose they believed I was young enough to enjoy some prospects, either another marriage or a modified career once the children were older. What they couldn't accept was why you did it. It wasn't a clean suicide with a medical basis. You had reasons.

It took approximately three months for the facts to catch up to your death. Your father promptly had a heart attack. My parents didn't have the cover of illness to divert them; neither did I, but I was concerned about the children, particularly Matthew, and the tranquilizers I was taking insulated me from the magnitude of what had happened. But my parents weren't insulated, and they did react, only it was with incredulity, not compassion. 'Why didn't you let me know what was happening?' my father asked me, characteristically eliminating any tactful preliminaries. 'And why did Richard get himself involved in the first place?'

I ignored his second question and mumbled something about being unaware of what was going on.

My father thrust his face close to mine, as if the elimination of physical distance would somehow remove the actual distance between us. 'You were married to the man,' he said, his breath hot on my face, 'married to him. How could you not know?'

I couldn't answer. My father gave me a kind of wild-eyed look, as if he suddenly realized he had sired a dummy. 'This is incredible,' he said, raising his voice. 'I can't believe it. I just can't believe it. I thought Richard was smarter than that.'

'Richard didn't do anything wrong,' I replied, feeling defensive. 'People make mistakes.'

'That's no excuse,' my father said, unmoved.

'He paid for it, didn't he?' I asked.

'It was a stupid thing to do.'

'Other men have done a lot worse and I don't see you condemning them. Instead, you join them for dinner. You belong to the same clubs. Your wives work on the same charities,' I said, hoping I could make him see his hypocrisy.

'I'm not talking about men who have gotten away with things,' he yelled. 'I'm talking about Richard, who made a mess of things.'

That was it. You had made a mess of things. I knew there was no point in defending you, definitely not with my father as judge. If you had pulled a fast deal and had gotten away with it, you would have earned a modicum of his admiration, but because you failed, because your failure was public, and because you took too many important people on your downhill ride, there was no absolution. To my father, getting caught was what counted.

After the futile interrogation, the matter wasn't discussed again. My parents knew you had provided for us amply, so they more or less left me and the children to survive on our own. I wish I could point to something specific they did in their rejection of us, cruel words or a nasty incident, but my parents don't operate that way. They separated their lives from ours a stitch at a time. Phone calls decreased from daily to twice a week to once a week to once every two weeks to once a month. If I called them and broke the unwritten schedule, they were polite but distant, making it clear that my call was as welcome as an insurance salesman calling during the dinner hour to catch a prospective buyer off guard.

Visits became obligatory rituals played quickly and halfheartedly. We were undesirables. In my parents' eyes, I had fallen to Linda's level. I was another child who brought them grief in an unwrapped package, an offspring who disturbed their happy long-term dreams. But unlike my sister, who has made a career out of rebellion, I was cast out without choice and forced to take my children with me. I would have felt better about their rejection had I willfully caused it; there would have been a measure of satisfaction. As it stood, we had unwittingly become semi-untouchables, like my mother's aunts, Louise and Bess, who are seen only at weddings and funerals. Bess and Louise are never discussed at my parents' table. I sometimes wonder if they discuss me or Matthew or Catherine.

When I was down to my last pills in what must have been my hundredth bottle of tranquilizers, I decided not to reorder. I had experienced several frightening lapses of memory and had developed an irritating skin rash. My skin and my head cleared. I saw that we were alone and panicked without my cushion of drugs. I wanted to run. I picked up the phone, called a realtor, and put the house up for sale, not knowing where we would go or what we would do. Escaping from Eagles' Landing, with its electrical screen of animosity, and ridding myself of a house that had become a five-bedroom, five-bathroom mausoleum for three half-alive people was enough.

The decision to move to California was not conscious. It was the visceral reaction to something said in a telephone call. I hadn't told my parents that I was putting the house up for sale; our communication had been on a monthly basis for quite some time, and my last conversation with them had been two weeks before I stopped taking the pills. I wasn't going to call. They could hear the news from someone else or wait a few weeks to hear it from me. Actually, I knew they would hear it from someone else, but I didn't care. We, my parents and I, had been polite but distant for months. The woman at the cash register on aisle six of the supermarket was friendlier than they were, and I didn't tell her, either. There was no one to tell.

Apparently I was still newsworthy. When I heard the unfamiliar ring of the telephone late in the afternoon the day after I listed the house, I knew who it was. Both children ran to answer with looks of excitement on their faces. It was an event, the ringing of our telephone.

'Wait,' I said to them, 'I'll answer.'

They were upset. 'But Mommy,' they wailed in unison.

I interrupted. 'If it's someone you know, I'll let you talk later.'

I sat down and picked up the receiver to talk to my mother. 'Jennifer,' she said, dispensing with formalities, 'why didn't you tell us you were planning to sell the house? Eleanor Walmond called twenty minutes ago, annoyed because I hadn't mentioned it at lunch. Can you imagine how I felt? I didn't know. What was worse was that I couldn't tell her that I didn't know. How could you put me in such a tacky position? How could you?' She waited for my answer. I had nothing to say.

'I called your father,' she continued. 'He was as taken aback as I was. Really, before making a decision as major as selling the house, you could have at least given your father the courtesy of a call to ask his advice.'

'Why?'

'Because you have no experience in these matters. Absolutely none. You've never sold a house before. You know nothing about it.'

'I'm not stupid,' I replied. 'The house is in the hands of a good realtor. When the right offer comes, I'll take it.'

'Just like that,' she snapped. 'Putting your house up for sale without even mentioning it to your parents.'

'I didn't think it was necessary.'

'Courtesy in a family is always necessary. Loyalty. Basic consideration. I'm surprised at you, truly disappointed. Linda might have done something as impetuous as this, but not you. And not in this way. We spoke to you only a few days ago. You could have mentioned it then,' she said. I could visualize her holding the phone in her left hand, the receiver in her right, taking short, quick steps back and forth as she always does when she is angry.

'Well, why didn't you mention it?' She was pushing now and the overcultivated voice she uses when she's angry became sharper, almost shrill.

'I didn't talk to you a few days ago, Mother. It was more like several weeks ago,' I replied.

'You could have said something then.'

'I didn't know then.'

'When did you know? On what day did you receive this mighty revelation?' She was definitely beginning to sound shrewish.

'I decided to sell the house on Sunday,' I said, standing up. 'I called the realtor Monday morning. It is now Tuesday afternoon and you know. If you hadn't heard today, you could probably have heard tomorrow.'

'I didn't want to hear it from someone else,' she said. 'I wanted to hear it from you.'

'Then you should have called yesterday. But you wouldn't have called. It wasn't a full month, was it?' Bitterness like hard phlegm started to plug my throat.

It was her turn to be silent. I waited. I don't know what I expected. I knew it wouldn't be an apology, for I was sure she had managed to rationalize her withdrawal by convincing herself we had to learn to become independent. She has always had a remarkable facility for rationalization; it has been the trump card of her life. Still, I hoped. A small acknowledgement would have been sufficient.

Finally, she spoke. 'Courtesy is courtesy,' she said, as if it were some kind of sacred oath, an incantation she could use to reverse the flow of guilt.

I didn't reply. Perspiration was forming between my breasts, as it always does when I'm nervous or upset.

'And just where are you planning to move?' she asked.

The walls of my mouth felt like rough parchment.

'Well?' she demanded. 'Are you going to move into an apartment or are you going to do something outlandish like your sister Linda and traipse off to a commune to eat nuts and wear rags? You have two children, you know. You can't move around like a gypsy.'

The perspiration between my breasts started to trickle down my midriff. Where was I going to move? I hadn't thought about that.

'Well?' she said.

'I . . . I'm going to move to . . . to California,' I managed to say.

'California! Why California? We have no one in California.'

'Because,' I said, 'California is the last place to go.'

'It's the what. . .'

I interrupted. The glands in my mouth had started functioning again. 'The children are standing next to me. They have been waiting patiently to talk to you. Here's Catherine.'

I handed Catherine the receiver and walked into the kitchen. Catherine started chirping brightly into the phone. Matthew ran into the library to pick up an extension. I took some ice out of the freezer and made myself a drink.

While the children were talking, I started thinking about California. The prospect was pleasing. We would escape the hard northern winter: no more leaky boots, dripping snowpants, or runny noses. And the distance was appealing. We would be three thousand miles away from Eagles' Landing. Anything over five hundred miles seemed safe. Three thousand miles was a bonanza. I lifted my glass and congratulated myself.

I think I was premature.

California is a strange place. I can't seem to find my

bearings here. There are moments when I don't know who I am or where I am going. Any roots I had have shriveled under decaying stumps; there is nothing left to nourish Matthew and Catherine. It worries me. If I have lost my sense of place, how can I help them find theirs? My sister Linda is twenty-nine now, and the last I heard she was still running, looking for a life that doesn't exist. Linda could even be in California. It would be a logical place for her to go. There is this feeling here of living close to the edge.

At least I know why I'm in California. I am here because I had to be somewhere. That's as good a reason as any I can think of, although you would argue that it wasn't a reason at all. I suppose you would be right. You once said that I had more impulse than thought.

It is close to dawn, a time that is neither morning nor night, a time of gray light. For an instant, I thought I saw you rise out of the early morning mist in your gray pinstripe suit. A corner of your mouth was raised in an I-told-you-so smirk. You don't have to tell me, Richard. I know. I started to perspire when I wrote about my conversation with Mother.

Catherine won a coloring contest. She got off the bus and ran up the walk screaming, 'Mommy! Mommy! I won! I won!' Then she started to laugh, a fabulous world-conquering laugh, free and innocent, a laugh one never hears coming from adults. She laughed so hard that Matthew had to tell me what she won. I could see his pride in his sister when he told me, and he hardly paused or blocked. I could have cried.

We may have messed up our lives, Richard, but there is a chance for our children to remain whole. The question is, how do I keep them that way?

Our next-door neighbor, Mrs Feltcher, heard the commotion and came out to investigate. Catherine had recovered by that time and told her jubilantly that she had won a coloring contest. 'How wonderful!' exclaimed Mrs Feltcher. 'Your mother must be so proud of you.'

'Matthew and Catherine make me feel very proud,' I said.

'Oh,' replied Mrs Feltcher wistfully. 'These are the best years of your life, the best years. When your children are young. If only I had...'

She sighed. Poor Mrs Feltcher. She was going to say, 'If only I had grandchildren,' and caught herself. The words did slip out once, and she bit her lower lip so hard I could see the indentation that her teeth left.

Catherine caught Mrs Feltcher's hesitation. Our daughter has inherited your uncanny instinct to pinpoint and test weaknesses in conversational walls. 'If what, Mrs Feltcher?' she asked.

'Nothing, Catherine,' I said. 'Now go into the house and change. Maybe we'll have a big treat later.'

'W-What kind of treat?' asked Matthew. 'F-F-For me, too?'

'A treat for all three of us,' I assured him. 'Now let's go in and change. Please excuse us, Mrs Feltcher.'

Mrs Feltcher said, 'Of course,' but her eyes told me she was disappointed at her exclusion. I glanced back before I stepped inside and thought I saw her shoulders droop as she walked away.

The children's treat was my punishment. I took them to Burger King for dinner, and they celebrated Catherine's victory with Junior Whoppers, french fries, and milkshakes. They were ecstatic. I had a double meat hamburger which I didn't eat. The bottom of the roll was soaking wet, and the hamburger looked as if it had been recycled. I ate a few french fries. They weren't bad: a little too light, not crisp as I like them, but they weren't soggy. Catherine was oblivious to the fact that I wasn't eating; Matthew noticed. 'Is-Is-Isn't your h-h-h-hamburger good?' he asked, concern making maps on his face. I told him I wasn't hungry. It was the truth. I lost my appetite after I picked up the wet hamburger.

We don't often go to fast-food places, maybe once a month at the most, so dinner at Burger King was an occasion. Matthew and Catherine adore going to drive-in places for what I have started to call 'stand food' – hamburgers, hot dogs, pizza, tacos, submarines – starch standing in soggy paper wrappers. I don't know which appeals to them more, the wrappers or the food that's inside, but they love it. Every paper product has a logo on it, and there is paper everywhere – wrappers, napkins, cups, straws, hats, babies' bibs. Eating is a long commercial, a constant promotion. When America sinks, it won't be due to a nuclear attack. We shall be suffocated under an avalanche of fast-food wrappers. If I weren't patriotic, I'd write to the Russians and tell them to be patient.

You never minded fast-food places, did you? Matthew remembers that. Occasionally he talks about his daddy taking him out to lunch for hot dogs on Saturdays, usually when I refuse to take them. You used to come home each time with burned fingertips from peeling his hot dog because he wouldn't eat the charcoaled skin. He still won't, but I'm not as patient as you were so we just don't go out for hot dogs.

You were patient, Richard, and you were a good father when you took the time to be a father. I'll tell the children about your burned fingertips from peeling hot dogs when I finally answer their questions, not to make them feel guilty but to show that you wanted them to be happy.

Actually, I should be grateful for fast-food places; they are a form of insurance. When I have run out of ideas for the weekends, or when I'm too tired to battle tourists and traffic, I take the children to a fast-food place. It is an easy, if nauseating, way to divert their attention from the fact that they do not have a daddy picking them up to take them someplace special. They are not fooled, but a taste of the forbidden does ease their longing. And they don't seem to ask as many questions.

An awful thought: I'm buying our children off, filling

their mouths full of junk food to keep their tongues silent. I wonder if they know.

I think they do know.

You see, Richard, we are carefully balanced.

I was selfish today. We could have celebrated Catherine's honor after school and invited Mrs Feltcher to join us. It would have been the nice thing to do, and I know she would have enjoyed it. But I am avoiding Mrs Feltcher. I have been avoiding her for the past few months. It wasn't that way when we first met.

The day after we moved into Sherwood Village, Mrs Feltcher came over with a cake, a sweet, old-fashioned gesture that I have since discovered is as rare here as it is in Eagles' Landing. In California, it is possible to live on the same street with the same people for ten years and never see the inside of their houses. Perhaps the people who move here can't break the habit of running, so they run in place.

I invited Mrs Feltcher in and offered her a cup of coffee. She seemed eager to stay, almost anxious to talk. She tried, in an unsophisticated, earnest way, to pump me for the details of my life – where I had come from, why I was in California, etc. – not maliciously or to place me socially but curiously, as if the details would somehow add interest to her day. I kept my answers simple, saying as little as possible. Interpreting my reticence as shyness, she leaned across the table to encourage me, her ample figure straining against the wood, her sharp-featured, birdlike face, tiny in comparison to her body, looking at me hungrily. Without thinking, I pushed my chair back, feeling that I was about to be devoured. Suddenly conscious of my rudeness, I forced myself to smile and asked her if she would like another cup of coffee. She said she didn't drink more than two cups of coffee a day, and she already had a cup at breakfast. But today would be an exception; she would have exactly one-half of a cup, if I didn't mind.

Mrs Feltcher watched me pour the coffee with the concentration of a chemist supervising an assistant in the final step of an experiment. She told me to stop, thank you, at precisely one-half cup. Then she started to talk. They, Mr Feltcher and herself, had moved from the East when her son was given a parish in California (he has since been transferred to Detroit). 'My son is a priest. We, my husband and I, had the one child. There were problems, and I couldn't have another. Are you Catholic?' she asked.

When I said no, she seemed disappointed. I didn't volunteer more. She would have been offended if I had told her that I came from a family of occasional Presbyterians, the occasions being weddings and funerals.

'My religion has been a great comfort to me,' she continued, 'a great comfort. Do you belong to a church?'

'Not yet,' I answered evasively. 'We just moved in yesterday.'

'Oh,' said Mrs Feltcher, 'I do hope you will become affiliated with a church soon. One cannot let matters like this slip when one has children. Like they say on television, a family that prays together stays together.

'We always went to church with our son. Never missed a time he served at Mass. Not that we thought he would become a priest or that we pushed him. We just wanted to give him a proper religious upbringing: the best parochial schools, attention to his prayers, faithful attendance at confession. He makes a fine priest.'

'I'm sure he does,' I said.

Mrs Feltcher took a deep breath and continued. It soon became clear that she was embarking on a complete oral history of her family. I thought of the full cartons waiting to be unpacked and inwardly groaned. Mrs Feltcher was sitting solidly in her chair, as if she planned to stay for hours.

Catherine came into the kitchen just as Mrs Feltcher had finished giving me the details of her grandparents' courtship. 'Hi, Mrs Feltcher,' she said. 'Mommy, you promised you would take us to the playground. We've been waiting and waiting. Can you go now?' Catherine ended her question with a whine.

I turned to Mrs Feltcher. 'I'm sorry,' I said, 'but I did promise the children. The moving van didn't arrive until ten o'clock last night, and they are anxious to become acquainted with their new home.'

'I understand,' she said. 'They are such cute children, and they have lovely manners. Do you know what Catherine said to me yesterday when I met them outside? She said I was their first friend in California. Can you imagine that? And I only gave them a few cookies. Aren't children wonderful? If I only had grandchildren.'

After Mrs Feltcher said grandchildren, her teeth clamped shut on her lower lip with such force that I winced. She got up quickly, thanked me for the coffee, and left. There were deep tooth marks on the skin under her lip, deep enough to look as if she had a good start at eating herself up alive.

Mrs Feltcher forced me out of Sherwood Village and into Briarhill sooner than I would have ventured forth on my own. Outside of daily Mass and the compulsive cleaning of her immaculate rooms, she has little to occupy her days. I became her main form of recreation through Matthew and Catherine. She would come over to tell me that she had seen something happen when they were playing or inquire about their health if she didn't see them or report 'the cutest thing' that one of them had said (she was sure I would want to write their words verbatim). I had to mirror her concern or pleasure with each report. Was I not the mother of these lovely children, these 'gems' as she calls them?

I love the children, but they're nothing new. And they aren't always gems.

If Mrs Feltcher had concentrated solely upon the children, lavishing more grandmotherly attention on them than either one of their natural grandmothers had been motivated to do, I probably wouldn't have been so eager to escape her daily presence. She is, after all, a grandmotherly figure, and the children have no one but me. They can function without a grandmother, but it is nice to have one, even if she is a surrogate. Mrs Feltcher, however, wasn't content to concentrate upon the children. I, too, became an object of her attention. She brought me things: arrangements of plastic fruit she had varnished, coasters she had woven out of discarded plastic bread wrappers, fabric flowers made out of scrap material and wire, eggshells she had painted and decorated with ribbon and beads. Instead of a card, advice was tucked into each piece of handiwork. I was lectured on the importance of a proper schedule for the children (children need schedules to function well), the necessity for discipline (happy children are children who know what is expected of them), and nutrition (the healthy body, healthy mind bit). Each platitude was garnished with the image of Mrs Feltcher's son, the well-disciplined child of a conscientious mother.

I could have tolerated Mrs Feltcher's well-intentioned, if unsolicited, advice longer than I did had it not been for the needle of religion working its way through the cloak she was wrapping around us. When was I going to take the children to church? What did I intend to do about their religious upbringing? I gave her opaque answers and escaped to Briarhill.

I thought of Mrs Feltcher again tonight when I was putting Catherine to bed. She asked me if Daddy knew she had won a contest. I didn't know what to say, so I followed what is becoming a pattern and answered her question with a question. 'Why, Catherine?' I asked.

'Because I want Daddy to know that I won. It would make him happy,' she said.

'Yes, it would,' I replied.

'Well, how can we tell him? How can we know that he knows?'

'I don't know,' I said, 'but if there is a way for Daddy to find out, I'm sure he will.'

'How will he find out?' she persisted.

'He will simply know,' I said, 'and he will be very proud of you.'

'But HOW will he know?'

'There are some things I can't explain, and this is one of them,' I said helplessly, realizing with a pang that Mrs Feltcher could have answered her questions. 'Now go to sleep. It has been an exciting day.' I kissed her good night and left the bedroom door ajar.

Catherine won't sleep with the door closed. I must keep her bedroom door open and the light in the hall burning all night. If the bulb goes out, she awakens instantly, crying that she can't see to sleep. The last time it happened, I was on a ladder changing the bulb at four o'clock in the morning. I nearly fell off the ladder. When the new bulb was in, I put her back to bed and asked her what she sees when she sleeps. 'My dreams,' she said matter-of-factly, looking at me with somber brown eyes as if I were the child and she the parent.'

'Oh,' I said with a nod of understanding. I didn't understand at all.

Catherine came home from school with a note yesterday. It seems she is to be awarded a prize at a special assembly. Her teacher wrote a note on the bottom of the mimeographed notice:

Dear Mrs Weaver,

I hope you can come to the award assembly. Any friends and relatives who would want to come would be most welcome.

Catherine's winning the coloring contest is quite an honor. The contest is for primary grades, one through three, and no one can recall a first grader ever winning. The entire primary wing is excited about it.

I shall look forward to seeing you on the tenth.

Sincerely,
Violet Eberhard

Well, Richard, we have a winner, a little girl who can stay within the lines. Neat. Precise. The way you were with figures. Catherine may look like me, but inside, she's your child.

I worry about Catherine. She's too neat, and she tries too hard. I have watched her doing math papers at home. They are nothing more than simple drills, but she works on each one as if it were under consideration for hanging in the Louvre. If she has to draw six apples and three apples, the apples are of uniform size and are lined up as if they were sitting on invisible shelves. Matthew's papers were different at that age. If he had to draw apples, some of them looked like pears, some like lemons, and a few like bananas. The only unifying quality the apples had was their color, and that varied in intensity from apple to apple. His papers were messy, but there was a comforting normality in them.

It isn't the care Catherine takes with each thing she does that disturbs me. I want her to care. Rather, it is the manner in which she pushes herself, demanding perfection in the execution of the simplest things. She ties her sneakers so the loops in each bow are of equal size. When she sets the table, the napkins are folded exactly in half. She brings papers home from school that are painfully perfect: all of her *i*'s are dotted, and her *t*'s are crossed. Her letters look like they have been drawn, not written, and her number papers are neat enough to have passed inspection in your office. It doesn't seem healthy, at least not for a six-year-old. Not for anyone of any age. You were a perfectionist, but even you weren't that compulsive.

Maybe you were that compulsive but were more adept at concealing it.

I tried discussing Catherine's perfectionism with Mrs Eberhard at our parent-teacher conference. She is a pleasant, wiry woman who looks like she's close to retirement age, but I doubt that she'll retire until the law forces her to leave the classroom. Mrs Eberhard is full of kinetic energy. She sits on the edge of a chair looking as if she is ready to leap up in an instant; her crossed leg is a perpetual-motion machine, swinging back and forth to its own rhythm, and her hair is in frantic gray curls all over her head, bobbing about as if they can't contain what is going on beneath them. I found it impossible to relax with her.

Mrs Eberhard took charge of the conference immediately. She ushered me into a seat facing her, flashed a quick smile that revealed a set of small, rather yellowed teeth, and took off on her report.

'Catherine is a delightful little girl,' she said, 'just delightful. She doesn't seem to require any outside motivation. Catherine is interested in everything and has the self-discipline of a much older child. She follows things through to their completion without having to be pushed or prodded, most unusual for a child of her age. I know. I've been teaching first grade for twenty-eight years.'

She flashed me another quick smile, took a deep breath, and plunged on without waiting for my response.

'Catherine's work is beautiful. Just beautiful! It's a pleasure to correct her papers. She takes great pains with each one. You know, Mrs Weaver, I've been looking forward to meeting you. It makes me feel good to talk about a child like Catherine, one so bright and caring. It's a joy to have her in my class.'

Mrs Eberhard rested a moment (her leg swung at a half-time beat) and waited for my response. What could I say? I was happy that Mrs Eberhard had given me a glowing report on Catherine, but the characteristics she was thrilled with – the unusual perseverance and perfectionism – were the very things I was concerned about. I hesitated. I didn't want to mar Catherine's accomplishments, to diminish her in Mrs Eberhard's eyes by suggesting that the qualities she was so taken with could possibly be unhealthy.

'I'm glad Catherine is doing well,' I began.

'Doing well!' Mrs Eberhard exclaimed. 'She's doing

better than well. Catherine is functioning to the optimum of her capabilities. She has considerable ability, Mrs Weaver.' Mrs Eberhard gave me a look that told me she wasn't pleased with my response.

'That's good to hear, but is it possible that she could be pushing herself too hard?' I asked tentatively. 'You did say it is unusual for a six-year-old to be as motivated as Catherine is, to follow things through the way she does.'

'It is unusual, but it's nothing to worry about. Catherine's fine, just fine. Look at her folder. In twenty-eight years of teaching, I have never presented a parent with a folder of papers as perfectly done as these.'

It was as if Mrs Eberhard hadn't heard me at all. I took Catherine's folder and went through her papers. They *were* perfect. I could see her working on them in my mind's eye: Catherine's tongue sticking out slightly in concentration, the shadow of a crease on her forehead, her hand gripping her pencil hard, the knuckles white with effort. I could almost feel the image physically, a hollow nausea close to fear. Or was it fear making me nauseous?

I handed the folder back to Mrs Eberhard and tried again. 'Catherine's papers are beautiful, but aren't they almost too beautiful?'

'Oh no,' she replied. 'BELIEVE ME, Mrs Weaver, Catherine is doing remarkably well. I can't understand why you seem to be concerned. My years in the classroom tell me you have nothing to worry about.'

I thanked her and rose to leave. Mrs Eberhard leaped off of her chair, bounced to the door in her crepe soled shoes, walked me out, and greeted the next parent – all in a single burst of energy. I left the building feeling exhausted, concern about Catherine beating against my temples to the rhythm of Mrs Eberhard's swinging leg. I felt as if I had failed her. But what could I have said? Mrs Eberhard must have thought I was an overanxious mother or that I was minimizing Catherine's accomplishments to encourage her ecstatic praise. But Mrs Eberhard hasn't seen Catherine crying when she can't make her hands do what she wants them to do. She hasn't seen Catherine rip up a picture she isn't satisfied with or throw puzzle pieces in the air because she can't fit them together. If Catherine would scream, if she would stamp her feet and holler with frustration, I wouldn't be so concerned. But Catherine doesn't stamp her feet or scream; she's too self-contained. Instead, she weeps, saying: 'I can't do it right. I can't do it,' over and over again. I worry.

I talked to Catherine about the word 'perfect,' explaining that nothing is perfect: not a tree, a flower, a person, or a paper for school. 'Everything is just a little bit different from everything else,' I told her, 'and nothing is perfect. Sometimes when people try too hard, they can't do anything right. Trying too hard makes people tense, and then it's even harder to do what they want to do.'

'But I have to try, Mommy,' she replied earnestly, 'and things have to be good enough, not just different. Good.'

I can't change her, but I have found that I can cut her drive for perfection before it erupts into tears. When I see that she is becoming frustrated, I remind her of our talk. 'Nothing is perfect,' I say. 'Now don't spoil the world by trying to make the first perfect thing in it.' If I'm not too late, it works. Sometimes.

Other than coping with her drive for perfection, I have found Catherine an easier child to raise than Matthew. She can amuse herself to some degree; he cannot. And she can size up a situation, particularly if it's tacky, almost immediately. It is as if she can see the invisible lines around everything outside of herself. Trouble finds Matthew before he knows that it has been there all the time, standing behind him.

I shouldn't compare them. Comparing one's children is probably the grossest sin of parenthood. My parents compared me and Linda constantly; we never had a chance to be friends. There wasn't enough time between rounds of sparring to get to know each other. Linda is my sister, my closest biological relative, yet if someone were to ask me about her, I could give them no more than a few outdated physical statistics.

The assembly in which Catherine is to receive her award is scheduled for the same time as the fashion show at Briarhill. I don't know how I'll manage the conflict, but I must be there when Catherine receives her prize. I'll talk to Jim Gentile and the owner of the store supplying the clothes tomorrow to see if it is possible to switch the time of the show. It shouldn't be too difficult to handle. Certainly a lot easier than fielding how-and-why-did-Daddy-die questions.

Everything went wrong today. It started with the car, which wouldn't start. I called six gas stations before I could find one that would send somebody out. A man on the telephone promised me I wouldn't have to wait more than a half hour.

Then I called Briarhill to tell them I would be late. Ellen, Jim's secretary, reminded me that I had an activity scheduled for ten o'clock: a local backgammon expert whom I had worked on for weeks was finally coming to teach the residents the fine points of the game. Some of Briarhill's players had let me know that they knew more than he did and that they were going to attend only to find out for themselves how much my expert didn't know. The enthusiasm the elderly have for proving people wrong has an intensity that puts color in their cheeks.

I told Ellen I would be there as soon as possible.

When thirty minutes became forty, I called the gas station. The man who answered said he was doing the best he could. I waited another fifteen minutes and called again. The same man answered; he was furious. I told him I had to be at work, that I was already late. 'Look lady,' he said, 'I just sent a fella out. Be patient. This ain't room service.'

The mechanic, a boy in his late teens whose blond hair

hung down past his shoulders, must have come by way of Disneyland. The gas station is five minutes away, and it took him twenty minutes to get here. I waited for him outside, gave him the keys to the car, and ran inside to call Briarhill again. It was ten o'clock. Jim Gentile got on the phone. 'Where are you? Your speaker is here, and everyone is seated in the game room, anxious to begin.'

'I'm sorry. My car wouldn't start, and I've been waiting all this time for a mechanic. He's here now. If he can fix it quickly, I should be there soon. Could you please introduce Mr Cole and apologize to him for my not being there?'

'It's not my job, but I'll do it as long as you don't make a habit of this kind of thing. It's bad public relations to invite someone to Briarhill and not be here to greet him. Try to get here as quickly as you can.'

'I'll do my best,' I said and hung up. I felt like telling him to go to hell.

I went back outside. The boy from the gas station had cables hooked up to the battery. 'If it isn't the battery,' he said, 'I'll have to tow it in.'

A glance at his hands let me know that he was telling the truth. For a mechanic, he had the cleanest hands I'd ever seen; there wasn't a speck of grease under his fingernails. With the possible exception of connecting the battery cables, he looked like he didn't know any more about cars than I did.

He told me to get into the car. He jumped the battery, and it started. 'Keep it running,' he said.

He removed the cables and walked to the side of the car. 'That'll be fifteen dollars. You were lucky, lady.'

Some luck.

Mr Cole, the backgammon expert, had finished his talk by the time I arrived at Briarhill. I saw him in the main lobby, a diminutive man with an unusually large head, and apologized for not being there to greet and introduce him, explaining that I had had car trouble. He accepted my apology graciously, then said, frowning: 'I wonder if I should have come today. There were several people in the group who argued with everything I said. It's hard to believe, but I think they came to hear me looking for a fight. I don't blame you, but I intend to stick to younger groups in the future.'

After Mr Cole left, I headed for Jim Gentile's office to tell him that I had to switch the time of the fashion show. I met Mr Gallisdorf in the hall. He was more agitated than I had ever seen him, quite unlike the reticent man who wheels himself silently through Briarhill's halls.

'I missed you at the backgammon lecture,' said Mr Gallisdorf. 'Mr Cole gave a nice talk. He certainly knows the game. I would have liked to invite him to come back and play a game with me sometime, but I felt I couldn't after several people in the audience started riding him. They deliberately picked on things he said like children spoiling for a fight.'

'I heard about that. It's too bad. Perhaps it wouldn't have happened if I had been there, but my car wouldn't start,' I replied.

'It wasn't your fault. You couldn't have prevented it unless you had taken them out of the room bodily. The individuals who were disruptive today – I won't name names – are always disruptive. They look for an argument just to make themselves heard, never thinking, not once, that they may be spoiling someone else's time. Such rudeness!' he exclaimed, gesticulating wildly with his right arm.

I tried to calm him by suggesting that he confront the troublemakers. 'It might make you feel better,' I said, 'and if they know how it upset you, perhaps they wouldn't do it again.'

'No,' he replied emphatically. 'They already had their good time, and they'll do it again. You can't change people. Whatever they are, they become more so with age. I am certain that the residents who were rude today were the same ones who were always getting into scrapes on the school grounds when they were youngsters. Personalities don't ripen like fruit; they deepen, become rutted like a heavily traveled dirt road. Talking to them wouldn't make a bit of difference.'

Mr Gallisdorf's good side, his right side, seemed considerably higher than his left, and his face was pale with exertion. I didn't want to leave him. 'Would you like to sit with me in the solarium?' I asked.

'If it wouldn't be detaining you,' he answered gratefully.

He refused my help with his wheelchair and apologized for his outburst: 'Forgive me. I didn't mean to run on. Those people this morning, interrupting the way they did, bothered me more than usual. I try to be overlooking. When one lives with strangers, one must be tolerant. Unfortunately, tolerance is an attribute I have been short on all my life,' he said ruefully. 'I have no right to criticize others when I consider my own shortcomings.'

I told him about Catherine's award and the conflict in time between the assembly and the fashion show while we sat in the solarium. Mr Gallisdorf seemed sincerely pleased that Catherine had won and apologized again for detaining me. He looked totally spent, exhausted from the morning's irritation. When he started to doze, I pushed his wheelchair out of the sun and asked an aide to check on him.

It was close to noon when I entered Jim Gentile's outer office. I had hoped to avoid him by telling Ellen about the change in scheduling, but she wasn't there. Instead, he was standing at her desk with a paper in his hand and a scowl on his face.

'Well,' he said, 'I see you finally arrived.'

'I told you I'd get here as quickly as I could,' I replied coldly. 'I didn't plan on having car trouble.'

'When was the last time you had the car serviced?'

'I had the oil changed a few months ago.'

'Just the oil?' he asked with raised eyebrows.

'It didn't need anything else.'

'Women don't take care of cars and then they act

56

surprised when their cars don't work. Like I've been telling you, Jenny, you need a man to watch out for you.'

I felt like telling him I'd hire a mechanic to service me and my car, anyone but him. However, I kept my mouth shut.

'Will you type this form?' he asked. 'You just have to fill in the blanks. Ellen stepped out, and I'm in a hurry. I have a lunch meeting.'

'Sorry,' I said, remembering his response when I asked him to introduce Mr Cole, 'but I don't type. I came in to tell you that I have to change the time of the fashion show. It's scheduled for Tuesday morning, and I can't be here. I must be at my daughter's school that morning.'

'What do you mean, you must be at school? You have a job. Schedule your conferences on your own time,' he said, looking first at me, then at the form in his hand. 'And why don't you type?'

'I don't type because I don't type. And I'm not going to my daughter's school for a conference. She won an award. There's a special assembly, and I have to be there.' I was too irritated to worry about what I said to him.

'What kind of remark is that: You don't type because you don't type? You aren't at a society tea party. You have a job,' he yelled, his face blotching.

'I don't type because I never learned to type. Besides, I wasn't hired to type. And I don't think I'm at a society tea party. Briarhill is no tea party, not for the people who really work here,' I said, glaring at him.

'You don't have to get nasty,' he replied, backing off. 'Now, what did you say about the fashion show?'

'I have to change the date.'

'You can't.'

'Why not?'

'I've arranged to have the evening paper cover it. The store wants free publicity, and it will be good public relations for us; our petition for a zoning variance to expand is coming up before the city council. I want a picture of happy old ladies prancing around in new clothes in the paper before our lawyer presents it. The council meets on Wednesday.'

'Oh,' I said, 'I didn't know. But I must be at school for Catherine. I'll call the newspaper and the store and rearrange everything.'

'If you can't rearrange it, you'll have to be here for the show. I'll be back at two. You can let me know then.'

I said nothing and walked back to my office, fuming. Instead of eating lunch, I spent the next two hours on the phone getting the fast shuffle from the newspaper. They weren't sure, they said, if they could send anyone to Briarhill on Monday. Something was always happening on Mondays, and they didn't want to commit themselves. I must have talked to everyone on the paper from the copy boy to the women's editor, a woman with a mint julep accent who writes sob stories every Sunday about the tragic lives of discarded wives and the evils of alimony. In her Thursday columns, she writes stories featuring nuns who live in peace and tranquility doing God's work. She was as aggravating as her articles. 'Ah'm sorry ah cain't help you,' she drawled, 'but there's nothin' too excitin' about fashion anymore, not in these relative times, and especially not for old ladies. It's the seventies, and there's a lot happenin'.'

I silently cursed her and hung up.

At two o'clock I finally called the city editor in desperation, a man named Nat Witton, and explained my problem – the entire problem – including Catherine, her assembly, the fashion show, and the petition for a zoning variance. He was reasonable.

'Look,' he said, 'what is your name?'

'Weaver,' I replied, 'Jennifer Weaver. Sorry for the omission. I've repeated my problem so many times to so many people that eventually something was going to be left out.'

'I understand. I'm not promising anything definite, but I'll try to help you. Covering fashion shows at nursing homes is the responsibility of the women's editor or the society page.'

'I talked to the editor of the women's section,' I said wearily.

'And?' he asked.

'Don't ask,' I said.

He laughed. 'I won't be able to send a reporter to cover the show, but I could send a photographer to take some pictures if you would jot down enough information to give us a decent caption.'

'I'll write anything you want,' I said, 'anything.'

'That's an extravagant promise,' he replied, 'and not necessary, but I like your enthusiasm. I'd like to hear some of our reporters say that.'

Embarrassed, I thanked him quickly and hung up.

The store owner was impossible. He didn't know if he could have everything ready for Monday. He talked about the pressures of business, impossible customers, slow deliveries, absorbing alteration costs (which was a lie), and plans to spend Sunday at his beach house (which was the truth). 'I can't have the clothes ready by Monday,' he said.

'If I come in late Saturday afternoon and get the clothes together myself, can you do it?' I pressured him. 'You'll get free publicity. The city editor promised me he'd send a photographer over on Monday, and I'll arrange to have the name of your store in the caption.'

He agreed.

It was two thirty, past the time for me to leave, when I started looking for Jim Gentile. Ellen hadn't seen him; neither had anyone else. I ran around Briarhill for fifteen futile minutes and returned to his office. He still wasn't there. I finally asked Ellen to tell him that everything had been changed to meet his satisfaction and rushed out. The children would be home in ten minutes. I was late. I ran to the parking lot, got into the car, and turned the key in the ignition. It wouldn't start.

I sat behind the wheel, momentarily frozen with panic,

then rushed back into the building and frantically called Mrs Feltcher. She's always home, but today no one answered. It was three o'clock. The children were already off the bus, and they didn't have a key. Worse than that, I had never been late. They expected me to be there. They *knew* I would be there. Since we have lived in California, I have always been there. With the exception of two or three evenings, they haven't had a babysitter since you died.

I called a cab company and asked the dispatcher to send someone in a hurry. It was an emergency, I told him. The dispatcher decided to be cute. He wanted to know if I was having a baby or a heart attack.

'Neither,' I said, 'but close.'

'Either you're having a baby or you're not having a baby, lady.'

'I had the babies,' I screamed. 'Now I'm having the emergency.'

'Crazy,' he said, 'they come out here, and they get crazy.'

I went outside and paced up and down the front walk while I waited for the cab. It pulled up just as Jim Gentile turned into the drive in his green Cadillac, looking bloated and sleepy. I didn't wave.

It was three thirty by the time I got home. The children were sitting on the concrete step, huddled together and shaking as if they were freezing under the hot sun. Catherine was sobbing; her face was red and puffy under her blond bangs. Matthew looked like he needed a transfusion.

'Wh-Wh-Wh-Wh-Wh-Where were y-y-y-y-y-y-y-you?' he asked, blinking hard. 'W-W-W-W-W-W-W-We did-did-did-did-didn't know wh-wh-wh-wh-wh-wh-where you were.'

Matthew hadn't blocked that severely in months.

I held them tightly and explained. 'I'm so sorry,' I said. 'I'm so sorry. I didn't mean to be late. The car wouldn't start. I'm so sorry. Really, I am.'

I kept apologizing, but Catherine couldn't stop crying. She spoke between sobs. 'I was scared, Mommy. I was scared. What if you never came back? What if you died like Daddy and never came back? I asked Matthew. He didn't know if you died, either. And Mrs Feltcher wasn't home. We were going to go to Kerry and Steve's but didn't. We were afraid to leave. Then you wouldn't know where we were. Maybe you'd think we were dead, too.'

I hugged and kissed her and explained again, but I couldn't seem to reassure her. Then I looked over at Matthew. He was standing rigidly, pale and silent as a sphinx.

Suddenly Catherine looked down and started weeping fresh tears. 'I wet my pants, Mommy. I got so scared, I wet my pants.'

Poor Catherine. She has never had an accident, not from the time she first wore training pants; her pride wouldn't allow it. She was devastated.

I unlocked the door, ran a bubble bath for Catherine, and gave Matthew a snack. He sat at the kitchen table wordlessly, drinking his milk in gulps and halfheartedly picking at a cookie. I sat down opposite him. 'Matthew,' I said, 'I know how you felt. I understand. But I couldn't help what happened. The car didn't start this morning either, and I was late for work.'

No response.

'I tried calling Mrs Feltcher to tell her I would be late, but she wasn't home.'

Silence.

'I hope it never happens again, but it could happen. Machines don't always work. If the car had started, I would have been home on time.'

Still no response. He finished his milk and mashed the cookie into bits, his eyes concentrating on crumbs he was rolling between his fingers.

'You are eight years old, Matthew. I think you are able to understand how these things can happen. They aren't pleasant, but they do happen.' His silence had planed my voice into sharp edges.

'Would you like to have a key? I think you're old enough to have your own key, and I know you'll be responsible with it. I have confidence in you. You won't lose it. Then you won't have to worry about me being late anymore. I'll always try to be here, but if I'm not, you'll be able to let yourself and Catherine in. You can wait inside for me, and I'll call to tell you where I am.'

He pushed the crumb-covered napkin toward me. 'C-C-C-Catherine would l-l-l-like that,' he said. 'Sh-Sh-Sh-She k-k-k-kept crying and crying. I-I-I-I couldn't m-m-make h-h-h-h-her stop. Sh-Sh-She was sc-sc-sc-sc-sc-scared.' His speech-contorted face didn't relax when he finished; I could see the tension in the muscles of his neck.

'I know she was scared,' I said. 'I was scared, too. Not scared, really, but worried. In fact, when I called the cab company and told the man I had to be picked up right away because it was an emergency, he thought I was going to have a baby.'

He finally raised his eyes; they were a solid, churning gray. 'A-A-A-A-Are you g-g-g-going to have a b-b-b-b-b-baby?' he asked, pressing his forehead with his hand while he spoke as if to make the words come out of his mouth smoothly.

His question was so innocent and full of pain that I answered him seriously. 'No, I'm not going to have a baby,' I said, thinking that my mother's eighty-year-old Aunt Bess has as much of a sex life as I do, maybe more. 'Why would I have a baby?'

'M-M-M-Maybe you f-f-f-found a new f-father,' he said solemnly.

'No, Matthew, I haven't found another father. But I'd better find that spare key and get your sister out of the tub before she shrivels up from sitting in the water too long. Do you want to change and go out to play?'

He nodded, got up from the table, and went to his room to change.

Catherine wouldn't get out of the tub. 'You've been in there long enough,' I said, taking one of her hands in mine. 'Look at your fingers. They're wrinkled. I'll get your clothes, and you can have a snack and go out to play. Matthew's changing now.'

'No. I want to stay in the tub.'

'You've been in the tub too long.'

'No,' she insisted, sticking her chin out.

'Come on,' I said, bending down to pick her up.

She gripped the handle of the soap dish with both hands and started to scream.

'Please, Catherine.'

'No. I won't get out. *I won't get out. I'm never getting out. I'm going to stay in here forever.*'

Richard, she was hysterical. And I couldn't get her out with threats or promises. The harder I tried, the more hysterical she became. She wouldn't budge. Her lips started to turn blue with cold.

The telephone rang.

'I'm going to answer the phone, and when I come back, you are going to get out of the tub.'

It was Jim Gentile. 'Ellen told me that you were able to switch the show to Monday. Is the newspaper covering it?'

'Yes.'

'What's wrong with your car? I saw you getting into a cab.'

'It wouldn't start.'

'I'll take care of it,' he said. 'I'll call the garage across the street. You can pick it up there tomorrow. Since you'll need a ride to work, I'll stop for you on my way in.'

The thought of fielding him off at eight thirty in the morning made the acid in my empty stomach bubble. 'No, thank you,' I said. 'I'll manage.'

'How will you manage? A cab again? Free with your money, aren't you?'

'No,' I lied, 'a neighbor will drive me.'

After I put the receiver down, I went back to the bathroom. 'It's time to get out now, Catherine,' I said, 'and I don't want any arguments.'

She started to cry, which made me feel awful.

'Please stop crying and get out of the tub. You have to get out. It's almost dinnertime.'

Her teeth were chattering, and her sobs came out punctuated by clicks. Sob. Click. Sob. Click.

'Now, Catherine!'

She moved to the far side of the tub, gathering courage for a desperate last fight. I couldn't be angry with her; she was too pathetic.

'It's almost time for dinner, and I haven't prepared anything. Let's go out to eat. We can even go to McDonald's if you'd like,' I said, inspired.

'We can't,' she cried.

'Why not?' I asked in a half-shriek. McDonald's was my last hope.

'We don't have a car,' she said flatly. She stopped crying. Apparently my oversight was enough to plug her tear ducts.

'We can ride our bikes.'

'It's too far.'

'It's not too far. I'm going to change and find Matthew. We are going to ride our bikes to McDonald's. If you want to come, you can. We'd like you to eat dinner with us.'

'You don't like McDonald's,' she said suspiciously. 'You're just saying that to get me out of the tub.'

'*I love McDonald's*,' I screamed. '*I love it*. I just don't like Whoppers, that's all.'

'McDonald's doesn't have Whoppers.'

'They do, too.'

'They do not. They have Big Macs.'

'Catherine, I'm not going to argue with you. I'm tired, I'm hungry, and I'm going to McDonald's.'

'I won't go,' she said. 'McDonald's has takeout bags.

64

Can you get me a chocolate milkshake, french fries, and . . .'

I interrupted her. 'I'm not going to bring McDonald's home. Either you get out of the tub and come with us, or you stay in the tub and miss your dinner. I'm going to change.'

I left her in the tub, went to my bedroom, and collapsed on the bed. Within minutes there was a noise, the sound of water draining from the tub. I waited. The toilet flushed. McDonald's had accomplished what I couldn't manage on my own.

We rode our bicycles to dinner. I think the children enjoyed it, but somehow it wasn't the same for them. This afternoon upset our balance. They sat across from me in a booth, staring as if they expected me to disappear, to turn into a french fry or dissolve into a milkshake or become a logo on a Styrofoam container.

I am not overdramatizing, Richard. That's what you would say if you were here. Whenever I recounted a story or an incident that upset me, you always commented on the actual telling. 'Stop the melodrama,' you'd say, or 'Your imagination is riding in high gear,' or, if you were angry, 'Cut the crap!'

It isn't crap. And I'm not being melodramatic. The children were bone marrow scared, and it will take them a long time to recover. I'm sure a portion of their fright came from the stretching of your death scars; they haven't healed as they should. But it is more than that. They conceived the idea, the possibility of my mortality today. I could die, Richard. A drunk driver could kill me or I could be sardined in a freeway chain-reaction accident. It is not uncommon. There are more ways to die in a car than the one you selected.

And there are other quick ways to die: freak accidents to the head, unsuspected blood clots like malevolent rubies looking for a permanent setting. It's frightening. I would not have time to prepare the children and, more important, prepare for them. What would happen to Matthew and

Catherine if, one day, I didn't come home? If I died instantly and unexpectedly? Matthew's key would unlock the door but that is all it would do. Instead of waiting for me outside in fear, they would be waiting inside. Waiting for the ring of the telephone. Waiting for a call from a dead woman who was their mother.

Perhaps I am being melodramatic, but what would happen to them? Would they sit at their stations by the phone until hunger took them to Mrs Feltcher's door? What then? Your parents couldn't take care of them. They are barely managing to take care of themselves. My parents would make arrangements – boarding schools or hired sitters – but arrangements are fixed and cold. Who would care for them? Who would love them, Richard? Who?

I took a cab to work this morning and had the driver let me out a block away from Briarhill. Jim Gentile usually doesn't come in before nine thirty, but I didn't want him to see me getting out of a taxi. His remark about my being free with my money irritated me more than I thought it would.

I was early and walked to the gas station before going to Briarhill. The car was sitting in midair in one of the bays; the tailpipe plus other pieces of metal were lying on the grease-coated floor. It looked ominous, like the car's intestines had been removed.

'Is that wagon yours, lady?' a voice asked.

I turned around. A tall, angular man wearing dirty olive-green coveralls approached me. 'Yes,' I said, 'I've come to pick it up.'

'It isn't ready,' he said. 'It needs a lot of work. A tune-up. A new exhaust system. New shocks. We haven't finished checking it over yet.'

'The car was running well until the battery died,' I said, 'and I had it charged yesterday.'

'We had to put in a new battery. The battery was dead.'

'Couldn't you just have charged it again?'

'Nope,' he replied. 'No point in charging a bad battery. One of the cells was gone.'

'Couldn't you have replaced it?'

'Nope. Can't replace one cell in a battery. Battery cells are in sequence. When one goes, the whole thing goes.'

'Why is the tailpipe off?' I asked, hoping for an answer that wasn't prefaced by the word 'nope.'

'You had a hole in your exhaust system. We had to take it off. The system's shot.'

Suddenly I found myself preferring his nopes. 'It worked fine yesterday,' I said, suspicious. 'Can you just put it back on the car so I can take it out?'

'Nope. Can't let you drive around with a hole in your exhaust system. It's against the law.'

'How much will it cost to fix?'

He looked at me, then fixed his eyes upward as if he were reading his estimate from randomly scattered clouds in the brilliant California sky. 'One hundred sixty-five dollars,' he said, his enormous Adam's apple bobbing while he spoke.

'For a new battery and a new exhaust system?' I asked incredulously.

'Nope. Just for a new exhaust system. The battery is separate.'

'How much for the battery?'

He took a grease-spotted pad out of the breast pocket of his coveralls and flipped a few ragged pages. 'Seventy-eight dollars and thirteen cents for the battery.'

'I don't want to spend more than that,' I said. 'I'll pay you for the new battery and take the car.'

'You can't take the car without the exhaust system. You can't run it.'

'Put the exhaust system back on,' I ordered. 'No one asked you to take it off.'

'Don't get huffy, lady. I can't put the exhaust system back on like that,' he said, snapping his fingers. 'The hole has to be welded; the muffler, tailpipe, and crossover pipe have to be put on. I can't work for nothing.'

'How much?' I asked.

'Forty dollars to put the exhaust system back on with a temporary weld, but it won't hold,' he warned.

'I didn't authorize you to take the exhaust system off,' I said, starting to perspire.

'You had the car towed in, and you didn't give us written instructions telling us what to do. The car wasn't working. We just checked it out, that's all.'

'Checking it out isn't the same as taking it apart.'

'Sometimes you can't find out what's wrong with things unless you take them apart.'

He had me. 'How much will all of this cost?' I asked nervously.

'Like I said: $78.13 for the battery, $165.82 for the exhaust system, $25.50 for the tow. That's for starters. The tune-up, the shocks...'

I interrupted him. 'Forget about the tune-up and the shocks. I've had enough shocks, and I'm spending more money than I want to spend as it is.'

'It's your car,' he shrugged.

'When can you have it ready?'

'Tomorrow.'

'I need it today. This afternoon,' I insisted.

'Nope. I can't do it,' he replied implacably, stuffing the pad into his pocket with bony, grease-embedded fingers.

'But I must have the car,' I pleaded in earnest. Then, to my horror, my lower lip began to quiver.

'Oh, Jeezus,' he said disgustedly. 'You're not going to cry on me, are ya, lady?'

Richard, it was awful. That scarecrow in coveralls had intimidated me to the point where I couldn't fight back. Instead of threatening him with a call to the Better Business Bureau or a lawyer, I stood there like a helpless idiot, fighting tears. Then I started to hiccup.

'Oh, all right,' he said, raising his arms as if he wanted

to push me out of his sight. 'I'll have the car ready this afternoon.'

I turned and ran all the way to Briarhill. By the time I reached the front entrance, I was gasping for breath. My hiccups stopped.

The shaking started after I was safely inside my office. I must have leaned against the locked door for ten minutes, just shaking. I don't know why I shook, if it was anger, humiliation, or fear, but I know how I felt. I was so vulnerable, so utterly alone. I felt completely unprotected for the first time in my life. It was one of the worst moments I have experienced since your death.

After I calmed down, I added the cost of the car repairs: $269.45. It was an outrageous sum, more money than I earn in a month. And the car is old. If you hadn't died and we were still in Eagles' Landing, we wouldn't have kept the car. No one in Eagles' Landing had a car that was more than two years old unless it was a legitimate antique, like the Foxes' 1932 Rolls-Royce. I remember when they remodeled their third garage for the car; they put up a partition and installed a heater and a tile floor. The garage was kept cleaner than their house. Dale and Penny cared more for the Rolls than they did for their children. Every time it coughed, sputtered, or clanked, they had a mechanic work on it. Penny resented staying home to wait for a serviceman to fix her washing machine, but she never complained about waiting for a mechanic to check the Rolls.

Less than a month after you died, the Foxes' youngest child, four-year-old Danny, complained of a sore throat for several days. He had a fever and was hoarse, but Penny assumed that it was a cold. She was working on the annual fund raising drive for the Philharmonic and was too busy to take him to the pediatrician. When Danny began to have difficulty swallowing, she asked Dale to take him to the doctor. Dale decided to wait a day; he had to leave to drive the Rolls to a vintage auto show. Poor Danny was left at home with a babysitter and aspirin, which was common-

69

place in Eagles' Landing, but Danny's sore throat wasn't common. When police summoned by the babysitter arrived to rush him to the hospital, Danny had stopped breathing. He died of asphyxiation from a quinsy throat.

Danny didn't have to die. If he had been taken to the doctor when he first complained, he would still be alive. Penicillin would have saved him.

The upstanding residents of Eagles' Landing added an extra finger of liquor to their drinks when Danny died, but they weren't drinking to him. They were attempting to anesthetize their individual consciences: what happened to Danny could have happened to one of their children. The air was saturated with booze and unarticulated guilt. Everyone was solicitous toward Dale and Penny, including the authorities. His death certificate was stamped DUE TO NATURAL CAUSES, and his coffin was closed. The magic of Eagles' Landing produced another perfect illusion. If Danny had been a ghetto child, the Foxes would probably have been charged with neglect.

I wish I could say that I was immune to the trauma of Danny's death, that the tranquilizers I was taking to cope with your death kept his from touching me, but they didn't work, even when the dosage was increased. The reason for Danny's death – I should say the lack of reason – penetrated. The Foxes cared for their children the same way everyone in Eagles' Landing cared for their children: they were fed, clothed, and babysat. The children were loved, but the actual loving, the giving of time and affection, was a matter of convenience. It wasn't always convenient. You know what I mean, Richard. Quick good night kisses sandwiched in between cocktail parties and late dinners. Children coming home to empty houses or hired sitters.

We were no better than our neighbors. Now that I am alone with Matthew and Catherine, I am ashamed of our treatment of them. We had time for everything and everyone but our children. I can still hear Catherine's screams each time she saw us put our coats on, and I remember how Matthew often ran upstairs so he wouldn't have to see us leave. Other times he watched us sullenly, his eyes old with the understanding that we were abandoning him in favor of a life from which he was excluded.

And I can recall our guilt at the start of our third year in Eagles' Landing, our halfhearted attempts to rearrange our schedules so that we could eat together as a family. The dinners weren't too successful. I experimented a few times with sophisticated recipes that were practice runs for dinner parties, but the children picked at the unfamiliar food. Mostly the dinners were hurried affairs, for Catherine had an early bedtime, and you were spending longer hours at the office. There were nights when our meals at home were twenty-minute rush jobs from start to cleanup; I nearly always had indigestion later.

I thought of Eagles' Landing when I called Mrs Fry's eldest son today. If he grew up in California, he must have been raised in a West Coast version of our former suburb. Mr Fry is definitely Eagles' Landing material. All he needs is a little polish, which the grind of a few hard northern winters could give him.

I made the unauthorized call because I wanted Mrs Fry to be in the fashion show. It occurred to me last night that she is doing more for me than I am for her. I'm not exactly sure of what I mean, except that Mrs Fry's life seems to be defining mine in some way. At any rate, I thought modeling might help restore some of her self-respect. I told Mr Fry who I was, described the fashion show briefly, and asked him if he could visit his mother on Saturday or Sunday. 'It wouldn't have to be a long visit,' I explained, 'but every time you come, she seems to feel better.'

'I can't make it,' he said curtly.

'Just a short visit,' I pleaded, 'a few minutes of your time.'

'Who are you again?' he asked.

'The recreation director.'

'She's not sick, is she?'

'No,' I said, 'but modeling in the show would be a positive experience for her.'

'Look, Mrs Whatever-your-name-is. My mother's too old for positive experiences. I visited her three weeks ago. My brother takes the next visit. Call him.' The receiver clicked hard in my ear.

I didn't call Mrs Fry's younger son. He wouldn't have been as pleasant. But I didn't give up on Mrs Fry, either. Instead, I asked Ellen to call the younger Mr Fry. 'I think it's his turn to visit his mother,' I said, 'and I'd like him to visit this weekend.'

'Why?' Ellen asked, looking so much like Aunt Maggie that it hurt to see her. 'Is she falling apart again?'

'She isn't falling apart yet, but she is disoriented. I'd like her to model in the fashion show. If her son comes for a visit, his attention will glue her back together in time to model on Monday.'

'Sorry, I'd like to help you, but I can't. The Fry brothers left definite instructions not to be called unless their mother is one step away from being sent to the second floor. They didn't say it like that, but their message is clear. It's considerably more expensive on the second floor, and they would have to pay for the difference out of their own pockets. They have already let us know that they aren't pleased with the prospect. If she does become completely unhinged, they may take her out of here and put her in a less expensive place rather than support her at Briarhill. There isn't too much of her husband's estate left, and I think they might even try to get some of the initial deposit money back.'

Jim Gentile walked in while Ellen was explaining the Fry situation. 'Why are you asking about Mrs Fry?' he wanted to know.

I told him.

'Leave the old lady alone,' he said, 'and for God's sake don't decide that she can be helped and call her sons. You'll only cause trouble.'

'But she can be helped.'

'There is nothing anyone can do for Mrs Fry but keep her clean and take her to the john so she doesn't add too much to our laundry bills, and that's not your job,' he said with his usual class. 'You're in charge of recreation. You're supposed to keep everyone happy. Mrs Fry is beyond happiness.'

Jim dismissed Mrs Fry's life with a wave of his hand and asked about my car. Without giving him the details of what had happened to me, I told him that I felt cheated. 'I'll call the gas station right now,' he said, 'and knock their price down.' He marched into his office like an aging Lancelot, pulling in his paunch, straightening his shoulders, his flat feet toeing out on the brown shag carpet, one step after another, striding to battle. He failed. I couldn't hear what the gas station mechanic said, but I did hear Jim. He bellowed into the telephone like a castrated bull and accomplished nothing. I winced when he slammed the receiver down. He mumbled something about thieving bastards and said he had work to do. The man wore his defeat as awkwardly as he wears his polyester leisure suits.

The car was ready at two o'clock. I handed the man his check without looking at him, and I was home, waiting for the children outside, before their bus arrived. Mrs Feltcher saw me and came out to chat. When I mentioned that I was late for the children yesterday, she seemed honestly upset. 'I was at church,' she said, 'working on a bazaar. I would have come home early if I had known.'

She would have, Richard. She's that kind of woman. Caring. At times, oppressively caring. I thanked her and, on an impulse, invited her to come to school with me to Catherine's assembly. Mrs Feltcher was thrilled. 'Thank you,' she said. 'I'd love to come. I'd just love it.'

Mrs Feltcher's enthusiasm makes me feel as guilty as my mother's criticism always did.

Matthew jumped off the bus steps with his hand in his pants pocket. I understood. He was holding the key I had given him. When he saw me, he pulled his hand out of his pocket and smiled.

I wonder if he was holding the key as a talisman, keeping it in his hand to ensure my presence when he came home.

Or was he holding it because he wanted to use it, because he wanted to feel grown-up?

I can't remember when I first felt grown-up. It was probably for a frivolous thing like wearing lipstick or eye shadow, a young girl with the tribal markings of adulthood. I must have acted unbearably sophisticated. After what happened to me today, I'm not sure that I am grown-up.

Richard, I'm not going to find the truth by writing it down, because I'm not writing everything down. I'm holding back. And I can't afford to hold back. If I do, I'll lose Matthew.

Matthew and I had a fight tonight over 'Ringer's Night at the Races.' He turned it on while I was cleaning up after dinner. When I heard the announcer say, 'Check your purple tickets for race number two...' I went into the living room and switched the channel. 'I want you to watch something else,' I said. 'I don't want you watching Ringer's Races.'

'I-I-I-I like the r-r-races,' said Matthew.

'But I don't like them.'

'E-E-Everyone watches Ringer's Races. K-K-K-Kerry and Steve are w-w-w-watching.'

'I don't care what Kerry and Steve are doing. You can watch something else.'

We continued arguing until I had had enough. 'You are not watching the races and that's final,' I yelled.

'E-E-Everyone watches Ringer's Races,' he yelled back. 'If-If Daddy were here, h-h-he'd let me watch.'

'No, he wouldn't.'

'Y-Y-Y-Yes, he would. Y-You don't even kn-kn-know

how he died. Y-Y-Y-You always say something else when we ask. M-Maybe Daddy really isn't dead. M-Maybe he's alive, and y-y-you just brought us here so we c-couldn't see him anymore.'

'That's not true.'

'Th-Then what is true?' he asked, his eyes blazing.

'Your daddy died in a car in Eagles' Landing, the place where you used to live,' I replied, the words coming out of my mouth in a long spasm, 'and he wouldn't want you to watch Ringer's Races.'

'H-H-How did he die in the car?'

'He fell asleep.'

'B-B-B-But the car wasn't smashed. It-It was in the g-garage until G-G-Grandpa drove it away. I-I-I saw G-Grandpa driving Daddy's car.'

'Maybe you don't remember, Matthew. Sometimes we get confused.'

'I'M NOT CONFUSED. I REMEMBER. G-G-Grandpa drove D-D-Daddy's car away. H-H-How could D-Daddy fall asleep in the car and d-d-d-die if the car wasn't smashed?'

'He died from fumes that were coming from the car.'

'L-L-Like pollution?'

'Yes.'

'Th-Th-Then why didn't G-G-Grandpa die when h-he drove D-D-Daddy's car?'

'Because Grandpa knew about the fumes.'

Then Matthew saved me. 'G-G-Grandpa would let m-me watch Ringer's Races. H-H-He wouldn't care.'

'Let's call Grandpa and find out,' I suggested with relief.

We called my parents but no one answered. Ringer's Races were over by that time, and the past had taken a step back. I don't think I'll be as lucky the next time.

I'm afraid, Richard. Matthew is getting older and more assertive. I can no more control his thoughts than I can his questions. He wants to know what happened to you, and it is, in a perverted way, his birthright. If I only knew what

he is thinking. His face often wears a mask of inscrutabil-
ity, as yours did. I had no idea that he remembered my
father driving your car away.

What does Matthew remember?

I am afraid to know.

I am also afraid of the truth. I keep doling it out in
carefully measured portions, like a hostess who isn't sure
she has enough food for all of her guests. But this isn't a
party. My purpose in writing to you is to tell the whole
truth, not just a portion, so I can tell Matthew and
Catherine. That means I must tell you about Danny Fox's
death. Everything about Danny Fox's death. Until now I
haven't let myself think about Danny, although he was one
of the most beautiful children in Eagles' Landing – blond
and bright and sweet-tempered.

I told you that Danny stopped breathing when he was
with a sitter, but I didn't tell you who the sitter was. The
babysitter who was with him when he died was Ginny, our
Ginny. She was one of the spoils of your death, and Penny
Fox, who was always quick to sense an opportunity,
grabbed her.

Ginny's move from our household to the Foxes' seemed
logical at the time. I couldn't quite pull myself together
after you died and told everyone that I was dropping out
temporarily. I stopped all of my charity and organization
work; there didn't seem to be a point to it anymore.
Without you, I felt that I had lost my place. Since I was
no longer out every day, I didn't need a sitter. Penny Fox
was forever having sitter problems. You remember the
rumors about Penny and her sitters, don't you? Whenever
Penny lost a sitter, and it happened often, there was usually
a crack about her expecting two days' work and a pint of
blood for a six-hour job at less than the minimum wage.

Enough about Penny. The truth. Ginny's presence, her
role in Danny's death, is what disturbed me. It still
disturbs me.

Ginny started sitting for the Foxes three weeks after you
died. Danny's death neatly rounded out the month. The

residents of Eagles' Landing would have commented more on the month itself, marked as it was by death, if their attention hadn't been focused on the circumstances of Danny's passing. They didn't talk about the Foxes' neglect, of course, for to talk about that would have forced them into some form of self-acknowledgement which would have been inadmissible. Discussing the circumstances of Danny's death was a comfortable alternative.

The rumors started before Danny's funeral, and the telephone bells in Eagles' Landing chimed overtime. Our telephone rang, too. It was before I had become a suburban pariah. Danny's death wasn't discussed in detail on our phone because your death was fresh, but Ginny was discussed. I was asked question after question about Ginny. What was she like? Was she stable? Did she really drink? How much? After the second or third call, I pleaded exhaustion and excused myself.

The rumors continued after Danny's funeral. Some said that Danny's speech had become garbled and that Ginny was too drunk to understand him. Others theorized that she was napping when Danny died. All believed that Danny was dead before the police were summoned. The Foxes said nothing; neither did I.

It is time I said something, Richard. Not for Danny, because it is too late for him. It is time I said something for me. For Matthew and Catherine.

We knew Ginny drank. You caught her when you returned home unexpectedly one morning to pick up a file. There were two glasses of orange juice on the kitchen counter, one for Catherine and one for Ginny. You saw Ginny give Catherine one glass, then pour vodka in her own drink. I was conducting a tour of the art gallery when you had me paged. You were furious. I could hear Ginny and Catherine crying in the background. 'Come home now, Jennifer,' you ordered. '*Now.*'

By the time I got home, Ginny was a slobbering mess. The house wasn't big enough to contain your rage. 'You left my daughter with a drunk,' you shouted. 'Ten in the morning and she's drinking screwdrivers. She's probably out of her gourd by two in the afternoon. I wanted you to see her before I threw her out.'

'I didn't know, honestly I didn't. I never saw her drinking.'

'The liquor,' you reminded me. 'Didn't you notice the missing liquor?'

'No. You stock the bar. Didn't you notice it?'

While we stood accusing each other, Ginny struggled to regain some semblance of propriety. She tried to straighten her wrinkled print blouse, blew her nose, wiped her swollen eyes, and pushed her lank brown hair off her face. Then she swore on her father's grave, her mother's life, and her son's new car that she wouldn't drink at our house again if we would give her another chance. I had a busy week and couldn't find another sitter who had her own transportation, so we agreed to give Ginny a last try. That was more than a year before you died.

We knew she continued drinking. At least I knew. I checked the liquor, but I didn't say anything about the descending levels of the vodka and gin bottles. Ginny preferred her liquor clear. I did put a few ads in the local paper for a new sitter, but they were unsuccessful, so Ginny stayed. I talked to her about her drinking and warned her that she'd lose her job, but she knew I was bluffing. Sitters with their own transportation were as rare in Eagles' Landing as teetotalers. Her job was safe. If Ginny did conk out during some period of the day, she always managed to look conscious when we came home.

Maybe you didn't know Ginny was still drinking. It is possible.

The Foxes knew Ginny drank. You told everyone after you caught her. There was a party that evening at the Springers', and the Ginny story was the night's big news. Our fight was eliminated from the telling, but Ginny's tears, her tall glass of orange juice laced with vodka, and her fervent protestations were described in detail. You told the anecdote well, pausing for the desired dramatic effect, controlling your voice to get the greatest play from your words. The evening was yours.

You always could tell a story, Richard. Better than anyone.

The Foxes didn't mention Ginny's drinking when they hired her. Penny called before I officially dropped out and asked if I were planning to keep Ginny. When I hesitated, she asked if I would mind if she hired her. I said no, and the matter was settled. The transfer was painless. I didn't even have to fire her; Ginny just parked her car in front of a different house.

I wonder if the Foxes ever think about Danny's death as I am thinking about it now, if they can see Ginny as I see her, sleeping off her day's allotment on the sofa while their son is struggling for air, trying to breathe through a pus-swollen throat. They are still in Eagles' Landing. That fact may be all the protection they will ever need.

Matthew and Catherine stayed with Deirdre Cohen yesterday while I went to La Belle Fashions to get the clothes ready for the fashion show. There really wasn't too much to be done; the store wasn't busy, and a clerk was available to help me. I selected a dress that I think will fit Mrs Fry, but I doubt she'll be well enough to wear it.

I haven't told you about Deirdre Cohen. Incongruous name, isn't it? When she introduced herself to me, I was taken aback. Her maiden name was Irish, O' something or other, and Deirdre fit. It also blended fairly well with her first husband's name, Jamison. But Deirdre's second husband was Herb Cohen, and since she hasn't married again or changed her name legally back to one of the first two, Cohen it will stay.

Deirdre laughs about her name. 'People remember me,' she says. 'With a name like Deirdre Cohen, how can they forget?' She has a quick sense of humor and continues with a grin: 'I'm worried about my name. I don't want it to become ordinary, and it will if Jewish people keep naming their kids Scott and Heidi, Italians name their children Tammy and Kevin and Poles use names like Colleen and Craig.' Then she recites a few choice examples like Heidi Goldstein and Colleen Skrzyniecki to make her point.

In Eagles' Landing, Deirdre's name would be an eye blinker, but it isn't here. Babies born in California are named for the days of the week, the seasons, colors, abstractions (Peace, Hope, and Charity are the most common), and material objects. I wonder when Californians are going to discover standard brands. The next generation might have names like Tide Shroeder, Colgate Newman, or Frito Winkowski. Can you imagine them growing old, a dowager named Listerine Greenberg or a dignified banker called Dr Pepper Wakefield? At least the banker would have a head start with Dr in front of his name. A thought: name a child Judge, Doctor, or Lord to give it a jump on its contemporaries.

I can laugh at California names, but there are times when I think I don't belong here, when I feel like the palm tree outside my Tudor window: I don't fit.

Deirdre Cohen is my only female friend in California. We are a year apart in age (I'm older) and both have two children. Deirdre's sons are eight and five: Kerry by her first marriage to Ken Jamison and Steve by her second marriage to Herb Cohen. I complain about my weekends, but I shouldn't when I consider Deirdre, whose weekends are often disastrous.

Herb Cohen's visiting day for Steve is Saturday, and he is generally reliable. Steve is picked up after breakfast and returned at dinnertime, unless Herb doesn't have a date and decides to keep him overnight. Herb is a dentist, and he keeps Steve supplied with sugarless gum, toothbrushes, and little red tablets he is supposed to chew before he brushes his teeth to see whether he is brushing well. Catherine discovered those little red tablets and ate six before I caught her. We had to scrub her teeth until our arms ached to get them clean. Catherine wouldn't open her mouth to speak or smile, and I couldn't blame her; each one of her teeth was grotesquely framed in red. She could have easily passed as Count Dracula's daughter.

Herb Cohen also keeps Steve oversupplied with expensive toys, a source of trouble between the half-brothers. Deirdre has implored Herb to keep the toy-buying to a minimum, but he ignores her. If he has had to skip a Saturday, he arrives the next weekend laden like a Jewish Santa Claus.

Deirdre and Herb were standing outside talking late one Saturday afternoon when I happened to see them. I was riding my bicycle to Sherwood Village's play area (cutely named the Village Green) to call Matthew and Catherine home. I waved and Deirdre motioned me over to introduce me to Herb. I must have been staring at them without realizing it, for they seemed blatantly mismatched. Deirdre, who is tall, stood eyeball-to-eyeball with Herb, talking to him earnestly; she must have been saying something about Steve's toys. But it wasn't their closeness in height that made me stare. Deirdre was speaking animatedly, but Herb remained impassive. He is a dark, sallow-complexioned man, squarely built in contrast to Deirdre, who is slender and fair. Her high cheekbones were flushed, while his face, even when speaking, was expressionless. As they walked up to me, I noticed that Herb moved with a cautious heaviness, unlike Deirdre, who glided with a dancer's grace.

After Herb left, Deirdre said, 'I know what you're thinking: Herb and I don't look right together. Everyone I knew thought it was odd when I married him. There were moments when I thought so, too, but we had a lot in common then. Guilt mainly, although we mistook it for something resembling love. In the house where I grew up, sin was served along with salt at the dinner table. I think my mother felt it was her holy obligation because my father refused to go to church or confession. I don't know why, but he wouldn't go and wouldn't discuss it. My mother became pious enough for both of them. That's why I couldn't wait to leave Gary, Indiana. The nuns at school were softer and more approachable than my mother was. When I called to tell her I was marrying Ken Jamison, the first thing she wanted to know was his religion. I told her he was Protestant. She asked if he was converting. I said no, and she hung up. We didn't speak to each other again. She died nine months before I married Herb.

'I don't know why Herb has this guilt thing. It could be because of his parents, but I was never sure. They wouldn't accept me. I think he knew they wouldn't from the beginning, although he refused to discuss it. I often wondered if their lack of acceptance made me somehow more desirable. Anyway, Herb was the kind of person who couldn't seem to let go. If his life was going well, then the world was in bad shape. I never understood him. His toy buying for Steve is a guilt trip, too. Thousands of men are divorced and see their children on weekends, but Herb is the only one I know who is constantly compensating for it. He didn't want custody of Steve because he couldn't devote enough time to him. Herb was actually gracious about the divorce after I promised that I would stay home with Steve until he entered nursery school. I think he was relieved. Steve looks so much like Herb that he must have felt as if he were abandoning himself. His money supports us, not Ken's. If I had to depend on Ken, I wouldn't be living in a place as nice as Sherwood Village or going to school. I would be struggling to survive.'

That's the way Deirdre is, Richard. Open. She sensed my curiosity about Herb and gave me a rundown on their relationship. I didn't ask, and it was clearly none of my business, yet she told me. She also told me about her first husband, Ken Jamison.

I have seen Ken Jamison twice and remember each time. He is extraordinarily handsome. Tall and dark, with a classically featured face that looks as if it had been chiseled by a master carver, Ken is the kind of man a woman can't help staring at. At least Deirdre could understand my unabashed curiosity in his case.

Ken is Kerry's father, not that Ken always remembers.

82

He is supposed to pick Kerry up every Sunday. Sometimes he shows. Most of the time he forgets. Herb's visiting day for Steve was on Sundays, too, but Deirdre had him switch to Saturdays because of Ken and Kerry. Both boys would be ready for their fathers to take them out on Sunday mornings: Herb would come five minutes early, and Ken wouldn't come and wouldn't call. Kerry would be crushed, and Deirdre would be beside herself trying to distract her disconsolate son. As she said after one of Ken's missed Sundays, 'What can I tell Kerry after he sees Steve and Herb leave? He sits by the window or goes outside, straining for a glimpse of Ken's pickup truck. An hour passes, then two, until he realizes that his father isn't coming. At that point he sits by the telephone waiting for Ken's call – an excuse, the promise of another day, anything to show that his father remembers him.

'Ken only called once. It was three in the afternoon, and Kerry was sleeping. He was exhausted from an hour of crying. I wouldn't wake him up, and Ken accused me of trying to keep him from his son. I told him he was a bastard for disappointing Kerry. He called me a bitch and told me that I was feeling sorry for myself because I didn't have a free day. It was like being married to him all over again.'

Things aren't much better when Ken does remember to come for Kerry. Ken is a potter, or he thinks he is a potter, or he pretends to be a potter. According to Deirdre, he's a dropout who plays with clay. He lives in a dilapidated farmhouse with a young girl, a potter's wheel, and no telephone so he can concentrate on the clay or the girl, whichever comes first. Ken takes Kerry out to the farmhouse and lets him run wild. Anything the boy wants to do is fine. A few days after one of Kerry's visits to Ken's, Deirdre caught him urinating outside. She was furious and told Kerry she never wanted him to do that again. He was old enough to know better, and if he had to go, he was to come in and use the bathroom. Kerry sassed her back with: 'My father says it's OK. He lets me pee anywhere I want. He doesn't keep telling me I can't do things like you do.'

Ken's purposeful lack of censorship makes Deirdre look like an ogre. As far as I know, it's the only thing he has given to his son, that and his face. Kerry is a miniature of Ken Jamison.

Deirdre's candor is what amazes me most about her. She holds nothing back. I had known her for a brief time when she related the story of her marriage to Ken. Deirdre spoke as if she weren't a principal player in the drama, as if she were talking about a woman in an article she had read.

'Ken and I just slid into marriage,' she said. 'We were young and came to California to escape. Everyone comes to California to escape, to look for something new, something better than what they have. Sometimes I think people come looking for miracles. I don't know why, but it is that way, although times have changed. My brother went to Atlanta, and my sister went to Phoenix, but the idea is the same. Once you do your leave-taking, all places are California. I came here to escape from my mother's house and had dreams of becoming a dancer. I knew what my fate would be if I stayed in Gary: a tract house, marriage to a steelworker, and romance magazines. I couldn't wait to leave.

'I didn't have any skills when I came here, so I did what women without skills do if they want to stay legitimate – I served. The choice was being either a maid, a waitress, or a clerk in a store. I waited on tables during the day and took dancing lessons at night. That's where I met Ken. He was taking dancing lessons to improve the way he moved. Ken grew up on a farm in the Midwest, watched the land drain his father, and came to California to become an actor. He drove a florist's truck to keep himself in acting and dancing lessons. We started to dance together. That was the only time I was ever really happy with Ken. When we were dancing. Sometimes he would bring me flowers he had pinched from the bouquets he was delivering. Those flowers were the closest things to a present that he ever gave me. The flowers and Kerry.

'As I said, we slid our way into marriage. Or danced our

way into it. I managed to find some work as a dancer – a bit part in a movie, a nightclub review, dancing in the chorus line of a local play. Ken couldn't find work as an actor. I know you think he's great looking, and I suppose he is, but there are hundreds of men just like Ken who think they are going to be the next Rudolph Valentino because they have perfect faces and lean bodies. That's their problem. They have the right faces but nothing else: no charm, no charisma, nothing that makes them special. After a while, they become indistinguishable. A man can be just another pretty face, too.

'I think Ken's resentment made me pregnant. Not literally, of course. He caught me off guard when things started to break for me. I don't kid myself. I know I would never have become famous as a dancer. I wasn't good enough. But I did make a start. Kerry ended it.

'After Kerry was born, Ken started working in the bar of a fancy hotel. I thought he was a bartender. He wasn't. I called the hotel one night, frantic when Kerry had a bad attack of croup. He was turning blue, and I couldn't reach the doctor. I gave my name and asked if Ken Jamison was available. My call must have been transferred three or four times; each time I asked to speak to Ken the call was transferred again. Kerry was getting worse, and I was becoming panicky. Finally, a man answered who seemed to know Ken. "May I help you?" he asked. I told him it was important that I speak to Ken Jamison, that I was having a crisis and it was urgent. The man laughed. "That's what they all say," he replied. "Ken is completely booked for tonight. Can I get you someone else?"

'I started arguing with the man, telling him that there was some mistake, that he was thinking of the wrong Ken Jamison. How dumb I was! "Only one Ken Jamison works here," he said, "and he's not available tonight. Do you want to book him for later in the week?"

'I put the receiver down in shock, but I didn't have time to think about Ken, the hotel, or the man I had spoken to.

Kerry looked like he was ready to give up. I called the police. They came and rushed us to the hospital.

'I took a cab home at five o'clock in the morning. I didn't even have enough money to give the driver a tip. I never had money when I was married to Ken'except when I went food shopping, and even then I didn't have enough.

'When I unlocked the apartment door, I found the lights blazing. Ken jumped off the sofa and leaped at us in a rage. "Where have you been," he wanted to know, "running around with my son all night?"

'I walked past Ken toward Kerry's room to put him into his crib. Ken followed me. "Well, where were you running around with a baby? Even a cheap whore doesn't do that."

'"I'm not the whore," I said.

'"What does that mean?" he yelled.

'I thought of what the man at the hotel said. Then I thought of the nights Ken came home and took me without showering first. I couldn't make it to the bathroom. I threw up in Kerry's wastebasket.

'There was another thing Ken gave me besides Kerry and the flowers. He gave me syphilis. I went to a doctor the next day to be checked. I had had a sore that I thought was the aftermath of giving birth. Finding out about Ken made me realize that the sore could have been something else. The doctor called me personally to tell me that the test was positive. "Mrs Jamison," he said, "I must know whom you have been having relations with. It is extremely important. They must be treated."

'The doctor said *they* as if I had been screwing the entire West Coast. Ken Jamison was the only man I had ever slept with. I felt unclean, like those whores in the Bible. Fallen women my mother used to call them. "I'll tell my husband," I said.

'I started on penicillin and left Ken the same day.

'I was nicer to Ken than he was to me. I don't know why, but I left him a note telling him about the syphilis. I think

I did it for Kerry. I wanted Kerry to have a father even if he was a bastard.

'I'm not sure I did the right thing.

'Now tell me, Jenny, does Ken Jamison still look smashing to you?' Deirdre asked when she was finished.

I stared at her in disbelief.

In her casual way, Deirdre has tried to befriend me. I met her through the children, and aside from Mrs Feltcher, she is the one adult in Sherwood Village who has shown signs of life. There are rare hellos and occasional smiles or nods of greeting, but generally the adult inhabitants of Sherwood Village pass each other without acknowledgement. Their behavior seems to change, however, when they are out riding their ten-speed bicycles, jogging in their Adidas sneakers, or driving their cars. Then they wave. They are big on waving. I suppose there is safety in motion; it eliminates any chance of contact. As for my isolation, it is probably a blessing. Sherwood Village has allowed me to reside quietly and keep the history of my life in a plain brown wrapper.

Deirdre's life has purpose. She is going to school to become a social worker, and she'll be a good one. Deirdre is perceptive. At times, I think she is practicing on me. She knows I don't like talking about myself and hasn't pushed me directly, but she has asked me questions like: 'How long are you going to remain in seclusion at Briarhill?' or 'When are you going to let me fix you up on a date again?' I try to avoid her questions. I spend a good portion of my life avoiding questions.

Deirdre is also anxious for me to get into a self-help program. 'I don't know how you can live without expanding your self-awareness,' she says repeatedly, shaking her head as if I am in mortal danger. 'Everyone needs something.'

I've replied by telling her I have the children, but she says they aren't enough. 'Everyone needs something,' she asserts, 'for the self.'

Deirdre's something is yoga. She is as devoted to it as

Mrs Feltcher is to the church. 'Yoga isn't a religion,' Deirdre explained. 'It is a philosophy that enables you to get in touch with yourself. You'll learn how to relax, how to eat, how to breathe...'

'I already know how to breathe,' I interrupted. 'I've been breathing for years.'

'That's what you think,' she replied. 'The only time you come close to breathing properly is when you sleep. Yoga teaches deep, rhythmic breathing. Your lungs absorb more oxygen, which makes your mind sharper. It also improves the functioning of your body. After I meditate, I feel recharged.'

I was tempted to ask whether yoga helped hiccups but decided against it.

Deirdre insists that yoga has changed her life. 'I am able to face reality now,' she said. 'I have learned to relax, and I am learning to forgive. At one time I couldn't utter Ken Jamison's name without crying or swearing. Today I can talk about him. What he is doing to Kerry makes me angry, but I can cope with it. I can fight back because Ken can't touch my inner being, my inner self. If it weren't for yoga, he would have destroyed me long ago.'

I have a book on yoga that Deirdre brought for me to read, but I haven't opened it. A blurb on the cover says: *Yoga is a way of life.* Since I'm still trying to adjust to California, I thought I'd better wait. I don't think I could handle adjusting to more than one way of life at a time.

Richard, I don't know why I told you about Deirdre and her marriages. It wasn't necessary.

Maybe it was necessary. It bothers me. Not because Deirdre needs sympathy or wants it. She would be appalled at the suggestion. And not because it is mildly titillating. Deirdre isn't the first woman whose husband gave her venereal disease; there were rumors of cases in Eagles' Landing.

Why does it bother me? You didn't give me anything as awful as venereal disease, and you certainly weren't a male prostitute. The thought of you catching the first or employed as the latter is so completely out of character that I would laugh if I weren't scared.

Is it Deirdre's candor, her openness that disturbs me? No. I admire it.

If it isn't for any of the above reasons, then why did I say I was scared?

I think I know why. Deirdre can talk about what happened to her because *it did happen to her*. She didn't cause it.

I am scared. But why? I wasn't the one who set up the Bestmark Partnership. You did.

I don't want to think about it. I won't.

Mrs Fry wasn't well enough to model in the show. I left for work as soon as the children's bus picked them up so I could check on her condition and found her sitting on a chair in her room. The odor in the room was strong.

Mrs Fry recognized me. 'Oh, Jenny,' she said in a quavery voice, 'have you come to talk about our boys? It is a lovely morning. They can spend the day playing outside.' Then she hesitated. 'Is it a school day? I can't seem to remember if it is a school day.' Without waiting for my reply, she turned to stare out the window and lost everything, even the awareness of my presence, in a matter of seconds.

I waited for her mental return, but she simply sat there, a shell of a woman, shredding a tissue she had taken out of the pocket of her robe. Bit by bit the pieces fell, tiny pieces of white tissue, some clinging to her robe, others landing on the floor.

I left Mrs Fry's room tasting my morning coffee, feeling that my entire breakfast would come up if I didn't get outside for air. I hurried down the corridor and ran out the front entrance. Cars were zooming past. People were going to work with their radios blaring, their vehicles gleaming like huge enameled insects under the perfect California sun. The people behind the wheels looked young and invulnerable, as if they would always be competent, as if they would always be able to control their lives as they were controlling their speeding cars. I wanted to run down the steps to the curb, wave my arms and scream at them to stop so I could tell them about Mrs Fry. I wanted them to know about the woman I had just left, a woman who had once driven a car and had known the date, the time, the temperature, and the ages of her sons. Like a half-crazed gypsy fortune teller, I wanted to give them a free reading into their future. I stood on the steps gulping in carbon monoxide and struggled to control myself.

There are times, Richard, when I think I may be cracking up.

I spotted Jim Gentile's green Cadillac before it turned into the front driveway and went back inside. One of the aides, a pleasant woman who seems to have a smile for everyone, stopped me as I was heading toward my office. 'I saw you coming out of Mrs Fry's room,' she said. 'The old lady had a bad night, real bad. That bed reeked. What a mess! I told them, told them last week that they should call one of her hotshot sons. But do they listen? Hell, no. Why should they listen? They ain't the ones that has to clean her up or change those stinking sheets. Now I'll get her dressed, but I don't know what for. She ain't goin' nowhere, that lady. Tell them in the office, will you? Tell them to call one of her sons. They'll listen to you.'

'I called one of her sons last Friday and asked him to visit,' I replied, 'but he refused. He said it wasn't his turn.'

'Which son?' she asked, frowning.

'The older one. I thought he'd be more sympathetic.'

'Her sons are bad news, both of 'em. The older one acts nice when he comes, but he don't mean it. He runs outa here like his pants was on fire.' She shook her head sadly. 'I'd better go in there now. Been puttin' it off long enough.'

What the aide said surprised me. I was under the

impression that the professional staff – the nurses and visiting doctors – listened to the aides. It is a reasonable assumption. The aides have the most contact with the residents. Now that I think about it, I haven't seen the nurses doing much of anything other than paperwork and carrying trays with tiny paper pill cups on them. Perhaps I'm being unfair. I don't see too much of what actually goes on at Briarhill because my work is confined to the public rooms. Still, Briarhill is supposed to be the country club of residential-nursing homes. If it is the best, the others must be gray hells.

The fashion show was a success, but there were a few tense moments. The newspaper photographer didn't arrive until the show was almost over, and Miss Manfred, who insisted upon wearing her highest pair of heels, lost her balance while she was pirouetting in a blue dress that matched her eyes and hair. She landed spread-eagled on the floor. Luckily, the dress had a pleated skirt; all that was damaged was her dignity. The fall must have been her first, for she went down relaxed as a baby and declined help when she rose, bones intact.

Everyone in the audience gasped with fright when Miss Manfred fell. Any fall in a nursing home gets as big a reaction from the staff and residents as a six-alarm fire would in a fire station; adrenaline flowed hard in the room. I caught the panic of the residents and looked around, fearing I would see someone having a heart attack or worse. When the elderly gather together, there is always the real possibility that one in the group could drop dead, a possibility that I have been dreading. Can you imagine planning an activity and literally exciting a participant to death?

Fortunately everyone survived, but I don't think I'll plan another extravaganza at Briarhill. It's too risky. A diet of craft demonstrations, sing-alongs, movies, and bridge tournaments will have to be standard fare for a while. If there is a death at a bridge table, it will be a murder, and for that I can't be held responsible.

I asked the photographer to take a picture of Miss Manfred for the paper. The fall took more out of her than she would admit. She insisted that she was fine, but her face was pale and the rouge spots on her cheeks had evaporated. When I told her that she would probably be in the evening paper, she perked up and posed, but I don't think her heart was in it. Miss Manfred became aware of her vulnerability today. Even among the aged there can be a coming of age, the recognition of one's human frailty. I hope Miss Manfred regains some of her spunkiness. I would hate to see her go the way of so many of the others, to live without her spicy, independent personality.

The photographer took pictures of several residents besides Miss Manfred, and I gave him enough information for ten captions, although I knew only one picture would be run. After last week's aggravation, I didn't feel I could risk omitting anything. I was actually apprehensive when the evening paper was delivered, afraid that Nat Witton had forgotten his promise. He didn't forget. There was a good-sized picture of Miss Manfred opposite the Women's Page, with a decent caption underneath, and a brief article alongside the picture. Mr Witton must have had someone write the article from my notes. I wrote a thank-you letter and mailed it to him after dinner.

Tomorrow morning Catherine will receive her award. It is all she can talk about. She must have repeated 'I'm going on the stage' dozens of times from the moment she arrived home until I finally got her into bed. Catherine wouldn't go to bed after her usual stalls because she found another one, good for at least an extra half hour: the tearing apart of her closet, which she managed with the efficiency of a veteran sales clerk taking inventory. 'I have nothing to wear,' she said in disgust while surveying her full closet, 'that is just right for the assembly. How can I go on the stage with nothing to wear?'

'You could always wear nothing,' I suggested, trying not to laugh at the ageless lament of females coming out of a six-year-old mouth.

'Nothing!' she shrieked. 'You mean go on the stage BARE NAKED?'

'If you can't make up your mind with all the clothes you have, then don't wear anything at all. Everyone will notice you.'

Her face twisted in an effort to hold back tears. 'You don't care about me being on the stage. You're being mean.'

I shouldn't have teased her. You used to tease me for the same complaint, only it wasn't always teasing. In the beginning, it was irritation coated with teasing. After we moved to Eagles' Landing, it was undisguised anger. I remember how I rationalized the bills that made you blanch each month. 'The clothes are necessary if you want us to be accepted,' I explained. 'I'm seeing the same women week after week. They've made careers out of dressing themselves. You can't expect me to wear the same outfits repeatedly. I'm building an image, and clothes are a part of that image.'

There were also vague feelings of uneasiness that I couldn't explain, which I quelled with trips to the local stores. The uneasiness was loss, although I didn't recognize it then. I missed Catherine's babyhood. Ginny witnessed her first steps and heard her first words. And there was Matthew, who was becoming increasingly withdrawn. Whenever his eyes met mine, they were dark with disappointment, so I avoided him and shopped. I filled my walk-in closet with designer outfits, but the clothes didn't make me happy.

Richard, now that you are gone, I wear jeans, with the exception of a few skirts and blouses for work. I haven't shopped in months.

Catherine started to cry. 'I'm sorry,' I apologized guiltily. 'I do care, but it is late. If you don't go to bed soon, you will have circles under your eyes, and that won't look nice no matter what you wear.'

She put her hands on her tearstained cheeks, her fingertips searching under her eyes for dark rings.

'No, you don't have circles yet, and you won't if you hurry to bed. Let's pick three outfits, and you can choose the one you want to wear in the morning.'

We selected three outfits and hung them importantly on one side of the closet. Finally, she climbed into bed. It occurred to me that we might have a problem in the morning if she had trouble deciding among the three. 'Catherine,' I said, 'will you surprise me in the morning by picking out your dress all by yourself?'

'Just me decide?' she asked. Her brown eyes opened wide, like bright pennies.

'Just you. Come downstairs all dressed and surprise me.'

'Can Matthew help?'

'No. Surprise him, too.'

She started to giggle. 'I'll even surprise me,' she said.

I kissed her good night, burying my face in her soft blond hair; nothing is as delicious as the fragrance of a child fresh from a bath and shampoo. When I started to leave the room, she sat up in bed. 'Mommy, who is coming to school tomorrow besides you and Mrs Feltcher?'

'No one. Aren't Mrs Feltcher and I enough?'

'Some daddies are coming. Lots of people are coming. Mrs Eberhard said you could invite friends.'

'I did. Mrs Feltcher is coming.'

'Not just Mrs Feltcher. Other friends. Why couldn't you invite other friends like ... like Mrs Cohen?' Catherine tried to think of other friends but couldn't; there are no other friends.

'Mrs Cohen has to go to her own classes,' I said.

'I wish Daddy were here. He'd come,' she said wistfully.

'Yes, he would. Go to sleep now.' I left her door ajar and turned the hall light on.

Tonight was the first time Catherine wanted you here for a specific reason, Richard. It will be the first of many times, I suppose. Her memory's picture of you is hazy, but the picture isn't important. It's the need that matters:

needing you to witness the events of her life, to confirm the genes that link you, life affirming life.

It could be worse. Matthew and Catherine could be victims like Kerry Jamison, who has a father that doesn't give a damn about him and wouldn't show for any event in his life if it weren't convenient. There are thousands of fathers like Ken Jamison, just as there are men like my own father, who put business above school plays and assemblies. I managed to survive. Catherine will, too.

Again, death protects you. You can never disappoint your children because you aren't here. They can embellish their slivers of memory of a father until the slivers become mighty trees, giant sequoias that dwarf everything around them. I took the children to see the redwoods, as much for myself as for them. The trees are awesome, so massive that a human eye can't contain one in a single, close image. You could become a myth to your children, the greatest of fathers as the sequoia is the mightiest of trees, if they would only stop asking questions.

Maybe death isn't final after all. It has potential. Think of what you can become if I can give our children the right answers. If there are right answers.

This is unfair. The marriage has ended, and I am still responsible for your image.

I wonder, Richard. Would you have come to Catherine's assembly if it conflicted with the scheduled meeting of an important client? Don't answer. I believe I know.

Catherine came downstairs beaming this morning. She had brushed her hair until it shone, scrubbed her face pink, and put on a yellow dress with white trim that made her look as fresh and perky as a daffodil. All that was missing were her socks and shoes. In her excitement, she had forgotten them.

'How do I look?' she asked. 'Did I make a good choice for the stage?'

The *stage* is beginning to take on an aura not unlike the presidency.

'You look wonderful,' I said, 'but didn't you forget something?'

'What?' she wanted to know.

'Look at your feet.'

She looked down and put her hand over her open mouth. 'My feet,' she giggled. 'They're bare naked.'

She ran upstairs to finish dressing.

Catherine has become fascinated with nakedness and uses the words *bare naked* constantly, as if the word naked isn't sufficient. She was one of his witnesses the day Kerry Jamison decided to relieve himself outside, and the forbiddenness of his act impressed her. After years of taking Matthew for granted, she became suddenly curious and peeks in on him whenever she can. Matthew isn't modest yet, but one of these days she'll be greeted with a closed door.

I try to be casual about the whole business, but one day I asked Catherine why she uses the words *bare naked*. 'Naked and bare mean the same thing,' I said to her. 'Why do you use both words?'

She thought for a moment. 'When you're naked, some things are showing. But when you're *bare naked*, everything is showing. Everything. And when you can see everything, then you're really bare naked.'

I didn't argue with her. In a strange way, her childish logic seemed to make sense at the time, even with the redundancy. It was jarring at first, but now when she says *bare naked* the words pass almost unnoticed.

Mrs Feltcher arrived at my door early, chattering away. There was a flush of excitement on her face, and she kept moving her handbag, a sensible black purse loaded with zippers and compartments, from one arm to the other. I didn't have to say a word. Her monologue amply filled the time it took to drive to school, park the car, and get seated in the auditorium. Mrs Feltcher talked about rude shoppers in the supermarket, the price of meat, the yearly threat of brush fires – 'It's unnatural for nature to burn itself up' – kids smoking pot the way boys used to smoke Lucky Strikes and Chesterfields behind the drugstore when she was a girl, and the apathy of young people in her church. 'All they do is bounce around in sneakers from one game to another,' she said. 'Why, some of them even wear their sneakers to church, if they bother to come. It's disrespectful. And the services! There's no Latin, and instead of the organ, we get guitar music. Can you imagine guitar music in church? They have it at the late Sunday service. I won't go to that one. There are some things I can't overlook. Church is going to turn into a rock-and-roll concert or one of those folk-song festivals. It's a big mistake, this idea of keeping up with the times. In a few years, the traditions will be gone, and then it will be too late. The young people will discover that they have lost something, but they won't know what it is that they have lost, so they won't be able to find it.'

I hadn't realized it before, but Mrs Feltcher is unhappy living in California.

'I'm tired of these sunny days,' she said, sighing and clutching her handbag. 'One day after another without a break. It's like being forced to live your life under a light bulb; you can't turn it off. And the seasons! I miss the seasons. It doesn't feel right doing spring and fall cleaning when one day looks like the next. It should be spring when you do spring cleaning – the crocuses should be coming up through the snow. That's a sign to begin. Out here, I have to live by the calendar. Except for the dry spells and the rainy season, one month is like the next. I have to rip pages off the calendar to find out where I am in the year.'

By the time we were seated, Mrs Feltcher had regained her earlier enthusiasm. 'I can't wait to see Catherine. It's too bad her grandparents aren't here today.' Her sharp-featured face peered inquisitively at the adults around us. There were perhaps a dozen parents sitting with bored expressions on their faces. 'You know, Jenny,' she observed, 'I don't see too many people who look like grandparents, maybe just that woman over there.'

Mrs Feltcher was looking at Mrs Eberhard. 'She is Catherine's teacher,' I said.

Mrs Eberhard walked over to us. 'I'm so glad you could come, Mrs Weaver. Is this Catherine's grandmother?' she asked, waiting to be introduced.

A merry-go-round of emotions – longing, a mild embarrassment, and pride – each took a turn playing on Mrs Feltcher's face.

'This is Mrs Feltcher, our neighbor and friend,' I explained.

Mrs Feltcher seemed pleased with her introduction.

'The turnout is disappointing,' said Mrs Eberhard. 'Fewer and fewer parents come each year. You'd think they would want to be here when their children are spotlighted. I suppose it can't be helped. Most parents work today, both mothers and fathers.'

'Then one of the parents should take time off,' said Mrs Feltcher positively.

'I agree,' replied Mrs Eberhard, bobbing her gray curls.

The two women warmed to each other instantly and traded doomsday visions until Mrs Eberhard excused herself to help the other teachers shepherd children into the auditorium.

Matthew came in with his class first. He spotted me, started to smile, then turned away, marching straight ahead. Matthew's getting older, Richard. I think he felt that recognizing his mother would be babyish. I understood, but it hurt.

Catherine entered the auditorium exuberantly, her dark eyes shining. She saw us and waved. I smiled and held up my hand to return her greeting. Mrs Feltcher waved both arms and hit the head of the woman who was sitting in front of her with her purse. 'Excuse me,' she said. 'I'm sorry. I got carried away seeing Catherine. She's going to get an award today.' Mrs Feltcher would have said more, but the woman rubbed the back of her head and dismissed Mrs Feltcher with a look of annoyance.

The world may be in a continual state of flux, but school assemblies remain essentially the same from one generation to the next. It was comforting for its familiar monotony. The program included the Pledge of Allegiance, *The Star-Spangled Banner* sung off-key and out of sync, the standard brain-numbing opening speech by the principal, self-conscious performances of wiggling children, and the presentation of awards. Catherine's name was one of the first to be called, and she practically danced across the stage.

It's a shame you couldn't have been there to see her. She was radiant.

Mrs Feltcher clapped the entire time Catherine was on the stage. It was all I could do not to tell her to sit on her hands, but she means well.

Sometimes meaning well can be a curse.

I drove Mrs Feltcher home before going to work. 'What's that blinking light?' she asked, pointing to the dashboard. The square marked ALT was flashing on and off.

'I don't know,' I said. I felt like cursing the damn car but didn't. Mrs Feltcher would have started making preparations for my direct descent to hell.

'You should have it checked,' she said. 'I don't know anything about cars because I don't drive, but a flashing light is a warning. Your brakes could fail, or the car could explode.'

I told her I would take care of the car and found myself relieved when I dropped her off. 'Thank you for taking me,' she said effusively. 'I had a wonderful time. That Catherine is such a gem! Matthew, too.'

'I'm glad you could come,' I said, anxious to leave.

Mrs Feltcher stood next to the car, gripping the door handle. 'Aren't you going to eat lunch?' she asked.

'I'll grab a sandwich at Briarhill.'

'It is bad for your digestion to eat in a hurry. Ruins the

stomach. Did I ever tell you about my uncle with the stomach problems? He had ulcers, indigestion . . .'

'I'm sorry,' I interrupted, 'but I really must go now. It's close to noon. I've already missed half a working day. Perhaps you'll tell me about your uncle another time.'

Mrs Feltcher let go of the door handle reluctantly and watched with disappointment as I pulled away. I felt ungracious, as if I had ruined her morning. She really enjoyed the assembly, and it was kind of her to attend. If she would only give me room!

Later in the day I found Mr Gallisdorf reading in the solarium, so absorbed that I had to tap him on the shoulder to get his attention. When he looked up, his eyes were misted with tears.

'I didn't mean to disturb you,' I said.

'It's perfectly all right,' he replied. 'I just read something terribly moving. I'm glad you're here. I have a tendency to dwell on things these days.'

'Are you reading a novel?' I asked doubtfully.

'No. It is a biography of a man named Turner, Frederick Jackson Turner. I was just reading about the deaths of two of his children in 1899. He only had three. A loss like that is a terrible thing. It almost destroyed him, yet he pulled himself together and went on with his career. Did you read Turner when you were in school?'

'No,' I replied, 'I wasn't much of a history student. The memorization of names and dates of battles bored me.'

'History is more than names and dates. You would find Turner interesting. He had difficulty writing his theories down, but what he wrote still makes sense today.'

'What did he write about?'

'The frontier,' said Mr Gallisdorf, closing the book after marking his page with a worn leather bookmark. 'He wrote about the importance of the frontier in promoting democracy and developing our national character. Each time Americans moved west, there was a resettling. Civilization met savagery. There were clashes, conflicting values, and necessary adaptations between the old and the new. Settlers had to adjust, not only to a new physical environment that was often harsh, but to each other. They were people formed by their pasts, diverse pasts, and all were seeking a decent future. The old frontier was indeed volatile.'

Mr Gallisdorf paused, reflecting. 'It is considered a uniquely American thing, the frontier, the continuous expansion west. Europeans thought of us as killers because of our guns. Some of them think of us as savages to this day. But we weren't just gunslingers, although the film industry makes our past look as if it were peopled by trigger-happy cowboys. Our people were individuals, brave enough to begin over and over again.'

'But the frontier is gone. Didn't America lose its last frontier when California was settled?' I asked.

'Some historians think so, and if one considers the frontier in strict geographic terms, I suppose it is gone. There have always been arguments against Turner's theories. Men are writing books to prove him wrong today, but I don't agree with them.'

'Why not, if the frontier is gone?'

'Because I don't believe the frontier is gone. Not in America. It is if one thinks of the frontier as virgin territory and homesteading for free land. However, Americans are still moving, today more than ever, and with these moves they are finding their own frontiers. Different local customs, new job challenges – the frontier all over again.'

He cleared his throat and stroked his mustache. 'When I was a young man and traveled in Europe, I visited towns where the inhabitants knew the history of their own and everyone else's family. Those Europeans could go back three or four hundred years as if it were yesterday. I don't think they did it intentionally, but they made me feel inferior, as if my country were populated by a bunch of upstarts. I found myself apologizing for being an American, something I am ashamed of to this day.

'I was in Europe for a long time. It took me a while, but

I finally saw beyond their mesmerizing stories. I looked at the people themselves, at their progress. You know, those small European towns stayed essentially the same from one generation to the next. If I had to describe their life in a word, I'd call it predictable. Some towns were actually stagnant. Nothing had changed and anything that was new was brought in by outsiders.'

'A sense of place is important,' I said, feeling the emptiness that my own lack of place has created within me. 'I've always had respect for old families, for people who have lived a long time in one area and made a place for themselves there.'

'There is a difference between the place in which you live and a sense of place that you find within yourself as a human being,' replied Mr Gallisdorf.

'Aren't they tied together, your geographical roots and your emotional roots? When people live out their lives in one area, they carve a position for themselves. They know who they are, and their knowing comes both from themselves and from the place in which they live.'

'It's fine to stay a long time in one place if it works for you,' said Mr Gallisdorf, 'but for some people, it doesn't work: they have to leave to live. Look at you, Jenny. You came from a place on the opposite side of the country, a good three thousand miles away. As I recall, it had a very American-sounding name – Eagle something. You moved, and you're making a new life for yourself and your children. California is a frontier for you. You are adjusting to a new environment, different ideas and local customs. Life style, I think they call it today.'

'Yes, I suppose California is a frontier of sorts for me.'

'Of course it is, and you'll meet the challenge,' he said positively. 'I have a frontier of my own, you know. I had an awful time adjusting to this [he pointed to his wheelchair with his good right arm] until I started reading Turner. The man gave me an idea. I began thinking about age as a frontier. Instead of continuing to fight my

102

infirmity, I began to work with it, trying to adjust and adapt. Why, I believe I am a pioneer, too. Not in a big way. Just for myself, an old man trying to meet a challenge.'

Mr Gallisdorf looked so gallant sitting there, a frail wisp of a human being meeting life with half a body and the courage of ten men in their prime, that I impulsively bent down and kissed his cheek.

'Oh my,' said Mr Gallisdorf, nonplussed. 'What did I do to deserve that?'

'You were being yourself,' I replied, embarrassed. Mr Gallisdorf is reserved. I suddenly felt that I had overstepped and didn't know what to do to correct it.

'You are kind,' he whispered. His eyes glistened.

'I'll see you on Thursday,' I said, turning to leave.

Mr Gallisdorf didn't reply.

I carried our conversation with me for the remainder of the day, unable to accept the idea that all of our pioneers were bravely seeking prosperous new lives. I believe that many of them were doing exactly what I am doing, simply looking for a place in which to hide. It would be interesting to know how many of them succeeded.

I also began to wonder about the quality of their lives, if they lived as I am living now, an alien in a strange place, observing rather than participating, always watchful, ever on guard. Sometimes I feel like a prisoner of the past, that I shall never be free because I ran away. I am not proud of running; it wasn't the bravest choice I could have made. Maybe I was wrong. But you killed yourself, and that certainly wasn't right. I suppose we all have to choose our own means of escape. For you, it was easier to die than to run.

Now that I think about it, your choice of suicide was almost frighteningly predictable. I remember how you always snickered at California. You used to say that every jerk you knew moved to California at one time or another. Someone would mention a name, like Harry Grubman, and you would say, 'Oh, Grubby Harry. I remember him. He moved to California and changed his name to Harris

Gray. Charlie saw him a couple of years ago when he went out there to close a big franchise deal. He was in a restaurant, one of those little "in" places, and who should be at the next table but Harry Grubman. Charlie recognized him right away. "Why it's Harry," he said, "Harry, Harry Grubman." Grubby pretended not to notice, but Charlie's a persistent guy. "Harry, Harry Grubman," he said and went over to Grubby's table to shake hands. Friendly, you know. Grubby looked him right in the eye and said, "I am afraid you are mistaken. I am not Harry Grubman."

'Charlie knew he was Harry Grubman. Custom jeans and a professionally styled haircut don't change a guy that much. Anyway, Charlie took a burn. He wouldn't have bothered with the jerk back home but to be snubbed like that was ridiculous, so Charlie said, "Be glad I didn't call you Grubby," and he walked away. Grubby nearly had a heart attack.'

Everyone in Eagles' Landing thought the Grubby story was hilarious. It was perfect for cocktail parties. You always stopped at that part of the story. The rest wasn't amusing. You didn't tell them about Harry Grubman/ Harris Gray locating Charlie later and explaining his rudeness.

They met that evening at a bar. Harry/Harris was a shattered man; his custom jeans no longer fit. He told Charlie he had come to California to lose Harry Grubman. 'I was always on the outside,' said Harry, 'a walking joke, a jerk with a jerk's nickname.'

Harry created Harris Gray. The man gave birth to himself. He was happy for the first time in his life, until he met Charlie in that restaurant. The people at Harry's table, people he had worked years to cultivate and whose respect he had finally earned, knew that Charlie had spoken the truth. Harry could tell. Charlie named him and resuscitated Grubby Harry. 'How can I still be Harris Gray?' he asked mournfully.

Charlie apologized, but like most apologies, it was too late. The damage was done. Words can't erase words.

Charlie told us that story when he was drunk. I remember the evening vividly. It was the first time he had dinner with us after we moved to Eagles' Landing. You had been upset because Charlie had avoided our invitation for weeks. 'Charlie is in the throes of divorcing Doreen. He hasn't been himself,' you said, excusing his stalls.

Richard, you were the one who needed the excuse. Charlie was your best friend. His reluctance to come to dinner in our new home had cut you deeply.

Charlie arrived that night with a magnificent porcelain vase for a house gift. You took him on a tour of each room, and I can recall the expression of pride and pleasure on your face when he told you the house was elegant. No one's approval meant as much to you as Charlie's. He also warned you, in a joking manner, that it would be expensive to furnish. 'You'd better not try to fill it up all at once. You might have to buy a furniture store to do it.' Charlie was looking at me with his cool green eyes when he said that.

Charlie drank all evening, which was unusual for him. You commented on it after he polished off a bottle of wine before we were finished with our main course. 'Take it easy,' you warned him. 'I haven't seen you drink like this since our engagement party, and you've gained a few pounds since then. I doubt that I could get you home.'

'Don't worry,' said Charlie, waving an empty glass in one of his immense hands. 'I've got a big frame. It would take a case of this stuff to knock me out. It's just pop with a little kick.'

The effects of the liquor hit Charlie after dinner. He didn't pass out, as he had promised, but his eyes lost their sharpness, and he became unusually loquacious, actually expansive. I found it hard to believe that careful Charlie could be so animated. Just before he left, he told us the Harry Grubman/Harris Gray story. Charlie's face was slightly flushed, and he was perspiring. Still, I thought I saw the rivulet of a tear on his face. It was possible, for

Charlie spoke in a voice of broken dreams and left immediately afterward. I went to bed thinking that I had misjudged him; Charlie Pritchard was human after all.

I never told you, but I knew why Charlie avoided our dinner invitations. He had called me early one morning from his office months before, after you dropped off the contract to purchase the house and lot in Eagles' Landing. 'I want to talk to you about the house,' he said.

'What about it?' I asked, surprised that he wanted to speak to me.

'I don't know how to say this tactfully, so I'll come right out with it: the house is too expensive. I know you want to live in Eagles' Landing, but you'd be better off building somewhere else.'

'Richard wants to live there, too,' I said defensively. 'The decision is as much his as it is mine.'

'You can't afford it,' Charlie said flatly.

'Have you been going through our bank statements?' I asked, bristling.

'I'm familiar with Richard's assets, if that's what you mean,' Charlie said. 'Remember, I'm his best friend as well as his lawyer.'

I didn't need or want to be reminded. 'Then why didn't you tell him we couldn't afford it when he dropped off the contract?'

'Richard knows how much you want the house, Jenny. He's crazy about you. He'll give you anything you want.'

'You're making Richard sound like a lovesick imbecile. Don't insult him. Or me. Richard wouldn't build the house if he thought he couldn't handle it. We have a substantial down payment. There isn't a bank in the city that would refuse us a mortgage.'

'You have to live after you move in,' Charlie argued. 'The taxes on that house will be astronomical, at least four thousand dollars a year...'

'We'll be able to pay our taxes,' I interrupted.

'It isn't just the taxes. The house will have to be

furnished. Knowing you, it will be furnished with nothing but the best. You have never been one to settle.'

'I'm not planning to furnish it all at once.'

'But you'll want to after you move in. There will be other expenses, too. Eagles' Landing is very social. You and Richard will join a fancier country club, go out to dinner more often, and give expensive parties.'

'How do you know? Are you omniscient?' I asked angrily.

'No,' he answered. 'But I am practical. I have to consider all of the facts.'

The dry, logical tone of his voice infuriated me. 'Joining a country club and doing expensive entertaining is supposition, not fact. We haven't moved in yet,' I said, trying to keep my voice as modulated as his. I didn't want to give Charlie the satisfaction of hearing me scream into the telephone.

'I'm making an accurate projection,' he said. 'It will take money, a lot of money to live in Eagles' Landing. Richard can't afford it right now. He should be able to swing it in a few years, if all goes well.'

'You sound so positive,' I replied. 'It must be nice to know everything. Maybe you should have been a fortune teller instead of a lawyer.'

Charlie ignored my outburst. 'As I told you,' he said dryly, 'I must consider all of the facts.'

I don't know why I didn't tell you about Charlie's telephone call. I almost said something at dinner that night, but I was so angry and full of resentment that I held my tongue. You and Charlie were such good friends; anything I said would have come out as an attack. And I believed that Charlie was wrong. He put the full responsibility for the house on me, as if I were leading you down a long road toward doom. You were the one who picked the lot and approved the final plans. The house was yours, too.

Richard, he hedged for weeks before coming to dinner because he didn't want us to build that house; we were where Charlie felt we shouldn't be.

There is something else I didn't tell you. When the mail came the next day, there was a long white envelope with Charlie's office address printed on the upper left-hand corner in dignified black letters. It was addressed to me in Charlie's legal scrawl. Inside, there was a note and several sheets torn from a yellow legal pad on which itemized figures were written. The note read:

> Jenny,
>   Perhaps you'll reconsider after reading the enclosed figures, which I believe are a conservative projection of the expenses you will incur if you build the house in Eagles' Landing. I'll hold off sending the contract to the builder in the hope that I'll hear from you.
>
>   Charlie

I sat down and studied the figures. Charlie had estimated our building, living, and furnishing expenses for the first two years in the Eagles' Landing house. The totals were astronomical. He's crazy, I thought, crumpling the yellow papers in anger. I threw everything – Charlie's note, the envelope, and the papers – into the garbage, thinking that I'd be damned before I'd call him, even if only to tell him that he was absolutely wrong.

Charlie wasn't wrong, Richard. As much as it hurts me to admit this, he had estimated our expenses accurately and conservatively. At the end of our second year in Eagles' Landing, we had spent three thousand dollars more than Charlie said we would.

The car broke down again. This time it was the alternator. Now I know what the ALT window on the dashboard means.

I planned to have the car checked after I finished my Wednesday errands. The alternator light was blinking, but the car was running well so I thought I could postpone going to a garage until I was through. After what happened to me at the gas station last week, I wasn't looking forward to dealing with another mechanic.

The car died in a supermarket parking lot. It didn't die, actually. It just wouldn't start. After struggling with the ignition for at least five minutes, I threw my keys into my purse and ran back to the store to use a pay phone, concerned about my groceries. There were seven full bags in the back of the wagon, and the temperature outside was 78°.

This time I called an Oldsmobile dealer. I fried in the parking lot for twenty minutes until their tow truck came. A heavyset boy of about eighteen got out of the truck. 'Are you Mrs Weaver?' he asked without interest.

'Yes. Can you start the car?'

'No,' he replied, 'I don't work on cars. I just tow them in.'

Can you believe it, Richard? In California, there are a bunch of kids driving tow trucks who know nothing about cars. It must be a new career. There could even be a course called 'Towing Dead Automobiles.' Anything is possible here.

'I have perishable groceries in the back of the wagon,' I said. 'Could you stop and let me unload them before taking the car in? It's on the way, and it would only take a few minutes.'

'Your groceries!' he exclaimed, staring at me as if my nose were growing before his eyes. 'I deliver cars, not groceries.'

'I'm not asking you to deliver my groceries, just to stop so I can put some of them away before they spoil. I really don't live far from here.'

He mumbled something about not running a grocery delivery service. I suppose I deserved it. This is the age of specialization.

I opened the passenger door of the tow truck. 'What are you doing?' he asked.

'I'm getting into the truck.'

'It's against the rules.'

'If you're taking my car and my groceries, you can take me, too.'

'I can't do that.'

'Then unhitch my car, and I'll call someone else.'

'Oh, all right,' he said disgustedly, 'but when we get there, tell them you insisted or they'll have my ass.'

I looked at his coarse features, his erupting skin, and his lumpy body, which was encased in a sweaty gray T-shirt and filthy jeans. No one would want his ass. 'Don't worry,' I replied.

He climbed into the truck and flipped a transistor radio that was sitting on the dashboard to blasting before starting the engine. It was nostalgia hour. 'Now for some golden rock oldies but goodies,' the announcer crooned. 'Our first trip back is with a classic done by the great group CHICAGOOOO.' The record started to play, and the boy's eyes glazed. He gunned the motor of the truck to the beat of the music and took off to the lyrics: *Does anybody really know what time it is? Does anybody really care?*...

When we arrived at Ripley Oldsmobile, nothing was said about me being towed in with the car. I waited in the garage watching wet circles spread on the brown grocery bags. Mechanics emerged occasionally from under cars as if they were ants crawling out from under rocks; they would get a necessary tool or part, then disappear. There were no other signs of life.

Finally, a serviceman appeared. 'Can I help you?' he asked, squinting at me impatiently. His forehead was extremely low, so that his eyes appeared almost closed.

I explained who I was and pointed to my car.

'We're real busy now. I can't get someone on it right away.'

'My groceries are spoiling,' I said. 'Your garage will start to smell of spoiled food soon if I don't get them home. Can you lend me a car while you're fixing mine?'

'Our loaners are out.'

'I must have a car,' I insisted.

'I'll see what I can do,' he said, walking away.

I signed a work order, and he loaned me a battered tan Chevrolet that sounded like it needed a vacation for all of the choking and wheezing it did, but it ran. When I called this afternoon to find out what was wrong with my car, the service man told me that I need a new alternator and that it will cost $185.76. With the cost of the ruined groceries, this latest disaster will come to over $200. It's ridiculous. I would trade the car in, but I've spent so much money on it that I feel forced to keep it.

I don't know what you would do about the car if you were here. It was my choice, not yours. I remember how we battled over the car. You said that we couldn't afford a new one when I needed it. 'Money is tight,' you said. 'We just bought a house.' Two weeks later you purchased a Mercedes for yourself.

'How could you?' I asked, feeling more betrayed than angry.

'It was necessary,' you replied. 'A Mercedes says something; a Buick doesn't.'

'But my car skids all over the road.' It was late in October, and I was already dreading another winter of struggling to control my car on icy roads.

'You can get a new car next year,' you said.

When the new cars came out the following September, I reminded you of your promise. 'I'd like a new car,' I said late one night as we were getting ready for bed.

'Let's wait,' you replied, lining up the creases on your trousers before sliding them on to the hanger.

'You promised, Richard.'

'Don't be a child, telling me that I promised. I know I said you could get a new car, but money is still tight.'

If you hadn't called me a child, I would have suggested that we buy a decent used car. 'Hasn't your Mercedes said enough to improve things or does it have laryngitis?' I snapped, kicking my shoes off.

'I'm trying, but you're not.' You stalked out of the

bedroom, went into your study, and returned with a handful of bills. 'Look at these,' you ordered, waving them in my face. 'You charged over six hundred dollars' worth of clothing last month.'

'More than half of those bills are for the children's things; they had to be outfitted for the fall. I only bought what I needed. I'm going to meetings every day of the week – in a car that won't stay on the road. And I have more carpools this year,' I added. 'If I wind up in a ditch with a car full of kids, we'll really have problems. We'll be sued into bankruptcy.'

'No, we won't. Our insurance will cover an accident.'

'In other words, you're saying that it's okay for me to have an accident. The insurance will cover it.'

'I didn't say that. Stop being dramatic.'

'I'm not being dramatic. The Chevelle is unsafe, and you know it.'

'You've been able to manage. You can manage for another year,' you said, the green specks of anger in your eyes flashing me a warning.

'Then find another hostess for yourself. I'll be damned if I'm going to give parties if we can't afford a new car,' I threatened, half-hoping you would release me from the obligation of entertaining. I would have been willing to trade a new car for the relief of never having to give another dinner party. In Eagles' Landing, the parties were more like gourmet cooking contests, each hostess trying to outdo the other. I studied gourmet cookbooks for weeks before our dinner parties, planning the menus more carefully than I did our wedding, then was sick with worry that I would have an unexpected failure. Even now the thought of those parties makes me shrivel up inside.

'We can't afford not to entertain. You know that as well as I do,' you said icily, marching to the bathroom.

Yes, there were certain facts of life that we both knew. You bought the Mercedes for the same reason we belonged to the country club, for the same reason we entertained the right people at parties we couldn't afford, for the same reason I donated my time to the 'in' charities. I'm beginning to think of it as Weaver's Law: spend money to show that you have money you really don't have. The law was all I needed to know to get a new car.

'How do you think it will look for your wife to be driving around in a Chevelle with rusting doors and fenders again this winter?' I asked after we were in bed. 'It doesn't add to your image.'

You didn't answer right away. Instead, you moved your legs restlessly and bunched the pillow under your head. I waited. I knew you weren't asleep. 'Well, Richard?' I asked into the darkness.

'You can have a new car,' you said finally. Your voice was unusually low, barely audible.

'I want an Oldsmobile station wagon.'

'They're expensive.'

'They're less expensive than a Mercedes-Benz and hold more,' I retorted.

I didn't ask where you got the money for the car, and you didn't tell me.

I should have asked.

Without knowing why, I became defensive about the car. Surprisingly, you weren't. In fact, you seemed rather pleased that we had bought it. When we pulled into the driveway one Saturday with the children, Bruce Lynch walked over. 'Nice car,' he said.

'Thanks,' you replied.

Bruce walked around the car as if he were appraising it for an auction. He actually had the audacity to peer inside to see what extras the car had. 'A Custom Cruiser with all the options,' he commented. 'I can see things are fine at the Weavers'.'

The expression of approval on Bruce's long face irritated me. 'We're not going to apply for welfare until next week,' I said jokingly. 'When we do, can we hide the car in your garage?'

You waited for Bruce's reaction. He laughed. I knew he

would, but I hate to think of what you would have said to me later if he hadn't.

I didn't enjoy the car, although there was no reason why I shouldn't have enjoyed it. It drove well and had every luxury I wanted, even some I didn't want, but somehow it made me uncomfortable. I would get into the car, close the door, and feel trapped. Through the entire first winter I had the car, I couldn't drive it without keeping the window open – completely open. The children complained that it was too cold. I turned the heat up and kept my window down. It was as if I couldn't breathe in that car without a fresh stream of bitter winter air.

Deirdre Cohen called late this afternoon. 'I've been trying to reach you,' she said.

I told her that Matthew has speech therapy on Thursdays.

'My consciousness-raising group is meeting tonight. Can you come? One of the members, Glenda Miller, left last week. Her husband was transferred to Montana or Minnesota – someplace with an M. Anyway, there's an opening now, and I think you'd like it. It's a terrific group. We have two lesbians.'

'Thanks for inviting me, but I can't come,' I said, thinking about the lesbians. Deirdre made it sound as if they gave the group credibility, that the two lesbians were wanted not for themselves but because they were different.

'Why not?' Deirdre pushed. 'Look, Jenny, you have to get out. This is an ideal place to start. You'll jump in all at once. I told everyone about you, and they're anxious to meet you.'

I shuddered. From what I've read about consciousness-raising groups, I wouldn't be able to test the water with my big toe before being totally submerged. 'What did you tell them?' I asked with trepidation, wondering if they wanted me to become their token widow.

'Nothing much. That you're new in California and don't know too many people yet.'

'There are thousands of new people in California. Why would they be anxious to meet me?' I asked, suddenly nervous.

'I told them you have a degree in psychology.'

'It's an old degree, and I haven't used it. Everything has changed.' Now I was really wondering what she had told them.

'Freud and Jung haven't changed.'

'Is that what you talk about, Freud and Jung?'

'No, we don't talk about Freud and Jung specifically, or Laing either. You know that. I've told you about the group. We talk about ourselves as women. We share our experiences, relating them to each other as human beings, female beings, and to the specific circumstances we have found ourselves in. The group has really helped me. I have a greater awareness of myself as a person than I did before. You must come. I even have a sitter lined up for you,' she said.

Deirdre always makes the group sound like a psychological vitamin pill in megadose form.

'I can't, as much as I'd like to. My car broke down yesterday, and it might be ready tonight. If it is, I'll have to pick it up.'

'What time are you going? If it isn't too late, you could still come. We have a rule that everyone must be there on time. That way nobody feels left out or that they have missed anything.'

'I don't know. I haven't had time to call,' I lied. I had called, and the service man said the car would be ready at four thirty. I told him I had to take my son somewhere, so he said I could pick the car up anytime until eight o'clock; a salesman would give me my car and take the loaner back.

'Why don't you call now and call me back? The meeting tonight is going to be interesting. It's a topic night.'

'A topic night?' I asked.

'Sometimes we have general discussion. Other nights we have specific topics. Tonight's topic is orgasms.'

'Oh,' I gulped, 'I don't think I could talk to a roomful of strangers about orgasms.'

'You don't have to talk if you don't want to. You can listen. And learn. That's the point of a consciousness-raising group: you're not *forced* to talk. But you will. Everyone does,' she promised.

'What time is the meeting?'

'Eight thirty. Please try to come.'

'I'll call you back,' I said. My mind was busy framing my regrets.

I waited a safe ten minutes and called Deirdre back. I told her that my car would be ready at eight, which would make it impossible for me to join the group. Although I tried to sound as convincing as I could, I knew the excuse was transparent.

Deirdre was too polite to confront me with my lie, but she let me know that I hadn't fooled her. 'I see,' she said in a cool voice. 'What dealer did you say it was that has mechanics working at nights? Well, never mind. Maybe you can attend our next meeting.'

'Thanks for asking me,' I said, surprised at finding myself grateful that she had left the matter open.

'I'm not going to give up on you, Jenny. I'm going to get you out and into the world of the living if I have to drag you bodily,' Deirdre threatened before hanging up.

Deirdre's consciousness-raising group is one of her favorite topics of conversation. She hasn't divulged the names of the women or their specific stories, but she has told me some of the things they talk about. Men, children, men, job situations, men, female discrimination, men, and sex are big topics. From the way she has described the meetings, it sounds as if the participants are talking to themselves as well as to each other.

I shouldn't be critical. My assessment may be wrong. Besides, talking to yourself is cheaper than therapy and sitting in a group somehow makes the whole business of

116

talking to yourself seem legitimate. I certainly have no right to pass judgment on them. Here I am writing to a dead husband, which is a form of talking to yourself taken to the extreme. Maybe I am crazy.

I am not crazy. Not yet.

Unless any of the women in Deirdre's group are widows who have already spoken, I could contribute a bit of information that would raise their collective female consciousness to an earsplitting pitch. I could tell them that death doesn't sever a woman's identity with her husband. When a man's wife dies, she's dead. Widows' husbands linger.

When you were alive, I was accustomed to being identified as your wife. It bothered me at times to have my own accomplishments ignored, but my identity as your wife was my role, and I liked it. Why not? Your success was my success. If you had been a failure, it would have been different. No one wants to be identified with a failure, not even the failure's wife. Especially not a failure's wife in Eagles' Landing. Remember Vera and Seymour Darby? When Seymour lost the drugstore her father's money had bought for him, Vera threw him out.

I knew Seymour was going under long before the bankruptcy was rumored. Whenever they went somewhere together, Vera stayed as far away from Seymour as she could. She didn't speak to him in public or mention him when she was alone. I recall telling you one night after we came home from a charity dinner that Seymour was in trouble.

'How do you know?' you asked.

'Vera is treating Seymour as if he has a communicable disease. Haven't you noticed?'

'Maybe they're having marital problems,' you said. 'Vera's a bitch who puts on a saccharin smile for company.'

You never liked Vera, not from the time you were a child and she lived a few doors away from your parents' house on Locust Street. Something must have made you feel so strongly about her, but you never told me what it was. Instead, you offhandedly mentioned that I should watch my step around Vera, then characteristically let the matter drop.

'No,' I disagreed, 'If they were having marital problems, Vera would continue with the public masquerade of their marriage until they separated. She's disassociating herself; Seymour is in trouble. I'll bet his drugstore is going under.'

Seymour lost the drugstore, and Seymour and Vera were separated by the end of the first year we lived in Eagles' Landing. Seymour's loss was my gain. You came home one night and told me that Seymour had filed for bankruptcy. 'You were right, Jenny,' you said, looking at me with new respect. 'There is something to the idea of woman's intuition.'

It wasn't intuition, Richard. I had merely observed the behavior of two people. One person, actually. Vera. But I didn't say that to you. You had been pushing me to do my share to get us established in Eagles' Landing, and I resented it. I wanted to choose for myself, not have you do it for me. Seymour gave me credibility. For a while, at least, you let me pick and choose for myself. And you listened to me. Suddenly my judgment was respectable.

I couldn't tell that story to Deirdre's consciousness-raising group. They would blast me out of the room for docilely agreeing with you that I had woman's intuition. It was an insult, really, your thinking that what I knew came from a mythological instinct rather than from my own mind.

I just realised something: until this moment, I didn't think that telling a woman she had good female intuition was an insult. Perhaps there is a certain validity in talking to yourself.

If I had the courage, I would tell the consciousness-raising group that marriage doesn't end in death, that my life is still linked with yours. You have been dead for almost two years, and people I meet want to know about you. They want to know how long you've been dead, how you died, and what you did for a living. They don't ask one question after another because of my grieving widow performance, but the questions manage to weave their way into the cloth of casual conversation. You're dead, I'm alive, and people want to know about *you*. I feel like a spider caught in another spider's web.

Amazingly, our intertwined identity goes beyond people's questions. They observe where I live and how I live, drawing conclusions. Even stupid Jim Gentile estimated your success when I applied for the job at Briarhill. After he told me there were women waiting to grab the position, he asked: 'Why do you want the job?'

'I want to work,' I said, as if it weren't obvious.

'Do you need the money? It doesn't pay much.'

'Everyone can use money,' I replied obliquely.

He appraised me openly, puckering his fleshy mouth. 'You don't look like you need money. What was it you said your husband did for a living?'

I hadn't said. 'He was an accountant,' I replied resentfully.

'Hmmmm. He must have been successful. Left you well taken care of, didn't he? You live in Sherwood Village, a nice place. Not cheap, either.'

I didn't reply.

Jim still makes occasional references to what he believes was your success by commenting on my secure widowhood, and has gone so far as to tell me that I am a successful widow.

I am not a successful widow. You were a suicide, and by its very nature, a suicide can never be a complete success. People will always wonder if the death couldn't have been prevented, if the survivors hadn't somehow failed, or, worse, if the survivors were somehow to blame.

Richard, the only success that has come out of your suicide is that it has joined us in life and in death. We have more than fulfilled our marriage vows.

I had trouble falling asleep last night. It has been happening often lately. I go to bed, then toss and turn, unable to lose consciousness. It is as if I can't find a place for myself. My mind races at full speed: images, thoughts, contradictions flash off the walls of my skull like silent movies flickering on a screen. They are gone before I have a chance to fully comprehend them.

Maybe I don't want to comprehend them. I evade the past and sleep evades me. It is just retribution.

Last night was different. I knew why I couldn't fall asleep. Until she caught me in my lie about picking up the car, I hadn't been aware of how important Deirdre's friendship is to me. She befriends me, yet I have nothing to offer her: not social position nor entrance into a club nor a seat on some Junior Board. Deirdre wouldn't be interested in that menu if I did have it to offer. She'd laugh and say: 'Who needs it?' Deirdre seems to care about me as a person. I have come to realise that her caring is a rare thing, a delicate flower my recalcitrance could crush. I don't think I could handle the loss of her friendship.

We thought we had friends in Eagles' Landing. They were earned friends, worked-for friends, not real friends like Deirdre. We were fools, Richard.

You would argue with me if you were here. No one could intimate that you were a fool and get away with it. But you were a fool. So was I, and I am not overdramatizing. Would you believe that one of your carefully cultivated friends (I use the word 'friend' reservedly) put a price on your life?

I told you that the upstanding residents of Eagles' Landing built a wall of ice around me and the children once the reason for your death became known, but I didn't tell you what occured after I listed the house. The foreign sound of a ringing telephone was heard again at 103 Eyrie Road. After not speaking to me for months, our neighbors, who were once our friends, discovered that they indeed had something to say to me. With the exception of a few minor variations, the calls were identical; they all could have been reading from the same prepared speech.

First, I was told that the Weavers had caused enough trouble and enough pain in Eagles' Landing. This verdict was delivered with the solemnity of a judge sentencing a criminal to one hundred years in jail with no hope of a pardon for good behavior. A lengthy pause followed. I believe they felt the pause was necessary to give me time to complete the implied equation: trouble + pain = money. It was not difficult to compute. I met their silence with my own.

After the caller decided that my time to reflect was sufficient, I was advised on the sale of the house. It was not friendly advice. Since the Weavers had proved themselves to be undesirables, the least I could do, I was told, was to make sure the house wasn't sold to other undesirables. I was to understand that this meant the house could not be sold to 'niggers or Jews.'

I hung up in disgust after the first calls, too shocked to reply. Then I started thinking: Barney Leadman is Jewish. What difference would another Jew make? According to our neighbors' standards, Eagles' Landing was already sullied. When the telephone rang again and the content of the previous calls was repeated, I struck back. 'Barney and Sara Leadman are Jewish. You call him for free medical advice and entertain them in your homes.'

'Barney is a doctor,' was the reply, 'an internist. He's acceptable.'

Lucky Barney. He has the right degree and a useful specialty.

The calls continued over a two-week period, coming every other day or so. It was as if they were deliberately timed to ensure my remembrance of the message. I felt like exploding each time I answered the phone and did explode with the final calls. 'You didn't mention Indians,' I said testily. 'Will they meet the Eagles' Landing purity standard?'

Silence came before the replies. 'Do you mean Indian

R.-E

Indians or American Indians? American Indians are okay, but Indian Indians are definitely out. They're worse than niggers. Besides, there's no need to worry about Indians buying in Eagles' Landing. Indians don't live around here.'

'But they will live here,' I said, 'now that the new hospital wing has been completed, and the research facilities have been expanded.' I was regretting my work for the hospital building fund.

'No Indians,' was the verdict, 'except American Indians.'

'An American Indian wouldn't live in Eagles' Landing,' I shouted before slamming the receiver down. 'American Indians have taste.'

American Indians were temporarily chic in Eagles' Landing because their jewelry was popular that year. And it was safe to say that American Indians were acceptable. An American Indian couldn't afford to buy our house unless he was a doctor, and there aren't too many American Indian doctors around. I doubt that they'd think Eagles' Landing was heaven anyway.

I prepared myself for Bruce Lynch's call, sure that it would come. I knew he wanted to be the last one to deliver the message. I was right.

Bruce began as the others did, then added the obvious fact that our lot was adjacent to his. 'I want my property protected,' he said. 'Richard cost me more than his life was worth.'

I gasped. Nothing could have prepared me for that statement. To Bruce Lynch, your life wasn't worth fifty thousand dollars.

'Did you hear me? Am I making myself clear?' Bruce demanded.

'You said Richard's life wasn't worth fifty thousand dollars. What kind of man are you, you ... bastard?'

'Hah,' said Bruce. 'The refined Mrs Weaver isn't so grand, is she? You can just stop calling me names because I'm telling you what to do, and you'd better listen.'

'I can't listen to you, Bruce. You're not a man, and you'll never be a man,' I blurted.

'What is that you said, you bitch?' Bruce yelled.

'I said you're not a man, and you'll never be a man. You are your father's puppet. A parasite. A sponge. If you were kicked in the balls, you wouldn't flinch because nothing's there, absolutely nothing. Someone else had to father your son. You can't create life because you don't have the equipment to do it with. That's why a hand in your pocket hurts more than a knee in your groin.'

It was Bruce's turn to be stunned. I didn't wait for him to recover. Our conversation had ended.

I was cruel, Richard. Bruce didn't know that Adam wasn't his son. I don't think anyone knew but Sylvia and me, and I happened to find out about Adam and Bruce during the course of the most bizarre afternoon I spent in Eagles' Landing. It was one of the rare times life penetrated through my cocoon of tranquilizers.

Sylvia came over early in the afternoon approximately six weeks after you died. She was wearing grayish satin scuffs that had once been white and a mauve peignoir with brown stains dotting the front; her hair was uncombed, and she wore no makeup. There were dark smudges under her eyes, traces of mascara that had not been removed from the day before, and black roots were visible at the base of her scalp that made her copper hair look metallic. 'Is anyone here?' she asked, looking around glassy-eyed. 'Where's Catherine?'

'In nursery school,' I said, shocked at her appearance. Whenever Sylvia stepped outside her house, even if it was only to garden, she was appropriately dressed and immacualately groomed.

Sylvia walked unsteadily into the family room and held out her hand as if it were circling a glass. 'I need a drink. Gimme a drink.'

I gave her a drink against my better judgment and put on a pot of coffee. Sylvia must have consumed a quart of liquor before arriving at my door. I had never seen her even slightly tipsy, not after having seven or eight stiff drinks during an evening of bridge. We had this theory about Sylvia, remember? We said scotch went directly to her boobs so that the rest of her body could remain unaffected. We called her chest the Seagram reservoir. No one in Eagles' Landing could hold their liquor like Sylvia Lynch.

While the coffee was perking, I sat with Sylvia in the family room. She downed the drink I had given her in greedy swallows and held the glass out for more. 'I wanna 'nother drink,' she demanded.

'Why don't you wait until you've had some coffee,' I suggested. 'You'll feel better.'

'Nothing'll make me feel better 'cept a drink.'

'If you have more scotch, you won't be able to feel anything.'

'That's the idea. Yer a smart girl. Gimme scotch.'

If she had been able to get up and navigate to the bar, Sylvia would have poured her own drink, but she couldn't. She had a vacuous expression on her face, and her limbs looked boneless, like those of a rag doll. I stalled until the coffee was ready. When I came back from the kitchen, she was lying in a sprawl on the sofa. 'Sit up,' I said, putting the tray down on the coffee table in front of her.

'A drink,' she gurgled, looking at the pot of coffee with distaste. 'I wanna drink.'

'You have to drink this first,' I said, helping her up. Then I forcefed her the coffee a teaspoonful at a time. Her mouth opened and closed around the spoon automatically, like a baby's.

After Sylvia finished a second cup of coffee, she began to speak. At first her words were nothing more than incoherent mumbles; tears started rolling down her cheeks, and she picked up the hem of her peignoir to blow her nose. I was flabbergasted. The haughty Mrs Lynch was behaving like a common drunk. I was also curious, so I waited until the coffee began to take effect, then carefully pried out the reason for Sylvia's drunkenness. I can't tell it to you as she told it to me because I had to extract the story piece by piece, constantly reassembling it in my mind until the pieces locked into a completed puzzle.

Sylvia had started drinking when she finished talking to her father-in-law early that morning. The senior Mr Lynch had phoned minutes after he knew his predictable son had left for work. The old man was furious over the cost of a sun room Bruce and Sylvia added to their house. He told her that it was an unnecessary expense and that she should be grateful for the house as it was, because it was a damned sight nicer than the house Sylvia had grown up in. Mr Lynch told Sylvia she couldn't have a skylight cut into her bedroom ceiling as she had planned and that the decorator she had hired was to be fired. Sylvia would not be redecorating. Further, Mr Lynch told her that, if she didn't cut down on her spending, he would personally close all of her charge accounts. If necessary, he would even block Bruce's bonuses. Since his son couldn't keep his wife in line, Mr Lynch would do it for him.

Apparently Sylvia had argued back. She told Mr Lynch that the Lynch family had their own bank full of money, and she could see no reason why some of it shouldn't be spent. After all, what was money for, if not to be spent? Besides, the house was her hobby. Mr Lynch was depriving her of her only creative outlet. She could express herself through the house. What was he trying to do, stifle her creativity?

Mr Lynch became enraged. He said he'd like to stifle her and told her she was stupid. Nothing more than a pair of teats, he said, and they'd fall eventually. But his bank wouldn't fall, he assured her, and neither would his money be spent wantonly. Lynch money would be spent prudently. It was not to be wasted on whimsies. He had their bills on his desk from the last three months, and all he could see was wasted money. If she wanted to express herself, she could write a letter to the editor of the weekly shopping news since that was the only paper she seemed to read.

Sylvia tried reasoning with her father-in-law, rationalizing her expenditures by telling him that money spent on their house was an investment: it would bring returns when the house was sold. Mr Lynch told Sylvia that the house was not going to be sold. He had personally selected their lot for its investment value, and they were to stay until he decided they could move. As far as he was concerned, there would be no reason for them to move until his grandson Adam went away to college. Unless, of course, something unforeseen happened to threaten property values in the area.

Before hanging up, Mr Lynch made Sylvia repeat everything he had said to make sure she understood his warning. 'I had to repeat everything,' Sylvia cried, 'everything. The old man forced every word out of me. It's not fair. I've paid.' The coffee had finally coordinated Sylvia's tongue.

On cue, I nodded sympathetically, but I was dizzy with the confirmation of facts I had been surmising for so long. All I had believed about Bruce and Sylvia Lynch was true: they were living on doles from Bruce's father. I had often wondered if Bruce came even halfway toward earning his salary at the bank. I had doubted it before, but now I felt sure that Bruce wasn't worth a teller's salary. His position as some kind of vice-president was probably a joke, an excuse for his paycheck.

I sat looking at Sylvia dumbfoundedly, reliving our cultivation of the Lynches – the torturous dinners, the endless evenings of bridge, our forced laughter at Bruce's stale jokes, and, worst of all, your benign attitude toward Adam Lynch's cruelty at Matthew's expense. We all paid, Richard, for nothing. You would never have been able to get business from the Lynch bank because the women who washed the bank's floors and dusted the antique walnut desks in the lobby performed a more valued service than Bruce Lynch did.

Hysterical laughter rose in my throat. I had told you, over and over again, that Bruce was a nothing, a nonentity

126

with an important name. 'The name is what counts, Jenny,' you had said, dismissing my arguments. 'Remember that.'

Oh, I remembered. My laughter became uncontrollable when it occurred to me that I didn't even have the satisfaction of saying 'I told you so.'

Sylvia watched me, still glassy-eyed. 'Why are you laughing?' she demanded, insulted.

'I ... I'm laughing because you can't make your father-in-law be reasonable,' I said, 'and he thinks he's such a reasonable man.'

Sylvia's drunken laughter mingled with mine. 'Ya think that's funny,' she said. 'I'll tell ya something that's a riot! Gimme another drink, and I'll tell.'

I couldn't resist and went to the bar to refill Sylvia's glass. She took the drink with a shaking hand and downed the scotch. Strangely, the liquor seemed to have a stablizing effect on her. 'I fooled the old man once,' she boasted. 'I did. I'm not stupid.'

'How?'

'Adam. I fooled him with Adam. Ya know, Jenny,' she said, putting her face so close to mine that her breath nearly overpowered me, 'the old man didn't want Brucie to marry me. He didn't!'

Sylvia waited for my response. I clucked sympathetically.

'Yeah,' she continued, 'can ya imagine that? The old man wanted Brucie to marry Barbara Brewster from the utility company. He wanted a goddamn merger, not a marriage. But Brucie wanted me. It was the only time he talked back. A while after we got married, the old man started looking at my belly. Then he started asking. He'd ask anything, that man. Anything! "When're ya going to have a baby? When?" he'd ask. I wanted to tell him that it was none of his goddamn business. Brucie said, "shuddup," so I shuddup. I wanna drink.'

'You've had enough,' I warned her.

'Just a swallow,' she pleaded.

I went to the bar and brought back the bottle of scotch, wondering what Sylvia had to say that took so much alcohol to get out.

'Two years went by, then three. No baby.' She shook her head. 'No baby. The old man was getting angry. I wanted a house. He said I couldn't have a house until I had a baby. A baby for a house.'

She emptied her glass, then looked at me. Her eyes were dark pools of disappointment. 'How could I have a baby?'

'The same way everyone has a baby,' I said, thinking that Sylvia was even drunker than she appeared, if that was possible.

'No, you don't understand,' she said. 'I didn't know about Brucie. When we were dating, he treated me like . . . like I was a virgin queen . . . like those ladies on a pedestal. All he wanted to do was put his head between my boobs, so I let him. He was nothing like the creeps I had to fight off. It was nice. I didn't find out until after we were married. Brucie has only one. And that one was ruined by the mumps. The other one isn't real. When he was born, only one came down.'

'Only one what?' I asked.

'Ball,' said Sylvia.

'You mean he had an undescended testicle when he was born?'

'That's what they call it. The old man knew. What did he want from me, a goddamn miracle like the Virgin Mary? Anyway, I didn't know because Brucie had had an operation. I guess they couldn't find the other one, so they put a false one in. He didn't tell me about his mumps, either. But the old man was talking about a baby all the time. I wanted a house, and he was talking about a baby. He even sent me to a doctor.'

Sylvia slammed her fists down on the coffee table. 'Relax,' I said, 'it's all right.'

'NO,' she shouted, 'it's not all right.' Tears of anger ran down her face. 'Ya know what the doctor did to me? Do ya know what he did, that fucking bastard? He pumped air up my tubes like I was a tire, and there was no place for the air to go. Pain. Pain in my shoulders, in my neck. And that's not all. He cut me. He went in and cut tissue from my uterus. The pain nearly killed me. I kept yelling "STOP," and the goddamn bastard wouldn't stop. I thought he was going to pull my insides out and lay them on the exammmmm . . .'

'Examining table?' I guessed.

'Yeah,' said Sylvia, nodding her thanks. 'I told Brucie that I wouldn't go anymore. "You go," I told him. "It's easier to test you. All you have to do is come." He wouldn't go. I told him I would leave if he didn't go. I packed my bags. Brucie got scared. Then he told me about his mumps and his ball. A false ball.'

Sylvia held out her glass for a refill. I poured her another drink, watching the golden liquid rise.

'The old man knew,' she said between gulps of scotch. 'Their family doctor told me about the mumps after I had Adam, so he had to know. He knew and made me go through that torture. And there are some things he didn't know, like me reading those porno stories out loud to Brucie to get him to do anything. Brucie can't get it up without a story. I had to hide those magazines all over the apartment so the cleaning lady wouldn't find them. Do you know how hard it is to hide magazines in an apartment?'

Sylvia waited for me to show my appreciation for her difficulties. 'It's hard,' I said, unable to resist laughing at my pun.

'It's easy for you to laugh,' she said resentfully. 'You had Richard. Too bad he's gone. Richard was a man.'

I stopped laughing. Drunk as she was, Sylvia had spoken the truth. You were a man, Richard. I ached as I recalled the feeling of your body against mine. Through my pain, I thought I saw a glint of envy in Sylvia's eyes.

'That's better,' Sylvia commented on my silence. Then

she continued. 'I wanted a house, and I was gonna get one. Do ya know what I did? I started taking my temppp . . .'

'Temperature,' I supplied.

'I took it every day to see when I was fertile. I made a chart. After three months, I could tell to the day. Then I made plans. I called an old boyfriend in New York from a pay phone and told him when I'd be coming in. I made myself sound sexy. I teased. He couldn't wait for me to fly in. Then I told Brucie and his father that I was going to New York to see a doctor. They believed me. The old man even smiled and said I was a good girl. He's not so smart! Adam was born nine months later. All I had to do was read Brucie a story when I got home to make it legitt . . .'

'Legitimate.'

Sylvia polished off her drink. 'He had red hair, my old boyfriend. Mr Lynch was upset when he saw Adam's red hair. "What about my family?" I asked. My family didn't count. Mr Lynch remembered that his grandfather had a red beard. He said Adam's hair came from his grandfather's beard.'

Sylvia looked at me shrewdly through her drunken cloud. 'You won't tell, Jenny. I know you won't tell. Yer a lady.'

Sylvia was right. And I wouldn't have told if Bruce hadn't said your life wasn't worth fifty thousand dollars. He provoked me, and I lost control. I don't regret it. I never told anyone else. Loaded as she was, Sylvia knew her secret was safe.

Sylvia fell asleep on the sofa after she told me I was a lady. I left her there until it was time for the school bus to arrive, then had an awful struggle getting her up, out of our house, and into her own home. It would be better, I had decided, to let her sleep it off where she belonged. Bruce Lynch wasn't going to be given the opportunity to blame me for something that started under his roof.

Sylvia's behavior toward me remained the same as it had before that revelatory afternoon. She reappeared sober and resumed her position as the queen of Eagles' Landing. I did overhear her say that she was going to postpone redecorating because it was too much of a strain on her delicate constitution. 'I just can't take any aggravation now,' she said. The women of Eagles' Landing, like ladies-in-waiting, all nodded in unison to show their appreciation of the difficulties of decorating. It was as fine a display of fawning as I had ever witnessed. Sylvia was so secure that she didn't even bother glancing in my direction to gauge my reaction.

When the news hit Eagles' Landing that the Bestmark Partnership had collapsed, Sylvia joined Bruce in leading the icy vendetta against me. I don't know why, but I was shocked. Perhaps I thought Sylvia would be kind to me. After all, I did know her secret. More important, I lost a husband. What greater payment could the Weavers make to Eagles' Landing than to give a life?

I was wrong. Drunk as she was, Sylvia's judgment was better than mine. She knew I wouldn't talk, and later she made sure I had no one to talk to, which was perfect insurance.

This has been painful for me, Richard. I didn't want to go back and relive that afternoon. I didn't want to look through someone else's scotch-filled glass and see the hopeless waste of our ambition. And I didn't want to feel the pain I felt when Sylvia acknowledged my loss, my having had something she didn't have – a man.

I am beginning to question the wisdom of writing to you. It seemed like a good idea when I started, but now I find it more difficult than I had imagined it would be. Tonight brought me nothing but pain and regrets. I think I would be happier sitting alone with the hiccups.

The most incredible thing happened tonight, and I am not quite sure how to handle it.

Our Saturday started out normally. We ate breakfast, then I did some fast dusting and vacuuming and was ready to take the children out for their Saturday treat before noon. Matthew had been nagging to go to a skateboard center. I don't believe you ever saw one, Richard; skateboard parks hadn't reached the East before you died. They are vast, undulating seas of concrete, and they are big in California. If they are big in California, they'll become big across the country. Fads travel east, not west as when we were children.

I fought with Matthew for weeks about going until it became an issue, which was my mistake. 'They're dangerous,' I said.

'N-N-No, they're not,' Matthew argued. 'I-I-I can rent everything. C-C-Crash helmets. Knee pads. A-Arm pads. Th-Th-They're safe, and I-I-I-I want to go. Y-Y-Y-You're turning me into a b-b-baby. Y-Y-You say everything is dangerous.'

He hit the right nerve with excruciating precision. Whenever Matthew asks for permission to try something new, I usually tell him that it is dangerous. I have developed a fear for Matthew's safety that is ridiculous. It started in Eagles' Landing and hasn't stopped. There are afternoons when I see him playing outside happily and find myself wanting to call him in, to admonish him one more time to be careful. If I can't control my fears, I'll either transfer them to him or raise a son filled with resentment toward an irrationally overprotective mother.

After we moved to California, I must have automatically told Matthew to be careful every time he went out to play. I hadn't been aware of saying anything until Matthew opened the door to go out one afternoon and said, 'I know. Be careful.' There was a weary, impatient sarcasm in the tone of his voice that stopped me cold. The realization of what I was doing to him suddenly hit me. Now I try to keep my mouth shut. It's difficult. I tell myself that he is safer here than he was in Eagles' Landing because he's three thousand miles away from Adam Lynch. Sometimes it helps.

We stopped for lunch at a taco stand, a perfect way of avoiding McDonald's without an argument, and went on to a skateboard center. Catherine and I watched Matthew for a while. It was difficult to pick him out of the crowd of children whizzing by, all suited up to battle with concrete. Then I took Catherine to the beginner's area and watched her struggle to keep her balance. She managed quite well, but I think she was scared. Her tongue was sticking out from between her lips the entire time she was on her skateboard, and she slept in the car all the way home.

Matthew was exuberant. He had emerged from the concrete battlefield with several brush burns, nothing more, and during our ride home assured me that he wouldn't have fallen if another boy hadn't run into him. 'H-He didn't know wh-wh-what he was doing,' Matthew said scornfully. 'Th-Th-They shouldn't let those kids on.'

Matthew had his afternoon of skateboarding, and I survived. There is hope.

The children played outside until dinner. After we finished eating, the phone rang. 'It-It-It's for me,' Matthew said, jumping up to answer.

I was surprised. Usually his friends at Sherwood Village ring our doorbell. I heard him say, 'Yup, I've got it. I-I-I'll tell you tomorrow.'

At seven o'clock, Matthew walked over to the television set determinedly and turned on 'Ringer's Night at the Races.'

'What do you think you're doing?' I asked.

'I-I-I-I am going to w-w-watch Ringer's Races,' said Matthew defiantly. 'I-I-I have a t-t-ticket.' He pulled a green ticket from his pocket.

'Where did you get that?'

'I-I-I-I found it on m-m-my way to the Village Green today,' he said. Matthew was holding on to the ticket so hard that the tips of his fingers were white.

Catherine chimed in. 'Matthew did find it, he did. I wanted the ticket, but he said no. Matthew's lucky. Can we watch? Can we see Matthew win money?'

'No. Matthew isn't going to win money.'

'How do you know?' Catherine asked, pouting.

'I just know,' I replied. 'Now turn to another station.'

'I-I-I have a ticket, and I-I-I'm going to watch,' Matthew challenged.

He stood glaring at me, and Catherine was close to tears. I decided that reasoning with them might help to end my battle with Ringer's permanently. 'Look,' I said calmly, 'Ringer's Supermarkets give away thousands and thousands of tickets every week, and almost all of them wind up in the garbage. The races are a promotion for Ringer's, an advertising gimmick. Some people have ten or more tickets and have to throw them away. Now why don't you watch something else so you won't be disappointed?'

'B-B-But my ticket might win,' Matthew insisted. 'I-I-I have a chance. It's my chance.'

'It's a slim chance, so slim that searching for one particular grain of sand on a large beach might be easier to do than win a race with Ringer's Supermarkets,' I warned. 'Besides, it's gambling, and I don't like gambling.' My calm attitude was evaporating faster than a shallow puddle on a sunny afternoon.

'What's gambling?' asked Catherine.

'Gambling is hard to explain,' I thought aloud. 'Sometimes people gamble by betting money. They buy a racing ticket for money or play dice for money or play cards for money. They put their money down hoping to win more money. If they lose, their money is gone, and they walk away with empty pockets.

'There is another kind of gambling, the kind where people take chances hoping for something in return. The something can be anything; it isn't always money. These people take great risks, some even risk their lives, taking a gamble that is almost impossible. They are so anxious to win that they forget how hard it is to do the impossible, and because they forget, they usually aren't prepared to lose, which makes losing even harder. They often end up paying with more than money, for they have risked more.'

'W-W-What do they p-p-pay with if they d-d-don't pay with money?'

'They pay with their happiness,' I said. 'They pay with their dreams.'

'That's silly, Mommy,' giggled Catherine. 'You can't pay for anything with a dream. Dreams are for free.'

'When you are little, your dreams are free. When you grow up, each dream has its price.'

Matthew was getting impatient with dream talk. He wanted the action of Ringer's Races. 'I-I-I can't lose anything by w-w-watching the races. I-I found my ticket. I-I-I didn't pay for it.'

'But how will you feel if you lose?' I asked.

He shrugged his shoulders.

'You'll be disappointed, won't you?'

'Y-Y-Y-Yes, but it'll be worse if I-I-I don't watch.'

'Why?'

'B-B-Because then I'll never know if-if-if I won or not. I want my chance. It's mine. I-I-I-I want to know for m-m-myself.'

I could see that it was pointless to continue our argument. If I had been stronger, I could have issued a flat *no*, but it didn't seem fair. It was, after all, Matthew's chance. He flipped the television on just as the second race was starting. The announcer appeared on the screen holding up a handful of green tickets that matched his green plaid jacket. 'Are you ready for race number two?' he asked with oily professional enthusiasm.

'Yes!' Catherine answered, sitting down two feet away from the screen.

I left the room and went upstairs, hoping my absence would make an impression on them. They didn't notice.

It couldn't have been more than fifteen minutes later when I heard their screams. 'Mommy! Mommy! Where are you? Come quick. Matthew's ticket won!'

I ran downstairs. They were jumping about wildly in the

living room, Matthew waving his ticket in the air and Catherine laughing hysterically. A glance at the television told me that a commercial for Ringer's Supermarkets was playing: cartoon robots with RINGER painted on their chests and backs were racing up and down supermarket aisles filling enormous carts with groceries. I couldn't hear through the children's pandemonium. The announcer returned to the screen. 'Be quiet,' I yelled.

'Well, that's it for tonight,' said the announcer with a patronizing grin. His teeth seemed to have a greenish cast. 'Some lucky winner with . . .'

I grabbed Matthew's ticket.

'. . . number 706495 WON ONE THOUSAND DOLLARS tonight. Can you imagine that, folks? Another big one for Ringer's. See you next week, your chance to ring one up with Ringer's.'

It was true. Matthew had won.

'I'm rich,' Matthew shouted, 'I'm rich! I-I-I can buy anything in the whole world.'

I didn't know how to react, whether to smother the joy on his face by killing his win with the truth, the fact that one thousand dollars couldn't begin to buy him his 'anything in the whole world,' or to share his bizarre victory, a gamble that I did not approve. I sat down on the sofa, rejecting responses as fast as they came into my head until I had nothing to say.

'Mommy, what's the matter? Why aren't you happy? Matthew won. He really won!' bubbled Catherine.

'I don't like gambling,' I said. 'I'm happy for Matthew because he wanted to win, but I'm not happy with this kind of winning.'

'B-B-But that's the way everybody w-wins when th-th-they bet on the races. It was fair.'

'No, Matthew, you don't seem to understand what I mean. You won, but not everybody wins. Thousands of people lose for every person that wins.'

'W-W-Who cares? I was the person who won. Th-Th-That's all that counts.'

'To you,' I whispered under my breath.

I couldn't get them to go to sleep until after ten o'clock. They expended more energy enjoying Matthew's win tonight than I expend in a year. Besides running around like playful squirrels, they talked. They couldn't stop talking. Matthew spent his winnings twenty times over. With Catherine's help, of course. She was busy trying to wheedle a few prizes out of his money for herself. I finally shut them up by threatening to put every penny of the thousand dollars in the bank. Catherine cried and Matthew became so upset that he took his ticket to bed with him and put it under his pillow. I'm exhausted.

Richard, this never should have happened. I should have been firm and simply forbidden them to watch Ringer's Races. But I wasn't. I don't know why.

I do know why. If I had said no, Matthew would have hated me. Not forever, but for a while. I was afraid of his temporary hate. It was easier to say yes, to be a likeable parent. There is nothing unusual in wanting him to like me.

I am defensive. Also, I am tired. Tired of being a single parent, tired because of today, tired of coping with a life I didn't choose. Dammit, Richard, what right did you have to choose this life for me?

I'm going to bed. Alone. And I didn't choose that, either.

Matthew has become the celebrity of Sherwood Village; Catherine and I are minor celebrities by association. I certainly didn't plan on anything like this happening, but I don't think I could have prevented it unless I taped both children's mouths shut and kept them in their rooms for the next two years, which I would never do, although the thought was tempting.

I shouldn't joke about locking the children up. A number of child abuse cases have been featured in the newspapers since we moved here. Children have been found dying of starvation in bare rooms, some of them locked in closets and fed only bread and water. In the most recent case, a girl had been incarcerated in her bedroom for five years and no one reported her missing, not even neighbors who had lived next door to her parents' home for eight years. Police had come with a search warrant to investigate the girl's father on a drug charge and found the child unconscious, lying in her own filth. She died in a hospital a week later. Local television stations sent out their reporters and camera crews to question the neighboring families. They all gave the same response. With a shrug of their shoulders, they said: 'Well, come to think of it, we hadn't seen her around for a while. Shocking news. It's really too bad.' They stared into the television cameras with proper solemnity and, cleansed by their public condolences, continued their daily lives that had been briefly interrupted.

As annoying as she can be at times, I think every street in California needs someone like Mrs Feltcher.

We slept late this morning – all of us – for the first time. Oh, how I miss sleeping in on Sunday mornings. I've been up with the children every Sunday morning since you died, although I've tried everything possible to get an extra hour of sleep. Late Saturday evening I set the kitchen table, put out boxes of cereal and bowls, and lay the children's clothes out. They get up in the morning, go downstairs to watch cartoons, then wake me up. Usually Catherine comes bouncing into my room to ask me a very important question, like: 'Can I have two glasses of orange juice?' or 'Can I wear shorts instead of jeans?' or 'Can we get new toothpaste? Can we get mint Crest this time?' Sometimes they come in together, arguing over whose turn it is to watch a certain cartoon show.

I miss our alternate Sundays, each of us taking a turn getting up with the children so the other one could sleep late. During that last year, I believe our alternate Sunday arrangement was the single remnant of what had been our marriage.

Instead of making breakfast this morning, I made brunch. Matthew put his winning ticket in the middle of the kitchen table. I started to eat with them, but the presence of that bilious green piece of paper, growing mold in my mind like a piece of stale bread, killed my appetite. I excused myself and let them finish eating alone. They continued last night's conversation as if it hadn't been interrupted by sleep and spent Matthew's money with fresh enthusiasm. When they were done, Matthew grabbed the ticket and headed toward the door, Catherine following close behind. 'I-I-I-I'm going to Kerry and Steve's now,' said Matthew.

'Me, too,' echoed Catherine.

'Are you going to take your ticket?' I asked. 'You might lose it.'

Matthew paused with one hand on the doorknob, the other hand holding the ticket. His body swayed, each hand pulling him toward a different decision, until the hand holding the ticket won. 'I-I-I'll leave it here. K-K-Kerry and Steve saw it y-y-y-yesterday anyway.' He dashed out, Catherine close behind.

They were back in minutes, Kerry, Steve, and several other children in tow. 'I-I-I just want to show them the w-w-winning ticket,' said Matthew.

He repeated the same refrain for the rest of the day. Every child in Sherwood Village must have been in our kitchen today: short, tall, freckled, dark, gap-toothed, pudgy, and bony-kneed children of every description, size, and age made their pilgrimage to see the ticket enshrined on our kitchen table. Matthew, who seemed to have acquired the polish of an experienced master of ceremonies, shepherded each group around the table so that the ticket was in full view for proper adoration. 'Th-This is it,' he said, his voice rich with pride. The children gaped in reverence.

I called him aside after the fourth or fifth group. 'Matthew, I have to change the beds and do some laundry. It's going to be impossible to get anything done if you keep bringing groups of children in to see the ticket. Can't you simply tell them that you won?'

'T-T-Telling isn't the same as seeing. Th-Th-They want to see the t-t-t-ticket.'

'Haven't enough of them seen the ticket?'

'N-Not everyone.' Matthew's eyes pleaded with me. He was king of his peers for the first time in his short life. The green piece of paper gave him something I could not give; now I wanted to dim his temporary spotlight. I yielded. 'Just a few more, okay? Give me a chance to finish.'

He agreed, then asked, 'W-W-When are we g-g-g-going to get the money?'

'Tomorrow, after school.'

Mrs Feltcher came over to offer her congratulations. She was wearing a matronly navy blue dress with white lapels that rested on the shelf of her bosom. 'I heard when we came back from church. Isn't it wonderful that Matthew's so lucky?' she exclaimed.

'I guess so.'

'What do you mean, you guess so?' she asked, frowning at me. The white lapels of her dress seemed to accentuate the sharpness of her nose and chin. 'It was the big race, wasn't it?'

I nodded affirmatively.

'Then why aren't you thrilled? It's as exciting as Catherine winning the coloring contest. You're a fortunate young woman to have two children that are winners.'

'Matthew won something by chance; he didn't earn it. I don't approve of Ringer's Races,' I said.

Mrs Feltcher studied my face with concern, as if I were ill and she was contemplating taking my temperature. 'Well, he did get something for nothing, but what of it? Someone would have won, and I'm glad it was Matthew. It's just harmless fun, like bingo at church or a raffle; there's always a winner. That's the way things are. Some people have terrific runs of luck. Maybe Matthew's on a winning streak. Back home, I was once on a winning streak that lasted almost three months. It was the happiest time in my entire life. Some weeks I would go from church to church, playing bingo every night, calling out one winning card after another. People began to know me and would try to get seats next to mine for luck. I was famous. Until I stopped winning, that is,' she said, sighing.

'Maybe it will happen again,' I said.

'Do you think so? Do you really think so?' she asked, brightening.

'Sure,' I replied. I left her standing on the front walk, lost in a bingo reverie.

When Deirdre rode over on her bicycle at three o'clock, I was still changing the beds. 'You're the mother of a celebrity,' she kidded. 'This is no time to be making beds.'

'Don't remind me.'

'What's the matter, Jenny? You sound angry. People around here have been asking about you all morning, trying to identify the woman who is Matthew's mother. I've been outside for a good part of the day and have spoken to more people in Sherwood Village than I have since we moved in two years ago. I feel like your press agent.'

'Why were you out?' I asked, upset that I had become a curiosity.

'Ken hasn't shown up for Kerry in three weeks, and the poor kid has been beside himself. It's affecting him more now that he's older. I had hoped it would be the other way around, that he would grow accustomed to the fact that Ken doesn't care. I thought he would adjust, but he hasn't. It's starting to get to him physically. He had diarrhea yesterday, and I knew that it was nerves, not a bug. Anyway, Kerry wouldn't wait for Ken inside. He insisted upon waiting outside, as if there were some magic in being outside that would draw Ken here. I didn't want him to wait alone, so I waited outside with him.'

'Did Ken come?'

'No,' said Deirdre through clenched teeth.

'How did Kerry take it?'

'Badly, as always. I don't know what to do. How can I be a social worker if I can't handle my own problems? Kerry is starting to take his hurt out on Steve. He's been teasing him unmercifully and hitting him whenever he thinks he can get away with it. The only time Kerry treated Steve decently in months was the one weekend Herb skipped. Kerry really isn't mean, or wasn't mean until he realized that his father doesn't give a damn about him. He's punishing Steve for having what he doesn't have. It has been awful, and it's affecting me, too. Every time Steve cries, I blame Kerry. Once it wasn't his fault. Steve tripped and fell down the back steps. I heard him crying and rushed out screaming at Kerry, but Kerry wasn't there. He had already left to play at the Green; Steve fell rushing to catch up with him. Damn Ken,' she cursed, 'his absence is hurting my life as much as his presence did. More, actually, because he's hurting Steve, and he has no right to touch Steve's life in any way.'

'Can you get his visiting rights taken away? He hasn't paid support money for Kerry, has he?'

'No, but what good would that do? Kerry knows Ken is his father, and he wants him. Every boy wants a father, even if the father is a bastard. Fathers aren't much different. They may not admit it, but they look upon their sons as an extension of their manhood. Ken wouldn't relinquish his claim to Kerry any more than Kerry would want him to.'

'You could try to reach some kind of workable arrangement, maybe monthly visits,' I suggested, feeling the quick pain of your permanent separation from Matthew in the hard tightening of my chest.

'I don't think it's possible. Ken would fight any attempt I made to cut his visiting rights, just on principle, and Kerry would blame me for keeping him from his father. He needs to blame someone, and I'd be the one. There is no way I'm going to play the heavy in this mess. I'm the ogre in Kerry's life as it is.'

142

'No, you're not,' I said. 'Kerry is old enough to realize that you are the one who cares for him.'

'That's the point,' Deirdre replied, raising her arms in a gesture of frustration. 'I am the one who cares for him, which means I am the one who disciplines him. Ken is the good-time parent. When Kerry is grown, he'll remember Ken for his occasional fathering and me for saying no. It will be the same with Steve. I can see it coming. Steve will associate Herb with amusement parks and extravagant presents; he'll think of me as the parent who insisted that he hang up his clothes and straighten his room.'

'I hadn't thought of it that way,' I admitted.

'Jenny, you're looking at me sympathetically. Don't feel sorry for me. I was able to get custody of both boys without having to go through messy court battles. The problems I have now are part of the package.'

'But it isn't fair,' I protested.

Deirdre smiled, but her hazel eyes were serious. 'I suppose I did sound bitter. Actually, I'm lucky. There are a lot of women who have it worse than I do; their ex-husbands use visiting days to pit their children against them. They court the kids with junk food and presents, then tell them how rotten their mothers are. I've heard stories from the women in my consciousness-raising group that have made me want to vomit. An ex-husband of one of the women told their kids that she arranged to have their dog run over because she didn't want to take care of it. Another ex-husband complains about how lonely he is, then cries and tells the children that he doesn't think he can go on living. The kids come home terrified that he'll kill himself, which he threatens constantly. Meanwhile he's out every night with a different woman, spending more money in bars and restaurants in a week than he spent on his ex-wife in a year when they were married,' she said with disgust. 'Those kids will fill psychiatrists' waiting rooms when they grow up. And do you know who'll be blamed? I'll lay you odds it will be their mothers if those doctors are anything like the psychology instructor I have this semester. Did I tell you about him?'

I shook my head.

'His name is Ralph Gates. I'd guess he's in his late thirties, not bad looking, either. He's conducting a one-man crusade, crucifying women for obsessive mothering. He says women nurture the need to be mothered in men, that historically women created a cult of mothering because they had nothing else to do. He says it has been going on for centuries and loves to talk about a woman named Volumnia in one of Shakespeare's plays who made her son into a warrior so he could carry her sword. I started to read the play – *Coriolanus* – and found out that the son's father was dead. When I mentioned it in class, the instructor said that it made no difference: Volumnia was a frustrated warrior and fought her battles through her son. Period. I didn't finish reading the play, but I did wonder about Shakespeare's mother. Do you know anything about her?'

'No, I said. 'I don't think anyone does, other than the fact that she existed.'

'From the little I read, I'd guess that she was a bitch.' Deirdre chuckled. 'No man could create a mother like Volumnia without knowing her well. The instructor may be partially right about mothers and mothering, but in the end, boys look over their mothers' heads into their fathers' eyes for the recognition that means the most to them. They want their daddies to be proud. Did I tell you that the psych instructor asked me out? He followed me one day after I started arguing with him in class.' Her face assumed an arrogant expression. '"I like your spirit," he said, "even if you are wrong."'

'Did you go out with him?'

'No,' she laughed, 'I told him I couldn't go because I was too busy mothering.'

When my laughter joined Deirdre's, I suddenly realized that I hadn't laughed in days. The skin on my face felt tight, like a hard rubber mask, and my facial muscles pulled with unaccustomed strain. It was frightening.

There is more wrong with my life than my avoidance of the past, Richard. A lot more.

'Let's talk about Matthew's winning ticket,' Deirdre suggested as our laughter ebbed. 'Why don't you join me for a bicycle ride and meet the neighbors who have been ignoring you for a year?'

'Frankly, I'm not interested in meeting them. I've grown accustomed to being ignored. Besides, it has been a rough day. Matthew personally escorted the entire juvenile population of Sherwood Village into our kitchen to see the ticket, and I haven't been able to get anything done. Now I'd just like to relax.'

'Yoga would help,' Deirdre said. 'I can't relax without it.' Then she studied my face. 'You don't seem happy that Matthew won. Does it bother you?'

'I can't stand Ringer's Races. The show encourages children to bet as if they were adults. They can't lose money because the tickets are free, but it's the principle that I'm concerned about, not the money. Matthew and Catherine scream for horses like seasoned pros at the track. Now that Matthew has won, he's already beginning to believe that he can get something for nothing. It's wrong, and I can't fight it. Each penny of his winnings speaks more eloquently than I can.'

'He'll forget it in a few months and latch on to something new. That's the way kids are. What I want to know is why you're so down on gambling. You talk about it the same way a reformed alcoholic puts down booze. Who was the gambler? I don't think it was you. Did your husband play cards or dice or leave you alone to spend nights at the track?'

It was the first time Deirdre had asked a direct question about you, Richard. I answered truthfully. I told her that you didn't play cards or throw dice or abandon me for horses. I actually laughed when I tried to picture you at the track in one of your impeccably tailored vested suits and silk ties screaming for a horse to come in. It was impossible. Then I tried to imagine you getting down on your knees to shoot dice and laughed harder at the thought of you ruining the knife-edge creases in your pants. Even my imagination couldn't put you down on your knees.

Not knowing what else to do, Deirdre laughed with me. 'I don't know what's so funny, but I can see that I was wrong,' she said.

Deirdre wasn't wrong, exactly. After she left, I poured myself a glass of wine and sat down to read the paper, but I didn't read. Instead, I thought about gambling, about how people commonly think of gambling as dice or cards or horse races. Computing the odds in a horse race may be complicated, but the concept is breathtakingly simple: pick an animal and hope it runs faster than the other animals, a matter of flesh straining to outdistance flesh. It happens and it's over. A ticket is purchased, a race is timed, and a final answer, win or lose, is given without making promises.

You gambled, but I didn't think of it as gambling then because it wasn't called gambling. It was called investing, a normal, approved extracurricular activity for an accounting major at Wharton, and you were a star player, as good at interpreting profits and losses and price-earning ratios as a star quarterback is at calling the plays in a big game. I sat in the late afternoon quiet remembering how proud I was of your investment ability and how I used it to defend you years ago. You never knew this, Richard, but my father wasn't ecstatic over the prospect of having you for a son-in-law.

I shuffled through the cards of my memory to a humid evening in August before my senior year in college. My mother was out playing bridge, Linda was staying in Florida with Aunt Maggie, and my father and I were sitting in the backyard under the cool green shade of the elm tree. It was growing dark, and I asked him for the time. 'Richard's picking me up at nine,' I said.

My father held his chin and cleared his throat importantly. 'I want to talk to you about something, Jenny. It won't take long.'

I was surprised. My father hadn't made an effort to talk to me, father to daughter, since I had developed breasts. Our conversations, if they could be called conversations, had consisted mainly of political arguments at the dinner table and had usually ended with his lectures and my resentful silence.

He spoke to me softly so his words wouldn't travel out of our backyard into the thick night air. 'Next month you'll be going back for your last year at college. I want you to have fun. Go out and enjoy yourself. You're young and pretty. I can say so even if you are my daughter. It hurts me to send you away to a fancy school in Boston knowing that you aren't going out the way you should, that you're staying in your room nights writing letters to Richard Weaver.'

'I date,' I protested.

'I know you date, but I can guess that you let the boys know you aren't interested in them. No one has to tell me. I know by knowing you. You've been seeing Richard since you were in high school, and you've never given another boy a chance. It's not that I have anything specific against Richard. It's just that I don't want you to limit your choices to one boy. Look around at some of those Harvard fellows. They can think circles around Richard any day.'

'They cannot,' I argued defensively. 'Richard can think circles around them. He's been investing in the stock market, and he made six thousand dollars this year.'

My father chuckled sarcastically. 'How much capital did he start out with, five thousand dollars?'

'No, he started out with five hundred dollars.'

'Not bad, not bad at all. But I never said Richard wasn't sharp. He's smart. Maybe I'm so accustomed to Richard that I underestimated him. Still, I want you to date other boys with an open mind. I'm not telling you to marry them, just to enjoy yourself. You're young.'

My father paused reflectively, and when he spoke again,

his voice was uncharacteristically tender, soft and rich as the late summer night. 'You'll be graduating in June, and you can start thinking about more schooling or starting a career. Your life is beginning now. Think of the world as a gigantic room, a room that you can take your time walking around in to find the most comfortable spot for yourself. Don't hug the walls or linger in the corners. Walk around in the middle with your head high, touching and examining, thinking about who you are, where you are, and where you want to be. You've earned the privilege. I know I haven't told you because I'm not good at that sort of thing, but I'm proud of you. You've been a good girl, and you'll be a fine woman,' he said, swallowing.

I sat under the elm tree deeply moved, feeling his embarrassment and mine, or was it love, sifting through the rustling leaves of the elm in the darkness of that August evening.

I found my place next to you at nine o'clock that night in your new convertible, the gleaming red-and-chrome trophy won from your first investments. You smiled at me as you backed the car out of the driveway, a quick, possessive smile that made my heart swell. I looked at your strong, even teeth, gleaming as they caught the light from the lamppost in front of our house, and leaned my head back against the black leather upholstery. At that moment, I knew I had found the most comfortable spot in the world.

The children came running in. 'When's supper?' asked Catherine.

'Soon,' I said.

'Mommy, why are your cheeks wet? Are you crying?'

I reached over and pulled her on to my lap. 'No, not crying. Just remembering.' I hugged her tight.

Catherine wiggled away impatiently. 'I'm hungry,' she said, running toward the kitchen.

'So was your daddy,' I muttered under my breath.

You told me after the holidays. I don't know whether you picked the first week in January because you didn't want to spoil Christmas or if it was simply a matter of opportunity. We had been out partying almost every night during the month of December, and when we weren't being entertained, we were entertaining. It seemed that nearly half of my waking hours were spent with a napkin-wrapped glass in my hand wishing everyone in Eagles' Landing good cheer. We were so busy running from party to party that I don't believe we had sex more than two or three times the entire month. Even now I can't recall much about that Christmas; you and the children are still a distilled blur in my memory.

But I do remember the evening you told me. You called from the office late in the afternoon. 'I won't be home in time for dinner,' you said. 'Eat without me.' I was about to suggest that we have a late supper together when the receiver clicked in my ear.

It was close to nine thirty when I heard your Mercedes pull into the garage. I was sitting at the game table in the family room studying travel brochures. We hadn't made winter vacation plans, and whenever I had mentioned a trip, you had been noncommittal. At first I had attributed your evasiveness to preoccupation, to the long hours you were spending in your new office and to our frenzied holiday activities; you were keeping the perfect schedule for an early coronary. But my sympathy started to wane when you continued to evade me, and by the first week in January, I was ready for an answer. I had spent December listening to the detailed vacation plans of everyone in Eagles' Landing and was tired of hearing myself say: 'Richard has been so busy with his new office that we haven't had time to make plans.' It was partially true, but I was becoming increasingly defensive. And resentful. I wanted a vacation. I had also worked damned hard, and I was exhausted.

You walked directly to the bar, put your attache case down, and poured yourself a double. 'Aren't you going to take your coat off?' I asked.

You swallowed a mouthful of scotch. 'In a minute,' you replied. 'Are the children in bed?'

'They've been asleep for an hour,' I said, walking over to the bar. I made myself a drink, acidly noting that you hadn't asked me if I wanted one.

'Good,' you said. You tossed your coat on one of the game table chairs; it knocked a travel brochure for sunny Grenada on to the carpet. I noted that, too, and added it to my list of complaints rather than bother to wonder at an act so contrary to your compulsive neatness. I realize now that I was spoiling for a fight, but I didn't know it then. Nor did I see what was coming.

You picked up your attaché case and sat down at the far end of the sofa. 'I have something to tell you,' you said, 'and I don't know how to say it.'

If I hadn't been upset over our lack of vacation plans, I would have heard the weariness in your voice. I would have noticed your eyes, which were unusually flat in color – a solid gray without flecks of brown or green in them – and the uncharacteristic lack of tension in your shoulders. But that night I had tunnel vision and focused on all of the wrong things. It was the vision of habit.

When you continued to drink your scotch wordlessly, I became impatient. 'We haven't made plans for a winter vacation...' I started to say, gathering up the travel folders.

'There are no possibilities,' you interrupted. 'There will be no vacation.'

The emphatic tone of your voice made me stop short. I dropped the folders and watched you concentrate on your remaining scotch. You swirled the liquid in the glass, then drank it slowly, as if you were alone in the room. 'What do you mean, there are no possibilities?' I asked.

'Sit down,' you ordered, motioning me toward the sofa opposite you. Then you snapped open your attaché case and withdrew a sheaf of papers. 'Perhaps these will tell you better than I can.'

You handed me the papers. I saw page after page of neat

columns of itemized figures in your handwriting with subtotals on the bottom. You had listed all of our expenditures from the time we had signed a purchase contract to build the house: the landscaping, the carpeting, the draperies, and the furniture, starting with the grand-father clock ($3,243). There were pages for our living expenses – entertainment, clothing, club dues, liquor, property taxes, domestic help, utilities, medical expenses, insurance premiums, charitable contributions, and babysitter costs. Every nickel we had spent, even the fifty-five dollars for my I.U.D., had been meticulously recorded.

You watched me while my eyes traveled down the columns of figures. I felt as if I had been handed indictment papers.

'Concentrate on the last two pages,' you commanded.

Itemized subtotals were on the second last page. I saw with shock that we had spent three thousand dollars more than Charlie had predicted we would. What was left of our assets was on the last page. The paper was almost blank.

Then you started to talk. 'We have to sell the house. I can't swing it any more. I didn't tell you, but I reinvested in the stock market last year. We were spending at such a fast clip that I got nervous and tried to make some quick money.'

The words 'quick money' went off in my head like an alarm, for you had always preached that the stock market was for investing, not speculating. 'How much did you lose?' I asked.

You winced. 'Twenty-seven thousand,' you said, your lips barely moving.

'Twenty-seven thousand,' I repeated. 'How could you?'

'By the end of our first year in Eagles' Landing, we had spent close to thirty thousand dollars more than I had earned,' you explained. 'It seemed to be the most logical way to supplement our income.'

There was an infuriating ring of piousness in your voice.

It was as if you were saying that the decision to gamble in the stock market was justifiable because you had made it. 'You had no right...' I exploded.

'I had every right,' you interjected. 'Where do you think I got the money to put us in this house? No one handed it to me, and I certainly couldn't have done it on the thirty-two thousand a year I earned at Wilson, Clarke and Turner. The big money I made came from the stock market. You don't have to tell me that I made a mistake this time. I know I did, and crying about it won't get the money back. I'm sorry, but we'll have to leave Eagles' Landing. I've already discussed it with Charlie, and he agrees with me.'

'Charlie.' I spit his name out like an epithet. 'Instead of talking to your wife before you invested, you ran to Charlie.'

'I didn't discuss this with Charlie until tonight,' you replied, trying to appease me. 'That's why I was late. Charlie had an arbitration that he couldn't reschedule. Anyway, Charlie says our best move is to sell the house. As it stands now, we can get out with a profit and live comfortably somewhere else. It takes time to establish a new accounting firm, but with the contacts I've made in Eagles' Landing, the office should be sailing within a year or two. Then we can live wherever we want. It will just take us a little longer to arrive, that's all.'

'"Charlie says..." Who in the hell is Charlie?' I yelled. 'God?'

'I know you're disappointed,' you said wearily, 'but don't blame this on Charlie. I didn't ask him to make the decision. I just wanted a confirmation of my own thoughts on the matter. I told Charlie because I trust his judgment. I always have. Charlie was against the house from the beginning. I should have listened to him.'

'Then you're blaming me for this mess,' I concluded.

'No, I'm not blaming you. We made the decision together to build in Eagles' Landing.'

'Are you saying that the decisions you make with Charlie are better than the decisions you make with me?'

'I've tried, Jenny,' you answered evasively. 'I've worked damned hard.'

'And I haven't? What do you think I've been doing for the past two years? Do you think it's fun smiling at obnoxious people until your face hurts? Do you think I've enjoyed volunteering for the crap work on committees to inch our way in? You opened your fucking office on clients I cultivated. Damn you, Richard, you used me and now you're blaming me. It's convenient, but it just won't work,' I shouted.

My accusation jolted you out of your weariness; the familiar tension in your body returned. 'That's unfair,' you charged in a voice kept deliberately low to make me feel like a fishwife.

'And it was fair of you to tell Charlie first?' I retorted.

'I tried to tell you.'

'When?'

'When I went over the bills each month. What the hell do you think I was talking about when I kept asking you to take it easy? You were spending money as if you had unlimited funding from the Lynch bank.'

'And you weren't? A Mercedes for over twenty thousand dollars isn't what I would call an economy car. If you wanted to go foreign, you could have bought a Toyota,' I lashed back.

'A Toyota?' you said with distaste, as if I had suggested that you walk to work with a brown-bag lunch in your hand.

'Yes,' I snapped. 'You could have started a new fad in Eagles' Landing – buying cheap.'

'That isn't funny,' you snapped back.

'Telling me that we can't afford to live here after telling Charlie first isn't funny, either.'

Then it started, Richard. We both began talking at once, each reciting our private list of grievances. That night we bared the scars we had accumulated during the years of our marriage, the surface wounds and deeper lacerations which had continued to fester because they could only be healed from within. I heard what you were saying, but I didn't acknowledge you; nor did you acknowledge me. We alternately talked and shouted in unison, our voices rising and falling in cadences set by the other like rival preachers competing for the same congregation. You told me that, to buy my new car, you were forced to borrow money from a client who had cash he couldn't declare, while I told you that you were the only man in Eagles' Landing who turned his back to me when I spoke to him. You complained about my extravagances while I complained that you never talked to me unless it was about money. You asserted that everything, all of the work you had done, was for me, while I charged you with locking us into a life I hadn't chosen. As I was speaking, I started to understand that the growing sense of loss I had felt since we moved to Eagles' Landing was loneliness; there had been no one with whom I could share the thoughts that were important to me. A new, unfamiliar emotion, the strength of which made me feel physically ill, came with the realization of what had happened. The emotion, Richard, was hate, but I didn't recognize it then. I fled the room and left you talking to yourself.

I wasn't going to write to you tonight, Richard. There are a number of reasons:

1. I think this writing is causing my insomnia. The insomnia isn't too bad yet, maybe an hour's struggle before falling asleep, but I know it will get worse. I can't stop thinking when I stop writing. Mornings have been awful; every pore in my body screams for sleep. This morning I dropped a full pitcher of orange juice in the kitchen. It splashed everywhere: on the walls, the appliances, me, the children. Even a section of the ceiling was dripping. It took close to an hour to clean up. The children almost missed their school bus, and I was late for work.

2. The writing is becoming a crutch. Let me try to explain: when things happen to me during the day, I don't always think about them. Instead, I postpone my thinking for later when I can write it down. This means I am living my days twice, days that are generally aggravating. The punishment is hardly worth it, which brings me to the next point:

3. I am reliving past unpleasantness. If my present were in any way pleasurable, it wouldn't hurt as much to relive the past. But it is not. I feel that I am wedged in between the worst sides of both lives, past and present. Yesterday and last night are perfect examples of what I am talking about.

4. This reason is difficult for me to articulate without sounding crazy, but I'll try. There have been times when I have expected you to answer or have hoped that you would answer. I know it is ridiculous. You cannot answer because you're dead. Then why do I expect you to answer? Or want you to answer?

Don't answer!

5. This solitary writing is defining my loneliness. I have no one to talk to but you (which could be the reason I want you to reply), and my loneliness has become almost physical, a gnawing ache that is growing like a tumor.

6. I am afraid to continue. If I leave the past unexcavated, it cannot hurt me. If I do not, if I keep digging, I may find myself in a crater so deep that there will be no escape. I am not a masochist, nor am I a heroine. I do not want to dig my own grave.

7. There are some things I don't want you to know.

8. There are some things I don't think I want to know.

There are more reasons than I thought there were. When I started the list, I could think of three. I finished with eight. Now can you understand what this writing is doing to me?

Count the above as the ninth reason.

As long as I started, I might as well finish.

Matthew was anxious to return home before he left for school this morning. He wanted to know when we would go to the nearest Ringer's Supermarket to collect his one thousand dollars. It occured to me then that he was planning to spend all of the money (which I knew I would not allow), but I didn't say a word to squelch his plans. There would be enough time after school to discuss the money. Memories of bitter early morning fights with my mother when I was a child, tears and angry words that clung to me like pieces of lint on a dark dress for the remainder of the day, harnessed my tongue.

I suppose there are times when memories can be instructive.

While driving to work, I pondered over how to handle Matthew and his money, whether to let him spend a portion of the winnings or to insist that he put every penny in the bank. It didn't seem fair to demand that he bank the whole amount, but I didn't want him to take a large sum of money and squander it thoughtlessly. I started to play with figures, juggling percentages of one thousand dollars that Matthew might feel was a fair settlement, but I couldn't make a decision: what I felt was fair, Matthew would probably think was unfair. The debate continued in my head until my mind was fractured into opposing camps, and by the time I parked the car at Briarhill, I had the promising start of a healthy headache. I took two aspirin as soon as I reached my office and decided to discuss the problem with Mr Gallisdorf. That done, my headache showed signs of disappearing, due either to aspirin or the thought of Mr Gallisdorf, and it would have been gone by noon if it hadn't been for Jim Gentile.

The activity for the morning was a duplicate bridge tournament, and the players were working on the last hand when Jim came in to see me. 'How's about going out for lunch?' he asked, thrusting his hands into the pants pockets of his leisure suit, a hideous plaid in mustard, brown, and robin's-egg blue.

'I'm sorry. I can't go out today,' I said.

He took his hands out of his pockets and placed them on his hips. I noticed that the weekend had added weight to the gut pillowing out of his open jacket. 'Why not?' he asked, pouting like a spoiled child.

'I have some work to do.'

'It can wait.'

I was firm. 'I'm afraid that it cannot wait. It's important.'

'What's so important that you can't go out and celebrate?'

'Celebrate what?'

'The zoning variance. Our lawyer called this morning – it was passed. Now we can go ahead with the new construction. He told me that the coverage of the fashion show in the paper helped push it through. The council was impressed. I knew they would be. Frankly,' he said, lowering his voice, 'I think they were relieved just seeing the old ladies up and around. You can consider the lunch a bonus.'

I felt my eyebrows raise. 'A bonus? Since when is a free lunch a bonus?'

'There could be more,' he said suggestively, edging closer.

'I'm sorry, but I can't go out for lunch with you today,' I said, stepping back. I felt like adding 'or ever' but didn't.

'It's your loss,' he called out sulkily before slamming the activity-room doors.

I found Mr Gallisdorf in a corner of the solarium with a book on his lap. His eyes were closed, as if in thought or sleep. Miss Manfred was sitting on a chair on the opposite side of the room staring at the expansive back lawn that will shortly disappear under a crush of bulldozers. Suddenly I was sorry I had pushed so hard to get a picture of the fashion show in the paper. In my eagerness to do my job, I hadn't realized what the new building will mean. Soon the residents of Briarhill won't have more than a few tiny strips of grass, areas no bigger than grave plots once paths are put in, to look at or take a stroll on if they are up to it. They will die, brittle-boned and weary, walled in by bricks and concrete.

I was (and am) disgusted with myself, although my part in pushing the new building through could be rationalized. Eventually the Gentiles would have found a way to get the land rezoned without my help. They can afford persistence. That thought hurts even more. For the meager salary I earn as their employee, I saved them thousands in bribes and legal fees.

The pattern of my life repeats. I embrace the challenge at hand and think about consequences after I act. I still haven't learned to consider the effects of my actions. Perhaps Mr Gallisdorf is right: people don't change.

Not wanting to be rude, I walked over to Miss Manfred before talking to Mr Gallisdorf. 'How are you today?' I asked.

'Fine,' she replied absentmindedly.

There was something distinctly different about Miss Manfred, more than her response, which lacked the brightness and vitality I have come to expect of her. She turned in her chair to speak to me and shuffled her feet. Then I knew. Miss Manfred was wearing sensible, low-heeled black shoes styled with a wide strap across the instep; she had abandoned her high heels to shoe herself in fear. Miss Manfred had joined the others, becoming one with Briarhill.

I exchanged pleasantries with Miss Manfred, then excused myself to talk to Mr Gallisdorf. He was awake and smiling a crooked half-smile in my direction. 'I wasn't really dozing,' he joked. 'I usually save that for after lunch.'

'It's lunch time now,' I said, glancing at my watch. 'Are you planning to leave for the dining room?'

'I can wait. I don't need to eat much now that I can't walk. Besides, I'd rather talk to you.'

It didn't take long to tell Mr Gallisdorf about Matthew winning Ringer's Races. 'I really don't know how to handle this,' I said, 'not the money nor the concept of the whole business. I don't want Matthew to grow up believing the world is easy, that he can expect to get something for nothing because he's Matthew Weaver.'

'He won't,' said Mr Gallisdorf. 'He'll learn soon enough that it takes more than a spectacular win to get what he wants out of life. There is a whole world out there [he gestured with his good arm toward the lawn] waiting to tell him so.'

'But what if he doesn't learn, what if he grows up truly believing that prizes will fall in his lap?' I asked, thinking of the continuous stock market windfalls you and I had once expected to last forever.

'Explain it to him as best you can. Don't underestimate Matthew. And don't be too hard on him. Give him a fair portion of the money,' said Mr Gallisdorf positively. 'When a parent kills a child's joy, the child never forgets; neither does the parent. You can lose your son, young as he is. Don't do it.'

It was the strangest conversation I have had with Mr Gallisdorf. I tried to continue talking to him, but he didn't respond. Instead, he sat in his wheelchair as if he had been transported to another time or place that the sound of my voice could not reach. I don't believe he even heard me say good-bye.

Now that I think about it, it was unusual advice for a man to give who had no children of his own. He spoke with the sure pain of experience. Perhaps he was hurt as a child. The elderly seem to have an amazing facility for remembering what happened to them sixty years ago, yet they are frequently unable to recall what they ate for dinner an hour after the meal. That has to be the explanation. Mr Gallisdorf told me his marriage was childless, and I believe him.

Jim Gentile confronted me outside the solarium. It was apparent that he had been standing there for a while. 'So you didn't have time to go out to lunch,' he said sarcastically. 'I can see why. You prefer talking to an old, half-dead man than a real man, because a half-dead man is safe. Is that what's the matter with you, Jenny? Can't you handle a *real* man?'

'It's none of your business,' I replied coldly.

'So I'm right,' he gloated. 'Your late husband couldn't have been much of a man. What did you do, give it to him on birthdays and anniversaries like it was a special prize? Did you wrap yourself up in a ribbon, too? Your husband must have been a real jerk to take that kind of crap.'

My voice was hard with leveled anger. 'You are the jerk, Jim Gentile, and don't you dare mention my husband again. Ever.'

Jim's face became a mosaic of red blotches. 'I could fire you,' he threatened.

'For what?' I asked, taken aback.

'Insubordination,' he roared.

'I was hired to provide entertainment for the elderly, not for you,' I snapped, feeling my headache return in fresh prisms of pain. I stormed off before he had a chance to reply, took two more aspirin, made several calls, and waited until it was time to go home. While waiting, I decided that I would ask for a raise. And a bonus. The Gentiles can consider the whole package combat pay.

Our doorbell started ringing minutes after the school bus arrived. A parade of strange children came to the door, some of them much older boys, to call for Matthew. I could hear the excitement in his voice when he told them he could play as soon as he came back from Ringer's.

I overrode the children's protests and insisted that they have a snack before going to the supermarket to claim Matthew's prize. We had to discuss what was to be done with the money. Matthew wanted to spend all of it, the full one thousand dollars. 'No,' I said, 'it is too much money to spend.'

'B-B-B-But it's mine,' Matthew protested.

'I know, and I understand how you feel, but we have to save some of the money for college.'

'W-W-W-Whose college?'

'Yours . . . your education. It costs a lot of money to go to college. We'll put some of the money in the bank in your name, and you can keep the bank book and watch your money earn interest.'

'W-W-W-What's interest?'

I explained interest, telling them that, if Matthew put one thousand dollars in the bank, the bank would give him close to sixty dollars at the end of a year. Both children became quite excited. The sixty dollars sounded almost as important to them as the original thousand.

'W-W-What happens after you g-g-g-get the sixty dollars?'

'You get more money. The longer you keep your money in the bank, the more interest you earn.' I sounded like a commercial.

'I-I-I-I-I think I'll put all of my m-m-money in the bank,' Matthew decided. 'I-I-I'll get really rich.'

'Oh no,' Catherine wailed. 'You promised me a present. Now I won't get a present, and I won't get interest.'

Catherine started to cry; Matthew looked stricken. 'D-D-D-Don't cry, Catherine. P-P-P-Please don't cry. I'll get you a present.'

'You will?' Catherine asked through her tears.

Matthew nodded. 'I-I-I-I-I'll get you a s-s-skateboard for your very own,' he said generously.

Catherine gave him a glorious, wet-cheeked smile and ran over to hug him. 'D-D-D-Don't get mushy,' he said, wriggling away from her. 'Y-Y-Y-You know I don't like mushy stuff. L-Let's go now.' He got up and headed toward the door, Catherine following.

I was touched by Matthew's generosity, and proud. There have been moments like that with the children, times when they have been kind and compassionate toward one another, that have taken the edge off the other times, the times when they are cranky, whining, or generally miserable. I cherish the special times as rare gifts, tentative confirmations that I am not botching the job of parenting.

161

On the way to the supermarket, I asked Matthew if he wanted a present for himself. He told me he wanted a ten-speed bike like the big boys, but he wanted the interest on his money, too. The disposal of the money was decided by the time we parked the car: Matthew would get a ten-speed bike, Catherine would get a skateboard, and the remainder of the one thousand dollars would go into a bank account. Every year Matthew would be allowed to spend the accumulated interest on something that he wanted. He agreed that, if he had nothing specific in mind, he would keep the interest in the bank. But I doubt that he will. Every toy manufacturer in the country is waiting to take it away from him.

Once inside the supermarket, we went directly to the enclosed platform that serves as an office, and I asked the girl behind the glass if I could speak to the manager. She said he was getting ready to leave and wanted to know if she could help me. 'I-I-I-I got the one thousand dollar t-t-ticket,' Matthew shouted excitedly. The girl said she would get the manager right away.

People in the store heard Matthew, and a crowd started to form. We were completely surrounded by staring shoppers by the time the manager arrived. I don't think I have ever felt so self-conscious. There was no place to hide, and we stood like animals in the zoo, caged in by metal carts, the targets of impersonal eyes. Some of the people were eating while they hunched over their carts watching us.

'Excuse me,' the manager said, pushing his way through the wall of shoppers. He was a stocky, middle-aged man with black hair and a carefully trimmed salt-and-pepper beard. 'Do you have the winning ticket?' he asked.

'I-I-I-I do,' said Matthew, proudly holding up his ticket.

'You mean you're holding the ticket for your mother.'

'N-No,' said Matthew. 'It-It-It-It's *my* ticket. M-M-Mine.'

An immediate buzzing sound came from the crowd. I heard snatches of 'it's the kid's ticket' and 'the kid won.'

'Okay people. Let's break this up,' the manager said, waving his arms to disperse the onlookers.

'Are ya gonna give the kid a thousand dollars?' asked an anonymous voice.

'Ain't it against the law?' asked another voice.

There was a chorus of 'yeahs,' and the buzzing increased. Matthew blanched. 'It-It-It-It's my ticket, Mommy.' He was close to tears.

I put my arm around him and bent down. 'Don't worry,' I whispered.

'All right, everybody. You're blocking the aisle. People can't get out with their groceries. Let's move it.' The manager's voice was increasing in volume.

'Naw, we wanna stay,' someone said over the buzzing. 'This is almost as good as TV.'

The manager tried pushing some of the carts away, but they returned to their former positions as if they were on springs. He turned to me. 'This is a mess,' he said disgustedly. 'Take your kids through those doors, and I'll meet you there.' He pointed to double doors at the far end of the produce aisle, then said to the crowd: 'Move aside. Let these people through.'

The carts moved grudging inches to let us pass.

It was damp and chilly in the cavernous produce room. Girls were trimming heads of lettuce and packing Brussels sprouts into pint containers. Catherine walked over to watch the girls working on the Brussels sprouts. One girl scooped the miniature cabbages into a container, shaking off the excess with a snap of her wrist, and another covered the filled container in plastic, sealing the bottom on a hot pad without a single wasted motion. There was a synchronized grace to their labor, the packing and sealing accomplished to an even quarter-time beat. Fill, cover, smooth, seal. Fill, cover, smooth, seal. Catherine was mesmerized.

Matthew was too upset to watch the packers. 'W-W-

Why did the m-m-m-man tell us to come in h-h-here? W-W-W-Why were those p-p-p-p-people in the store looking at us, t-t-t-t-talking about me winning? Wh-Wh-What's wrong?'

'Let me see your ticket,' I said.

He handed me the ticket. I scanned it quickly and found the clinker. On the top half, in minuscule print, it read: ONE WINNER PER TICKET – ADULTS ONLY. I should have realized that Matthew would be ineligible to win. The mess was my fault.

'What does this say, Matthew?' I asked, putting my finger under the words ADULTS ONLY.

'D-D-D-D-Does that m-m-m-mean th-th-th-they w-w-won't g-g-g-g-give m-m-m-m-m . . .' He couldn't finish and started to cry.

My headache returned with renewed vitality. 'No, you'll get your money,' I assured him. 'I'll tell the man that it is my ticket. But I want you to understand that it is not the truth. I'll be lying, and I don't like lying. It's wrong. I'll do it because you're counting on the money, but you will have to give me a promise.'

'W-W-W-What?' he asked, pressing his hand against his forehead, as if the gesture would somehow stop his awful blocking.

'You'll have to promise me that you won't watch Ringer's Races again. They are not for children, and it says right on the ticket that children can't win. Do you promise?'

'Y-Y-Yes. I-I-I-I-I'm sorry I-I-I-I'm making you l-l-l-l-lie. R-R-R-Really I am.'

I was too harsh. Matthew's face had a pinched look, like a wizened old man's.

The manager swung through the double doors of the produce room carrying a clipboard in one hand and a camera in the other. 'You created quite a scene out there,' he said with irritation. 'Now what's this business about the ticket belonging to the boy?'

'I'm giving you the ticket,' I said.

164

'Did you win or did the boy win?' he asked, taking the ticket. He checked the number against a sheet of paper held by the clipboard.

'It says ADULTS ONLY on the ticket. Obviously, my son can't win.'

'I want to know who the ticket belongs to,' he persisted.

'Why? So Ringer's can save one thousand dollars? Who do you think watches Ringer's Races? The show isn't exactly quality adult entertainment.'

'What is your name?'

'Weaver, Jennifer Weaver.'

'Look, Mrs Weaver, I don't have the time or the energy to debate the merits of Ringer's Races with you; either you won or you didn't win. Which is it?'

I hesitated. Matthew's eyes became round with pleading. 'Is there a form I have to sign?' I asked.

'It's right here.' He held out the clipboard and marked an X on the bottom line of a printed form. 'Sign there,' he said, handing me his pen. 'Fill in your address and phone number underneath.'

I scanned the form, a legalistic scrap of double talk stating that the undersigned was not an employee or relative of an employee of Ringer's Supermarkets, its advertising agency, or the participating television station. It further stated that the undersigned was of legal age, had not altered or mutilated the ticket, and was aware of the laws governing the races in the state of California. I signed.

'All right now, if you'll step over there please.' He pointed to the far wall of the produce room and snapped a flash cube into the camera.

'I don't want my picture taken,' I said.

'It's a formality. Our big winner appears each week in the Ringer's Circle of our lead ad. Now cooperate and walk over to the wall. The light's better there.'

'You don't seem to understand. I don't want my picture in a Ringer's ad.'

He let out an exasperated breath. 'Mrs Weaver, every big winner of a Ringer's Race gets a picture taken for the ad. It's part of the promotion. Please cooperate. You've caused enough trouble in the store already.'

'I don't want my picture taken, and you don't have my permission to use it in your ad.'

He started to read the form I had signed. 'There is nothing in the form that says you can use my picture,' I said.

'Don't give me a hard time. I'm already late to pick my son up from practice.' Without giving me warning, he held up the camera and the flash went off in my face. 'That's it,' he said. 'We're finished. You can pick the check up here on Friday.'

'Look Mr – . What is your name?'

'Broylin, Arthur Broylin.'

'Mr Broylin, I suggest that you destroy that film. If you use my picture without my permission, I'll sue Ringer's Supermarkets.' My voice rose an octave as I spoke.

'There is nothing you can do to prevent it, Mrs Weaver. So long,' said Mr Broylin, pushing open the double doors.

The girls in the produce room stood idly and stared. We had interrupted their interminable rhythm.

Our ride home was silent; we were each cocooned in our own thoughts. When we pulled into Sherwood Village, a group of children were waiting for Matthew. They reminded me of baby vultures. 'There he is,' yelled a boy of eleven or twelve, pointing to our car. 'Hey, Matthew, did ya get the money?'

Matthew tucked his body into a corner of the back seat and stayed there until the car was parked. 'Let's go in for a few minutes and talk over what happened before you go outside to play,' I said, turning off the engine.

Once inside, Matthew asked if I were mad at him. I knew I looked grim. My face felt tight, and my jawbone was rigid as steel. 'No,' I said, 'not at you.'

'W-W-W-W-What about the p-p-picture?'

'Don't worry about the picture,' I said determinedly. 'It won't be in the paper.'

'B-B-B-B-But the m-m-m-man said . . .'

'I don't care what the man said. It won't be in the paper.'

'If-If-If-If-If the kids s-s-s-s-see it, th-th-th-th-they'll think y-y-y-y-you won instead of m-m-m-m-me.'

So that was what he was worried about – the kids thinking that I won. I exploded. 'Matthew, doesn't it bother you that I lied and signed a paper saying that the ticket belonged to me?'

'Y-Y-Y-Y-Yes, but I'll st-st-st-st-still get the m-m-m-money.'

'There are some things that are more important than money. Telling the truth is one of them. Do you hear me?' I shrieked.

He started to cry.

'Dry your tears and go out to play. I'll call you in for dinner.'

Richard, I am a hypocrite. I talk to the children about truth and lie to set an example for them.

But I had to claim the ticket. If I didn't, Matthew wouldn't have won the prize.

Matthew would have survived without the prize money, and I could have exposed the negative influence of Ringer's Races on children.

Who am I kidding? I am one of those people who can plan a great crusade for someone else to fight.

Why did fate play this perverse trick on us? Real people don't win prizes in supermarket promotions. To my knowledge, no one in my family ever won anything. But I am forgetting something. Matthew is your child, too. I'll blame this on your side of the family. It's fair. You blamed Matthew's stubbornness on mine.

The anonymous voice in the supermarket today comes back to mock me. 'This is almost as good as TV,' the voice said. Even at its most ridiculous, my life isn't quite up to a listing in the Nielsen ratings.

I wrote a letter early this morning and sent it, special delivery, to the executive offices of Ringer's Supermarkets before going to work.

Gentlemen:

Yesterday my picture was taken by one of your store managers, a Mr Arthur Broylin, for use in a Ringer's ad. I told Mr Broylin that I didn't want my picture taken. He said it was customary to feature winners' faces in your advertising format and took the picture without my cooperation and over my protests.

As ridiculous as it may sound, I believe that my face belongs to me. You may not purchase it for your use for the sum of one thousand dollars. Further, the form I signed does not give you permission to use my picture as a part of your advertising campaign. To put it succinctly, you did not and cannot buy the rights to use my face or person in your promotional advertising.

I am sending this letter to inform you, in writing, that Ringer's Supermarkets does not have my permission to use my picture in their newspaper, television, or slinger ads. If you do use my picture, I shall consider it a breach of my privacy and shall be forced to sue your corporation.

I am retaining two copies of this letter should the need for litigation arise, and, I assure you, I shall definitely sue Ringer's if my picture is used.

This letter will be posted in time to prevent the use of my picture. I shall also call the newspapers in which you advertise, apprising them of the fact that Ringer's Supermarkets does not have my permission to use my picture.

I trust that you will respect my person and my privacy.

Thank you for your cooperation.

Sincerely,
Jennifer Weaver

I think it's a terrific letter, Richard. In fact, I know it's terrific because the telephone was ringing when I came home from work today. A Mr Anderson, the public-relations director for Ringer's Supermarkets, was on the line. He said that he had been trying to reach me for hours.

'We received your letter, Mrs Weaver,' he said, 'and it distresses us greatly.'

'The manner in which my picture was taken distressed me. You aren't going to use it, are you?'

'That's why I'm calling. We at Ringer's are sorry if Mr Broylin upset you, but we do want to use your picture. I'm sure you'll understand when I explain that it's a tradition to use winners' pictures in our ads. We have always featured winners' pictures. It is a nice way for them to receive recognition, and the ads make terrific mementos. Think of it: the ad featuring your picture will be cherished by future generations of your family. Some of our winners have even framed the ads. If you would like, Ringer's would be delighted to present you with a profession-ally framed picture of yourself featured in the Ringer's circle.' Mr Anderson's delivery poured smooth as liquid plastic.

'I do not want my picture used in your ads,' I said firmly.

'But it's a tradition at Ringer's to feature winners' pictures.'

'How can it be a tradition when you've only been running the promotion for a few months? I thought traditions took years to evolve, not weeks.'

'In today's fast world, traditions are born instantly.'

'Well, I don't call it tradition. I call it promotion, and you do not have my permission to use my picture.'

'That's too bad, Mrs Weaver. Ringer's is being generous with you. Your check for one thousand dollars has already been issued and signed. Couldn't you cooperate to show your appreciation?'

'No.'

'According to Mr Broylin there seems to be some question over the ownership of the ticket, if it was indeed your ticket at all. There was some mention of the ticket belonging to your son.' The tone of Mr Anderson's voice underwent a subtle change as he spoke. It was still smooth, but there were knives under the opaque plastic of his words.

I held the receiver, remembering how you taught me to anticipate. 'The secret of one-upmanship,' you said, 'is to do the unexpected. If you think someone is going to snub you, embarrass you, or say something that you don't want to hear, act before they can. Call their shot. Then they will have to retrench. Usually they can't, because they've been taken off guard.'

I called Mr Anderson's shot. 'Mr Anderson,' I purred, 'I hope you're not implying that the ticket did not belong to me. You know that it's illegal for minors to bet in California, yet I am sure thousands of children watch Ringer's Races every Saturday night with tickets obtained in your stores. In fact, I have seen children take tickets from your cashiers after their parents' groceries have been purchased and bagged. Your stores are encouraging children to gamble and are giving them the material to do it with. An impartial observer might say that Ringer's Supermarkets are actively engaged in the corruption of minors, some of them no more than five or six years old. Do you happen to know the law concerning the encouragement of gambling among minors?'

'Uh, well, I don't,' Mr Anderson said. His voice lost its sheen.

'I'll be watching your ads, and I don't want to find my picture in them. Also, I would appreciate it if you mailed me the check. It will save me the trouble of picking it up.'

'You can do your shopping after you get the check,' he suggested.

'I shop for food on Wednesdays, and according to Mr

Broylin, the check won't be in the store until Friday. Good-bye, Mr Anderson.'

'Don't hang up,' he said nervously. 'I don't know how to tell you this, but your picture has already been included in the paste-ups for next week's ads. The newspapers have them by now.'

'I strongly suggest that you correct your ads by removing my picture. It isn't too late. If you don't, I'll be forced to sue.'

'I'll try my best, but I can't promise anything,' he said wearily.

I would have called the newspapers, but the children came home before I had a chance. Then the doorbell started ringing. It was a repetition of yesterday. Unfamiliar faces were at our door, boys of every age looking for Matthew. Some of them were too old for him, twelve or thirteen at least, and several looked tough.

'Who are these boys?' I asked. 'Where did they come from?'

'A-A-A-Around here. Th-Th-Th-They're new friends,' Matthew said proudly.

'What about Kerry and Steve? Where are they? Aren't they your old, good friends?'

'Y-Y-Y-Yeah, but they're too little. I-I-I-I like the b-b-b-big boys.'

'Matthew, do the big boys want to play with you because you won Ringer's Races?'

'N-N-N-Not really,' he said, squirming.

'Are they being friendly to you because you promised them something?'

Matthew hesitated. 'N-N-N-N-No. Th-They like me. N-N-N-Now I'm one of the b-b-b-b-big boys.'

'That's not so,' said Catherine. 'Matthew told the big boys he was going to have lots of money to buy things. I heard.'

Matthew glared at her. 'Sh-Sh-Sh-Shut up, Catherine.'

'No, I won't. It's true, Mommy. It's true.'

I silently cursed Ringer's Races. The past few days I have

cursed them as often as an old lady says her rosary, pausing on each bead. 'Matthew,' I said, sitting him down on the sofa, 'I want you to stop telling strangers that you are going to have a lot of money to spend. You are not going to spend the money on anything but a bike and a skateboard. Is that clear?'

He nodded and started to rise.

'Sit down. There is something else I want to tell you. I don't want you to make friends with kids who are interested only in what you have to give them. They aren't real friends; they are bought friends. A real friend will like you even if you didn't win Ringer's Races. Your real friends are Kerry and Steve. These other boys want something from you. If you can't give them what they want, they'll hurt you later.'

Matthew understood what I was saying, but he didn't want to believe it. Lately he has shown signs of what I am beginning to think of as 'selective understanding.' He understands only what he wants to understand. If he disagrees, he tunes me out. Later in the afternoon, I saw him playing with the older boys. He was more of a mascot than a participant. I watched from the kitchen window, stifling the urge to call him inside. I have this terrible premonition that Matthew is going to be hurt, and there is nothing I can do to prevent it.

I called the newspapers this morning after the children left for school. The morning paper assured me that Ringer's had eliminated my picture from their ad, but the evening paper gave me the same runaround I had gotten from them when I wanted to get coverage of the fashion show. They all must have taken lessons in the art of the brush-off, for everyone I spoke to referred me to someone else. I finally hung up in disgust and decided to go grocery shopping at Ringer's arch rival's store. I was so annoyed that the thought of suing became quite pleasant.

While I was out, I remembered Nat Witton and called

him when I returned. After I told him who I was, he asked: 'Are you having another fashion show?'

I don't know why, but I was embarrassed. 'No,' I said, 'there won't be another fashion show for a long time, at least not under my supervision. I'm calling for another reason. I hate to impose, but I don't know anyone else on the paper.'

'What's the problem?'

I gave him a brief rundown on the Ringer's mess and told him that I didn't want my picture in their ad. 'No one on your paper will tell me if the ad has been changed. They are guarding the information as if it is a Pentagon secret. Is there any way you can find out?'

'Sure, but why don't you want your picture in their ad? It's just a harmless promotion, and you'll be a celebrity in your neighborhood for a day or two.'

'I don't want to be a celebrity and certainly not a celebrity through Ringer's Races.'

'You sound as if you're sorry you won. Are you?'

'Yes.'

'Why?'

'It's a long story. Can you find out?'

'I'll check on it now and call you back.'

I gave him my telephone number, and he called back within minutes. 'Your picture was taken out of the ad,' he said. 'It caused quite a stir this morning.'

'Thank you. I hope I won't have to bother you again.'

'It was no bother, but now I'm curious. Why are you going through this trouble for one picture in a supermarket ad? I could understand if you were a fugitive and the picture would lead to your capture, but I know you're not a fugitive.'

'How do you know?'

'Fugitives don't write thank-you notes,' he said, laughing.

'It's too involved,' I replied, 'and I've taken up enough of your time already.'

'Don't be so sure. There could be a story here. Are you at work now?'

'No, I'm at home.'

'Could you come down to the paper? I'd like to talk to you. It wouldn't take long.'

I wanted to refuse but didn't. The day was already shot. Besides, Nat Witton had helped me twice. I felt that I owed him something.

The newspaper offices weren't what I had expected. I had imagined them to be either drab and smoke-filled or ultrasleek and sparkling. Instead, they were ordinary. The floor on which Nat Witton works is dominated by an enormous room filled with desks, wastebaskets, and other office clutter. People were working concentratedly, seemingly undisturbed by the various noises around them. I don't know why, but I almost felt cheated. The offices weren't at all as romantic as I thought they would be.

I must have appeared confused when I walked into the room, for a young woman came up to me and asked if she could be of help. I told her I was looking for Nat Witton. 'Oh.' She smiled knowingly, as if we shared a secret. 'He's over there.' She pointed to two men talking on the far side of the room where there were glass-partitioned offices.

'Which one is Nat Witton?' I asked.

'The tall one,' she said, surprised. 'I thought you knew him.'

I thanked her and started walking across the room. It could have been nothing, but I thought I saw a glimmer of curiosity in her eyes or an acknowledgment of some kind. No one else paid attention to me.

I approached the two men. 'Excuse me,' I said. 'I am Jennifer Weaver, and I have an appointment with Nat Witton.'

Both men turned to face me. The shorter of the two was middle-aged and balding. 'Some people around here have pleasanter work than others,' he quipped.

'It pays to play your hunches,' said Nat Witton.

I felt myself flush. Can you believe that, Richard, at my age?

Nat Witton introduced me to the other man, an Ed something-or-other, and ushered me into one of the glass-partitioned cubicles. 'I'm glad you could come,' he said. 'Sit down and tell me about Ringer's Supermarkets.'

I sat down on a chair in front of the desk. Suddenly I was uncomfortable. My feud with Ringer's seemed too trivial to warrant a trip to the newspaper.

'Tell me about not wanting your picture in the paper,' he said, leaning back in his swivel chair. He looked at me appraisingly.

'Where do you want me to start?' I asked self-consciously.

'Anywhere you want. You can start with the picture and work back if you like. Speaking of work, aren't you still working for the nursing home?'

'It's my day off. I work there part-time.'

'Would you like a cup of coffee? I think I would.'

'Yes, please.'

I was relieved when he left the room. Nat Witton is attractive in a tall, loose-limbed sort of way. His face is too craggy to be called handsome, but it's interesting, and he has the most unusual eyes. They are a clear, penetrating blue, the sky color in travel brochures. His age could be anywhere between thirty-five and forty-five. He has the kind of face that makes gauging age difficult.

He came back with the coffee. My uneasiness must have been obvious, for he started talking about other things, including my thank-you note. 'I hadn't seen a thank-you note in years,' he said, 'not since I left home. I had forgotten that there were such social niceties. My mother believed in thank-you notes and God, in that order. "A decent upbringing," she used to say, which was her pronouncement of respectability.' He mugged a stern expression, and I laughed.

'You have a nice face,' he said. 'Why don't you want it in the paper?'

I told him the whole Ringer's story. 'That's it,' I said, finishing. 'The ticket really wasn't mine. I didn't want my son to watch the show in the first place. But he did watch, and he won. I couldn't take it away from him. We've been having a running battle over Ringer's Races since it went on the air. Have you watched the show?'

'No.'

'I didn't think so. I don't believe one adult in ten thousand watches that program. Ringer's Supermarkets are corrupting children under the guise of entertainment. When I stopped shopping in their stores, which was my form of protest, the children were furious. They wanted their weekly tickets to the races. It's sick.'

He looked directly at me with his perfect-weather eyes. 'I agree,' he said seriously. 'What does your husband say about this business?'

'I'm a widow,' I replied, lowering my eyelids.

'Oh,' he said. 'Forgive me for asking, but was it recent?'

'Almost two years ago.'

Nat Witton had taken the next line in my widow routine. I decided to change the subject rather than let him pursue it. 'It's getting late,' I said, looking pointedly at my watch. 'I have to be home in time for my children.'

'How many do you have?'

'Two. A boy and a girl.' I stood up.

'Your angle on the Ringer's promotion is interesting. I don't know if I can do anything about it, though. Ringer's Supermarkets are heavy advertisers. It took me a long time to learn that journalism is less than an idealistic profession. The people who pay a newspaper's bills have silenced more typewriters than I would like to admit. Let me kick this Ringer's business around. One of our reporters is about to start a series on television programming. Would you like to know what happens?'

I told him that I would, and he said he'd call me.

I was stepping into the elevator when I heard my name called. 'Jennifer, Jennifer Weaver.' It was Nat Witton.

'Did you receive your check from Ringer's yet?' he asked.

'No, I think they're mailing it.'

'It would be a good idea if you held onto it for a while. If the powers-that-be decide to allow any critical reporting on the show, we might not be able to use your story if you've cashed the check. An article could be slanted toward the fact that you felt forced to sign for your son's winning ticket.'

I agreed not to cash the check.

While I was driving home on the freeway, I heard the sound of approaching sirens. Traffic narrowed to a single lane to pass an accident. A tractor-trailer had slammed into the rear of a compact car; the cab of the truck was resting on top of the crushed automobile's trunk like a giant predator about to devour its prey. I averted my eyes but not before I saw a lifeless body sprawled on the hood of the car, bathed in blood and splinters of glass. One of the victim's feet, cut off at the ankle, was lying on the highway in a sneaker. I gripped my steering wheel in horror and, gasping for breath, forced myself to drive the rest of the way to Sherwood Village. There were moments when I didn't think I'd make it. I have been terrified of the freeways since we have lived here but thought I could overcome my anxiety. Now I have doubts.

Deirdre stopped by late this afternoon. After I told her about the accident, I mentioned my visit to the newspaper and the possibility of a story on Ringer's Races. She was surprised at Nat Witton's personal interest. 'Don't city editors usually send reporters out on stories?' she asked.

'I don't know. You could be right.'

'Maybe he just wanted to meet you,' Deirdre teased. 'You have a sexy voice.'

'He's probably married,' I replied.

Nat Witton wasn't wearing a wedding band, but a lot of men don't wear wedding bands. You didn't. I was hurt when you refused to wear one. 'I don't like wearing any jewelry but a watch,' you said. 'Besides, a wedding band isn't insurance that a husband or wife won't fool around. A ring can be taken off and pocketed as easily as it is put on. The only thing that's permanent is a tattoo. Would you like me to get one? I could have a big red M tattooed on my forehead.'

You painted an imaginary M on your forehead with your finger. I laughed, and you kissed me. Life was so easy before we were married, love enveloping us like a down comforter. Oh, to know that feeling again!

I can never know that feeling again. It only comes, I believe, with innocence. I am no longer innocent.

I am not innocent.

I didn't ask for a raise today. When I arrived at work, Briarhill was in an uproar. Mrs Fry met with an accident yesterday, the repercussions of which have hit the nursing home like a series of mine explosions. I say 'met' because that is exactly what Mrs Fry did.

One of the nurses told me how the accident happened. It seems that an aide had washed and dressed Mrs Fry, then stripped her bed and left to get fresh sheets from the laundry. Instead of waiting for the aide to return as she was instructed, Mrs Fry had gotten up and wandered down the corridor to the front entrance; she was outside before anyone knew she was missing. Apparently Mrs Fry stood under the front portico until she saw a car turning into the driveway. She rushed down the steps calling 'Albert, Albert,' and literally ran into the car. The driver, a linen supply salesman, said he had just completed his turn and was going no more than five miles per hour. 'It was as if she came out of nowhere, calling "Albert, Albert,"' he said.

Mrs Fry ran into the left front fender of the car, fell, and fractured her skull. She is lying unconscious on the third floor.

Albert was the name of Mrs Fry's husband.

The nurse said several aides quit in sympathy with the aide who left Mrs Fry in her room. Jim Gentile had berated her unmercifully in front of the residents and staff. 'He was hysterical,' said the nurse, a sturdily built blonde with a flat Midwestern accent. 'He yelled at the poor woman so loud that you could hear him in every corner of the building. She was our best aide, and she really cared for Mrs Fry. She was the one who was always telling us to call Mrs Fry's sons.'

'Did she explain?' I asked.

'She didn't get a chance. He kept yelling, then screamed at her to get the hell out before he threw her out. I would have quit, too, but I need the money. My husband was laid off two months ago, and he still hasn't found work. I've already started looking for another job.'

'How did Mrs Fry's sons react?'

'They were both out of town; we expect them here this morning. They'll probably come in with their lawyers, prepared to sue. I'll bet they won't even bother to go up to see the poor old lady because she's unconscious,' said the nurse bitterly. 'That aide cared more for their mother than they did. But they'll meet their match. Simon Gentile was up and dressed early this morning. He's a tough old bird. No one will pick his carcass clean without paying in blood for each feather.'

I went to Jim Gentile's office to see if he wanted me to proceed with the day's scheduled activities. Ellen wasn't at her desk, and the door to his office was open. Simon and Jim were inside, arguing.

'I'll handle the Fry brothers,' said Jim with bravado. 'They'll regret messing with me. You're not up to it.'

'Like hell I'm not up to it. Now you listen to me. I'm going to handle this, and you're going to keep your mouth shut. Is that clear?' Simon ordered.

'But you're not well. You can't take excitement. Remember, you have a bad heart.'

'Stop reminding me, you jackass. I told you to write the

Fry brothers a couple of months ago to recommend the second floor for Mrs Fry. You didn't listen. But then, you never did listen.'

'It slipped my mind,' Jim said. 'I have a lot of responsibilities around here. I can't remember everything. And you don't have to call me names.'

'You can't remember anything; you're inept. But you'll remember this: I'm telling you to keep your mouth shut, and you'll keep your mouth shut,' warned Simon.

'But you're sick. I'm in charge now. Let me handle the Frys.'

'You're not going to be in charge until I die, and I'm not dead yet. With you running Briarhill, I may never be ready to die. And if you don't keep your mouth shut, you won't be running Briarhill. You'll be out looking for a job like the aide you fired. There was no need to chew her out in front of everybody – she was the best aide we had on the first floor. Furthermore, firing her was exactly what you shouldn't have done.'

'But she screwed up,' Jim protested. 'If it weren't for her, we wouldn't have this trouble.'

'You screwed up. I told you to inform the Fry brothers in writing that their mother needed custodial care, and you didn't. It's just damned lucky that I didn't trust you.'

'What do you mean?' Jim asked indignantly.

'I wrote them,' said Simon. 'Typed the letter myself. Made a copy, too.'

'When?'

'Three weeks ago. I told them to get in touch with me. They never did. They ignored the letter because they knew they'd have to ante up out of their own pockets for their mother's care.'

'Then I can certainly handle them,' said Jim excitedly.

'If you so much as open your mouth, I'll throw you out of here,' Simon threatened. Then, almost to himself, he said: 'How does life go wrong? Look at you. Look at the Fry boys. Albert Fry was a good man, a family man. He tried as hard with his sons as I tried with you. I knew

Albert Fry for nearly forty years, and I missed him after he died. Now I'm glad he's gone so he can't see what his boys have come to. Or his wife. He loved that woman. A long life can be a curse. A man can live too long, like me, and then he doesn't want to leave because he can't leave in peace.'

I hadn't meant to eavesdrop, but I listened, fascinated. Simon Gentile's voice was strong and sure in contrast to his son's, which was all bluster. I felt sorry for both men; neither one could look into the eyes of the other and find satisfaction.

Simon Gentile spun his wheelchair around when I knocked on the open door. 'Oh, it's Jenny,' he said with a smile. 'What can I do for you?'

I had never seen Simon Gentile dressed for business. He was wearing a conservative navy blue suit, white shirt, and maroon striped tie. His shoes were polished to a mirror finish, and there was high color in his cheeks. He looked vigorous and competent. Jim Gentile was slouching behind him blotchy-faced in one of his tacky leisure suits. He looked twice his father's size but half the man.

'I wanted to know if I should go ahead with today's activities,' I said. 'Everyone is upset over Mrs Fry's accident. I realise that I'm already behind schedule, but I hesitated because I thought the residents might be offended. They could think the activities were somehow disrespectful. In view of the accident, I mean.'

Simon looked at me shrewdly. 'What do you think you should do?' he asked.

'I think the activities would be a good diversion,' I replied.

'So do I,' he agreed. 'Thanks for checking first. You show good sense. If we don't give you a raise soon, you'll leave us.'

Jim Gentile shot a black look in his father's direction.

I forced myself to go up to the third floor to see Mrs Fry before I left for the day. I knew it wouldn't mean anything to her, because she had lapsed into a coma late in the morning, but I couldn't leave without seeing her.

Filtering through the odors of disinfectant, urine, and illness, there was another, more tenacious odor. The third floor smelled of death. I had never smelled death before, but I recognized it instantly. It is an indefinable odor, stale and gray, yet acridly pungent.

You were lucky, Richard, to have never known the smell of lingering death. You went out fast.

I hurried past the few patients who were in the corridors. They seemed more like lumps in wheelchairs than human beings, their deteriorating flesh reflected in lifeless eyes. I did not glance into any of the open-doored rooms.

A nurse took me directly to Mrs Fry's room. She was resting peacefully on the bed. If it hadn't been for the tubes connected to her body, she would have appeared to be in sleep.

'Do you want me to stay?' asked the nurse, a pretty, olive-skinned woman with large, compassionate eyes.

'No,' I replied. 'I won't be long.'

As I stood at Mrs Fry's side, I became aware of the woman she must have been prior to her husband's death. Mrs Fry was dignified in her coma. Her hair, which was always in disarray, had been combed, and the haunted look that marked her features was gone, the fear and loneliness wiped clean. I left the room glad that I had come. I know this sounds terrible to say, but I was happy for Mrs Fry.

When I passed through the halls to return to the elevator and glimpsed several bodies vegetating on hospital carts, their faces withered and sexless, I thought of Aunt Maggie and was glad for her, too. I didn't fully realize what she escaped until now. With everything that happened after Maggie's death, starting with her will, I wouldn't wish her back. Instead, I can remember her as she would have wanted to be remembered, as she was until the moment she died, a vibrant human being, fully alive.

An awful thought: I wouldn't have seen Maggie that one

last time if we had been able to afford to stay in Eagles' Landing.

An even worse thought: If we hadn't gone to Florida to visit Maggie, we wouldn't have met Anson Schuyler, and you would be alive today.

Mrs Fry is still in a coma, and the mood at Briarhill is one of solemn expectation. I had scheduled a craft demonstration this morning – flowermaking with fabric, wire, and glue – but the residents were apathetic until Miss Manfred suggested that the flowers be taken to Mrs Fry's room. Everyone embraced the idea instantly and worked with quiet intensity. The woman who gave the demonstration, a Mrs Tighe, was amazed at the women's diligence. 'I never would have believed it,' she said, looking at the rainbow of flowers produced out of scraps of organdy. 'Some of them could barely grasp scissors with their arthritic fingers, yet they managed to cut out one petal after another. It must have been excruciatingly painful. Tell me about this Mrs Fry. Is she a great favorite of theirs?'

'She was one of them,' I said.

'Then why didn't anyone volunteer to take the bouquet upstairs? It's gorgeous, something to be proud of. I asked for a volunteer when no one offered. The women froze. I couldn't get a response from any of them, not even the lady who suggested giving the flowers. I felt as if I had said something terribly wrong.' Mrs Tighe's round face grew rounder with bewilderment.

'The move of a resident to the third floor signals the end,' I explained.

'But they know their time will come,' she observed, arranging the flowers into an artful bouquet with her quick, competent hands. 'This is a home for the elderly. You would think they would want to give each other comfort.'

Mrs Tighe decided to take the flowers up to Mrs Fry herself. She stepped into the elevator wearing a bright smile and the robust self-assurance of a healthy woman in her forties. I met her in the corridor twenty minutes later. She was wan. 'I had to wait for a nurse to take me to Mrs Fry's room,' she said thinly. 'I had no idea, no idea at all.'

Mrs Tighe's craft store wants Briarhill's business, but I'm almost positive she'll send one of her employees to give the next demonstration.

No one knows what was said during the meeting between Simon Gentile and Mrs Fry's sons. The brothers went up to see their mother afterward but didn't come in today. I doubt that they'll visit Briarhill again. They probably feel that they don't have to bother because Mrs Fry can't acknowledge their presence.

Simon Gentile has taken over command of Briarhill. He seemed to be everywhere: in the offices, the corridors, the kitchen, the recreation area. No one has seen Jim, who stays behind his closed office door all day, and no one misses him.

The check from Ringer's came in the mail. I wasn't going to tell Matthew, but he remembered that we were supposed to pick the check up today and wanted to go to the store as soon as he came home.

'I have the check,' I said. 'It came in the mail.'

'I-I-I want to see it,' he said excitedly.

After I showed him the check, he said, 'L-L-L-Let's get my bike now and C-Catherine's skateboard. I-I-I-I need some money, too.'

I told him that we would get his bicycle and her skateboard tomorrow, thinking that it would be a good way to fill Saturday.

'B-B-B-But I *need* money *today*,' he protested.

'Why? You promised that you would put the rest of the money in the bank.'

I waited for him to answer, but he didn't. The doorbell rang while he stood squirming. It was one of the older boys who had been everpresent all week. 'Where's Matthew?' he wanted to know.

'He's busy right now,' I said.

'I wanna talk to him. He's supposed to get his money today, ain't he?' The tone of his unevenly pitched adolescent voice was more demanding than questioning.

I looked carefully at the boy slouched against the doorjamb. He must have been at least thirteen, and his chronological age was the youngest thing about him. Although his upturned nose and full, petulant mouth were childlike, his face had an expression of cultivated toughness as tight as his skinfitting jeans. This was one boy I didn't want to see again.

'What is your name?' I asked.

'Why? What difference does it make?' said super-tough, shaking his black hair out of his eyes with a jerk of his head.

'I like to know who I'm talking to.'

'Robbie.'

'Robbie what?'

'Robbie O'Connor,' he said begrudgingly.

'I would like to know why you're so interested in Matthew and his check. Aren't you a little too old to be playing with Matthew?' I heard Matthew groan in the living room and stepped outside.

'Matthew said he was gonna get money. He'll have a lotta money to spend.'

'Is that why you're playing with him?'

The boy shifted his feet.

'Do you honestly think I'd let Matthew throw around a thousand dollars? Would your mother let you have that much money to spend?'

Robbie O'Connor's eyes narrowed into black lines of resentment. 'She wouldn't care. I can do what I want with my money. I'm my own boss. No one can tell me what to do.'

He stood erect and thrust his thumbs into the belt loops of his jeans, as if to challenge me. I realized then that he could hurt Matthew, and I was frightened. There had to be a remnant of understanding in this boy that his studied toughness hadn't killed, a concept of fairness that I could appeal to.

'Robbie, you're much older than Matthew, so you've earned the right to spend a lot of money. You've probably been your own boss for a long time,' I said, trying to flatter him.

'That's right,' he replied with a swagger. 'My mother never knows where I am or what I'm doing 'cause I don't hafta tell her. She's never home anyway.'

'Well, I am home, and I know how much Matthew wants to play with you. Younger boys always want to play with older boys. I imagine you did, too, when you were Matthew's age.'

Robbie O'Connor didn't respond. I guess the admission that he was once young was too much of a strain for him. I tried a different approach.

'I'll tell you something if you promise that you won't repeat it to anyone,' I said. Then I hesitated, adding: 'I'd better not say anything. I don't know if you're old enough to keep a secret.'

'I can keep a secret,' he bragged. 'There's a lot I know that I don't tell.'

I motioned to him to come closer and looked around as if to make sure no one else was listening. 'I had to sign a statement saying that I won so Ringer's would give us the money,' I said in a *sotto* whisper. 'It's illegal for Matthew to have the money.'

The boy's mask of toughness cracked, slightly. 'Could they put him in jail?' he asked with relish.

'I don't know,' I lied. 'But now do you understand why Matthew can't have the money? He's going to get a new bicycle, but I'll have to pay for it myself. You won't tell, will you?'

Robbie O'Connor shifted his feet, considering what I had told him. 'How much is it worth to you to keep me quiet?' he asked greedily.

I was floored, then furious with myself for allowing a suburban tough to intimidate me. He was reciting clichéd lines from junk TV shows, and I was letting him get away with it. 'I hope I didn't understand you,' I said forcefully. 'If you're trying to blackmail me, I'll call the police right now. They can put you in juvenile hall, and you can wait there until your mother eventually comes to get you. She'll have to get a lawyer, too. It will cost her plenty, and you'll have a record. Is that what you want?'

He laughed nervously. 'I was only kidding.'

'I'm sure you were,' I said, 'and you're going to prove it. You're going to be nice to Matthew and make sure the other older boys don't come after him for money. Is that clear?'

He nodded and started to walk away. 'Wait a minute. Come back here. I'm not finished. I'll tell Matthew to leave you alone. I know he's too young for you and that you're not interested in him. But if he gets hurt and I find out that it was you or any of your friends, I'll blame you, and I'll make trouble for you that you won't forget.'

Robbie O'Connor glared at me with hate, the first honest emotion I had seen register on his face.

I went back inside; Matthew was crying. 'Dry your tears,' I ordered, 'and listen to me.'

He wouldn't stop crying or couldn't, I don't know which, and I was too angry to care. I shook him. 'Stop crying or I'll spank you,' I threatened.

He stopped.

'You are not going to be allowed to go out to play today,' I yelled. 'You lied to me! You promised the big boys money so they would play with you, and you told me that you didn't promise them anything. Why did you do it, Matthew? Why?'

'I-I-I-I-I wanted R-R-R-Robbie to l-l-l-l-like me. I-I-I-I-I wanted to be-be-be with the b-b-b-big boys.'

'That Robbie is awful. He's mean and nasty. If I see you near him or with him, you'll be punished. DO YOU UNDERSTAND?'

I lost control and continued screaming until Matthew started crying again. Finally, to escape my ranting, he ran upstairs to his room and slammed his door shut. Catherine, who had witnessed the scene, stood in a corner of the living room chewing her hair ribbon.

'Why are you standing there?' I screeched.

She looked up at me and started to cry. 'Are you going to yell at me, too?'

'No, Catherine,' I said wearily. 'Go outside to play.'

How can I do it, Richard? How can I raise the children all by myself? There was no reason for my performance this afternoon. I could have been angry without becoming hysterical, but I wasn't. I was in rare form – a perfect shrew – and I hate myself for it. Even my behavior toward that obnoxious Robbie O'Connor was detestable; I met him at his level. If I earned the reputation for being the bitch of Sherwood Village today, I deserve it.

I know I'm not alone. Deirdre gets uptight and screams, also. Our lives are tightly strung. We walk on tense wires, struggling to maintain our balance. It is not easy to be alone on the best of days, so when a child creates a problem or becomes the focus of a problem, we get upset, lose our balance, and take the child down with us. It is an ugly, but real, facet of our lives. I am worse than Deirdre, for I can't acknowledge it as openly as she can.

After Catherine went outside, I went upstairs to talk to Matthew. I wanted to apologise to him, to tell him that I understood his wanting to be one of the big boys. What he did was wrong, but it was normal. When I knocked on his door, he didn't answer. I called to him. There was still no answer. The anger I had felt came bubbling back, and I ran downstairs before I became hysterical again, this time screaming because he wouldn't open his door.

Matthew came downstairs for dinner with Catherine. He wouldn't leave his room until she went up to get him. Our meal was silent; the food on our plates was pushed around rather than eaten. Both children were wary, afraid to say something that would trigger my tongue. They looked so innocent sitting at the table, so young and vulnerable, that I was filled with self-loathing.

The children will forget. Tomorrow morning they will wake up smiling, eager to get their presents. It will be the same as it was before.

Or will it? Will they love me less?

I love the children, more now than I did when they were born, but it is hard to be alone with them. Sometimes I tell myself that we would have been divorced if you hadn't died, but I am not comforted. Contrary to what Deirdre says, I believe it would have been easier for me to survive with a divorced husband than with a dead husband. You would have been with them for part of the time; a portion of the responsibility for their lives would have been yours.

Why did we have children? I've gone back, trying to remember when I decided that I wanted to bear a child. I can't remember making that decision, nor can I recall you ever saying that you specifically wanted me to have a baby. All I can remember is a vague conversation after our first anniversary. 'Did you start taking your pills this month?' you asked.

'No,' I said. 'Today would be the first day. Should I start or skip it?'

We looked at each other. You grinned. I suppose I did, too. 'Surprise me,' you said.

'What does that mean?' I asked.

'Whatever you want it to mean.'

I stopped taking the pills. Matthew was born within the year.

Catherine was conceived so that Matthew wouldn't be an only child. Young American couples weren't supposed to have one child; they were supposed to produce two children within a decent interval. We never talked about it, for there was really nothing to talk about. We did what had to be done. But it was fine. We were in love, and we were going to live happily ever after.

While I was in the hospital after I had Catherine, I read a slick magazine article about a glamorous, rising career woman who chose not to have children. The woman was my age, and there was a picture of her on a sailboat, looking tanned and fit. I shall never forget the caption beneath that picture: 'I've weighed my future regrets against the life I'm enjoying now, and my life style today always wins. I'd rather be pursuing my career and sailing on our boat every weekend than chasing a toddler.'

The article threw me into a postpartum funk that lasted for weeks. I thought of that woman every time I got up in the middle of the night for a feeding, every time I changed a messy diaper, every time I picked up Matthew's toys and listened to Catherine's infant wails, and I shriveled up inside. You noticed. 'Is something bothering you?' you asked one evening after the children were in bed. 'You've been so quiet lately. And so grim.'

'It's nothing.' I said, 'just postpartum blues.'

'But Catherine is two months old. The blues don't last that long. Why don't you see the doctor? Maybe there's something wrong.'

There was something wrong, but a visit to the doctor wouldn't have made it right. How could I have told you or the doctor that I thought I had made a mistake? Two mistakes. How could I have admitted that I had two babies I wasn't sure I wanted? It would have sounded crazy and irresponsible. It was irresponsible. I produced two children without once asking myself if I really wanted them. There was no thought involved. But then, one doesn't have to think to produce a child: there is a brief act of conception, and the body does the rest.

We were fortunate, Richard. We had two beautiful, perfectly formed babies. How could I complain?

Someday when Catherine is grown, I'm going to talk to her about having children. I'm going to tell her that the decision to bear a child will be the most important one she will make in her life, more important than choosing a career or a husband, for once the choice has been made and the child conceived, the obligation cannot be broken. But I shall also tell her that there may come a time in her life when she will find herself alone, hungering for a comfort that only the flesh of her flesh can give. I know. It happened to me, and I was grateful for the warm touch of my children's hands.

Another Saturday. We went shopping to buy Matthew his bicycle and Catherine her skateboard. There was no problem purchasing the skateboard, but the bicycle was, as I had anticipated, a hassle. I knew Matthew wanted his bicycle immediately, an impossibility unless I could persuade a store manager to let me buy a floor model. I think it must be easier to separate freshly entwined lovers than it is to cajole a store manager into parting with his floor model.

Nothing seems to come assembled anymore. Large toys such as doll houses, wagons, scooters, sit-in cars, and bicycles are sold in cardboard cartons filled with a potpourri of mysterious parts and schematic diagrams of instructions that require an advanced engineering degree to decipher. There is always a teasing picture of the completed item on the outside of these cartons that hold nothing but frustration inside.

My first experience with an unassembled toy was with a crib for Catherine's dolls. The salesman handed me a flat, rectangular carton. 'This isn't a crib,' I said.

The salesman, a short, nervous fellow who wore thick glasses, held up the box. 'Look,' he ordered impatiently. A picture of a completed crib was pasted on the carton.

'But I want it put together,' I said, suddenly realising that you were no longer available to assemble it. The realisation was one of the first footnotes to my widowhood.

'No, you don't,' he replied. 'If it came assembled, it would cost you twice as much. You'd have to pay for someone else's labor and our storage. The store doesn't have that kind of space.'

The salesman convinced me that it would be easy to put

191

the crib together. 'Your little girl could do it,' he said. 'It's simple.'

An evening of aggravation was spent putting the crib together, but the time wasn't entirely wasted. Aside from discovering that there is a unique tool called a Phillips screwdriver (which I learned after I mutilated the heads of the screws with a regular screwdriver), I planned my future toy purchasing. I told myself that, if I couldn't buy a toy assembled, it wasn't worth buying at all. Since that time I have been able to wheedle fully assembled toys out of the most intractable store managers. Don't undervalue my accomplishment, Richard. It is one of the few skills I have developed since your death, a survival technique of which I am quite proud.

We were able to buy Matthew a bicycle at the third store we tried. The first store didn't have what he wanted, and the manager of the second store wouldn't part with his floor model. 'Floor models aren't for sale,' he said with irritation. 'It's a store policy. Your boy likes the bike. Buy it and we'll charge you a reasonable fee to put it together. You can have it in four or five days.'

'No,' I said, 'I'll buy it someplace else. Your store isn't the only one that carries this brand.'

I saw him hesitate as we started for the door, hating to lose a sale. Instead of pausing as I usually do (it is part of the technique), I continued walking. He had been unpleasant; I would find the bicycle elsewhere.

The bicycle was ten dollars less at the third store, and I offered to pay extra if we could take the floor model after I went through my helpless routine. It worked. The salesman explained the gears to Matthew and warned him that he must be careful. 'The gears are easily stripped,' he said. 'Don't let anyone fool around with the bike and be careful when you're riding it. You have to pay attention to what you're doing. Try to switch the gears as little as possible.'

Matthew promised. He was thrilled and bounced up and down on the back seat of the car all the way home.

The bicycle is too sophisticated for Matthew, but what could I do? I promised him any bicycle he wanted and couldn't talk him out of one with ten speeds. He is no more ready for that bicycle than he is to drive an automobile. The bicycle wavered slightly from side to side when he rode off on it, and I squelched the impulse to tell him, one more time, to be careful.

It was an expensive Saturday. I spent one hundred forty dollars on the children's toys, and I don't know if I'll be able to cash the check from Ringer's. Nat Witton hasn't called. If the newspaper does carry an article on Ringer's Races, I may not be able to cash the check at all. There could be fraud involved since it was Matthew's ticket, although I don't understand why I wouldn't be allowed to sign for him. I hope Nat Witton calls soon. And not only because of the check.

The money I spent today won't hurt us, but you already know that. Jim Gentile was accurate when he surmised that I am a successful widow, if success is measured in terms of dollars. You left us well supplied.

Then why don't I feel successful?

I suppose I should give you a rundown on the money and what I have done with it, but don't expect a formal statement with debits and credits itemised to the last cent. It isn't necessary. Besides, the years you insisted that I keep detailed household accounts made any kind of bookkeeping unpleasant to me. Today I do a minimal amount of record keeping and pay an accountant to take care of my tax return. He isn't as bright as you were, Richard, but he doesn't charge as much, either.

I sold the house for $197,000. Can you believe it? That's quite a jump from the $110,000 we paid. The house was your best investment. It's too bad you weren't around to give yourself a congratulatory pat on the back. The realtor's fee, six percent, came to $11,820. Luckily, our mortgage insurance held even though your death was a suicide. If we had built the house a year later, I would have come out with much less; our remaining mortgage was

$54,952. A man at the bank told me they were no longer offering mortgage insurance that paid off if the owner took his or her life. He made it sound as if suicides were becoming epidemic among property owners holding large mortgages.

Your insurance policy had an incontestability clause which stated that the owner or beneficiary would be paid in full if the policy had been held for a period of two years or more, regardless of the cause of death. Because you put the ownership of the policy in my name, a check was made out to me for the full amount, $150,000, but the insurance company stalled for weeks before sending it. I guess policies on suicides do not get preferential treatment.

I know you were aware of the incontestability clauses in the mortgage and life insurance policies. You had lightly underlined them in pencil as if to tell me not to worry, that the money would be forthcoming. I erased the penciled lines before turning the policies in, but they have not been erased from my memory. Even now I can see the faint lead tracings underscoring your death. Oh Richard, if the incontestability clauses had not existed, you would exist. You would be here because you would have been worth more in life than you were in death.

Our checking account was dangerously low; the savings account held slightly over one thousand dollars, and your remaining stocks didn't amount to more than thirty-five hundred dollars. Our assets were temporarily frozen because they were in both our names, so I had to borrow money from my father to cover the cost of your funeral and immediate necessities until I was able to sell the stocks. The death benefit we received from Social Security was two hundred fifty-five dollars, which wasn't enough to bury one leg let alone an entire body.

Living in Eagles' Landing for a year was expensive, but it wasn't nearly as expensive as it had been when you were alive. There were no more mortgage payments to make, no extravagant parties to pay for, no expensive evenings out, no babysitter bills, which had been running over ninety

194

dollars a week when we had Ginny, no liquor bills, which had sometimes run well over one hundred dollars a month. I resigned from the clubs when our dues became payable, thus eliminating another thirty-five hundred dollars in expenses, and cut the cleaning woman down from two days a week to one before I let her go completely. There was nothing for me to do anymore – no frantic scurrying from meeting to meeting, no committee calls to make, no parties to plan or attend – so I cleaned the house myself. I made a career out of cleaning. On my better days I tackled closets or cupboards; on bad days I did light dusting and vacuuming. Cleaning was something to occupy my time, and I found myself grateful for the sheer size of the house. With over five thousand square feet of living space to scrub and polish, I could work myself into exhaustion.

It could have been coincidental, but I decided to stop taking tranquilizers when I finished my last major project – cleaning the basement. There was nothing left to tackle. It was time to leave.

My mother noticed the difference in the house on one of her infrequent visits and wanted to know if I had found a new cleaning woman. 'Everything glistens,' she said appreciatively. 'My Maude is getting old. Does your woman have any free days?'

I told her that I was 'the woman.'

Mother's eyebrows reached for her hairline with that bit of news, and she made a caustic remark about her daughter 'the scrubwoman' which I tried to ignore. Clearly, the information did not please her. It was fine for me to live in an immaculate home, providing that each gleaming surface was the product of another's labor. I was a disappointment; I had not fashioned myself in her image.

My father sold your Mercedes and was so impressed with the price it brought that he decided to buy one himself. I was annoyed, for I remembered his cutting remarks about you trying to impress people when you originally bought the car, but kept my irritation to myself.

My father had generously offered to subsidise us beyond the money I had borrowed while I waited for the insurance check. It wasn't necessary because I was able to manage on Social Security benefits supplemented by the cash I received for your car, but I was glad for his offer and touched at his solicitude. His eagerness to give me money was the only possible way for him to show his love and concern. When I told him I could manage, he seemed disappointed and called weekly to reiterate his offer until the check came.

If I could have put the memory of his loving concern in water as one keeps freshly cut flowers, perhaps the collected anger of our later arguments concerning the insurance money would eventually have been forgotten. It was not. My father wanted me to invest in blue-chip stocks and Treasury Certificates. 'It makes good sense,' he insisted. 'Richard would want you to invest your capital for the highest percentage of guaranteed return.'

I refused. 'The money will go into the bank. I want security.'

He told me that I was being unreasonable. Stupid, in fact. The harder he argued, the more adamant I became. During our period of disagreement, the news hit town that the Bestmark Partnership had collapsed. After he grilled me about the mess, he left in disgust. The breach between us was complete.

I still haven't invested the money, but don't be upset. It is safe and provides us with a healthy income, more than enough to survive on without touching the principal. We live well, if modestly compared to our life in Eagles' Landing, and I am even able to save money that I plan to use toward the children's education. Here is a breakdown:

$9,480.00   Annual Social Security Benefits
17,000.00   Interest on long-term savings account, ($200,000) at 8.5%

8,400.00   Interest on shorter-term savings account,
($120,000) at 7%

$34,880.00   Total

I haven't added my income from Briarhill to the total. It is under three thousand dollars because I haven't worked there for a full year. However, I shall have to make a decision concerning the job before I reach the three-thousand-dollar mark. For every two dollars that I earn over three thousand, one dollar will be deducted from our monthly Social Security check of seven hundred ninety dollars. The government doesn't believe in giving its citizens earning incentives – to work is to be penalised. On days when my job at Briarhill becomes boring or frustrating, I toy with the idea of quitting. I don't really enjoy what I'm doing, and I'm certainly not paid a sufficient amount to learn to like it.

The decision to keep the money in separate bank accounts was difficult. I know I'm losing income in interest, but I need the feeling of security that the smaller account brings. Somehow it seems more readily accessible. When I tried to explain this to the man at the bank, he looked at me as if I were weird. He may have been right, but then, he doesn't have my history.

I shopped banks for the best interest rates and feel that I did well. If I had invested in stocks, I wouldn't have earned enough extra money to justify the risks involved. I'm not rationalising, Richard. I know you would be as angry as my father was if you were here. Don't deny it. You'd disagree with my handling of the estate. But you're forgetting something: I don't have earning potential at present, and I have two children to raise. I *need* to feel secure.

If there is one thing you cannot criticize in my handling of the money, it is the manner in which the accounts are set up. Both are Totten Trusts with me as trustee for the children. When I die, the money will automatically belong to them. Matthew and Catherine are protected.

A strange thing has happened. The money has become an abstraction. I live off the interest as if it were an allowance given to me by a doting uncle. Somehow it seems easier that way. Don't ask me why. I couldn't tell you.

Once I believed that a woman who was financially independent could do whatever she wanted to do. She could keep the wind at her back and spit on the world if the spirit moved her. Now I know that isn't true. I have the money, but I sure don't have the spit.

I want to be independent, not just secure, but I don't know how to go about it. Perhaps I'll begin by not writing to you tomorrow. It will be a start. I'll have to learn to talk to myself without a pen and paper.

My resolve not to write to you is a failure. I couldn't keep away for more than forty-eight hours, but there is a reason: Deirdre.

The telephone rang last night at ten thirty. At first I thought it was a crank call or wrong number. I said hello two or three times and hung up when there was no response. The telephone rang again. I was annoyed and grabbed the receiver. 'Who is this?' I demanded.

'It's me ... it's Deirdre.' Her voice was faint and strained.

'Was that you who called before? Is something wrong with your phone?'

'Please Jenny, can you come over here?'

'Now?' I asked. 'Where will I get a sitter?'

'Something's happened. Can you come?' she pleaded, almost in a whisper. Then she added: 'Do you have any tranquilizers or sleeping pills? If you do, please bring them.'

I knew I had to get there quickly. Whatever happened had affected Deirdre drastically. In the year I have known her, I have never heard her mention taking any kind of medication. She seems to shy away from drugs, to a point where she refused aspirin I once offered for a sinus headache, insisting that she wanted to save her pill allotment for a worthy illness, a 'big event' she called it.

I phoned Mrs Feltcher. Mr Feltcher answered. I apologised for the late hour and asked if I could speak to his wife. Mrs Feltcher must have been standing next to him, for she was on the line instantly. 'Jenny, is one of the children sick?' she asked with concern.

'No,' I said. 'A friend called, Deirdre Cohen. You know her. Her sons play with Matthew and Catherine. Something has happened to Deirdre, and I'm concerned. She wants me to come over with some medication. Would you mind staying here for a few minutes? I don't want to leave the children alone.'

'Sure I'll come,' she said, 'but I have my bathrobe on. It's almost time for the eleven o'clock news.'

'No one will notice,' I assured her. 'Thank you.'

I didn't have any sleeping pills, but I did have a half bottle of Librium, which I slipped into the pocket of my jacket before the Feltchers arrived. They came over together. Mrs Feltcher had put a loose-fitting black coat over her flowered pink robe, and when she took it off, she looked like an inflated rosebush. 'It's dangerous to walk alone at night,' she said. 'My husband will take you over to Deirdre's.'

I hesitated. From the way Deirdre spoke, I sensed that she wanted me to come by myself. Besides, I doubted that Mr Feltcher would be protection. He's a delicately built man, a few inches taller than I am, with none of his wife's heft. Even his features are small, with the exception of his nose, which is as bulbous as his wife's is sharp. The moment became awkward when Mr Feltcher opened the door to escort me. 'Thank you,' I said, 'but I'll run over to Deirdre's alone. Sherwood Village is fairly safe, and I don't want to impose upon you any more than I have already.'

'It's no imposition,' interjected Mrs Feltcher. 'George

would be delighted to walk you over, wouldn't you, George?'

Mr Feltcher nodded; the poor man didn't have a choice.

Rather than argue, I walked out the door with him. When we reached the corner of our block of buildings, I stopped. 'Deirdre lives over there,' I said, pointing to the next quadrangle of buildings. 'Why don't you watch me run over. I'll be fine, and you'll be able to stay with Mrs Feltcher or go home before you miss the news.'

'I don't mind,' said Mr Feltcher. 'It's a nice night.' His voice didn't sound convincing.

'Yes, it is,' I agreed, 'but I've imposed upon you enough.'

Before he could reply, I started to run and waved my thanks. Although I didn't glance back, I was sure he waited until I reached Deirdre's, following his wife's order as best he could.

I knocked on Deirdre's door and saw a drape move before I heard the lock click open. Deirdre stood aside in the unlighted hall and motioned with her arm for me to come in. She closed the door and bolted it as soon as I was inside.

'Thanks for coming,' she said, walking into the living room. 'Did you bring the pills?'

Deirdre turned to face me without meeting my eyes. Her hair was wet, and her skin was tight and dry, as if dehydrated. Instead of holding her dancer's body as she usually does, with effortless grace, she was rigid. Standing appeared to be a strain for her, an exercise of will.

I reached into my pocket for the bottle of pills, not knowing what to say but realizing that I had to be careful. Deirdre was so like a piece of porcelain that I felt the wrong word might shatter her. 'Here are the tranquilizers,' I said, pretending to study the prescription label. 'They are Librium, twenty milligrams each. You can take up to four a day spaced at equal intervals. I didn't have any sleeping pills.'

Deirdre took the bottle from me and read the label, still avoiding my eyes. 'These pills are over a year old,' she said, hollow-voiced. 'Will they work?'

'They're good, if that's what you mean, but you can't expect a miracle from them. Have you ever taken tranquilizers?'

'No.'

'If you take the full dosage, four pills a day, your head will be foggy. Also, you can't drink. Alcohol and tranquilizers don't mix.'

While I was talking, Deirdre concentrated on sitting down. I say concentrated, because she didn't just sit. Rather, she gingerly engineered her body down onto a sofa cushion. Her head was bent, and she continued to stare at the bottle of pills in her hand. I waited for her to say something. She was silent. Finally. I spoke. 'I think I'll call Mrs Feltcher and ask her to stay a little longer.'

I went into the kitchen to call Mrs Feltcher. When I returned, Deirdre was as I had left her. I wanted to draw her out, yet I was afraid that I might push her further away. Pain reaches pain, I thought. It isn't a pleasant bridge, but it's one that I know.

I sat down on the sofa, far enough away from Deirdre so she wouldn't feel my presence as an intrusion. 'Deirdre,' I said softly, 'I was on those pills for almost a year after my husband died. I lived from pill to pill, swallowing one each time I felt a break in the fog they created. Even when the fog became frightening, I continued to take them. I didn't stop until I started to have blackouts. When my head finally cleared, I found that nothing had changed. I panicked, but I didn't go back on them. Not completely.'

'What did you do?' she asked in a faraway voice.

'I tried to function. It wasn't easy. After a few weeks, I reordered. That's the bottle,' I said, gesturing toward the pills in Deirdre's hand.

'Then you didn't give them up,' she whispered.

'Yes, I did. At first, I took one or two a day. I felt that

I had to take them. There were some upsetting telephone calls that almost unstrung me, so I started again. I took a pill, then another and another. I could actually feel myself becoming disconnected, so I stopped for good. Librium isn't a cure for anything. If you're temporarily upset, it will calm you down, but it won't heal your wounds. Tranquilizers are a fence; they enclose hurt, keeping it contained. But eventually the fence breaks. Then you must deal with what's inside. I know. I'm still trying to deal with it.' My voice was trembling.

Deirdre raised her head and looked at me. Her face was completely devoid of color. Then, averting her eyes, she said woodenly: 'I was raped.'

'Oh my god.' The words leaped out of my mouth. 'Did you call the police?'

'No.'

'Why not?'

'I couldn't.'

'I'll call,' I said, jumping up. 'I'll call right now.'

'No, Jenny. No. Please.' Deirdre began to sob. 'You can't call. You can't.'

I sat down and held her, not knowing what else to do. We remained there for what seemed like hours. Deirdre continued to sob, a deep, outraged weeping, and I became enveloped in her hurt and my helplessness. There was nothing I knew that I could do for her except to be there.

Richard, you can't imagine how devastating it is to hold someone who has been hurt beyond your powers to mend. Your helplessness becomes anger, and your anger rises like steam into unchanneled hate. You don't have to know what you hate to hate. It doesn't matter, for your anger propels you beyond reason. A moment comes when you want to lash out, when your morality evaporates, and the sensible words that have governed your life, words like respect, decency, and honor, become meaningless, equal in impact to a sticker marked FRAGILE pasted on a battered cardboard box. That instant of recognition came, and I knew, I finally understood how men are able to follow their leaders optimistically into battle. Destruction breeds destruction. There are excuses – rationales of boundaries, politics, and patriotism – but in the end, the old God Jehovah rules: an eye for an eye. And we call ourselves civilized.

There was no sign of a break in Deirdre's weeping. Afraid that she had gone beyond the point of stopping and frightened by my own reaction, I went into the kitchen for a glass of water. When I returned, I took the bottle of pills and removed two Librium. 'Here,' I said, offering her the pills and water.

She continued to sob. I withdrew her face from her hands as gently as I could. 'Take these,' I ordered.

She was so startled at the command that she obediently swallowed the pills.

'Where is your tea?' I asked. 'I'd like a cup of tea.'

'In the canister marked TEA on the counter,' she replied with a half-sob.

'That's logical,' I quipped.

Deirdre didn't smile.

While I waited for the water to boil, I glanced at the kitchen clock. It was after midnight. I suppressed an impulse to call Mrs Feltcher to ask for more time. Somehow I would make her understand later that I had had to stay with Deirdre, that I simply couldn't leave.

'Do you want to drink your tea in here or in the living room?' I called.

'In the living room,' was the reply.

Deirdre was huddled in a corner of the sofa in a fetal position. Her face was swollen, her eyelids crimson. I put a mug of tea on the end table next to her. She propped herself up and, leaning on her right elbow, began to sip the steaming liquid mechanically. We sat in silence, Deirdre sipping tea from the mug cupped in her hands. When she eventually spoke, it was in a choppy monotone.

'He came here at nine o'clock. The boys were asleep. I had put them to bed early. They were exhausted. We'd been out all day. I was getting ready to take a shower when the doorbell rang. I didn't expect him. He had never come here at night.'

She held her mug out for more tea. I went back to the kitchen, refilled it, and returned. Deirdre took the mug from me with outstretched hands, grateful, it appeared, for the warmth transfused through the glazed pottery surface. Cradling the mug, she continued. 'I was undressed. The doorbell rang again. I put a robe on and went to answer it. "What took you so long?" he wanted to know when I opened the door. I explained and asked him why he was here. He demanded to know where we were this morning, where Kerry was, and he marched into the living room as if it were his place, not mine. I told him it was none of his business. He said it was his business, that it was his son. He started to yell. I told him to be quiet, that he'd wake the boys. He said he didn't give a shit.'

Deirdre started to shiver. Soon her entire body was shaking, either from cold or the pain of fresh memory. I ran upstairs and found a pale green blanket in the linen closet. 'You don't have to talk about it,' I said after I returned and covered her.

She continued as if she hadn't heard me. 'He was like a wild man. He kept yelling at me. I couldn't reason with him. I tried to tell him how it is with Kerry. "You haven't picked him up for three weeks," I said. "He waits for you. He waits and waits, and you never come. Do you know what it's like waiting for a father who never comes? You're hurting him. You're making him sick."'

'He wouldn't listen. "Kerry's my son," he said, "and I can do what I damned well please with him. Do you understand? He's mine, and you have to make him available. You can't take what's mine away from me."'

Fresh tears pooled in Deirdre's eyes. She paused, then resumed speaking through heaving sobs. 'The harder I tried to explain, the angrier he became. I told him that I took the boys out because Herb was gone for the weekend. There was nothing wrong in wanting the boys to have a

Sunday outing together. After all, they are half-brothers. Aren't they entitled to know something of a family life? Must each weekend pull them further apart?' Deirdre asked, tears cascading down her cheeks. 'How was I supposed to know that he would show up?'

'You couldn't know,' I said soothingly.

'He told me that I had no right to take Kerry out. Then he said he didn't give a damn about Steve, that the thought of his son having a half-Jew for a brother made him sick. "That child's father supports your son," I said. "If he had to depend on you, he would have died of starvation long ago. You haven't given him anything. Men treat their whores better than you treat Kerry."'

'He hit me. I lost my balance and fell on my knee. My robe opened. I closed it and tried to get up, but he wouldn't let me. He unzipped his fly. "Blow me," he said.'

Deirdre started to gag. I thought she was going to vomit, but she didn't. 'I have nothing left to throw up,' she sobbed.

'He held me by the shoulders and thrust himself toward my mouth. I must have bared my teeth. I know I did. He pushed me down, furious. "One way or another you'll get it, cunt," he said.

'I couldn't scream. The boys were sleeping. If they heard me and came down . . .' She shuddered.

'He pinned my arms back and straddled me. An animal on top of me. I couldn't kick. His knees were on my thighs. I was dry. Ripping. I felt like I was being ripped apart.

'He spit on me. When he was finished, he got up and spit in my face. "Remember what I said, cunt," he called when he walked out the door.

'I lay on the floor for a while, unable to move. Then I crawled upstairs and got into the shower. I scrubbed myself until there was no hot water left. I scrubbed and douched, but I couldn't get clean. I don't think I'll ever feel clean.'

Deirdre had stopped crying. An aura of pathos emanated from her as ethereal as the glow radiating from candles in a darkened church.

We sat for a while longer. The white living room walls appeared gray and cold in the semidarkness. I struggled to say something comforting but couldn't find the right words. I don't believe they exist for what happened to Deirdre, so I sat holding her hands until she finally stopped shaking. Then I helped her to bed and went home.

I found Mrs Feltcher snoring soundly on a chair in front of the television set. I awakened her and apologized for taking so long. Mrs Feltcher heaved herself out of the chair and looked at her watch. 'My goodness! It's after two o'clock. What happened over there?' she asked, suddenly alert. Curiosity swept the drowsiness from her face, heightening the sharpness of her features.

I didn't want to tell her. 'Deirdre had an accident. I stayed with her until she was able to fall asleep.'

Mrs Feltcher wasn't put off. 'What kind of accident?' she wanted to know. There was a hunger in the tone of her voice that offended me, vibrations of Mrs Feltcher's appetite for the latest neighborhood dirt.

'I can't tell you what kind of accident,' I said. 'Deirdre wouldn't want it known.'

'It couldn't have been so bad that she wouldn't want anyone to know. An accident is an accident, nothing to be ashamed of. Life is full of accidents,' replied Mrs Feltcher, clearly miffed.

I couldn't get her to leave. She stood in the living room wearing her garish pink robe and a stubborn expression that told me she wouldn't budge until she knew exactly what had happened to Deirdre. I was too exhausted to fight. 'This is not to be repeated to anyone,' I warned. 'Deirdre was assaulted.'

Mrs Feltcher crossed herself. 'Where were the police? Why didn't she call the police?'

'She was afraid, too frightened to call them.'

'I'll pray for her,' promised a stunned Mrs Feltcher.

She left, forgetting her coat.

I went to see Deirdre today after work. She was withdrawn; there were lavender circles under her eyes, and the hollows beneath her high cheekbones appeared deeper, almost cadaverous. 'Do you mind if I take the tranquilizers for another day or two?' she asked. 'I didn't go to school. If I feel better, I'll stop taking them tomorrow.'

'You should see a doctor.'

'I don't like my doctor. He delivered Steve and wasn't a bit interested in my pregnancy. But he loved to ask me questions about my sex life. I couldn't talk to him,' she said.

'There is a female gynecologist who has come to Briarhill several times. She seems pleasant. Would you see her?'

Deirdre said she would, and I called Dr Emmond's office immediately. I couldn't get anywhere with the receptionist, so I left a message later with the doctor's answering service. She called while I was putting the children to bed. I explained the situation, and Dr Emmond agreed to see Deirdre tomorrow.

I couldn't persuade Deirdre to report the rape. She was adamant in her refusal and rambled on about Herb finding out, losing her support money, and Kerry hating her someday for jailing his father. Also, she reminded me that she had washed away the evidence. The police wouldn't believe her.

Deirdre wept quietly while she spoke. What she said may have been true, but her tears told me that the real evidence, the permanent evidence, would never be washed away.

Kerry and Steve had dinner with us. It was a meal full of happy children's chatter until Kerry said: 'It's fun when my mom's sick. We get to eat with you.'

I nearly jumped out of my chair. 'What an awful thing to say, Kerry. You should be ashamed of yourself.'

He was embarrassed and didn't speak for the remainder of the meal.

I shouldn't have chastised Kerry. What happened wasn't his fault, and I probably would have overlooked the remark if it had been made by Steve. The sins of the fathers...

I just realized something, Richard. Not once, through all of this, has Deirdre named him. Not once has she called Ken Jamison by his name.

I called Deirdre before I left for work this morning to find out how she was feeling and to offer to drive her to the doctor.

'I'm dopey,' she said, 'really slow. Your tranquilizers are like progressive embalming pills. If I keep taking them, my blood will stop circulating.'

She told me that she had already ordered a taxi. 'I'm afraid to drive. I feel rubbery, as if I don't have any reflexes. I'd get creamed on the freeway. Enough has happened already; a car accident would finish me.'

Deirdre sounded better than she did yesterday but far from her usual self. The familiar ring of cocky independence in her voice was missing. Perhaps the tranquilizers have temporarily suppressed it. I hope that is the answer. Deirdre has always struck me as being resilient, one of those women who is able to do more than simply struggle and endure, an updated version of Mr Gallisdorf's frontierswoman who can carve a life for herself out of our modern wilderness.

I am beginning to think of California as a wilderness of sorts, the future in a mad jumble of people and places that seem to have no relationship to one another, neither the people nor the places. Los Angeles is supposed to be a city, but it is altogether different from what I was taught a city should be, for it doesn't have a core, a discernable heart from which life radiates. Instead, the city is a twisted necklace, each town or suburb a bead strung on a rope of freeways. I couldn't have picked a more perfect place in which to hide. Although I didn't know it then, anonymity is almost a state of being in Los Angeles. The people who live here are rarely known outside of their places of work and freeway exits unless they are famous for some reason. As enterprising as he was, I doubt that even the legendary little tailor who killed seven in one blow would be recognized in Los Angeles. Some enterprising Californian would discover that the seven were flies before the little tailor had a chance to prove his cunning.

I don't read the children fairy tales anymore. Matthew has lost interest, and Grimms' stories have terrified Catherine to a point where she is positive that a witch, probably Rapunzel's, has taken up permanent residence in a corner of her closet. Before I can turn her bedroom light out at night, I have to check her closet a minimum of three or four times. Catherine supervises my closet check from the safety of her bed, and she makes sure that I am thorough. This witch business has been going on for nearly a week and shows no signs of easing up. No matter how hard I try to reassure her, Catherine remains convinced that a witch is in there. I'm beginning to lose patience.

Catherine has also been having a problem with her compulsive perfectionism again. Since she won the coloring contest, she has been driving herself even harder than she did before. After dinner tonight, she told me that she had to make a traffic-safety poster for school. I left her working at the kitchen table with a full pad of heavy white paper, crayons, pencils, and an eraser. When I went back into the kitchen an hour later, there were scraps of paper everywhere – on the table, the chairs, and the floor. Catherine was staring dejectedly at a picture of a traffic light with STOP FOR RED neatly lettered on the top and GREEN FOR GO clearly printed on the bottom. 'That's a terrific poster,' I said, wanting to compliment her before I asked her to clean up the mess. The poster wasn't original, but it was painstakingly drawn and colored, certainly exceptional for a child of six.

She looked at me, then at the poster, and before I could stop her, ripped the paper in half and crumpled it in her hands.

'Oh, Catherine, what did you do that for?' I asked.

'The light was crooked,' she said, throwing the wadded paper on the floor. Then she started to cry. 'I only have two pieces of paper left. Can we go to the store?'

I knew that she would stay at the kitchen table until she could no longer keep her eyes open, ripping her work into shreds, if I bought her more paper. 'You'll have to manage with what you have,' I said.

'I only have two pieces,' she howled, making me feel heartless.

'But you started with a full pad,' I said, trying to reason with her. 'And it's late. You have to go to bed soon. Besides, you're not remembering what I told you.'

'What?' she asked, sobbing.

'Nothing is perfect. You should be proud of what you've done if you've tried your best; no one expects more than that from you.' Then, suddenly suspicious, I asked, 'Is this poster for a contest, like the coloring contest?'

'No,' she answered.

'Then why are you pushing yourself so hard?'

'Because,' she said, 'I want my poster to be the best one.'

It was as if she hadn't heard a word that I said.

Children need more than one adult, Richard. I'm not saying that the adults have to be parents (although it would be preferable because the children would probably be loved), but the ratio of one adult to two or more children simply isn't enough. I feel that I'm not allowed the luxury of being tired or getting sick or losing patience or just holing up in my bedroom for an entire evening. It's been brutal being on call every day, a full twenty-four hours each, for two years. There are times when their problems overwhelm me.

I'm not complaining; I'm observing. There is no point in complaining about a situation I cannot change, at least for now. And not to you. Especially not to you.

My mother telephoned late this afternoon. It was an odd call. My father wasn't home as he usually is when she calls, and she seemed anxious to stay on the line. I don't know

why. She asked me questions that she has never asked –
about my job, the children's progress in school, the price
of groceries – and actually encouraged Matthew and
Catherine to have separate conversations with her (she
usually dismisses them perfunctorily after a minute or
two). This call didn't seem to have a specific purpose: it
wasn't anyone's birthday or a special holiday. If my
mother did have something to say I don't know what it
was, for she certainly didn't say it.

Or did she by not saying anything?

Is it possible, after all this time, that she has decided to
reclaim a daughter?

Probably not. She must be having a slow week.

Briarhill is engaged in a death watch. The attention of
everyone is riveted on Mrs Fry, with the exception of her
sons, who haven't come to see her, and Mr Gallisdorf, who
is conducting himself as usual, a wheelchair explorer in a
starched white shirt, tracking the footprints of history. He
remains, as always, a model of elegant decorum.

For the first time, I found Mr Gallisdorf's outsidedness
disturbing. His attitude toward me was the same, pleasant
and warm, but I expected more: a comment about Mrs
Fry, an expression of polite concern. There was nothing.
Finally, I asked him. 'You don't seem to be preoccupied
with Mrs Fry's condition like everyone else,' I observed.
'Doesn't it bother you?'

'Why should it bother me?' He seemed genuinely
puzzled.

'Because she's in a coma. She's dying,' I said, instantly
regretting my bluntness.

'When one lives in a place like Briarhill, one cannot
allow oneself to become consumed with each individual's
death. It is a natural occurrence here. This is a home for
the elderly, and death should be accepted as the inevitable
conclusion to long life.'

'But Mrs Fry is so pathetic,' I said.

'I am aware of that, just as I am aware of the fact that
everyone is buzzing about Mrs Fry's sons. They are adding

drama to the poor woman's death. Making a spectacle of it, seems to me. Please understand. My lack of preoccupation doesn't mean that I don't care. But I can't do a thing about her situation. I wasn't able to help her after her husband died, either. He was a decent man, Albert Fry. I knew him when we were much younger and watched her slide when he was gone.'

'Did you try to help her?'

'Yes, but she wasn't interested. I made suggestions, tried to draw her out. I told her how my history books had helped me. "Find an interest," I said, "something that appeals to you." It was no use,' he sighed. 'All she wanted to do was talk about Albert and their life together. She wouldn't let go.'

'Maybe she wasn't ready. Maybe she needed more time.'

'We all need more time. But the first step must be taken. If it isn't, there is no point in hanging on. And hanging on means grabbing hold of yourself, not your children or your relatives or people you live with. You must define yourself and realize that the definition is flexible, that it must change as circumstances in your life change. That's the trouble with most of the people in this place. They have stopped defining themselves.'

I didn't tell Mr Gallisdorf, but it's my problem, too. I lack a definition. To the outside world, I am a widow with two children. You and Matthew and Catherine have defined me. But I have to have more than an identity based on the existence – in your case, the lack of existence – of others. I need to be someone, a person in my own right. But who? I have been so busy running away from life that I haven't bothered to ask myself what I want out of it.

Richard, I didn't have to wonder who I was or what I wanted when you were alive, because you told me. You supplied all of the answers before I even thought of the questions. I asserted myself once – only once – during the years we were married, and when I did, the results were disastrous. Maybe I am hanging on to you, but at this moment, it is a lot safer than letting go.

I met Nat Witton for lunch today. He called early this morning, and I recognized his voice instantly, a deep bass with a trace of familiar Eastern flatness in his speech.

'I have some news about Ringer's that I think you'll like,' he said.

'Does that mean your newspaper will go after them?' I asked, trying to sound casual.

'Not exactly, but it is still good news. I'd rather not explain it over the phone. Are you free for lunch? As I recall, Wednesday is your day off.'

I was flattered that he remembered and agreed to meet him at a restaurant near the newspaper.

The prospect of having lunch with Nat Witton colored the entire morning a soft yellow. Even the sun seemed to reflect my mood, valiantly trying to show its full face through the gauze remnants of a dissipating smog. Rather than moving about mindlessly as I usually do on Wednesdays, a fully dressed somnambulist hiding behind dark sunglasses, I became suddenly alert and efficient. By eleven o'clock I was back home, having finished my errand-grocery shopping routine in half the time it normally takes. And I didn't forget anything – not milk, toilet paper, nor eggs. Lately I've been forgetting necessities. I don't write them on my list, and if an item isn't written down, I can't seem to be able to remember it.

I wasn't nervous until it was time to leave for the restaurant. Then an uneasiness started: my hands were cold, and I could feel flush marks creep up my neck and face, leaving pink imprints. I told myself that it was ridiculous, that I was only meeting a man for lunch. 'Stop reacting like an adolescent,' I said aloud.

My body wouldn't listen.

The restaurant was difficult to find, which was fortunate, for I had to concentrate on something outside of

myself. My adolescent jitters were gone by the time I
parked the car and walked a block to the restaurant, but
they returned when I entered and didn't see Nat Witton.
A hostess wearing a black dress with a V neckline that
plunged to her waist approached me carrying a stack of
menus on her arm. 'May I help you?' she asked.

'I'm supposed to meet someone here, a Mr Witton. Has
he arrived?'

'Not that I know of,' she replied. 'Would you like to
wait at a table or the bar?'

'At the bar,' I said, reasoning that if Nat Witton were
going to stand me up, I could leave inconspicuously.

I ordered a drink and waited. Soon the bar stools were
filled, and latecomers formed an irregular wall several
people deep around the bar area. I eyed the door every time
someone entered the restaurant, trying not to look
obvious. Then I glanced at my watch surreptitiously and
sipped the alcohol, which was acting like a grenade in my
stomach. After sitting for fifteen minutes or so, the man
next to me became friendly. 'Would you like another
drink?' he asked, sliding his bar stool closer.

He was a balding, broad-shouldered man with a
too-friendly gleam in his eye. His shirt was partially
unbuttoned to display a furry chest and an array of heavy
gold chains and pendants. I have noticed that the men in
California wear more dazzling jewelry than do the women.
At least it appears that way. Among the assorted rings on
his fingers, there was a wedding band. He was definitely
not my type, wedding band or no wedding band.

'No, thank you,' I said, deciding to leave. I opened my
purse to get my wallet, feeling both disappointed and
humiliated. Instead of meeting Nat Witton for lunch, I was
sitting alone at a bar looking as if I were out hunting.
Worse, I didn't even have a smart comeback for my
unwanted catch.

'If you don't want another drink,' said the jewelry box,
'then how about lunch?'

'No, thank you,' I repeated, praying that the bartender

214

would hurry and take my money. He was at the other end of the bar.

The jewelry box wasn't discouraged. 'It's no fun eating alone,' he said, putting his face so close to mine that I could smell the last swallow of his martini.

I felt a hand on my shoulder and jumped, nearly falling off the bar stool. 'She isn't eating alone,' a voice said. It was Nat Witton. Then, motioning toward my drink: 'I'll take care of that.'

The man shrugged and started to survey the bar for other lunch prospects.

'How long were you there?' I asked with a mixture of gratitude and relief as we walked to our table.

'A few minutes. I saw him start to talk to you when I came in.'

'Why didn't you let me know you were here? I was about to leave.'

'I know you were. I could tell by the way you grabbed your wallet when he started getting friendly. Sorry I'm late. We had a meeting that ran overtime. It's hard for me to keep appointments during the day. I should have warned you, but in a way I'm glad I didn't.'

'Why?'

'It was interesting to watch you try to fend him off. You're not used to that sort of thing, are you?'

'I don't pick men up in bars, if that's what you mean.'

There must have been an edge of resentment in my voice. 'Hey, don't be angry,' he said, smiling at me disarmingly. 'I learned a couple of interesting things about you, that's all. You have to expect that from me. Newspapermen are natural snoopers.'

'What did you learn?' I asked, feeling like the loser in a game of twenty questions.

He held up his left hand and marked each point he made by raising a finger. I noticed that his hands were well-formed, his fingers unusually long and slender. Artist's fingers, I thought. 'First, you don't do the bar scene. Second, you don't like being observed. The third observation comes from the second: you must have a strong sense of privacy.' He looked at his hand, then at me. His eyes were bluer than I had remembered. 'I have two fingers left. Is there anything you'd like to add?'

There was nothing that I wanted to add. Nat Witton had observed enough. Too much. He is bright and charming, his charm emanating from a deceptively relaxed manner. He has the body language peculiar to tall men who are able to carry themselves in an easy, rubber-limbed sort of way. You know what I mean, Richard. Men whose spines are so flexible that they can lean back in straight chairs, stretch their legs, and look like human slides. His conversation is the same, quick yet low-key. When he listens, he listens with his eyes as well as his ears. It is flattering, but it is also disconcerting. Nothing escapes him.

You were almost as tall as Nat Witton, but you carried yourself differently: whether you were sitting or standing, your spine was straight. There wasn't an ounce of rubber in your posture. Yours was a controlled presence with an energy so close to the surface that it could be felt without physical contact. It was exciting simply to be with you, to feel that incredible energy radiating from your body. Not once during the years we were married was I tempted to look with interest at another man. Even during that hellish last year we were together, you made every man I knew appear listless. I still haven't forgotten. Shortly after we moved to California, I was in a department store waiting for a sales clerk to help me. A man came up to the counter and looked into the display case. I only saw his profile, but I could feel, from several feet away, his energy. Your energy. The force of his presence was so great that I left immediately, finding it impossible to breathe in the suddenly charged air.

I don't know how much I should tell you about Nat Witton. To write of a new man when one is addressing a deceased husband is awkward, rather like walking in mismatched shoes. Even if one foot is eventually favored, there remains a discomfort, an imbalance due to the difference in lasts. But I have no one else to tell, so it will have to be you. I wouldn't have said much to Deirdre even if she hadn't been raped; now I shall say nothing. Nat Witton was right about my penchant for privacy, but you already know that. It is a trait we shared.

As I mentioned, Nat Witton is observant. My discomfiture at his remarks must have been as easy to read as one of his newspaper's banner headlines. He changed the subject adroitly. 'Your fight with Ringer's was effective,' he said. 'They felt your fury all the way to the board room.'

'But you said your newspaper wasn't going after them.'

'It wasn't necessary. I brought the subject up at an editorial meeting and suggested that we include an investigation of Ringer's Races and a local children's show in our TV series. As I expected, there was the usual talk about advertising revenue. Ringer's wouldn't cut their ads out of the paper, but they could certainly trim them down. We tossed the idea around and left a final proposal with the publisher. He contacted Ringer's and was told that they had already decided not to pick up their option for an additional thirteen weeks of the show as they had originally planned. They're dropping it next week. So you see, you were successful on your own. You didn't need the paper's help.'

I was pleased, but the results of my protests seemed to be out of proportion. 'That's terrific, but I really didn't feel as though I had any impact on them when I complained. Is there more to the story than what you've told me?'

He cocked his head to one side and looked at me thoughtfully. 'Yes, there is,' he replied, 'but it can't be made public.' He held his hand up again. 'Can I add keeping confidences to what I know about you? It will complete my hand.'

'How? What else have you learned about me?'

'You're intelligent. Most people would have accepted what I told them and been satisfied, but you weren't.'

R.—H

'I can keep quiet,' I said. What an understatement! I should have added that that's what I do best. I can't even repeat what I know to myself.

Nat leaned forward. 'A twelve-year-old boy had a winning ticket about a month ago. His parents cashed it, gave him one hundred dollars, and told him that they were going to bank the rest of the money in his name. Instead, they blew the money on a trip to Hawaii and left the boy at home. Somehow he found out that they used his money for the trip, and he started squawking. He began at the supermarket where his parents turned in the ticket. When the manager tried to brush him off, the boy created an uproar, to a point where I understand that he was removed from the store bodily. Enough customers heard the fracas to start unwelcome publicity. From the supermarket, the boy went to the police, demanding his rights and his money. He said he knew the law was on his side from watching cop shows on television. The people at Ringer's are sweating now. I think they'll be happier when that show is off the air than you will.'

'The boy was successful,' I commented, 'not me.'

'You helped. Your refusal to appear in their ads coincided with the boy's trip to the store and the police station.'

'What will Ringer's do about the boy's complaint?'

'I don't know, but I have the feeling that they'll buy him off with an additional thousand dollars.'

'They had better put it in the bank naming themselves as trustees or the same thing could happen again.'

'Their lawyers are working along those lines now. I almost forgot. Have you cashed your check yet?'

'No, you said not to cash it.'

'Well, go ahead. I hope you weren't inconvenienced.'

I told him about Matthew's ridiculous ten-speed bike, Catherine's skateboard, and Matthew's delight at learning that his money will earn interest. Nat was surprised. 'This is the first time I've heard of a child understanding the concept of interest,' he said. 'He must be bright.'

'Matthew comes by his fascination with interest naturally,' I replied wryly. 'His father was an accountant.'

I hadn't intended to mention you, Richard, and I changed the direction in which the conversation was moving before I found myself rowing against too strong a current. 'Why did you place the picture of Briarhill's fashion show for me?' I asked. 'Did I sound as desperate as I felt?'

He smiled. 'Pressured is the word, I think. Or harried. You definitely sounded harried. I get those calls every once in a while, but yours had a hook.'

'A hook?' I didn't know what he meant.

'A hook in the newspaper trade is the opening line of a story. It has to be interesting, a sentence that stands up and grabs or hooks the reader's attention so he wants to read on. Your main hook was Briarhill, but your voice helped. I like to listen to a woman with a soft, husky voice. It's sexy.'

If he heard me shrieking at the children, he wouldn't think my voice was sexy. 'People have more than one voice,' I said. 'There is a public voice and then there is another, unmodulated private voice that one hopes isn't overheard.'

'You mean a kind of primal yell like that new therapy?'

'That, too, but I was thinking more of an unguarded voice.'

'I see your point, but the quality of the voice, in your case the huskiness, the cloudiness, would remain – guarded or unguarded. Actually, it was your boss's voice that made me aware of Briarhill.'

'Simon Gentile? What's unusual about his voice?'

'Not Simon. His son, the gym teacher. When I first came to California, I did a friend a favor and covered a final game in high school basketball for him. Gentile was coaching one of the teams. He gave the most obnoxious performance I had ever witnessed in high school sports. I was on my high school's basketball team and hated my coach. We all did, but the bastard was a sweetheart compared to Gentile.

'The game was close, and Gentile's team was winning at halftime. He insisted that he wanted a big win and started belittling the boys during the break, haranguing them to the point where he knocked a win right out of them. Those kids spent their remaining energy hating Gentile rather than playing. A basket was blown every time they heard his yell, and he yelled solidly during the second half. My friend told me later that Gentile was probably the worst high school coach in the state. When Briarhill expanded, the paper ran a picture of Gentile in front of the main building. I saw it and groaned for those poor old people. I never forgot him. The day you called, sounding harried and mentioning Briarhill, you caught my immediate attention and sympathy. How does Gentile treat you?' he asked with what seemed to be honest concern.

'All right.'

'Why are you smiling? Has he changed that radically?'

'No, he's still a bully. It's just that . . .' I hesitated.

'That what?'

'That he'd like to treat me to himself, only I don't consider him a treat. I won't let him near me.'

'Unless I've misjudged the man, he's probably hurling insults at you now for rejecting him. But I can't blame him for trying,' he added.

He asked me how long I've lived in California and how I like it here. Hard as I tried, I could only give this place a mixed review, more negative than positive.

'You're still healing from the cutting of ties,' he said, 'old friends and family. Temporary alienation is common to people who move out here. Most of them find their groove. You will, too.'

'What happens if they don't find their groove?'

He shrugged. 'They move someplace else, I guess. We've become a nation of movers. We're already getting into disposable clothing and unassembled furniture, that stackable stuff. Moving may eventually become so simple that a family will decide to leave on a Saturday night and be able to deflate their chairs, disassemble their tables, and pack their belongings on Sunday morning to be off at noon, nomads with a car and an air pump.'

'I'd rather have a camel and a tent,' I said, laughing. 'It's a combination with more charm.'

Lunch was over too soon. As we were walking out of the restaurant, Nat said: 'I'd like to see you again without the excuse of Ringer's Supermarkets.'

I wanted to say 'Yes, call me.' Nat Witton is the first man I've met since you died that I wanted to encourage, but I couldn't. I didn't know if he was married and floundered unsuccessfully for a tactful way to ask. We had spent an hour together without my learning a thing about him except that he was extraordinarily appealing. 'I enjoyed our lunch,' I said lamely. 'Thank you.'

'You're not exactly encouraging.'

'I don't know if, if you're married,' I blurted, betraying my suburban sophistication. I could chair a Junior Board meeting, but I couldn't ask a man I liked a simple question.

'A proper lady, as I thought. No, I'm not married, or I wouldn't have asked.' He grinned. 'On second thought, maybe I would have asked.'

'Then I'd like to see you,' I said.

We emerged from the restaurant into a dazzling, early afternoon sun, which had burned away the last traces of smog. The day was temporarily painted with gladness, bright yellow and a clear, cerulean blue.

I stopped at Deirdre's to check on her before I went home, and the day's colors faded. She was sitting at the kitchen table, which was strewn with papers and books.

'I went to school today for the first time since last week, and I've really fallen behind,' she said, sighing. 'I have a term paper in sociology due on Friday, but I can't concentrate. All I have is an opening paragraph, and it stinks.'

'Ask for an extension,' I suggested.

Deirdre's eyes misted. 'I can't.'

'Why not?'

'I don't have an excuse that I would want to make public.'

'Tell the instructor that you had a family problem.'

'That would be terrific. He's big on family problems and would probably ask me to explain so he could use it for the course. Can you imagine a lecture hall filled with students discussing my rape as a violation of sociological mores? I'd be the walking symbol of a tribal taboo. No, thanks. I'll keep my rape to myself.' Deirdre's words were strong, but the tone of her voice had a passive bitterness that disturbed me.

I asked about her visit to the doctor.

'Dr Emmond said that I was all right physically,' Deirdre explained. 'The soreness is gone, and I know I'm not pregnant. I started menstruating today. But I can't cope. I keep thinking of this coming weekend and the next and the next. There will be years of weekends, and I'll never know if he'll arrive or what he will do. Herb is taking Steve this weekend, so I'll be alone with Kerry. I'm frightened.'

'Did you tell Dr Emmond?'

'Yes. She was kind and patient; I could respond to her. But she also had a hard practicality. "Your position could become untenable, if it hasn't already," she said. "Rape is not merely a physical act from which the body recovers and heals. It violates the victim mentally and emotionally, leaving wounds that eventually form what I think of as psychological scar tissue. A woman never forgets, but it is possible to adjust, to live with one's scars. In your particular case, the healing process won't begin until you confront your relationship with your rapist and resolve it. As the situation exists, you are in a position where you could conceivably be victimized again. This must change."'

'She's right.'

Deirdre became agitated. 'I know she's right, but what

can I do? I'm beginning to feel like the ultimate victim . . . like a prisoner waiting for the next drop to fall in a trial by water torture. I can't change the situation. If I move, Herb will want to know why, and moving wouldn't help anyway. He'll find me no matter where I go.'

'If he knows you'll have him arrested for so much as laying a hand on you, he'll leave you alone.'

'How can you be sure?' she challenged.

I wasn't sure. 'Tell him in front of someone else. Let him know that others know about him. It could scare him off,' I said, trying to sound convincing.

'I'll think about it,' she said doubtfully, 'after I finish this damned paper.'

When I left, Deirdre was staring at her typewriter. I walked home slowly, wondering why this had happened to her, why someone essentially good is hurt while others, shallow people like the Lynches, who think of nothing and no one except themselves, can go on living their selfish lives, unmarked by tragedy. Then I thought of you, buried in a cemetery three thousand miles away, and Matthew and Catherine, growing up fatherless, and concluded that there is no justice.

Mrs Fry died this morning.

The Fry sons and their wives alerted Briarhill's main floor by rushing in almost simultaneously from three different entrances. One of the wives was wearing a tennis outfit; the other was dressed for golf, and her shoes announced each hurried step she made down the waxed corridors to the elevator. It was the first and last visit the women made to see their mother-in-law, not that it mattered. Mrs Fry was gone before the elevator took them to the third floor.

The women left as quickly as they came, the Mrs Fry in the tennis outfit complaining that her morning had been ruined. 'I was in the middle of a set,' she whined, 'three games apiece. I had to forfeit.'

The golfing sister-in-law wasn't sympathetic. 'I was on the thirteenth hole,' she said, 'which amounts to being nowhere. You weren't the only one who was inconvenienced.'

I wonder if they will have the consideration, when they die, to take their last breath on a rainy day in those few minutes preceding dinner at the end of the cocktail hour.

After a skipped beat or two, Briarhill's pulse remained steady for the rest of the day. Another death, another acceptance on the part of the residents. I think it was the waiting that unsettled them. Or was it Mrs Fry's body, fighting death long after her mind had succumbed, that disturbing lack of harmony peculiar to our species? I have never heard of forests populated with animals – squirrels, deer, or raccoons – lingering for weeks in comas or wandering in aimless senility. Unlike us, their minds and bodies work in unison. We consider ourselves superior, yet our complexity betrays us.

My initial reaction to Mrs Fry's death was no different from the residents'. I was relieved, actually happy for her until I overheard her sons threatening the Gentiles. The four men were congregated in front of the main offices: Simon crisp in a business suit, Jim slouching behind his father's wheelchair, and the Fry brothers standing next to each other, elbow to elbow, facing the Gentiles with expressions of greed rather than grief on their faces. The younger Mr Fry, the stocky son with the fierce eyebrows who had been so short and hard-tempered with his mother, did most of the talking. 'You'll be hearing from our lawyers,' he promised, looking like a malevolent Cheshire cat. 'You're responsible for our mother's death, and you'll pay for it.'

Jim Gentile's face reddened. 'You . . . ' he started to say. A warning glance from Simon silenced him.

'I'm surprised and disappointed in both of you,' Simon cut in. 'Your mother hasn't been dead an hour, and you're already counting your profits. I'm glad your father can't see this, or have you forgotten him?'

224

The mention of their father briefly affected the Fry brothers. They glanced down, as if embarrassed, but their moment of remembrance lasted only a second or two. 'You were negligent,' accused the dapper elder son, squaring the shoulders of his custom-made suit. 'Our mother shouldn't have been left alone.'

'You were notified that your mother needed custodial care weeks before her accident,' said Simon, 'but you didn't respond to the letter. As it was, she received extra care on the first floor, and you weren't charged for it.'

'An aide was fired,' said the younger Mr Fry smugly, like a cat who had just swallowed a fat mouse. 'That's proof of your negligence.'

Jim Gentile grimaced. His father ignored him and turned his wheelchair so that it was directly facing the younger son. 'It would be unwise for you to sue,' he said, even-voiced. 'Most unwise.'

Simon edged his wheelchair forward; the Fry brothers moved back grudgingly. 'On the contrary,' said the older brother, raising his manicured hands so that his palms were level with Simon's face, 'a lawsuit seems to be reasonable under the circumstances.'

'Reasonable?' questioned Simon, rising out of his wheelchair, his spine straight as a steel rod. 'I'm an old man. At one time I thought I knew what was reasonable, but I don't know anymore. Not after listening to you. It would seem reasonable to me that you would have shown evidence of concern for your mother while she was alive, but you didn't. Instead, you paid her grudging visits only *after* we implored you to come. She needed custodial care that neither one of you was willing to subsidize.

'When was the last time either one of you invited her to visit you in your homes? If you didn't want her in your homes, couldn't you have offered to take her out for a drive? Did you ever bring your children – her grandchildren – to see her? I may be old-fashioned, but to me that would seem reasonable.'

225

A kaleidoscope of emotions played on the faces of the Fry brothers: anger, resentment, and finally guilt.

'We keep records at Briarhill,' Simon continued, his eyes riveted on the brothers, 'complete records, which will substantiate what I have stated. The records will tell the whole story. Any judge worth his black robe and gavel will be able to discern your lack of interest in your mother, your callousness toward her, after a cursory examination of the facts. I would welcome the opportunity to make those records public. They may not start a revolution, but there's a chance they could get a few sons like yourselves off their asses before it's too late. If one old woman is taken for a drive as a result of your lawsuit, it will be worth every penny of the court costs.'

'That's right,' Jim chimed in, 'and you'll pay the court costs, too.'

Simon turned to face his son. I thought he was going to strike him. 'Be quiet,' he ordered, his body shaking with anger. Then he faced the Fry brothers. 'I have nothing more to say to either one of you. You may speak to the secretary about removing your mother's remains.' He spun his wheelchair around and left the three men staring at each other.

I stood in an alcove during the Fry-Gentile confrontation. It was not my intention to eavesdrop, but there was no way I could have avoided it without disturbing them. The men had already gathered, blocking the office entrance, before I arrived. I would have looked foolish retreating down the corridor with papers in my hand, and I didn't want to ask them to step aside to let me through.

After Simon disappeared, the Fry brothers walked past me looking drawn. If I hadn't overheard their conversation, I would have attributed their sad expressions to grief. But I knew differently. Guilt and money inked the lines of misery on their faces. I watched them, remembering Mrs Fry sitting in a chair in her room absentmindedly shredding a tissue and asking me if it were a school day because she wanted her boys to play in the sunshine. The memory overwhelmed me. I ran into the ladies' room and wept.

I wish I could convince myself that I was crying for Mrs Fry, but I wasn't. I was crying for myself, for the possibility that Matthew and Catherine could one day leave me in a nursing home and walk out as the Fry brothers did today – uncaring. I'm not so much afraid of actual death as I am of dying unloved, unwanted, a human being whose lingering existence is an unwelcome burden and whose death is good news. What I want is the assurance that, when my time comes, there will be someone, somewhere, who will experience a single moment of honest grief at my passing. There will be no meaning to my death without that moment of grace. And if there is no meaning to my death, then what can my life have been worth?

This Saturday will mark the second year of your passing. Although yours was a suicide, it was still graced. Your children pay homage to you every time they ask how-and-why-did-Daddy-die questions. Even this writing is a form of acknowledgment. Your life has not been denied.

As painful as it was, I am glad I overheard the Gentiles and the Fry brothers today. I am especially grateful that I was able to witness the expressions of greed on the Fry brothers' faces, the same greed that showed on your face the day of Maggie's funeral when I signed a waiver against any claim to her estate. I have lived with guilt for so long that I had forgotten how you looked that day, how uncaring you were of Maggie's final wishes. I didn't expect you to grieve as I was grieving; she was my aunt, not yours. But you could have tried to understand, Richard, if not for her, then for me. I was your wife, yet you didn't care enough about me to respect my feelings. Instead, you balanced my promise to Maggie against her estate and the money won. Like the Fry brothers, you didn't give a damn.

I had the most unusual conversation with Simon Gentile today, and I am still not sure of what he meant. Perhaps if I can reconstruct it, I will be able to piece together Simon's elusive meaning.

He met me at the back entrance when I arrived this morning. 'Good morning,' he said. 'I've been waiting for you.'

I looked at my watch.

'No, you're not late. In fact, you are five minutes early, as I expected. I'd like to talk with you privately. It won't take long.'

I followed Simon's wheelchair down the corridors to his private quarters and was pleasantly surprised. The generous living area of the suite – an L-shaped combination living room and dining room – was elegantly furnished in an eclectic mix of expensive antiques and modern furniture. Everything fit, from the Eames chairs to the Georgian desk. The room was perfect, a decorator's dream in black, white, and the browns of rare hand rubbed woods. Simon noted my appreciation. 'You like it?' he asked.

'Yes. It's beautiful.'

'I've enjoyed living here. Designed the room myself. But a room like this can be a trap – it's almost too pleasing to leave. I can see that now.' He touched the rubber-rimmed tires of his wheelchair with gnarled arthritic fingers and laughed ironically. 'Now I can't even finish wearing out the upholstered furniture. But I didn't bring you here to complain. I don't feel sorry for myself. Don't have the time or the inclination. Tell me about the Frys. I want to know your reaction to what you overheard yesterday.'

I was too chagrined to reply.

'I can understand your embarrassment, but it wasn't your fault. I saw what happened. You were coming to the office with your schedule for next week, and you didn't want to interrupt us.'

'I could have walked away and come back later,' I said apologetically.

'But you didn't, and I'm glad. Now give me your opinion, Jenny.' His request was more like an order.

'I think the Fry brothers treated their mother horridly. You stated it very well when you spoke to them.'

'No, no, no,' said Simon impatiently. 'I know how they treated her, but that's done with. She's gone, and passing judgment on her sons won't make a damn bit of difference. Too many people do that: they pass judgment on others and elevate themselves to sainthood by comparison. It's a waste of energy, and exercise for fools. What I want from you is an appraisal of the situation. Do you think the Frys will sue us? And if they sue, will they win?'

Simon's sharp brown eyes measured my reaction to his questions. 'Cast your sentimentality aside,' he said. 'It only clutters the mind like needless bric-a-brac spoils a room.'

Without knowing why, I knew that my answer would be important to Simon. I felt that I was being tested, but images of Mrs Fry greeting me in the morning, Mrs Fry wandering addlebrained down the waxed halls, Mrs Fry clinging to her disinterested sons, Mrs Fry lost in shreds of tissue, cluttered my brain. Finally, and with great difficulty, I managed to force her out.

'I believe the Fry brothers have a good lawsuit,' I said cautiously. 'Briarhill was responsible for Mrs Fry, and her death was the indirect result of a lack of supervision. It was unintentional, but I don't think a court would look at it that way. A judge would probably rule that Briarhill was negligent. Also, firing the aide was a point for the Frys.'

Simon listened with inscrutable interest, his bald head cocked in my direction. 'Go on,' he encouraged.

I hesitated. 'I don't know if the Frys will sue. They were intractable until you threatened them with exposure. Then they backed off,' I reasoned aloud. 'Their image is important to them. If they sue, the case could get a lot of publicity. They'll look like bastards, which is exactly what they deserve.'

The strength of my answer surprised me, but it didn't faze Simon. 'Then you don't think they'll sue?' he asked.

'No, not if you keep pushing the exposure angle.'

Suddenly Simon's strategy made sense to me. In retrospect, his performance with the Fry brothers was superb. Yesterday I was impressed for the wrong reasons, moved as much as the others by what he said without understanding his motivation. His sympathetic speech about the abandoned elderly was an attack. The realization was a shock to me.

'Ah,' said Simon, reading my face. 'You understand. I knew you would. I've been watching you, Jenny. It's good to know that my judgment was correct.'

'I don't know what you mean.'

'There will be time enough for an explanation. That is all for now,' he said, terminating our conversation. 'I trust that our discussion will not be repeated.'

Simon's last words were delivered as an ultimatum. I was not, however, going to be dismissed so easily. 'That speech you made yesterday, all of that talk about Sunday drives and visiting grandchildren – did you believe any of it or was it simply an act?' I asked, recalling how the man sitting before me, crippled in his wheelchair, had stood straight-spined and formidable when battling the Fry brothers. It was almost as if I were remembering an illusion, the trick of a skilled magician.

Simon pursed his lips. 'You're entitled to an answer,' he said, 'but I don't know if I can give you a fair reply.'

'Either you believed it or you didn't.'

'It's not that simple. You want an absolute answer, and in life, there are no absolute answers. There is only recognition, the understanding of things as they are. Think of life as a game. You play to get through as best you can. Most people, including the Fry boys, aren't clean players. But they play anyway, hoping they won't get caught. To get caught, someone has to have the courage or good sense to call a foul. Timing is important. I would have sought the Fry brothers out yesterday if they hadn't come to me. The freshness of their mother's death was crucial to the naming of their attitude toward her. It's the same in a ball game. A referee can't call a penalty when the game is over.

'You're looking at me as if I'm not answering you, but I am. However, I don't think it's the answer you want. If I told you that I believed every word I said, you would walk out of here satisfied. Don't seek that kind of satisfaction. It's for dreamers and fools, for people who prefer to create their own reality rather than to live in the world as it actually is.'

'I think it's important,' I insisted.

'To whom? To Mrs Fry? What difference would it make if I believed what I said? It wouldn't bring her back any more than it would rectify those last years. I called it as it was, and I'm old enough to know that calling it won't mean a damn thing in the end unless it saves Briarhill's neck. Life will go on as it always has, a continuation of the same game. The players never change. Their faces may be different, or their clothes, but people are the same. That's why Utopian societies fail, why the most moving of church sermons doesn't last any longer than ice cream on hot pavements. Things are as they are, and neither fancy speeches nor grand philosophies can change them.'

'Why didn't you call the Frys on their attitude when Mrs Fry was alive? If you had said foul then, she might be here today.'

'You still haven't caught my meaning,' said Simon. 'The Fry brothers knew what they were doing to their mother. I told them; the staff told them. But they played the game out their way.'

'And their penalty?'

'Guilt,' said Simon flatly. 'Guilt and loss of face. Even if they don't sue, and I hope they don't, their mother's death will be an embarrassment to them. People who are aware of the situation, their friends, particularly, will wonder why they didn't pursue the matter. They will always question the Frys' lack of action, and that hanging question will be their penalty. As for their guilt, they'll slough it off in a day or two. That type always does.

'One more thing, Jenny. When you go to the office to pick up your paycheck, you will see that you've received a twenty-dollar-a-week raise. It's tardy, but I hope it isn't too late.'

I acknowledged the raise with a nod. Simon and I both knew that the raise wasn't a raise at all; it should have been my starting salary. But it was nice.

Our conversation stayed with me for the rest of the day. It kept repeating like an overseasoned meal, and I was unable to isolate the offending spice. Writing it down hasn't helped. I still don't know if there was honest emotion behind Simon's play for the elderly or if it was merely a game strategy, a speech made to save his own skin. Perhaps it was both. Simon told me that, in life, there are no absolute answers. He may be right, but I would like to know on which side the scale tips.

The telephone was ringing when I came home from work. It was Nat Witton wanting to know if I would go out for dinner with him tomorrow night. 'I'm sorry for the short notice,' he apologized. 'I had a last-minute change in plans.'

I told him that I might have difficulty getting a babysitter and asked if I could call him back. He gave me his home phone number. 'I don't want you to give up easily,' he said. 'It may take a few calls. If you can't reach me at the paper, call me at home.'

Nat was flattering. He made it sound as if I had, out of necessity, a veritable directory of sitters' names at my disposal. Actually, I've only used one sitter since moving to California, and that was months ago. I hunted for her telephone number, finally found it and dialed, only to be told by a recording that the line was no longer in service. Then I decided to call Deirdre for some names and telephone numbers. Unlike the women in Eagles' Landing, Deirdre is generous with her babysitter list, at least to me.

Maybe it's because she doesn't feel threatened. I haven't been a belle of the ball.

I heard someone knock at the back door while I was dialing. It was Deirdre. She looked tired and drawn. 'I was just calling you,' I said, noticing that she had lost weight.

'I've come to ask for a favor,' she said, her voice tight with pride. 'Will you and the children sleep over Saturday night? Herb is picking Steve up after dinner tonight and won't bring him back until late Sunday afternoon. I don't want to be alone with Kerry Sunday morning. Catherine can sleep in Steve's room, the boys will be fine in Kerry's bunk beds, and I'll sleep on the sofa. You can have my bed.'

I couldn't refuse her. My date with Nat Witton would have to be postponed. It was a last-minute invitation anyway. If he was that interested, he'd call again. 'That will be fine,' I agreed, 'only I'll sleep on the sofa.'

Deirdre smiled with relief and thanked me, then asked why I was calling her. It was a reasonable question, for we rarely telephone each other just to chat. Our calls almost always have a specific purpose. We're both out during the day and busy with housekeeping chores, preparing dinner, and spending time with the children when we come home. Deirdre has the added burden of homework. If we do visit during the week, it's usually outside when we're rounding the children up for bed.

'It was nothing,' I lied. 'I just wanted to know if you managed to finish your term paper.'

'Come on, Jenny,' she demanded, looking drawn and defensive again. 'Why were you calling me?'

I told her the truth. 'That's great!' she exclaimed. 'The hermitic Jenny Weaver is finally going out. It's been a long time. Close to a year, hasn't it?'

'I suppose so.'

'Well, I'll be your babysitter. The kids can have dinner with me, and you can bathe and dress in peace.' Then her eyes clouded. 'You won't mind coming back to my place?' she asked.

I assured her that I wouldn't mind. It occured to me after she left that Deirdre had, as Simon would have put it, called a foul when I lied. I was fortunate to escape without a penalty.

I waited until after dinner to call Nat Witton back. My mother's old lessons had been at work from the moment he invited me out. 'Don't make yourself too available,' she always said, as if reciting from the primary commandment for female desirability. 'If a boy thinks you are waiting for him to call, he will feel that he is doing you a favor. Don't ever put yourself in that position. *You* must be the one who is doing *him* a favor.'

Translated today, the commandment would have decidedly sexual undertones, but sex was the furthest subject from my mother's mind when Linda and I were growing up. We were to be ladies, and ladies were virgins until they were married. The translation we were fed with our orange juice became known in our house as the 'two-day rule,' which meant that a boy had to ask us out a minimum of two days in advance to be accepted. Twenty-four-hour notice was insufficient; if we accepted a date a day in advance, we were admitting our availability. To my mother, availability and unpopularity were synonyms, and she had not suffered through the agonies of childbirth to produce wallflowers. Her girls would be desired, and the two-day rule would ensure their desirability.

I never told you about the two-day rule, Richard. How could I when I used it on you?

The rule was so deeply implanted in my mind that I found myself rationalizing my acceptance of Nat's invitation. I chuckled to myself, realizing that the rule was ridiculous, but I also realized that his brief apology was necessary balm for my ego. I needed it, for the two-day rule was still at work.

Isn't it strange what women do to their daughters? It would be worse than it is, and it's bad enough, if their

234

motivation, for the most part, weren't well-intentioned. There were times when I wondered, though, whom my popularity was more important to: me or my mother. I'll add that to the list of things I'll never know.

Catherine won't be burdened with two-day rule. That is a promise.

Women haven't captured the market on absurdity; men are strange, too. My father once told me to think of my life as an enormous room, an area in which I could move about until I found the most comfortable spot for myself. Simon thinks of life as a game, a series of plays or confrontations that are scored according to one's ability as a player. Your concept of life was close to Simon's, I think. You played a game of commerce, and you played hard. What I want to know is why men feel compelled to make metaphors out of life that always seem to end in disappointment. Why can't life simply be life?

An awful thought: if my father's concept of life were combined with Simon's, the result would be a game room. Can you imagine hanging on until the end only to find that life is a Briarhill special with bridge, backgammon, and rummy at alternate tables?

I don't care what life is as long as I can live it without having to avoid the children's questions. After school today, Catherine told me about her new friend. 'My friend's name is Price,' she said.

The name seemed so preposterous that I had all I could do not to laugh aloud. 'Is Price a boy or a girl?' I asked, trying to keep a straight face.

'A girl, of course,' Catherine replied impatiently, as if the name were intrinsically female. 'She's six like me, and her father's dead, too. He got cancer.'

Catherine said the word 'cancer' matter-of-factly, almost happily. I was chilled. It wasn't her naiveté about the disease that disturbed me. She told me how her friend's father died as if the death were settled; there was nothing more to know. Then she added: 'Price asked me how my daddy died. I told her in a car like you said. She wanted to know just how. Just how did Daddy die in a car, Mommy?'

'He stopped breathing,' I said.

Catherine wasn't satisfied with my answer; neither was I.

Dinner with Nat Witton was pleasant. Actually, it was better than pleasant – a bonus – because I hadn't permitted myself the luxury of expecting anything. I have discovered that it is easier to survive with this attitude. By consciously denying myself the privilege of luxuriating in warm baths of expectation, I have developed a form of psychological insurance against disappointment. It is a terrific defense mechanism. When it works.

You, more than anyone, should be able to understand, Richard. Expectation was the cornerstone of our marriage. The expectation of fulfilled ambition. The expectation of a perfect life. So it shouldn't surprise you that I have taken the hard lessons of failure seriously.

The most difficult part of the evening occurred before Nat arrived, and it had nothing, or everything, to do with going out with him. Deirdre's gift of quiet time became a nightmare of indecision. I put makeup on, took it off, then put it back on again, settling for mascara, eye shadow, and blusher. I decided to let my freckles show; natural is 'in' in California. Once my face was finished, my body became a problem. My dresses date back to Eagles' Landing, and aside from being too big, they are out of style. I changed outfits five times and ran two pairs of pantyhose before settling on the one dress I purchased this year, my dating dress. It doesn't have a pleasant association for me, but it was the only sensible choice.

Finally ready, I looked into the mirror one last time. I was dissatisfied, but I have always been dissatisfied. Mirrors highlight my imperfections unmercifully, as if to say: 'Ha, ha, you thought you could pull a fast one this time, Jenny, but you're not fooling me. I've caught you down to the last flaw.' Then, as the light plays tricks, every mirror I have ever gazed into spotlights my stubborn chin, the less than adequate fullness of my lips, and my overwide forehead. In final insult, my freckles sit above the surface of my skin on invisible pedestals, every one prominent.

It was fortunate that I wasn't ready too far ahead of time. If I had been, the agonies of waiting would have been worse than they were, and they were bad enough. I sat alone in the living room in my dating dress and lit a cigarette. (I am smoking again, and I don't want to discuss it.) Then I snapped a mental picture of myself and took a good hard look at it. There I was, thirty-two years old and as anxious as a schoolgirl going on her first date. And that isn't all. I was waiting alone for a man to take me out on the second anniversary of your death. 'Dammit,' I said aloud. 'How did this happen to me? How in the hell did it happen?'

I remembered how nervous I was the first time I went out with you, but it was different then. Adolescence gave me an excuse. You did, too, for you were a teenage girl's dream, a winner with a handsome, blemish-free face, a letter sweater, high grades, and the treasurer of your graduating class. Every girl in Standish High School was aware of Richard Weaver, including me, an insecure freshman prematurely worried about gaining an acceptance into a prestigious college and forever concerned with my popularity. 'You can never be too popular,' Mother reminded me constantly, whether or not the telephone rang. So when you noticed me toward the spring of the year, my ecstasy was understandable. It was unheard of for a senior to pay any more than passing attention to a freshman, and for a senior the caliber of Richard Weaver, it was nothing short of a miracle. When you asked me for a date, my life would have been complete if it weren't for my nervousness; I was terrified that you would find me disappointing. Never, either before or since, have I wanted anyone's approval as much as I wanted yours.

I recalled the hours I spent dressing for our first date and remembered a small pimple that had erupted on my chin the day before, which I camouflaged with my mother's makeup. Rembrandt couldn't have worked harder painting his women's faces than I did covering that pimple. By the time you rang our doorbell, I was nearly catatonic with worry. My mother assured me that I looked fine (I had persuaded her to buy me a new beige and brown sweater with a matching brown wool skirt for the occasion), which was high praise in our house, but I didn't believe her. 'I don't know why you're so tense,' she said, getting up to answer the door. 'Richard Weaver can't be that special.' I stared at her as if she had just become a candidate for an insane asylum.

My father, who was watching us, remarked, 'Boys like it when girls smile. So do fathers, especially when they've spent a thousand dollars to straighten their daughters' teeth.'

I opened my mouth and displayed my teeth in a nasty grin, wondering how anyone that insensitive could possibly be my father.

I lit another cigarette, picturing you as you were that night. You wore gray flannel slacks and a V-neck cashmere sweater in a lighter shade of gray over a blue oxford-cloth button-down shirt. It was the standard uniform for a casual high school fraternity party, but I thought it was sensational because you were wearing it. When you held my coat for me before we left, I nearly fainted with happiness.

During the years you were away at Wharton, I dated other boys and saw you exclusively in the summer and on school holidays. I never suffered from a lack of invitations because the boys at Standish knew that you were interested in me. You gave me the impossible, Richard: female adolescent security. I began to understand my jitters while I waited for Nat Witton. Life was finally catching up, forcing me to pay my dues.

I knew that you dated other girls while you were away at college and later, when you returned and started working at Wilson, Clarke & Turner, Accountants, but I never worried. Nor was I upset when I sensed that you had lost your virginity sometime during your first semester at Wharton (I could tell by the way you held me during Christmas recess). It was as if the other girls existed for my benefit because each time you returned, your hands and mouth were more knowledgeable.

The boys I dated were of no concern to you, and I rarely spoke of them. Even then, we knew we would be married. Everything, including the timing of our lives, was perfect: you would earn your CPA the same year I graduated from college. We talked of our eventual marriage with the conviction of a couple sure that their union had been preordained.

I was so absorbed in our past that I was startled when the doorbell rang. To my relief, Nat Witton wasn't wearing bangles and beads. He was dressed in a navy blazer, gray slacks, and a white turtleneck sweater, and he was carrying a long, slender package wrapped in newspaper. I invited him in.

'Mmmmm,' he said appreciatively. 'You look good enough to take out to dinner.'

It may not have been an original compliment, but it was mine, a reward for two hours of hard labor. I accepted it graciously, inwardly grateful.

I offered him a drink. 'Scotch and soda will be fine, if you have it,' he said, looking around. 'I hadn't realized that these townhouses were so nice. Maybe it's the way you've furnished it. You have excellent taste. You like good things, don't you? The kind of furniture that's made to last forever, not that plastic stuff.'

I looked at the living room through his stranger's eyes. The quality of the furniture was so distinct that a price tag attached to each piece couldn't have made it clearer. And every item in that room had once rested on the oriental rug in our family room in Eagles' Landing. 'I don't care for plastic,' I said, trying to hide the defensiveness I felt. 'It has a sheen that bothers me.'

239

In case I haven't mentioned it, the bulk of our furniture is in storage back East: most of the living room furniture, the dining room breakfront, your den furniture, the library furniture including the Kittinger desk, the kitchen set, and our bedroom furniture. My bedroom is furnished with the set from our guest room. When we moved, I took the children's bedroom sets, the dining room table, chairs, and server, and the family room furniture, concerned even then about taking too much with me. The only furniture I've purchased is a new kitchen set. I left our Eagles' Landing set in storage, sure that it would be too large for a rental kitchen. Leaving it proved wise.

The couple who bought our house wanted the grandfather clock. 'It belongs in the foyer,' the woman said. 'It almost looks like the house was built around it.' They made a substantial offer which I accepted, even though the clock was our first major purchase after we moved in. Its chimes, marking every quarter hour, and the small symphony they made every hour on the hour, had become increasingly mocking. They echoed through the house, constantly reminding me that this was what I had wanted. 'Ea-gles' Land-ing,' they rang. 'Ea-gles' Land-ing.'

It was a relief to leave the clock punctuating Eagles' Landing time for someone else. I never told you, but I disliked that clock from the day it was delivered. The ad was what had originally intrigued me. It intimated that, if potential buyers had to ask the price, they couldn't afford the company's clocks.

There are times when the storage of our furniture bothers me. We had such lovely things; they should be used. When I saw our furniture, crated and stacked in storage, it reminded me of a lopsided headstone, huge and unwieldy in the cavernous room. It was weeks before I could erase the image from my mind.

Nat wanted to know where the children were. 'I brought something for them,' he said, indicating that the contents of the narrow package were for Matthew and Catherine. 'It's nothing much. The newspaper will be using kites in a promotion, and I grabbed a few before I left yester-day.'

He seemed disappointed when I told him they weren't home, which surprised me. I hadn't thought that men were particularly interested in other men's children. Perhaps his interest was a part of his natural curiosity. Nat Witton is curious about everything.

As I said, the evening was a success. At least it was for me, so I am assuming that it was pleasant for him, too. Again, there is that uncertainty of singleness where one can only guess what the other unattached party is really thinking. I may not have liked what you were thinking when we were married, but I did know where I stood. We both knew. There is comfort in knowing no matter how the other's thoughts run, and in the case of our marriage, they didn't always run well. But if we placed each other on low ground, our footing was reassuringly solid.

Nat had made reservations at a delightful Mexican restaurant. After we were seated, I told him that I was unfamiliar with Mexican food. He grinned. 'You're worried about getting a hot throat, aren't you?' he asked. 'Well, don't worry. This is a treat for me. I'm glad to be the one to introduce you to Mexican cooking. Everything they make here goes down easily. You'll like it.'

I did.

He ordered for both of us and did it graciously. I could detect none of the male pomposity I had come to expect in Eagles' Landing: Ike Springer's wine expertise, Bruch Lynch's obnoxious lectures on French sauces, and Barney Leadman's authoritative discourses on Italian food. Barney never left out an ingredient, always assuming that everyone within hearing range would be grateful to know exactly how the veal got to be picatta. Barney's descriptions were meticulous. There were times when I would have preferred listening to him read from one of his patient's hospital charts; it would have been more appetising.

For me, your star always rose on those evenings, and

you knew it. 'Food is food,' you said. 'If it's good, I like it.' But those were private words. You would never have uttered them publicly, for to do so would have meant embarrassment to men whom you felt were important.

I must change the subject. I could stop writing, but I don't want to. It's early, and I don't have a book to read. Television as a choice is out; I haven't watched in months. There was a time when television acted as a tranquilizer, a video-dose of Librium. I was lulled to sleep by a constant flow of inanities uttered by improbable characters, children in adult bodies who seemed determined to make public idiots of themselves. Now my mind tunes them out completely, and I sit, wide awake, staring at the walls, which are infinitely more interesting but not as safe.

I'll tell you more about Nat Witton. It may not be in the best of taste, but I don't believe there are precedents against it. In fact, it could be a first. I am relatively sure that even the thorough Miss Post overlooked this possibility. Besides, you already know about my lunch with Nat, so some of the initial uneasiness I felt is gone.

There were few pauses in our dinner conversation, and those few that I can recall seemed right. They weren't silences of boredom or embarrassment, sticky moments unattached men and women can spend together that seem to stretch like taffy into hours. I have become acquainted with those moments, and believe me, they are deadly.

Nat appears to be interested in everything and can talk as well as he listens, which makes him a natural conversationalist. He's been in California for five years and likes it here. 'I've never lived in a place like California,' he said. 'It's in a constant state of flux. Things change before you have a chance to become accustomed to them; even fads are out before half of the population knows they are in. Just keeping up is a challenge.'

As he spoke, I visualized an amusement park with people milling around confused, unable to leave because they couldn't find their exits, the places where they had originally entered. My thoughts must have registered on my face. 'You don't agree?' he asked.

I told him about the amusement park.

'There is nothing wrong with staying in an amusement park if you can relax and enjoy it,' he said, smiling. 'The fun is in the rides.'

'But you have to leave eventually,' I said. 'You can't stay in the park forever.'

The first pause in our conversation followed my remark. Nat's expression turned serious, then contemplative. I became aware of the lines in his face, faint etchings like leaf tracings extending from the outside corners of his eyes, and the deeper furrows between his eyebrows. It was a side of Nat Witton I hadn't seen before, and I liked it. But I also had the feeling that he didn't show this side of himself often, preferring to wear his mask of easy charm.

I encouraged him to talk about himself, which wasn't as simple to accomplish as it is with most men. He isn't a braggart, nor does he play upmanship games. Rather, he seems to live quite comfortably with himself. There was also the problem of contending with his curiosity. I knew he wanted to find out more about me, but I didn't want to talk about myself. It was my resistance, I think, that finally drew him out.

Nat is from a small town in central Pennsylvania. He left to go away to college and didn't return except for brief visits with his family. 'I wasn't particularly happy there, so I was eager to leave,' he said. 'Then a strange thing happened: I began to really see the town after I left. The farther away I went, the more I saw. My focus sharpened, but the picture remained the same. Each time I returned, everything was as I had left it – the people, the buildings – everything stayed in place. Life in the town moved to its own rhythm. After a while, the rhythm became reassuring to me. I'd go back just to check it out. I haven't been there in several years, but I'll bet it's the same.'

He went to Columbia ('New York was a shock to my nervous system,' he said. 'I had the feeling that I was running all the time, but I didn't know what I was running for') and met a girl from upstate New York who was attending Barnard. They were married after they graduated and moved to Utica. ('But we didn't know that Utica was dead. The place had died thirty years before we arrived.') Apparently they were both unhappy in Utica but stayed because Nat was doing well there. ('I couldn't fail,' he said, grinning. 'I was the only one working on the paper who hadn't retired.')

Nat's career blossomed, but his marriage fell apart after their only child died. 'She had a hard time conceiving,' he revealed. 'We were married for six years before our son was born. He had a congenital heart condition and was blue from lack of oxygen. There was a doctor in Buffalo who could have saved him if he had immediate surgery, but my wife was afraid. "He can't travel," she insisted. "He's only two days old. The doctors here can take care of him until he's a week old. Then we'll go." I agreed. The baby looked so fragile.'

Nat drained his glass of tequila. 'He lived for four days,' he said with the hollowness of loss in his voice. 'We were divorced within the year.'

Then: 'You know that doctor in Buffalo who could have operated on my son? He's still there, quietly mending nature's mistakes. I see his name every once in a while; the wire services occasionally run pictures of babies being transported to Buffalo so the good doctor can fix their hearts. Now some of them are only a day or two old.'

'You couldn't have known,' I said consolingly.

What followed was the second pause of the evening, and it came late, at the end of our dinner. Nat toyed with his empty glass, then looked directly at me. The candlelight highlighted his eyes. I felt myself becoming enveloped in layers of blue – the blue of the California sky, the shifting blues of the Pacific – a spectrum of blue in one man's gaze. A woman could drown in those eyes, I thought.

'I usually don't talk about myself,' he said.

'I know,' I replied.

He leaned forward. 'How do you know?' he asked, his eyes deepening in yet another shade of blue.

'Because you're naturally curious, and curious people like to hear others talk. Information is food to them,' I said lightly.

I was afraid that he might be offended, but he wasn't. Instead, he laughed. 'The next time, Jennifer Weaver, it will be your turn. You've left me a starving man whose curiosity must be fed.'

'We'll see about that,' I said.

The third silence of the evening occurred after we left the dimly lighted restaurant. There was a couple walking out directly ahead of us. The man, who was as tall as Nat, opened the door for his companion, then kept it open for me. I glanced up to say thank you and inwardly gasped. The lower half of his face was distorted by a livid purple birthmark extending from his mouth to his left ear, and his mouth was misshapen from what appeared to be a repaired harelip; keloids around the periphery of the birthmark outlined it hideously. I quickly averted my eyes, too shocked to speak, but not before I saw an expression of veiled defensiveness descend over the man's eyes. 'Thank you,' I heard Nat say behind me. 'I hope your dinner was as good as ours.' The man replied pleasantly, but I didn't hear what he said. I was so embarrassed by my rudeness and so taken aback with what I had seen that I kept walking, wanting to disappear into the night.

It took Nat a half dozen strides to catch up with me. We walked in silence to his car. After we were inside, Nat turned the key in the ignition, then turned it off. I knew he was looking at me, as if expecting me to say something. I was silent.

'Jenny,' he said in a low voice, 'forget it.'

'I can't forget it. I probably hurt that man more than if I called him ugly. I did call him ugly. I told him that he was grotesque by not saying anything at all. I didn't even thank him for holding the door open.'

'He understands.'

'Sure,' I said sarcastically. 'He knew exactly what I thought when I looked at him. If I had screamed, I couldn't have said it louder.'

'Look at me,' Nat said. He turned my face with his hand and held it gently. My eyes remained downcast.

'Look at me,' Nat repeated. 'That's better. Stubborn, aren't you? It's over. Instead of dwelling on it, try to understand.'

'What is there to understand? I know what happened.'

'You know what happened, but you really don't understand. The man knows what he looks like. He has a mirror. Even if he didn't, he'd know. He's been told hundreds of times by people who reacted as you did.'

'That doesn't make it right,' I said.

'No, it doesn't, but your reaction was normal. Human beings react to abnormalities in other human beings. If he had been a dwarf with a normal-sized woman, you would have reacted, too. In that case you probably would have looked at the pair with curiosity or amusement, staring at both of them in spite of yourself and wondering about all kinds of things. Interesting things,' he said teasingly.

'I would have preferred a dwarf; my behavior toward that man was inexcusable. How were you able to act nonchalant when I couldn't?'

'I had a second to prepare myself,' he admitted. Nat paused, then continued. 'There was a time in my life when people stared at me. I had one of the worst cases of scarring acne our local Pennsylvania dermatologist had ever seen. My face and the back of my neck were covered with eruptions the size and color of Bing cherries. I felt like a walking wound. But eventually I began to read the meaning in people's eyes, and it was the best learning experience I have ever had. Some people looked at me with curiosity, others with compassion, but the glances I understood best came from kids my own age who didn't know me. I saw identification in their eyes, and relief. They were glad that it was me and not them, and I couldn't blame them. I understood.

246

'That man understood your reaction tonight. He knows, and he doesn't feel malice toward you.'

During the ride back to Deirdre's, Nat told me that he underwent minor surgery to remove the outer, most scarred layers of his skin after he moved to California, which explains the cragginess in his face. 'My skin was literally sanded off. It's called dermabrasion. Some of the pits were too deep to remove, but I still consider the operation a success. I don't need an Ivory soap complexion in my line of work,' he joked, 'although for a while, I was painfully pink.'

I recalled my concern over my freckles earlier in the evening and said nothing. I don't believe I can remember feeling quite that small.

Nat wanted to know why I was staying at Deirdre's. I didn't want to tell him about the rape. 'My friend hasn't been feeling well and is expecting someone in the morning,' I said. 'She didn't want to be alone.'

'A former husband?' Nat guessed.

'Yes.'

'I'm going to give you some unsolicited advice,' he said. 'Don't get involved.'

'I'm not.'

'If you're there, you're involved, and it could get messy.'

'That's easy advice to give. Don't you ever get involved?'

'Not if I can help it,' he said, 'and only when I want to.'

Deirdre had given me a key. There was a single lamp lit in the living room, and she had made up the sofa with sheets, a blanket and a pillow. 'A monastic arrangement,' Nat observed.

The irony of his remark made me smile. After all, Richard, it has been a while. But there is time, and I'll see him again. I know I will. The signals were there when he kissed me good night.

Nothing happened this morning. Absolutely nothing.

Ken Jamison tooted the horn of his pickup truck at ten o'clock, and Kerry, who had been waiting for hours, bolted out the door. Deirdre and I stood in the doorway and watched Kerry climb in next to his father. There was an ecstatic expression on the boy's face that sickened me.

'See what I mean?' Deirdre asked bitterly as they drove away.

'Yes,' I said.

Neither father nor son looked back.

Later, Deirdre asked me to go with her to her consciousness-raising group on Thursday. 'You can't stay with me every weekend,' she said, 'but right now, I can't handle it alone. If I go to a meeting and have you with me for support, maybe I can find a solution to this mess.'

'I didn't think consciousness-raising groups solved problems,' I said.

'They don't, but it can't hurt to have my problem sifted through other people's minds. You never know. They could come up with something.'

'You mean, you'll tell them everything?' I asked incredulously.

'Yes,' she said, 'everything.'

'Wouldn't you be better off meditating? Yoga has always helped you. Telling the consciousness-raising group could be a mistake,' I warned.

'I can't meditate,' Deirdre said, bursting into tears. 'Yoga doesn't work anymore. If it's a mistake, I'll live with it. I'm living with my other mistakes, aren't I?'

'Aren't we all?' I felt like saying. 'Aren't we all?'

All of us except you, Richard, and tonight I'm glad I didn't choose your way out.

I hesitated to write to you tonight. There are things I want to tell you, but I don't know how to begin. Or where to begin. 'Begin at the beginning,' you would say with your infuriating logic if you were here. It isn't that easy. You see, Richard, your death marked the beginning. What I mean is that the things I am about to tell wouldn't have occurred if you hadn't died the way you did.

Maybe I'm wrong. One of them might have happened but not both.

I'm not sure. Maybe neither would have happened.

There is no point in debating the issue. What happened, happened. It is over and cannot be changed. If I have learned nothing else from writing to you, I have discovered that the past is inflexible. History can be written, rewritten, interpreted, and reinterpreted until it is ground into dust without changing anything. The facts are the facts. And in our case, the facts are as follows: you are dead, I am alive, and certain things have happened.

I realize that I haven't given you much in terms of preparation for what I am about to say, but I honestly can't think of a tactful approach. To be perfectly honest, I don't even know why I'm struggling to broach this business delicately. It occurs to me that you did not extend *me* the courtesy of preparation when *you* died. Your death was organized because organization was your signature, but your provisions for me did not include preparation. It would have helped. You could have said something, possibly dropped a few general hints at the dinner table, like: carbon monoxide is lethal in enclosed places; or, suicide is a tradition in Japan; or, a bit broader, no one lives forever. In the months I spent watching television, I saw a parade of policemen, doctors, and paramedics prepare families for bad news. With the pain of constipation on their faces, they all began by saying: 'I hate to be the one to tell you this, but . . .' Even strangers do that much for each other when they can.

Perhaps we were strangers, but I don't want to get into that topic. This is difficult enough as it is.

There have been men. Two. I shall tell you about the second man first; it will be easier. I know I once said the near past is more dangerous than the far past, but there are exceptions. This is an exception. Eventually you will understand why.

R.–I

Deirdre fixed me up with the second man, Craig Howard (nee Howard Smedley), several months after we moved to California. She knew without asking that I didn't have a social life and took it upon herself to get me started. I tried to resist her social work, but she was determined. 'You have to be with people,' she said. 'Days go by, and you don't have contact with anyone but the children and that old nun, Mrs Feltcher. You can't live like that forever; you'll go crazy.' It was before I was working at Briarhill, so I didn't have an adequate comeback. Not that I needed one, Richard. I was and am free to date. Remember, I am a widow.

Anyway, a fellow Deirdre was dating invited her to a party at someone's house. Deirdre's date, Lenny something-or-other, had a friend coming in from San Francisco. The friend was Craig Howard. Deirdre hadn't met him but assured me that he would be acceptable. 'If he isn't, I told Lenny I wouldn't go out with him again,' she said.

Lenny was crazy about Deirdre, so it wasn't a bad guarantee.

I was curious rather than nervous about my blind date, viewing it more as an adventure than a social engagement, so there was none of the anticipatory trauma I experienced before going out with Nat Witton. Deirdre told me to dress casually. Thinking that casual in California was the same as casual in Eagles' Landing, I wore a silk shirt and linen slacks and ended up being the most conservatively dressed female at the party. I felt positively staid, as if I had dressed in my mother's clothes, standing next to women wearing plunging T-shirts and scraps of expensive fabric joined together in what resembled halters, but Craig Howard didn't seem to mind. He looked me over carefully when he picked me up (nothing subtle about Craig) and said 'good deal' as if I were a surprise box lunch at a picnic that turned out to have his favorite goodies.

I wasn't as impressed with Craig, although he was nice looking in a clean, California way. He was of medium height and build, and it was obvious that he took extraordinary care of himself. His hair had just the right amount of sun streaks (I felt like asking him for the name of his beautician), his teeth were too perfect to be anything but capped, and his tan was gloriously rich and even. He was trim and wore an open shirt that revealed several gold chains and a well-muscled body.

Perhaps I wasn't impressed with Craig because everything in his manner told me to be impressed with him.

Maybe it was because I felt that he looked better than I did.

Craig also had a few words for Matthew and Catherine. They were watching television and eating potato chips when he arrived.

'What's that you're eating?' he asked after I introduced them.

'Pringles,' replied Catherine. 'Do you want some?' She offered him the can.

Craig took it and read aloud: 'Dried potatoes; partially hydrogenated cottonseed oil; mono- and di-glycerides; salt and dextrose. Whew,' he exclaimed, turning to me. 'How can you let your kids eat this garbage? It isn't even food; it's regurgitated potato.'

Catherine, who had a potato chip in her mouth, turned green and ran to the bathroom to spit it out. She came back into the living room crying. 'Will I die, Mommy? Will I die?' she asked, close to becoming hysterical.

Matthew glared at Craig and stalked out of the room; the babysitter looked as if she wanted to leave.

'No, you won't die,' I said, reassuring her. I felt more like slugging Craig than going out with him. She calmed down after drinking a glass of milk, and we left.

'I didn't mean to upset her,' Craig apologized, 'but she should be snacking on healthy food – sunflower seeds or raisins. I didn't think she'd take what I said literally.' He paused. Then, to justify himself, he added: 'Although the stuff she was eating was polluting her system.'

'Children take everything literally,' I replied.

251

'Oh, I didn't know that. I don't know much about children – none of my wives had them. At least not to my knowledge,' he joked, 'or I'd see it in my monthly payments.'

'How many wives have you had?'

'Only three. I'm a three-time loser.' Craig delivered that bit of information with a shrug, as if having three ex-wives were standard and his response was the accepted cliché.

During the course of the evening, I learned the rest of Craig's personal history. It wasn't difficult to extract. Craig's favorite subject, after health food, self-improvement, and how-to-do-it books, was Craig Howard. Craig, born Howard Smedley, was originally from Long Island and moved to California when he was in his early twenties. Like Harry Grubman, he sought a new identity and a new life. When I went out with him, he was thirty-eight (Craig told me his age and his original name in a moment of extreme confidence, as if he were giving me the combination to a safe holding royal jewels) and considered himself a supremely successful man. 'You must have heard of Howard's Health Food Stores,' he said.

I told him that I hadn't.

'You're new in California,' he said, excusing me. 'Everyone in San Francisco knows Howard's. You'll be hearing our slogan soon – "Go to Howard's for your health." Terrific, isn't it? We're opening here next month.'

Craig's enthusiasm saved him from being obnoxious. He was so utterly pleased with himself and his life that I found him pleasant, if different, company. The fact that he was pleased with me helped. He told me repeatedly that I was 'real class' and that he would make it a point to spend extra time in the area after his stores were opened. 'I like you, Jenny,' he said with gusto, 'and when I like someone, I reeeally like them.'

The people at the party ranged in age from their mid-twenties to mid-forties, and everyone was or had been into something, either est, TM, or yoga. There were a few people who swore by Esalen, one or two who felt that hot tubs were necessary to put one's mind and body in order, and still others who talked about rolfing. I wasn't going to betray my stupidity by asking for an explanation, but from the context of the conversations around me, I think that rolfing has something to do with getting your body in alignment. A woman who was convinced that rolfing saved her sanity said ardently: 'The only way to survive is to bring your body segments back together.' At the time, rolfing struck me as the ideal philosophy for a practicing chiropractor.

Almost everyone there seemed to be looking for a philosophy that would support them through life like a guaranteed annuity. Deirdre was into yoga, and Craig had his health food, his body building, and his self-improvement philosophy. 'I'm into building brick walls,' he said. 'I got this how-to-do-it book. You can't imagine the satisfaction you get working with your hands. And the results! To see something solid after a few hours of work, something that will really last. There is nothing like it.' He was so convincing that a woman who was into mud baths and a man who was disillusioned with est both asked him for the name of the book. 'After all,' said the woman, a well-built blonde in her thirties, 'mortar isn't that far removed in philosophy from mud.'

I wonder how a bricklayer feels at the end of the day, if his mind and body are in perfect working order or if he is subject to the same pressures as the rest of humanity. Perhaps getting paid for laying brick takes the philosophy out of the work. It would be interesting to know.

There was a dark-complexioned, powerfully built man at the party whose silence matched mine while the others were trading philosophies. He approached me after I left the group to sit on the terrace. 'Hi, I'm T.P.,' he said.

'Teepee?' I asked with disbelief, for he didn't look like an Indian. 'That's an unusual name.'

'They are initials,' he explained, his swarthy face

253

breaking into a grin. 'My name is too difficult for most people to pronounce.'

'Let me try,' I said.

'Timotheos Pegopoulos,' he enunciated slowly.

I managed to get it out, syllable by syllable.

'Not bad,' said T.P. 'How come you're so quiet?'

'I'm unfamiliar with the things they're talking about,' I admitted. 'Why are you quiet? Aren't you into anything, or are you keeping your philosophy a secret?'

He laughed, a deep laugh tinged with sarcasm. 'I don't need that shit,' he said. 'I'm Greek.'

It was the best prescription for survival I heard all night.

I would have liked to talk to T.P. a while longer, but a stunning brunette came to claim him after she heard him laugh. She stood between us, said, 'Hi, I'm Jeanette,' and led him away with a proprietary arm around his waist. I don't know what philosophy she was into, but Jeanette's territorial instincts were intact.

Their disappearance left me alone, so I went back inside to look for Craig and passed small cliques of people who were engrossed in private conversations. No one made an overture to include me. Several men smiled invitingly in my direction, but the women pointedly ignored me, which added to the feeling of outsidedness I was already experiencing, until I understood that their lack of acknowledgement was a form of acknowledgment. Still, it didn't make me feel any better.

On my way to find Craig, I saw a group of people who were getting high on cocaine. I had never seen the drug used before and stopped to watch, fascinated. Cocaine looks like sugar, and there are miniature spoonlike utensils used to scoop and sniff it. There was something about the actual sniffing of the drug that repulsed me, particularly when the women used it. It was almost as if they were picking their noses in public.

Craig was where I had left him, still demonstrating the fine art of laying imaginary bricks. I stood nearby and observed another activity at the party, a kind of sophisticated but undisguised sexual shopping. Although everyone had arrived with a date, that didn't preclude looking around to see what else was available, and some people did more than just look. Even the couples who were living together, married or unmarried, shopped. There were those, not necessarily individuals who had arrived together, who disappeared during the course of the evening, then returned with smug expressions on their faces. Others seemed to be unhappy, disappointed in either the party or the people around them, as if the affair were a poorly stocked store. Still others accepted the party as it was, appearing to be bored, happy, or indifferent. It was just another evening out, and they were testing the ground.

It probably isn't necessary to tell you that I was uncomfortable, Richard. You know me too well to have doubts on that score. I never learned the techniques of sexual shopping, and I never had time to devote to a philosophy that would get me through the day. I was too busy struggling to survive in Eagles' Landing to meditate on my position in the cosmos.

I wish I knew how to shop for sex. It is a necessary skill for widows and one that I do not possess. I have read books on widowhood, and they haven't taught me anything I really need to know. Either they are the how-to-do-it variety – how to cope with grief and loneliness, balance your checkbook, find new friends, look for a job, parent your children, and offer suggestions for time-filling busywork – or they are individual histories of crack-ups and disastrous love affairs. The latter are demoralizing, for they offer new widows a full spectrum of potential horrors that are not tempered by their pat endings. A woman cannot learn from another woman's love affair, but it can certainly scare the hell out of her. All that can be said for these books is that they have kept a lot of widows busy and solvent.

I am still waiting for the book that will give me shopping

suggestions. Don't laugh, Richard. It isn't easy. I am not the type who can pick a man up in a bar, and even if I were, there are still problems. How do I know if the man is clean? What if he has V.D.? I can't very well ask, nor will I carry condoms in my purse for 'just in case.' There is something new in V.D. now – herpes. Maybe it isn't new, but until I moved to California, I hadn't heard of it. People who have herpes get recurring genital sores that are excruciatingly painful, and some victims are troubled with the sores for years. There is no known permanent cure. Herpes is an illness that must have been designed as the ultimate punishment for sexual promiscuity, and it is big in California.

There is more to consider than veneral disease. What if a man is sick, a sexual psychopath who gets his kicks out of brutalizing women? Newspaper and television reports of the murders of women who have been sexually assaulted before their deaths have become quite common. I try not to be paranoid about this, but I can't ignore it, either. Look at what happened to Deirdre. She gave birth to Ken Jamison's only child, and even that didn't protect her from him.

So you see, there are problems. I am young and healthy, and your death hasn't quashed my appetite. My need for sex is urgently real, and although it is available everywhere, I am not psychologically constructed for a one-night stand. It would be too difficult, if not dangerous. I certainly couldn't bring a man home, for Matthew and Catherine must be considered. Once, in a crazy moment, I had a terrific idea: setting up a screening service for men so they could be certified healthy. It seemed sensible. After all, Nevada screens female prostitutes. But when I realized that I didn't want sex with a stranger, I became more depressed than ever. Still, there have been other times when any proficient man would have been welcome.

I wish I could discuss this problem with someone, specifically a woman, but it is impossible. Women may talk about sex generally, but they don't give details about themselves except in movies, books, and, according to Deirdre, consciousness-raising groups. And I doubt that they share everything they know even then. Until now, I am certain that I wouldn't have talked. I never have, not to anyone. Molly Springer was my closest friend in Eagles' Landing, and I knew no more about her sex life with Ike than she knew about mine with you. Molly wouldn't have told me what went on in her bedroom any more than she would have divulged Ike's yearly income. Some things just weren't said. Deirdre is my only female friend in California, and as candid as she is, she has never discussed intimate details concerning her relationships with the men she dates. The only woman I have ever heard talk, face to face, was Sylvia Lynch, and it took a quart of Seagrams to loosen her tongue.

I am telling you these things because I want you to know and understand why I went to bed with Craig Howard. I didn't especially like him, and I certainly didn't love him, but he was a man who was obviously safe. To put it bluntly, Craig was clean. There was nothing more important to him, aside from his health food stores, than the condition of his body and improving himself.

Craig courted me with bags of fresh alfalfa sprouts. He came laden with sunflower seeds, salted and unsalted, for the children. From him, Matthew and Catherine developed a temporary fear of white bread and sugar products. They wouldn't eat cookies, candy, or pre-sweetened cereal in his presence, which brought a new worry: I was afraid they would become food fetishists, for they started to read labels on canned goods and cereal boxes with the fanaticism of zealots. Neither child had the faintest idea of what the multisyllabled words meant, but they would pronounce the names of additives and preservatives phonetically, and their foreheads would crease. Catherine lost her normally healthy appetite, subsisted on Craig's sunflower seeds (which I supplemented with fruit, nuts, and raisins), and seemed to be leaping directly from childhood into a premature old age. In private, she referred to him as *the poison man*. Rather than say anything about Craig, Matthew simply glared at him whenever he was around. All of this happened within a three-week period of time, for Craig flew in every weekend to see me. 'I intend to court you,' said Craig, 'as you have never been courted before.'

He made his promise good. His bags of alfalfa sprouts and sunflower seeds grew heavier each weekend; Craig Howard gave me his deluxe treatment.

Craig called before he came in the last weekend we were together. 'I want to take you to a new organic restaurant,' he said enthusiastically. 'It's supposed to be terrific. I just made a reservation.'

I bought my dating dress, the one I wore when I went out with Nat Witton, for the organic dinner, and will forever associate it with that evening. Craig came to pick me up with dried fruit as well as his staples, the alfalfa sprouts and sunflower seeds, so I knew that this was to be the night. After our dinner (Craig was rapturous over the broccoli), we went to his hotel room.

I don't know how to tell you what happened, except to say that Craig tried. Oh, did he try! His penchant for reading do-it-yourself books and his dedication to self-improvement must have included sex as well as bricklaying. I wouldn't be surprised if Craig had, during his years of self-enrichment, read every sex manual ever written.

Craig's approach to lovemaking was distinctly geographic. It was as if he had mentally divided my body into erogenous zones, ranging from the arctic to the equatorial, and he was determined to pay scrupulous attention to anything in each zone that would be considered even faintly erotic. Instead of enjoying myself, I started to place mental bets on what spot he would hit next, my inner arm or my rib cage. By the time he reached the equator, I had become so self-conscious over the silver stretch marks on my belly that I was completely turned off. I did, however, fake a whopping orgasm to reward him for his efforts. It was easier to do than I had imagined, and I did a slick job,

258

if I do say so myself. Craig was ecstatic. 'You're terrific, Jenny,' he whispered lovingly. 'You're just terrific.'

It was an evening in which we were both cheated. Someday, if Craig is lucky, a woman will tell him the facts of life: that the arctic zone is as important as, if not more important than, the equator, and that it isn't the number of spots you hit that counts, but how you hit them. Perhaps he'll learn from his fourth or fifth wife.

I didn't see Craig again. Like Mrs Feltcher, he meant well, so I didn't want to hurt him. But Craig didn't make it easy. After a number of long distance calls ('I must see you,' he pleaded, 'I must'), I grew tired of making up excuses and became flippant. 'I don't like alfalfa sprouts,' I said. 'I just don't like them.'

Craig didn't reply. Instead, I heard a sound, like painful swallowing, before he hung up.

I sat by the telephone for a long time afterward, sorry for what I had done. Craig wasn't a bad sort; he certainly deserved better than a cute dismissal for his efforts. The sound of his hurt made me realize that men are as vulnerable as women. When I finally summoned the courage, I called him back to apologize. No one answered. I hate to admit this, but I was relieved, for I don't know what I would have said.

I'm exhausted, Richard. I'll have to tell you about the first man tomorrow night. It will be difficult, but I promise.

There is no way I can tell you about the first man except to come out and say it: I had sex with Charlie. That's right, Charlie Pritchard. I had intercourse with your best friend, and the memory still hurts. I can explain how it happened, though I realize that an explanation isn't an excuse.

Charlie avoided me after your funeral, and the first time I saw him, several months later, his eyes were accusatory and his manner distant. But he did make himself available on the telephone. I called him when I had an occasional

259

question concerning your estate, and he was most helpful. Charlie handled your final affairs with the same devotion and steadfastness he gave to you when you were alive. Of the two of us, Richard, you and I, you were the one who had a truly good friend. That fact says more about us as individuals than I care to contemplate.

We were always at odds, Charlie and I, with you in the middle. I know he was your friend first and that I was the intruder, but boys do grow up, discover girls, and eventually get married. The time comes, and it happens. I suppose Charlie just wasn't ready for me to step into your life. He always liked things as they were, and you had been friends from the time you could walk. If Charlie resisted anything, it was change. Unless, as he once put it, 'there was a damned good reason.'

When we were in high school, Charlie rebuffed my efforts to fix him up. I realized that he was shy, probably because he was so ungainly – six feet six, all hands and feet, with a long, serious face that had an appealing homeliness – but he was a good athlete and lots of girls would have been willing to go out with him. I tried to tell that to Charlie, but he wouldn't listen. The only voice Charlie listened to, outside of his own, was yours. No one could push Charlie, ever. He was a natural examiner of facts, a detective of innuendo, and he never made a decision until he was absolutely ready. It was as natural for him to become a lawyer as it was for you to become an accountant. The only time I can recall Charlie veering from character was when he impulsively married that awful Doreen after a vacation in the Bahamas. As Charlie said when their divorce was final: 'It had to happen. I didn't give the decision to marry Doreen the consideration it deserved.'

I tried to like Charlie during the years we were courting and after we were married, but it was difficult. Charlie never quite approved of me. There was always a hint of doubt in his manner, an air of reservation like a sheet of glass between us. Charlie never told me that he didn't like me, but he didn't have to; some people are able to articulate their feelings without uttering a word.

When we first started dating, I was insulted by Charlie's manner, and hurt. He made me feel flawed, as if I didn't measure up to some invisible standard that he alone understood. The worst part of it was that Charlie knew I was aware of his reservations. He didn't like his feelings acknowledged, at least not in the way I acknowledged them. I let him know that I knew he didn't like me. Charlie tried harder to be friendly, and I tried to respond, but it didn't work. And you were oblivious to what was going on between us, a tug of war in which you were the prize.

I thought, when you and I became engaged, that things would be settled between Charlie and me. Perhaps we could finally accept each other. But Charlie arrived late to our engagement party, avoided me all evening, and got roaring drunk. It was the first time I had seen him lose control. I steeled myself for an attack, an articulation of his disapproval, but nothing was said. Charlie passed out, and you left the party to take him home. We shared you that night, too.

The bond of loyalty between you and Charlie was so strong that I didn't dare voice my resentment of him until after we were married. For too long I had been tired of you quoting Charlie, of you conferring over business matters at lunch with Charlie, of your marathon Saturday afternoon squash matches with Charlie. I had had enough and told you so. I shall never forget the look of innocent surprise on your face. 'Charlie is my best friend,' you said. 'There will always be room in my life for him. Now that we're married, we should both make room.'

I was tired of making room, Richard, and I was angry. And jealous. I was your wife. Shouldn't I have been your best friend?

The second time I saw Charlie lose control was the night he came to dinner after we moved to Eagles' Landing. I was uncomfortable all evening. I knew Charlie wouldn't mention his telephone call or the note and estimated cost sheets he'd sent, but his presence in our house after weeks of avoiding our invitation was a reminder, especially when he started drinking. Normally, Charlie was as cautious with his liquor as he was with everything else. I wondered later whether the sadness in his voice when he talked about Harry Grubman was for us, not Harry. He didn't come over often after that, but whenever he did, Charlie and I were surface friendly and polite. It was the same as it had always been.

My attitude toward Charlie changed somewhat during the last year you and I were together. Everything was so strained, so difficult and complicated then. It seemed that Charlie's capable hands steadied your life, and I was grateful. You talked to him and met with him constantly. I know the meetings were mostly business, primarily the Bestmark Partnership, but steadfast Charlie was there as your friend, as well as your attorney. It wasn't until after you died that I realized he could be my friend, too. All of the legal work Charlie had done insulated me and the children from claims against your estate. He had constructed a protective barricade around us, as he had done for you during the war in Vietnam when he found a doctor who would certify you unfit for military service.

Charlie's face was the only one I remember seeing at your funeral, and it was ravaged with grief. The others, all family, were a blur. I was too numb with shock to speak to him, nor would he have wanted me to say anything if I could have spoken. From one glance, I knew your friend Charlie, that mountain of a man, all reserve and caution, was close to falling apart.

I didn't speak to him until several days after the funeral, and when he called, I knew that he was as far from recovering from your death as I was. He told me that he had a copy of your will and a list of your assets. 'I'll handle the estate for you,' he said, tight-voiced. 'That is, if you want me to. If you'd feel more comfortable with another lawyer, maybe your father's, don't hesitate to say so. I can transfer everything.'

'Richard would have wanted you to handle his estate,' I said. 'No one else would be acceptable.'

Charlie started to say something, but his voice cracked. He cleared his throat. 'I'll be in touch, Jenny. Call me if you have any problems or questions. Also, let me know if you need money. I'll get it over to you right away.'

That is the way it was between Charlie and me after you died. He watched out for your interests and mine from a safe distance, and he was dependably thorough. There was never a bill, either for filing your estate papers or closing the house. Charlie quietly absorbed the fees himself, and his manner let me know that I was not to mention it. Charlie wasn't comfortable with gratitude.

Charlie took Matthew out, once to a basketball game and once to a hockey match. He called in advance and planned their outings as carefully as he practiced law. You know how Matthew adored his Uncle Charlie; he came home ecstatic each time. After the second outing, I realized, how hard it was for Charlie. Matthew looks so much like you, Richard, that Charlie's face was lined with sorrow when he brought your son home. I felt that I had to say something. 'Taking Matthew out has been difficult for you, Charlie,' I said. 'I know it has. You don't have to do it.'

Charlie looked startled. 'Is it that noticeable?' he asked painfully.

'Yes, it is. Richard wouldn't have wanted you to suffer; neither would Matthew, if he knew.'

Charlie's long face relaxed slightly. 'I'm glad you understand,' he said with relief.

They didn't go out again, but Charlie did come by occasionally with small gifts for the children. I think the gifts were an excuse. Charlie was observing me; I know he was. 'Are you still on tranquilizers?' he asked each time, when it was obvious that I was peering out at him through a cloud of Librium. 'They can be habit forming.' Once he actually told me that he was worried. 'Call the doctor, Jenny,' he said. 'Have him cut your dosage.'

'It's all right,' I replied. 'I'll stop taking them soon.'

'When is soon?' Charlie wanted to know.

'Very soon,' I said obliquely. I had just taken another pill.

I called Charlie after I had listed the house to tell him what I had done. He hadn't seen me since I had been off the pills, and he was understandably surprised. 'What made you decide to sell?' he asked. 'Couldn't we have discussed it first? You're not...' He paused. Charlie didn't know how to tell me that I wasn't all there.

I told him I had stopped taking tranquilizers and that I knew what I was doing. 'You'll handle the closing, won't you?' I asked.

'I'll be over after dinner to discuss it,' he said.

Charlie arrived that evening when he knew the children would be in bed. We sat in the living room facing each other after I offered him a drink, which he refused. The grandfather clock serenaded a new hour. It was nine o'clock. I can still hear those damn chimes. Charlie leaned back in his chair, folded his hands behind his head, and studied me with his dispassionate green eyes. He had come to consider my plans, and I was uncomfortably aware that nothing I said would be considered lightly. Charlie never considered anything lightly. To a collector of fine detail, everything counts, and Charlie had always been a dedicated collector.

Surprisingly, I didn't resent his interest as I would have in the past. His presence indicated that he cared, if not for me, then for the children. At least someone cared, and that was important. Also, and to his credit, Charlie didn't bombard me with questions. Instead, he casually asked what my plans were. But I knew that my plans had better sound reasonable, for Charlie was there to see if I was fit to make any decision, let alone one of the magnitude of selling the house.

I began by telling him that the house was too large for

the three of us. 'We don't need this much space,' I said, 'and the realtor told me that it is an excellent time to sell. The market is in the seller's favor.'

Charlie seemed to agree. He nodded, then asked: 'Where are you planning to move?'

I had already spoken with my mother, so I knew where I was going. Although the initial choice was impetuous, I had become used to the idea of moving to California, almost charmed with it, and I told him. Charlie sat upright in astonishment. 'Why California?' he asked.

'Why not?' I replied. 'There is nothing here for me and the children.'

'Your parents are here. Your roots are here. I can understand your wanting to move out of the house, but you don't have to travel thousands of miles to do it. Buy a smaller house or rent an apartment in a different suburb. Move into the city, if you like. But California,' he said, leaping out of his chair, 'that's drastic.'

Charlie took two long strides and stood directly above me. He seemed immense, a judgment-day prophet demanding an explanation. I felt that I had no choice, so I told him how the children and I had been treated in Eagles' Landing after you died. I also told him what had happened between me and my parents, how our relationship had deteriorated into polite civility. I struggled to maintain control of myself and spoke in a crisp, passionless voice. Had I allowed emotion to creep into my words, I would not have been able to finish, and I was determined not to cry in front of Charlie.

'So you see,' I concluded, 'there is no reason to stay. The only people I have in the world are Matthew and Catherine. We could live anywhere, and it wouldn't make a difference.'

Charlie returned to his chair and sat forward with his elbows on his knees; he rested his forehead on the palm of one hand. When he finally spoke, he looked up at me with an expression I hadn't seen on his face before. I think it was compassion, but I'm not sure. His voice was kind. 'I had no idea that these things were happening to you,' he said. 'Why didn't you tell me?'

'There was nothing you could have done.'

'I could have spoken to them – to your parents, to those Eagles' Landing cretins who were supposed to be your friends.'

'And what would you have said, Charlie? Would you have told them to be nice to me even though they had lost...'

The ringing telephone interrupted me. It was the first threatening call I received after listing the house. I listened to the caller's vile message, put the receiver down in disgust, and returned to the living room. Charlie knew immediately that something was wrong. 'You're upset,' he said. 'Who was that on the telephone?'

I related the message, word for word.

'Bastards!' Charlie exploded, striding toward the kitchen. 'I'll stop those bastards now.'

I reached the telephone in time to stop him from calling anyone. 'No,' I said, 'leave it alone. I'll be gone soon, and this mess will end.'

'They can't do this,' Charlie bellowed indignantly.

'They can and they will and you can't stop them.'

Charlie put the receiver down; he knew that I was right.

Before he left, Charlie pleaded with me to move someplace other than California. 'I think I understand how you feel,' he said, 'but California is too far. It's too drastic a move.'

'My life has been rather drastic lately,' I replied. 'California may be just the place to finish living it.'

'You're not...' Charlie couldn't say it.

'No, I'm not contemplating suicide,' I assured him. 'I have two children to raise. They need me.'

Charlie's body heaved in a sigh of relief.

In the weeks following that evening, Charlie's attitude toward me changed from polite tolerance to an almost courtly chivalry. I began to wonder, as his calls became more frequent, if Charlie was being solicitous because he felt his best friend's widow needed protection, or if his concern was underwritten with guilt. Until that time, Charlie had made it clear in his handling of the estate that he was concerned about your affairs and your children; the fact that I had been your wife was incidental. Whatever his motivation, protectiveness or guilt, it no longer mattered. I was leaving, and my days were too full to dwell upon Charlie's extended hand of friendship.

After the house was sold and the closing date drew near, I asked Charlie if it was necessary for me to be present when the final papers were signed. I was anxious to be out of Eagles' Landing before the new owners took possession of our house. Charlie told me that he could easily handle the closing himself and that he would bring the deed and other papers for me to sign the evening before I planned to leave. I was so relieved that I forgot Charlie's unspoken rule and thanked him.

'It's nothing,' he insisted. 'Really, it's a common practice. Please don't thank me; it makes me uncomfortable.'

I apologized and didn't speak to him again until the night before we left for California.

My last weeks in Eagles' Landing were dizzy with activity. I arranged for our furniture to be put into storage and supervised its removal, finished packing for California, closed store accounts, contacted utility companies, obtained the children's school and medical records, made arrangements with several banks for the eventual transfer of funds, and, finally, visited your grave. I don't know whether it was due to the strain of my activities or to the soggy afternoon, but I came down with a throat infection the day after I visited the cemetery. I called the children's pediatrician (calling Barney Leadman was unthinkable), and he prescribed an antibiotic which made me feel better within twenty-four hours, although I was told to take the pills for ten days.

Charlie took us out for a quick dinner the night he

brought the papers for me to sign. There was no food in the house; everything was packed and ready for the movers, who were coming in the morning. It was a pleasant dinner. The children were excited about moving, and they talked animatedly. Charlie seemed to enjoy them, but he noticed that I was quiet. 'Is something bothering you?' he asked as we walked back to the car. 'You look awfully pale. If you're having second thoughts about California, it still isn't too late to change your mind.'

'I've prepared the children for California, and we're going,' I replied determinedly. 'I haven't seen them this excited and happy since before Richard died. If I've been quiet, it's probably because I'm tired. The past few weeks have been rough.'

He looked at me thoughtfully. 'You're brittle, so brittle that I've sometimes had the feeling that you could crack into a thousand pieces in front of my eyes.'

'I wouldn't do that to you, Charlie. It would make you uncomfortable,' I said, turning my face away from his so he couldn't see me blinking back tears.

Charlie helped me put the children to bed. He gave Catherine a piggy-back ride upstairs and wrestled playfully with Matthew before tucking him in with surprising tenderness. Charlie gave Matthew a last, lingering look before closing his door, and I'm almost positive that he saw you in your son's face.

I know he saw you, Richard. I could have reached out to touch his pain.

We went downstairs and sat in the family room; the living room and library furniture was already in storage. Charlie gave me the deed to sign, plus some other papers pertaining to the estate. After I finished signing, Charlie checked the papers, then returned them to a large manila legal envelope. 'I guess that's it,' he said. His voice sounded gravelly. 'If you need a lawyer in California, let me know. I have some friends who practice there.'

'I'm sure it won't be necessary. You've handled everything so well. I'm aware of all the work you've done, even if you haven't allowed me to acknowledge it. I appreciate it, Charlie, and I'm grateful.'

Before Charlie became too embarrassed, I went into the kitchen and took your watch out of the cupboard as I had planned, the gold watch your parents gave you when you graduated from Wharton. Charlie was standing when I returned to the family room. I handed him the watch.

'I want you to take this,' I said. 'I want you to have something of Richard's that he cherished. It has nothing to do with the work you've done. The watch belongs to you. It is the only piece of jewelry Richard wore, and he would have wanted you to have it.'

The wafer-thin gold watch rested in Charlie's massive palm. For a moment, I could feel you in the room, your energy, and I could see the watch gleaming against your wrist. Charlie must have felt the electricity of your presence, too. He thrust the watch at me so quickly that it seemed to leap out of his hand.

'I can't take it,' he said. 'The watch belongs to Matthew. Save it for him.'

'No,' I argued, slipping the watch into a pocket of his suit jacket. 'I've thought about this carefully. Richard's watch belongs to you. You don't have to wear it. You can keep it in a drawer if you like, but it's yours.'

'Then what will Matthew have to remember Richard by?' Charlie asked brokenly.

I hadn't considered Matthew. He was so young then, only seven. It would be years before he could wear the watch. By the time he was old enough, he might not associate it with the man who was his father. The realization that you had occupied only a brief period in his life overwhelmed me; Charlie and I would remember that watch on your wrist, but Matthew might not. To my embarrassment and Charlie's dismay, I began to cry. 'I can't argue with you,' I said, weeping. 'Please accept the watch graciously, if not for Richard, then for me.'

I didn't have a handkerchief and started toward the kitchen for a tissue, my face streaked with tears. I could feel their wetness on my blouse, on my hands when I attempted to wipe them away. The tears wouldn't stop. I had never cried in front of anyone before and was anxious to be alone.

'Here,' said Charlie, catching up with me. He held an immaculate white handkerchief in his outstretched hand.

I stared at the handkerchief dumbly, then covered my face with my hands. I don't know what I was thinking, if I was thinking at all, except that I wanted Charlie to leave so I could weep privately. But I couldn't move. I stood as if my feet had been woven into the rug. A wave of fresh sobs racked my body. I felt Charlie's arm around me, his free hand attempting to wipe the tears oozing out between my fingers.

'There, there,' Charlie said sympathetically, as if he were comforting a weeping child.

The tone of his voice was so gentle, yet sad, that I nearly collapsed. Suddenly the weight of that entire year, its loneliness and isolation, hit me physically, and I leaned toward Charlie feeling that I had been struck. Charlie put his arms around me. I could feel one of his enormous hands holding my head, the other rubbing my back soothingly.

'It's all right, Jenny,' he crooned. 'It's all right.'

I honestly don't know quite how it happened, how Charlie's comforting croons became sounds of love. All I know is that he was holding me, and I could feel his loneliness knit with mine. Charlie was warm, and he was holding me, and I hadn't been held in such a long time. I recall being vaguely aware that his tie and shirt were soaked with my tears. And I also remember feeling his growing hardness against my body and it seemed natural, so I didn't move away; neither did Charlie. I uncovered my face and felt Charlie's lips on my forehead, my cheeks, my mouth. My body began to respond with a hollow ache to Charlie's moving hands. There were tears, there was comfort, and then there was Charlie making love to me. And me responding.

The rest is a shadow. I don't remember walking to the

sofa or how I got undressed; it just happened. Charlie and I were on the sofa, we were naked, and he was in me, huge and insistent, and then we were coming with such intensity that both of us lay afterward in exhaustion, physically and emotionally spent.

I don't know how long we lay there, but it was for a long time because the skin on my inner thigh felt tight where Charlie's semen had trickled out and dried. Nor can I tell you what I was thinking. I was afraid to think, afraid to speak, so I concentrated on listening to Charlie's even breathing and waited. When his voice finally cut into the silence it was deep and tight, as if chained with emotion. 'I hadn't intended that anything like this should happen. I feel as if, as if . . .' He couldn't say it.

I understood. 'You feel as if you have betrayed Richard,' I whispered. 'So do I.'

'It was my fault,' he said with remorse. 'I was always afraid something like this might happen one day.'

I was flabbergasted and propped myself up on one elbow so I could see Charlie's face. He stared straight ahead.

'I thought you didn't like me, Charlie. If you had worn a sign hanging around your neck all of these years, the message couldn't have come through any clearer.'

'That's not true.' He paused, then turned his head to face me. Charlie's eyes were moist, the color of spring grass. 'There was something about you. It's difficult to explain.'

'Try,' I said.

'When we were younger and I saw Richard with you, he was so happy – so wildly happy. Richard was my first and best friend. I could almost understand what he was feeling because I knew him so well, but understanding another person's emotion isn't feeling it. I wanted to know that happiness myself; I wanted to feel it the way I saw Richard feeling it.

'There were girls, a lot of girls in college, but I never felt that way with them. I kept looking for the girl, the special girl who could give me that feeling of wild happiness, but

271

I never found her. I tried so hard that I ended up making a mistake. I still don't know why I married Doreen, unless it was because the weather was so terrific in the Bahamas that week, and I imagined that I was in paradise.'

'But you didn't like me,' I repeated.

'It isn't that I didn't like you,' he said. 'It's just that I had some reservations. I am that way. The only person in the world I never had reservations about was Richard. And when I couldn't find a special girl of my own, I guess I subconsciously thought that the one person in the world who was able to give that wild happiness was you.'

'Richard and I weren't always wildly happy,' I said, suppressing a wave of sudden bitterness.

'I know, but you were happy for a long time. Some people aren't that happy for more than five minutes out of their entire lives.'

I started to cry again.

'Please don't,' Charlie pleaded. 'I have to talk to you, and I can't if you're crying.'

I tried to stop but couldn't. Finally, between sobs, I told Charlie that I was going to take a shower and go to bed.

'But we have to talk,' he said. 'There is something we have to consider.'

'What?' I asked, sobbing while I gathered up my clothes.

'We didn't . . . we didn't take precautions,' he said.

Cautious Charlie's meaning drifted through my tears. 'I still have my loop,' I managed to say before going upstairs. Those were the last words I spoke to him.

Charlie must have left while I was showering, for I didn't hear the front door close or his car engine start. I went to bed and slept better than I had in months. In the morning, Matthew found your watch lying on the kitchen counter. He held it up curiously. 'W-W-W-Whose watch is this?' he asked. 'Un-Un-Un-Uncle Charlie's?'

'It's yours, Matthew,' I said, 'when you grow up.'

The telephone rang as I was closing our front door in Eagles' Landing for the last time, but I didn't answer it, so

I don't know if it was Charlie. We were behind schedule, and I wanted to begin driving while there was enough daylight to cover several hundred miles.

By the time we reached Chicago, I was a mess. I had foul vaginal discharge the color and consistency of spoiled cottage cheese and an excruciating itch that was constant. If I hadn't been driving, I would have torn myself raw. Unable to sit behind the steering wheel for another minute, I stopped and hunted through a telephone directory, praying that Chicago had physicians listed under specialties the way they are listed in the East. I was lucky. I bought the children ice cream cones and started calling gynecologists until I found one who would take me immediately.

The drive to the doctor's office was hell. I was positive that I had venereal disease, and I was alternately cursing Charlie, myself, and providence for meting out such an awful punishment. Then I thought of you and what I had done and how deserving I was to be so cursed. It serves you right, I thought to myself, it serves you right.

I almost fainted when I saw the doctor. He was young – my age – and attractive. All I could tell him was that I was from out of town and that I itched. I don't believe I have ever felt so humiliated, and when he started to examine me to get a sample of the discharge (forgive me), I wanted to die. I also wanted to scream because I was raw. I clutched the sides of the examining table and willed my feet to stay in the stirrups. After he finished, he apologized for hurting me and disappeared with the smear he had taken.

'Have you taken an antibiotic recently?' he asked when he returned.

I thought he had lost his mind. Then I remembered. 'I just finished taking an antibiotic for a throat infection,' I said.

'You have monilia, Mrs Weaver. It is a fungus disease frequently triggered by the use of antibiotics, and it is tough to eradicate but does respond well to conscientious treatment. I am going to give you prescriptions for pills, an external ointment, and vaginal suppositories. If you use them faithfully, especially the pills and suppositories, you should get rid of it; the ointment is to soothe and protect your skin. But I would suggest that you check with a doctor at a later date to have another smear taken. You will want to make sure that it is gone.'

I shall never forget a word that doctor said; his was a message of deliverance. No matter how uncomfortable or unpleasant the disease, and it was indescribable, monilia was not V.D., and I was not being punished for what I had done.

Or was I, Richard? Dammit, I wish you could answer.

After we arrived in California, I tried to forget Charlie, but I couldn't. I kept returning to that night, and I don't know why. It could have been my loneliness or my guilt, but Charlie was there, and he was hard to live with. The past is hard to live with; it crouches like a wild animal in the underbrush of the present, ready to pounce, and I am afraid that I will be devoured if I relax my guard for an instant.

I haven't seen or spoken with Charlie since we left. If he has been in California, he hasn't called me, and I am glad for that. I honestly don't know what I would do or say if I did see him again. What either of us would say. We don't correspond, but he did send me the papers and a check from the closing with a note attached saying that he hoped we were well. There have been a few papers since with similar notes. Whenever I have returned anything to him or written for information, I have assured him that we are fine. For now, I like the distance between us, and if it is kept, perhaps the past will eventually die.

The children will be awake soon. I have been up all night writing and remembering – you, me, and Charlie – and have felt the pull between us as it once was. Believe me, I found nothing, not a clue in Charlie's behavior or mine, to indicate that we would betray you. It simply happened.

We were thrust together by circumstance, by your death and our subsequent loneliness and vulnerability. Life can be that way, Richard. It isn't always reasonable, and no philosopher, lawyer, or CPA, living or dead, can make it reasonable. If Charlie did harbor thoughts about me, they were well-suppressed; you were the one he loved, the one who mattered. You were his best friend, and Charlie would never have done anything intentionally to hurt you or your memory. I imagine he has suffered more from that night than I have, and I have suffered. Perhaps it will satisfy you, if you need satisfaction, to know that we have paid.

I haven't written to you since Tuesday; that all-night session drained me. I went back to bed after the children left for school on Wednesday and slept until noon. When I realized how far behind I was, I decided to put an end to this nocturnal correspondence. Wednesday isn't a free day, Richard. I put our life in order on Wednesdays. I know it never meant much to you – the grocery shopping, the laundry, the cleaning, the errands – the dull, necessary chores that make life comfortable. I used to wonder how you managed in college, fending for yourself. I should have asked. After we were married, I watched you open your bureau drawers each morning, expecting to find them filled with clean shirts, underwear, and socks. You never stopped to think, not once, about how they got there. Here's a hint: the good fairy didn't put them there.

Yet here I am, writing to you. I need to talk. This written communication isn't exactly talking, and it certainly is one-sided, but it is all that is available to me. I hadn't thought of that before: death has made you available. When you were alive, we were seldom alone together. If you weren't working, you were at a meeting, or I was at a meeting, or we were out as a couple in the company of others. Now I can understand why some people habitually visit gravesites. The dead remain where they are placed; they can't escape or protest.

Last night I went with Deirdre to her consciousness-raising group meeting. I could have avoided going. Nat Witton called on Tuesday, excited because he had managed to get tickets for Thursday evening to a sell-out production of *Hedda Gabler*. Deirdre would have understood had I accepted Nat's invitation, but I refused him. The play, with its multiple suicides, does not appeal to me no matter who is acting in it or how skilled the performance. I have known the real thing and that is enough, thank you. However, I didn't say that to Nat. Instead, I told him I was sorry, but I had another commitment. He seemed disappointed and a bit surprised. Then he asked me if I were busy on the weekend. I said I was free, and we are going out tomorrow night.

Later, I thought about my mother's two-day rule and wondered if my unavailability on Thursday led to an early invitation for Saturday. I also started to wonder about the anonymous woman he would take to the play, if she were attractive and good company. But then I remembered my promise and began writing to you, forgetting her, Nat, and the play. Perhaps I was being compensated for telling you about Charlie.

I must discuss what happened at the consciousness-raising group meeting. Last night I walked out of a woman's apartment with Deirdre feeling confused and angry. Something unexpected happened that I can neither accept nor understand.

Deirdre's nervousness was as visible as fresh fingerprints on a highly polished table, so I suggested that we go out for coffee instead. 'I'm not trying to avoid going,' I told her as we drove to the meeting. 'Honestly, I'm not. But I think this idea of yours is crazy. How can you tell a room full of women about your rape, and what can they possibly do for you after you tell them? I've read that consciousness-raising groups can be dangerous, even when they're run by professionals. You're taking an awful risk; you'll be reliving that night all over again.'

'I'm reliving it now – every day – and I'll continue to relive it until the threat is gone.'

'The group can't remove either the threat or the memory.'

'You have to see how a consciousness-raising group works,' she said. 'The women help each other by sharing their experience and perspective. It's a collective effort toward understanding.'

I couldn't argue. Deirdre was determined to attend, but she did make one remark that puzzled me. She mentioned that she'd have to speak up immediately. Later, I understood why.

We were the last to arrive, so if there was any beforehand chatting, we missed it. Everyone – twelve women including Deirdre and myself – sat in the living room of a modest apartment in an irregular circle. There were glasses, a large pitcher of sangria, and assorted cheeses on a coffee table. I noticed that only one of the women wore a wedding band, and it may have been my imagination, but as each woman spoke to me, I had the distinct impression that she held a definite position within the group. It seemed that there was a pecking order among the women, for they introduced themselves randomly rather than naturally following each other around the circle.

An intense, sloe-eyed brunette named Monica, who was the first of the group to introduce herself, opened the discussion. 'It's not a topic night, so anyone who would like to begin, can.'

I glanced sideways at Deirdre. Her mouth was open and ready to speak when the woman wearing the wedding band, who was as small and slender as an eleven-year-old child, released a torrent of words in a single breath. 'You won't believe this, but Hal destroyed all of my poems, every single one of them,' she said, thrusting her tiny body forward as if to block any interruption.

The air was instantly filled with clucks of sympathy, and several women murmured 'Oh, no' and 'Poor Nikki.'

Nikki sat back in her chair, now sure of the group's attention, and continued. 'He came home from work and found me writing. "When's dinner?" he wanted to know. "I have a tennis game at seven. I told you this morning."

'It was close to six o'clock, and I hadn't started cooking. I forgot about his goddamn tennis match. I couldn't help it. The meat was thawing on the dish rack, and I was washing lettuce when I had the inspiration for a poem.'

She closed her eyes and began to recite:

> The meat bleeds its last crimson drops
> And the lettuce weeps in sympathy;
> String beans lie like fresh green spears
> Waiting it appears
> To puncture ripe tomatoes clustered
> In innocent repose,
> The chambers of a heart.

I can't quote the rest of the poem, but the gist of it was war in the kitchen with the poet, Nikki, as its intended victim. Frankly, I thought the poem was awful. The group, however, seemed to love it. Their praise was lavish, the consensus seeming to be that Nikki had captured the essence of a housewife's antagonistic environment.

I listened silently, inwardly smirking at the women's reactions. How ridiculous it was that eleven women could believe vegetables were out to get them, I thought. But when their comments took the poem out of the kitchen and into a world filled with inanimate, threatening objects, I remembered the grandfather clock in Eagles' Landing. Oh, how I had despised that clock! Then their remarks began to make sense to me, and I decided that there was something to consciousness-raising.

It was a premature decision.

Encouraged by their praise, Nikki continued. Her small, pointed face expanded with anger. 'Hal started yelling when I tried to explain that it was absolutely necessary to write the poem as soon as it came to me. "The muse," I said, "comes unexpectedly."

'"The hell with the muse," he yelled. "I was expected. If I brought home an unexpected guest, you'd sulk about it for days, but you think nothing of catering to an unexpected muse when I'm due on the tennis court at seven."

'He absolutely refused to understand and went upstairs. I thought he was changing for tennis until I heard the toilet flushing over and over again. By the time I got up there, it was too late. He had taken all of my poems, every one of them, and had torn them to shreds. He was sprinkling them into the toilet bowl, a handful at a time, and flushing when I caught him. "Stop," I screamed, pushing him away. The entire wastebasket overturned into the toilet, and the goddamn thing overflowed.

'"See," he said, "even the sewer rejects your poems".'

Nikki began to weep. 'Two years of work,' she cried, 'gone. He even destroyed my copies. I'm going to leave him.' She wrenched her wedding band off her finger and threw it into the middle of the room.

Three women walked over to Nikki to comfort her. Monica cleared her throat to get everyone's attention. I noticed that her eyes, which were heavily outlined with charcoal, sparkled with excitement. 'We're all familiar with Hal's treatment of Nikki,' she said. 'He has consistently refused to recognize her as an artist, as a creative individual who must express herself outside the narrow boundaries of marriage. Instead, Hal wants the traditional housekeeper-whore relationship that has silenced women's voices for centuries. I think the topic for tonight should be woman as artist.'

Monica looked around the room to see if the others were in agreement. Nikki continued to weep, Deirdre sat woodenly, and I avoided Monica's eyes. What she said and how she said it had made me uncomfortable. The tone of her voice was caustic, and she dismissed Nikki's marriage as if it were an afternoon soap opera with low ratings that was doomed to cancellation. (Deirdre told me later that woman as artist is Monica's favorite topic. She has had two husbands and written four unpublished novels, the failure of which she blames on her husbands for stifling her creativity.)

Everyone was momentarily silent, so I assumed that Monica's suggestion was accepted. Nikki dried her tears, and the discussion began. It continued nonstop under Monica's direction until a sandyhaired, attractive woman in her late twenties named Thalia asked: 'How will you survive if you divorce Hal, Nikki? The group has all agreed that alimony is out of the question unless it is absolutely necessary, as in Deirdre's case, and I've heard you say, time after time, that you wouldn't accept a penny from Hal if you left him. How will you live? You don't have any practical skills.'

'I'm an artist,' Nikki replied haughtily, but the pinched look returned to her face.

'Practicalities aren't topics for discussion, Thalia,' warned Monica. 'We agreed upon that. It's in the rules.'

'We've been ignoring the rules for months,' Thalia retorted. 'Nikki can't sleep on the freeway, and she has to eat. Even artists need calories.'

I mentally aligned myself with Thalia and waited in anticipation for what promised to be a knockout battle when Deirdre stood up. 'I have something to say.' Her voice was barely audible.

'You don't have to stand up,' said Monica, taken off balance. 'Besides, it's against the rules.'

Deirdre ignored her and walked to the center of the room, accidentally stepping on Nikki's wedding band. 'I was raped,' she said, just loud enough to be heard. The women all stared at her in shock; Nikki slumped in her chair like a marionette whose strings have been cut. Clearly, this would not be Nikki's night.

Deirdre explained what happened without going into detail, and I sensed a communal flow of sympathy rush toward her from every woman in the room. When she finished, Deirdre sat wearily on the floor. 'Please help me. Please. I must do something. I have to keep him away, but I can't because of Kerry. What will I do?' she asked, weeping.

I got up to help her back to her seat, but it was impossible. The women had surrounded Deirdre, all but Nikki and Monica, who remained where they were. The comfort she was receiving seemed to increase her sobbing rather than diminish it, so I walked over to the coffee table, poured sangria into a glass, and pushed my way through the wall of women. 'Drink this, Deirdre,' I ordered.

Deirdre took the glass and began to drink automatically; the women returned to their original places around the circle. Then the discussion began and that, Richard, is what I want to talk about. I can't remember what every woman said specifically, so I won't even try. But I do know what happened generally. Or what I think happened. I'm still not sure.

As I said, there was an overwhelming rush of sympathy toward Deirdre after she told the group she had been raped, and when the discussion began, it was clear that everyone knew Deirdre's personal history. An auburn-haired woman named Trudy said Ken Jamison had always been a bastard and agreed that he was capable of raping Deirdre again. 'Castration is too good for him,' she said, seething. 'Instead, they should cut his cock off. Completely off.' She made a downward chopping motion with her hand.

If 'they,' whoever 'they' were, wouldn't do it, I was sure that Trudy would.

Someone named Gail suggested that Deirdre seduce Ken, then call the police to accuse him of rape. The group turned on Gail in unison, and she apologized. 'I'm sorry,' she said, redfaced. 'It was a stupid idea.' Another woman suggested hiring an attorney to cut Ken's visitation rights, and Deirdre explained why she felt that was impossible. Even if she had agreed, she didn't have the money. A blonde named Salina told Deirdre to move without leaving a forwarding address. That suggestion was also rejected.

The discussion continued in the same vein for approximately ten minutes, everyone concentrating on Deirdre, until Monica interrupted. 'What we should talk about,' she said, 'is rape.'

'Yes,' someone agreed. 'What it all boils down to is RAPE.'

I wondered what 'it' was, and I didn't have to wait long to find out. Ten women began to speak simultaneously. There were no rules. There were no turns. There was no order. Instead, there was rape. Not Deirdre's rape, but a collective rape with every woman in that room feeling herself a victim. And rape grew into the shape of a man, any man and every man, known and unknown, until it became a metaphor, the violation of an entire society upon half of its population.

The women talked. They talked and talked, but no one listened to anyone else. There were ten women in that room who were talking to themselves, so absorbed in what they were saying that any pretense of talking to each other was totally abandoned. And the things they were saying! I still cannot believe what they were saying. I caught intimate fragments the women tossed out of their individual lives that astonished me – sexual intimacies, personal and financial disappointments, jagged pieces of unfulfilled dreams – a cornucopia of female intimacies in a room where intimacy was an illusion. It had to be an illusion. There can be no intimacy without communication, and the women in that room were all talking without communicating.

Deirdre, who had remained seated in the center of the room, stood up. 'Please,' she said in an anguished voice. 'I need your help.'

No one listened to her because no one was listening.

Deirdre's body tensed with frustration. 'LISTEN TO ME,' she screamed. 'I WAS THE ONE WHO WAS RAPED.'

The women stopped talking resentfully.

'Couldn't we talk about me?' Deirdre asked half-apologetically, now sure of their attention.

'Why you?' asked Trudy. 'At least you know *your* rapist. What about us?'

Everyone murmured in agreement.

I stared at the women in disbelief. They're crazy, I thought. 'Come on, Deirdre,' I said, walking over to her. 'Let's get out of here before rapists start crawling out from underneath the rug.'

We left unnoticed; everyone had resumed talking.

I mentally questioned whether Deirdre would be able to drive home, but there was no reason to be concerned. Instead of the sobbing I expected, Deirdre started swearing the moment we closed the apartment door behind us. I have never heard anyone swear like that before, so creatively and imaginatively. Without realizing what I was doing, I applauded. Deirdre stopped walking and turned to look at me. 'What the hell are you doing that for?'

I told her.

'Didn't you know,' she said, imitating a brogue, 'that the Irish are goddamn poets?'

Then she became serious. 'We're not like that titfaced Nikki and her pissing vegetables. We have real problems, we always have, but all we have ever been able to do about them is curse. And drink. My father drank; his nose was as red as one of Nikki's tomatoes. That man was miserable. Dammit,' she said, stamping her foot. 'I'm not going to grow old with a red nose, singing my father's curses.'

'What are you going to do, then?'

'I don't know. I thought I could get help from the group, but I should have known better.'

'How could you have known? You were so sure they would help you.'

'I was fooling myself. What happened tonight has happened before. The last time it occurred was when Thalia was undecided about having an abortion. The meeting ended in chaos, as it did tonight. That's when we adopted our new set of rules. What a joke those rules are! We're on our third set, and none of them works. The only time they're used is when someone wants to shut someone else up, and if the talker is strong, they're ignored anyway.'

We stopped for coffee, and I waited for Deirdre to say something about Trudy's remark that at least she knew her rapist, but Deirdre didn't mention it. Nor did she seem to feel that it was unusual for everyone to be talking at once with no one listening. Finally, I broached the subject. 'No one was really listening to anyone else,' I said.

Deirdre looked at me shrewdly. 'Do you really believe they weren't listening to each other?'

'It was obvious.'

'But they were listening. They were comparing their own suffering.'

'They were talking,' I insisted. 'They weren't listening.'

'Sure they were. They were doing the same thing old people do when they compare their operations. You could get a dozen together, all hard of hearing, who had the same operation, and they could all be talking at once, but each one would know exactly how many stitches the other one had. You can bet on it,' she said positively.

'How can you be sure?'

'Because things each woman said will come out in other meetings. It's happened before.'

'Then why didn't they seem to recognize each other?'

'They hadn't finished talking.'

I assumed Deirdre would drop out of the group, but she was undecided. 'Someone will call to apologize, probably Trudy. I might go back some day,' she said.

'How could you after tonight?'

'Part of it was my fault. I expected too much from them. I knew what might happen, but I didn't want to acknowledge it. They aren't bad people. They're just . . . people,' Deirdre said, throwing her hands into the air for lack of a better explanation.

By the time we pulled into Sherwood Village, Deirdre was calm. She was almost herself, the old before-the-rape Deirdre, although I know she'll never be quite the same again. There is a wariness about her that wasn't there before. But her powers of observation are keener than ever. As I got out of the car, she said, 'I think that meeting tonight upset you more than it did me.'

'Oh, no,' I protested. 'I was upset *for* you.'

'Are you sure?' she asked skeptically.

'Absolutely sure,' I replied, so unstrung that I forgot to ask her who the two lesbians were.

The babysitter told me that my mother had called while I was out. She answered on the first ring when I returned her call, as if she had been waiting by the telephone. Her voice sounded different – older, it seemed to me – and she was more snappish than usual. When she asked where I had been and I told her, she said: 'You're becoming a real California kook, aren't you, Jennifer?' I was so irritated that I cut the conversation short and didn't bother to ask her what her problem was, not that she would have told me. My mother follows her own rules, and keeping one's problems to oneself is as important as never crying in the presence of others. It is impossible to imagine her in a consciousness-raising group. If she did stumble into one, she would give no more than her name, and that only grudgingly.

An unpleasant thought: I must be like my mother, for I didn't contribute anything to that meeting except my name.

I spent a disproportionate amount of time in the public rooms at Briarhill today, hoping to hear a group of the residents expounding on their ills. I wanted to believe what Deirdre said, that people talking simultaneously were capable of listening. But I had no luck. The only group I found that wasn't sitting in the apathetic silence of the institutionalized aged was complaining about the fish at lunch. 'It was putrid,' said one resident. 'Vile,' said another. 'They should give us lobster every day for the prices they charge,' complained another. Then they got up and walked away from Mr Nowicki, a sad-faced man who was complaining that the fish gave him gas. 'You haven't stopped farting since you came to Briarhill,' said Mr Crandall, a potbellied, red-nosed man in his eighties whose favorite subject is America for Americans. 'You've got so much gas you should donate it to the government. Present yourself at the Pentagon in Washington, Nowicki. One whiff and they'll know what they've got. They'll ship you over to Russia and clear out the entire country, even Siberia, in a matter of days. Do you realize what that would mean? I could breathe fresh air in my old age, and my son could save on taxes because there would be no more need for a defense budget.'

The aged can be cruel. They have no place to vent their frustrations, so they take their unhappiness out on each other, particularly those like Mr Crandall, who, according to the staff, hasn't had a visitor in over a year.

'Just people,' Deirdre said. Then why don't I understand what happened at that meeting last night? The women in the group weren't different from me. Our backgrounds may not be the same, but every woman in that room was a woman alone as I am. How could they have taken Deirdre's rape and made it theirs? And how could each one hear what the others were saying if everyone was talking? Yet Deirdre insists that they did hear each other, and the fact that they identified with her rape didn't seem to faze her. Am I lacking somehow? Am I so insensitive that I am incapable of identifying with another human being? God, how awful if that is true.

But I did have compassion for Deirdre when she was raped. I still do. And I can recall that night, being so angry that I could have killed. The answer cannot be identification alone.

The women were all suffering, or they felt that they were suffering. That much I know. They each drew buckets full of pain from individual wells. Then why didn't they even pretend to recognize each other? Or did they recognize each other by not recognizing each other? Was it really a competition? Were they all saying: 'If you think you have suffered, listen to me, for I have really suffered?' Is that it?

That must be it: no one suffers like the sufferer. The pain we feel most is our own. Then Deirdre's rape must have been almost academic to them. They felt sorry for her, but in the end, they felt much sorrier for themselves.

I do know something about feeling sorry for oneself, Richard. There have been times these past few years when I have made a career of it. I am no better than they are.

Actually, I am worse. The night you told me we could no longer afford to live in Eagles' Landing, I behaved like the women in the consciousness-raising group. So did you. We recited our petty grievances and major disappointments, each blaming the other, both talking at once, until I fled the room. I was the one who ran. I was still running when I insisted, a month later, that we go to Florida.

The trip was my idea. 'If we go to Florida,' I argued when we resumed speaking to each other after two weeks of silence, 'we'll be able to save face. Our tans will give us credibility when we tell everyone we're moving because the house is too large for us. They know Ginny rests more than she works, and I can start complaining about cleaning up after the cleaning woman before we leave. We can say that our vacation gave us a new perspective on life – that we no longer want to live as encumbered as we have been – and be believed.'

You didn't want to go. 'The country is in the middle of an oil crisis,' you said. 'Haven't you heard about the embargo? What if we run out of gas in a godforsaken place in Alabama and find all of the gasoline pumps empty? I sure as hell don't intend to walk, and we can't afford plane tickets, even if we could get them. You're using Florida as a stall. You still haven't called a realtor, and if you don't call one within a day or two, I'll call myself.'

'No, you won't,' I said firmly, 'not until we come back.

You owe me that much. And we won't run out of gas. You can't believe everything you read in the newspapers.'

Actually, I wasn't sure that we would be able to buy gasoline, but I was determined to go anyway. The two weeks of silence after our blow-up had left me shaken. I was frightened, not only because of our precarious financial position, but because my life wasn't what I had imagined it to be: our marriage, our security, all of the things I had believed in were an illusion. It is a shock to be told in a few minutes that the life you are living is no longer possible, that it is nothing but a dream to be postponed until a later date. I am not saying that it was easier for you, but you did have the advantage of foreknowledge. You were braced for bad news; I wasn't.

The two weeks gave me my first lesson in silence. I learned to gauge the varying degrees of your daily anger, the stages of your withdrawal, the effect of our lack of sex upon you, the wordless intimations you sent out like sonar that indicated a willingness toward reconciliation.

I also learned something about myself. The silence showed me with no uncertainty that I was alone. You had Charlie to talk to, but I had no one. Discussing what had happened to us with anyone in Eagles' Landing would have been inconceivable, and going to my parents was out of the question. I knew that I would be unable to handle their predictable reactions, my father's smug justification for his years of probing questions concerning your finances, and my mother's disappointment in our fall from grace. We had eased out of our relationships with pre-Eagles' Landing friends, so my list of people to confide in was blank.

But by far, the worst lesson the silence taught me was the reading of my own emotions. I came to understand that it was hate that had made me flee the room the night we fought, and to hate the single person in the world with whom I could talk was more than I could bear. That is why I wanted to go to Florida, Richard. I was scared. The trip was a desperate hope, a chance to save our marriage.

We didn't want anyone in Eagles' Landing to know that we were driving to Florida or that we were staying rent-free in Sarasota with Aunt Maggie, so it was sticky when Ike Springer offered to drive us to the airport. You thanked him and refused, but Ike kept insisting. 'It will be my pleasure,' he said. 'You don't want to leave one of your cars in the airport parking lot for ten days, especially not the Mercedes. Besides, Jenny drove Molly and me to the airport when we went to Aruba. I'd like to return the favor.'

You shot me an angry look for placing you in an uncomfortable position, so I interceded and explained that my father had already offered to drive us. Then I realized that I would also have to excuse your missing car. 'Richard will be leaving his car at the dealer's for some minor adjustments. It isn't too far from my father's business,' I said, releasing you and satisfying Ike at the same time.

'I wondered how you were going to get out of that one,' you whispered later with grudging admiration.

'You underestimate me,' I replied.

We left before daybreak on a Saturday morning with a full tank of gas. Our drive to Florida was mostly silent. You kept your eyes on the road and the gas gauge, and when you did talk, it was to tell me approximately how many gallons of gas we had left. I knew you were waiting to find a gas station with empty fuel pumps so you could say 'I told you so.' I kept quiet, alternately praying for fuel and cursing Arabs, which occupied me until we reached Georgia. Then I started to relax and began to think about Aunt Maggie. She was my favorite relative, the only adult I could recall from my childhood who seemed sincerely interested in me as a person. Mother detested her, but I could never figure out why unless it was because she was my father's sister. Mother did not discriminate where Father's family was concerned; she detested every member equally. If Maggie had an edge on the others, it was because Linda and I adored her so openly. The few times Mother overcame her dislike occurred when she was having problems with Linda. Then she called Maggie to ask if Linda could come for a visit. Maggie never refused.

I started sharing my memories of Maggie with you when we crossed the Florida state line. I told childhood stories of Maggie taking Linda and me to circuses, plays, and tea rooms to have our fortunes read. Maggie liked circuses best and always tried to plan her visits, which were between husbands, when a circus was in town. We never left without having our programs autographed by center-ring performers, and one year she was able to finagle a ride for us on an elephant. It was the high point of my childhood. You ignored the gas gauge and laughed until you had to wipe tears from your eyes when I described Mother's reaction to our zoo smells when Maggie brought us home.

As we approached Sarasota, I forgot the reason we were in Florida and became anxious to see Maggie. When I had called to ask if we could come for a visit, her honest delight left me feeling guilty for the occasional spare letters I had written to her over the years. She hadn't traveled north since the death of her third husband, and I realized with regret that Matthew and Catherine hadn't met her; they knew her only through the Christmas toys she sent them each year. Maggie invariably selected their favorite presents. She always remembered me, too. Every year there was a special gift that was perfect for that moment in my life. Maggie had sent me my first makeup kit, my first grown-up nightgown, my first piece of real jewelry, a delicate gold bracelet which I shall give to Catherine when she is ten, the age I was when Maggie gave it to me. Her latest gift had been a Baccarat perfume bottle with a note that read:

To Jenny—
It is time to start your own collection so that when you are as old as I am, the gleam of crystal on your dressing table will divert your attention from the mirror above. One can never be over prepared!

Love as always,
Maggie

I smiled for the first time that Christmas day.

I was taken aback when I saw Maggie, unprepared for the change in her appearance. Although she was still a stunning woman – tall and fully fleshed without being heavy, and elegantly, if a bit flamboyantly, dressed – her tanned skin was deeply creased and her stylishly cropped hair was completely white. I noticed a slight tremor in her body when she held me in her usual ebullient greeting and remembered with dismay that she was twelve years older than my father. She's seventy, I thought. It didn't seem possible. Maggie was the youngest adult I had ever known. Seeing her as a white-haired, trembling matron was more than disconcerting; it was a change in image so drastic that mortality became real to me.

Maggie held you, too. 'I can't wait until I get to know you better, Richard,' she said. 'Any man who can capture my Jenny and hang on to her for as long as you have must be the world's greatest charmer.' I could tell by your expression when she took your arm and led you to the terrace for a welcoming drink that you had completely succumbed to Maggie's magic.

The terrace was as magnificent as the rest of the house. Maggie must have noted our admiration for her home when she took us to our room, which was in a separate wing complete with bath, dressing room, and a direct entrance to the beach. 'My last husband was the most financially comfortable of the three,' Maggie said with her usual candor after we were settled with our drinks. 'Walter had a knack for buying the right properties. It was a lucky thing, because he had an aversion to work. This house was Walter's wedding gift.' She squinted at the encroaching condominiums and highrise office buildings in the distance. 'Sometimes I'm glad he didn't live to see the mess they are making out of the Longboat and Lido Keys. Walter did so love the beach. My latest friend is different from Walter. I can't seem to convince him that too many buildings will spoil the land. You'll meet Anson tonight; he's coming for dinner. Anson is a compulsive builder. I've accused him of having had a deprived childhood, although he denies it. Once I bought him building blocks as a joke. "Play with these, Anson," I said, "and leave the land alone."'

Maggie sighed and gazed at the ocean. 'As much as I love life, there are times when I'm glad that I'll be gone before those damn buildings cast their shadows on my beach.'

My first impression of Anson Schuyler was different from yours. For a man in his early seventies, he was vigorous and attractive – broad-shouldered with a full head of wavy, steel-gray hair – but there was something about him, a sleekness that was too polished to be real. His dress, manners, and conversation were so impeccable that his smoothness began to rankle me before the dinner was half over. I began wishing that he would accidentally spill his wine on the Madeira tablecloth or catch a piece of meat between his irregularly spaced front teeth or burp aloud, anything to take the gloss off his sleek exterior, but Anson didn't oblige me. Nor was he unobservant. He noticed my aloofness and winked at me several times, as if to say, 'relax and enjoy the party.'

I never knew whether you liked Anson or not, but you were fascinated with the very qualities about him that irritated me. 'He could be the original prototype of the perfect salesman,' you commented when we were in bed. 'I didn't think men like Anson Schuyler existed anymore. He makes the corporate hustlers I know look like unpolished schoolboys.'

'Then why did you agree to go to Orlando with him? You accepted his invitation for both of us without asking me if I wanted to go. I don't like Anson Schuyler.'

'Come on, Jenny,' you said, rubbing my back, 'it's our vacation, probably the last one we'll have for a long time. We haven't seen Disney World. Everyone who has been there raves about it. It'll be fun, and we can check it out for the children. When things improve, we'll take them.'

Then: 'Did you notice his disappointment when Maggie politely shooed him out the door at ten thirty? Anson Schuyler expected more than dinner tonight.'

I had been thinking the same thing. 'Yes,' I said. 'It made me uncomfortable.'

'Why? Sex doesn't stop at sixty, or didn't your mother tell you about that, either? I'm going to make sure that Catherine knows everything by the time she's ten or eleven, otherwise some unscrupulous boy will give her the education of her life.'

'Like the one you gave me?'

'Yes,' you said, laughing. 'Now let's see if you can remember all of your lessons.'

After we returned from Orlando, I should have recalled what you said. Not about Catherine's sex education. About Anson Schuyler being the prototype of the perfect salesman. But I didn't.

We drove to Orlando in Anson's black Lincoln Continental. Aunt Maggie bowed out at the last minute; she felt the trip might be too much for her. I had noticed Maggie taking pills surreptitiously, and when I asked her what they were for, she explained: 'I've been having a little problem with my heart. It doesn't keep a beat like it used to. The doctors say it's from too many cigarettes when I was younger, forty-six years' worth. I quit last year, which helped some, but I should have done it long ago. You'd better quit, too, Jenny. Promise me that you will. It's the only thing I'll ever ask of you.'

It was the first and last time Maggie made a request of me. She seemed so concerned that I impulsively promised her I would quit.

'When?' she asked, clearly pleased.

'Today,' I replied, regretting the word as soon as it was out of my mouth.

'Wonderful!' Maggie said, beaming.

The ride to Orlando wasn't wonderful. I sat alone in the

back seat suffering from nicotine withdrawal symptoms and dreaming of cigarettes while you and Anson talked. I didn't listen to your conversation because I was busy chewing sugarless gum and consuming hard candies by the mouthful when I wasn't poking through Anson's ashtrays hoping to find a decent-sized butt. One ashtray held a crumpled Tums wrapper; the other contained a chewed cigar butt, several burned matches, a bobby pin, and what appeared to be ashes from a pipe. You glanced back at me occasionally to see how I was doing, but my cheeks were as full as a chipmunk's, packed with candy and gum, so I could only wave and grimace.

I was surprised when we stopped at a newly constructed and obviously unoccupied hotel. 'We're not staying here?' I asked after removing a wad of gum from my mouth.

'Weren't you listening, Jenny? This is Anson's latest motel,' you said.

'And my last,' interjected Anson. 'It's time to retire.'

The motel was more like a hotel, a massive six-story building constructed of smooth white concrete and decorative stone. A portico with a mansard-style roof leading to the glass front doors jutted out like an afterthought. The strong smell of fresh blacktop permeated the late afternoon air.

'We're behind schedule,' Anson said. 'I had hoped to be finished in time for this winter's tourist season and didn't make it. That's why I'm not putting up another building. It's become too difficult. Years ago I didn't have the union problems I have today. There were skilled men who could read blueprints and use their heads. Today workers are concerned with their Blue Cross benefits and the length of their lunch hours. They're prima donnas with absolutely no concept of what a schedule means; as long as their money isn't tied up, they don't care. This motel is a sure winner, but I'm going to sell it rather than run it myself as I had originally planned. It was going to be something to fiddle with in my old age, a form of longevity insurance. A man needs a business to keep him occupied. But this building will always remind me of the aggravation I had putting it up, and that will do me in quicker than retirement.'

Anson led us around the grounds. He showed us the landscaping plans, the oversized swimming pool in the rear, the kiddie pool, the shuffleboard courts, and the barbecue area. Then we entered the motel from the back to avoid the blacktop. The lobby was decorated in Florida pinks and greens, and white rattan chairs and sofas were stacked along the walls under plastic covers.

'The furnishings are being held in a warehouse,' Anson explained when he took us to the vacant upstairs rooms. 'There was no point in uncrating new furniture to let it collect dust.'

I could see that you were impressed. All I wanted was a cigarette.

As we were leaving, I noticed what appeared to be a pair of enormous curved swords facing in opposite directions. They were centered on a far wall in the lobby, their handles hidden under drop cloths. 'What are those?' I asked.

Anson walked over and pulled the drop cloths away to reveal the overpowering head of a steer, carved out of wood and painted gold. 'This will be placed dead center in the front of the building,' Anson said proudly as we stared at the monstrous, vacant-eyed head. 'The name of the motel is The Golden Steer. Do you like it?'

I thought it was the most garish object I had ever seen, but you loved it, Richard.

We spent the next few days in Disney World and met Anson for dinner. My body began to adjust somewhat to its lack of cigarettes, and although my nicotine craving was still strong, I found that my concentration had improved. Disney World was filled to capacity, and I marveled at the number of children who were absent from school. I missed Matthew and Catherine, who would have loved everything from the rides on the monorail to the gaily decorated, imaginative trash cans. 'I saw hundreds of children today,' I said at dinner, 'and school is in session everywhere.'

'You're absolutely right,' said Anson, surprisingly fresh after a full day in the sun supervising the landscaping. 'That is why I was in such a hurry to finish The Golden Steer. I wanted to catch the overflow from the Disney World hotels and Buena Vista Village. Disney World is the biggest constant draw in the United States. I'm within a thirty-minute drive, and most people come by car. The Golden Steer can compete easily by offering slightly lower rates.'

'What about the oil embargo?' I asked.

'Disney World is far from empty,' Anson replied.

Disney World certainly wasn't empty, I agreed.

Anson started talking serious business on our drive back to Sarasota. 'I put so much into that motel,' he said. 'I wish I could persuade a bright young man like you to take it over. I trust you, Richard. You'd do a fine job with The Golden Steer.'

'I don't know anything about running a motel,' you said. 'I'm an accountant.'

'Exactly. You have the skill and brains it takes. The actual running of the place would be done by a hotel management firm. They're professionals. The reading of the ledger sheets is what counts,' Anson said convincingly, 'and that is where your expertise comes in.'

'I'm afraid it's out of my league. I opened my own firm six months ago, and money will be a little tight until I'm firmly established.'

I didn't know whether to laugh, cry, or scream when you said that, Richard.

'Buying The Golden Steer would take a small capital investment for the right man. It could be done for as little as ten thousand dollars,' Anson offered tantalizingly.

'How?' you asked, ready to bite.

'Simple,' said Anson. 'A smart fellow could set up his own corporation and make a purchase offer to buy The Golden Steer with a ten-thousand-dollar deposit. The closing date could be set for six months, which would be ample time to find investors to raise the remainder of the capital. Syndication – it's become as common as cold breakfast cereal. The original corporation sets up a limited partnership selling shares in units, each unit worth a specific sum. To become a limited partner, an investor would have to buy a minimum amount of units. That keeps the total number of investors down. The original corporation would be a general partner receiving a percentage of ownership in shares plus a promoter's fee, all for ten thousand dollars. On a deal as big as The Golden Steer, if the corporation took as little as a ten percent promoter's fee, it would come to one hundred thousand dollars. That's a tremendous return on a six-month investment of ten thousand dollars.'

'How much money would have to be raised?' I asked, forgetting cigarettes completely for the first time in three days.

Anson stared at the road and pursed his lips while I waited for his answer. 'Roughly a million dollars,' he said finally. 'Three quarters of a million as a down payment and the rest for expenses – placement costs, reserves, working capital, closing costs, interest, and the like. Yes, on a three-million-five-hundred-thousand-dollar motel, a million would do nicely.'

'Who would hold the mortgage?' you asked.

'I would,' said Anson. 'You know, Richard, I envy you. There weren't the opportunities for me when I was a young man that there are for you today. I struggled with one building after another, doing everything from pouring concrete to welding beams, when I was your age. I was on a building site every day including Sunday and had the callouses to prove it. Syndication hadn't been invented back then. If it had, I would have let others build the buildings and earned my fortune finding investors for them.'

'But what if you couldn't have found investors?' I asked.

'It's easier than you think,' he said, adjusting an overhead visor to block the sun. 'So easy that good investments sell themselves. And for a man like Richard who, I am sure, has friends of means, it would require no effort whatsoever.'

Richard, I can't go on with this. I told you before that I am neither a masochist nor a heroine. I lived through the nightmare once, which was enough. Besides, reliving it won't bring you back.

It was a wonderful weekend, the happiest time I've had in years. Nat and I went to a movie Saturday night, then out for a drink afterward. He arrived early and spent time with the children before we left. Unlike most adults, he didn't make the mistake of talking down to either child, and his unabashed curiosity, so like theirs, became a common meeting ground. Even Matthew dropped his normal reserve and told Nat about winning Ringer's Races and his ten-speed bike. 'W-W-W-Would you l-l-like to s-see it?' he asked.

'Sure,' said Nat with a grin.

Catherine ran upstairs to get her skateboard and scrambled down again, calling after them, 'Wait for me. I've got something to show, too.' Nat extended his hand, and she took it, smiling triumphantly.

Catherine will not allow anyone to upstage her, not even her brother. She is all yours, Richard. The genes are there, and they don't tell lies.

'Your kids are nice,' Nat said after we left. 'I know it's none of my business, but has your son always had a speech problem?'

I suddenly felt protective toward Matthew. 'No,' I answered. 'It started after his father died. I take him for speech therapy every week. He seems to be improving, but he still has difficulty, particularly when he is excited or upset or meets someone new.'

Nat glanced sideways at me. 'You resented my asking, didn't you?'

I started to tell him that I didn't but changed my mind. 'A little,' I said.

'I'm sorry. I didn't mean to offend you. It's just that there is something about Matthew, a natural reserve, a reticence that reminds me of you, although there is no physical resemblance. Does he look like your husband?'

'Yes.'

'I'm jealous. He must have been a good looking man.'

'He was.'

Nat slowed the car down. I could feel him looking at me, as if he expected more than a brief response, but I was silent. 'I had better change the subject,' he said finally. 'If I continue in this vein, I'll be talking to myself.'

The movie was delightful, a funny yet poignant story of a love affair called *Annie Hall*, and I lost myself in it. There were even some scenes of a California party. It was more sophisticated than the one I went to, but the slickness and sexual shopping were all there. I knew exactly how Woody Allen felt – completely out of his element.

You never liked Woody Allen. 'He's paranoid,' you once said. 'There's nothing funny in other people's craziness.'

Nat likes Woody Allen as much as I do. 'I enjoyed the movie,' he said afterward, 'but you gave it stiff competition.'

I asked him what he meant.

'Your face,' he said, 'everything that played on the screen – every emotion – played on your face. After a while I didn't know which I should watch, your face or the film, so I divided my time equally. But if I had just watched you and listened to the sound track, I wouldn't have missed a thing.'

I became flustered. 'I didn't realize,' I started to say.

Nat interrupted me. 'Don't be self-conscious. This ability you have, this exquisite responsiveness, is a gift. I wish I had it.'

'Why?' I asked uncomfortably.

'Instead of editing news stories, I would be writing my own.'

He told me that he had wanted to become a writer and create his own Pennsylvania town, as John O'Hara had done with Gibbsville. 'I wanted to construct that town brick by brick and populate each house until the whole place became alive,' he said wistfully.

'You still could,' I said.

He shook his head. 'I tried, but it didn't work. The stories were missing something. The streets and the people never quite connected the way they did on O'Hara's Lantenengo Street. On any of his streets, for that matter.'

I asked him when he had last tried to write.

'After my divorce,' he said. 'It was a bad time to try, I suppose. I couldn't seem to stick with it and blamed my failure on the fact that I had moved and was adjusting to a new job and single life. But that wasn't the reason, not really. It didn't work because I just didn't have it in me; I wasn't able to create life on paper. My characters never breathed or coughed or sneezed. They just stood like chess pieces where I placed them.'

'Were you terribly disappointed?'

'I was at first,' he admitted. 'Almost everyone who goes into journalism dreams of writing a book, not fiction necessarily, but something solid with their name on the cover. But I got over it.'

'You're well adjusted,' I said.

Nat shrugged. 'I'm realistic. I like my job and have the ability to do it well, so I'm satisfied. Most people aren't that lucky. Even O'Hara had his disappointments.'

'I thought he was rich and famous.'

'He was, but he died waiting for a telegram from the Nobel committee that never came. I think he knew it wouldn't come, and that hurt more than he let on. Have you read O'Hara's stories?'

'I read one of his novels years ago and didn't like it.'

'His short stories are wonderful. He wrote them to pass

the time between his novels, just scribbling for his own amusement until he had enough for another collection,' Nat said. 'O'Hara's short stories are his best work.'

'I'll have to read them,' I said, wondering if John O'Hara's stories might tell me more about Nat Witton than I was able to learn on my own.

'I'll lend you a few collections,' he offered enthusiastically, unaware of the reason for my interest. 'I envy you, reading them for the first time.'

We stayed in the bar for several hours, talking more than drinking. The booth we were sitting in was just large enough for two, deeply upholstered in black, and the semidarkness of the room heightened a comfortable intimacy I began to feel growing between us. Our conversation slid easily from one topic to another but kept returning to the movie. When Nat told me he agreed with Woody Allen, that he felt it was almost as difficult to end an affair as it was to end a marriage, I didn't know how to reply.

'You've never had an affair, have you?' he asked.

'No,' I said, glad for the darkness of the room so he couldn't see perspiration forming on my upper lip. My admission made me feel deficient, as if I were the world's last remaining virgin. But then I recovered and said jokingly, 'Tell me about affairs.'

'Mine or anyone's?' he kidded, but his voice wasn't as light as his comeback.

I didn't know how far I could push, I did want to know about him, about how he felt and how experienced he was. I was half-afraid to ask, but for once my curiosity was as great as his. 'You can start with anyone's affair,' I said, 'or your own, if you prefer.'

'You really want to know?' he asked.

'I'm not a voyeur, if that's what you mean, so you can omit bedroom details. It's just that I've never heard anyone say that an affair was almost as difficult to end as a marriage,' I explained, beginning to regret my pursuit of the subject.

Nat picked up his empty glass and turned it around in his hands. 'That's one of the problems with affairs,' he said thoughtfully. 'No one talks about them. If a man is a gentleman, he keeps his mouth shut. Others may know, especially if a couple is living together, but men don't talk any more than I imagine women do. That locker room bit about men talking is a myth. A fellow might say something about a sensational one-night stand, but he's quiet about his affairs. You see, an affair isn't the same as a casual lay, but it isn't the same as marriage, either. There are no guidelines except those that the couple has agreed upon, and if it is a hot-and-heavy affair, more sex than talk, nothing is agreed upon. When you're married, there is a legal contract. At times it feels like a leash, but at least you know how tightly you can pull on it before cutting off your air.

'Then there is the intensity of affairs. Some are more intense than others, but few are the casual, let's-wait-and-see-what-happens variety. Affairs can peak fast, sometimes faster for one of the partners than the other; one may want out when the other one doesn't.'

Our waitress came over, and Nat ordered another drink for himself. I was still nursing mine. After she left, he continued. 'I never grow tired of the ocean, probably because I grew up landlocked in Pennsylvania. Sometimes I drive along the coast and stop to watch surfers. One day, while watching them ride the waves, I realized how much the affairs I've had have been like surfing. Surfers study the waves, waiting for a big one, then chase it until they can ride it through. You can actually see the incredible high they feel if they've been successful. But then the ride is over, the exhilaration is gone, and they must paddle out again to catch another wave. Surfers know when their ride is over, but you don't always know when you're having an affair. As a result, the spills from affairs can be a lot rougher than swallowing some salty water. You never know if you're going to be hurt, or if the other person is going to be hurt, or what the final damage will be. I've

302

never heard of an affair ending on a high note. The most that can be hoped for is an amiable separation and friendship afterward.'

'What you've said certainly isn't a recommendation for affairs,' I commented.

Nat smiled. 'I didn't say that I don't recommend them. Forgive the pun, but I love affairs. It's just that, in my experience, they start out much better than they end.'

I understood. Nat was warning me. He was telling me that he was the surfer, that he would want out once an affair had peaked for him. He was more sophisticated than I had thought. Perhaps I was foolish, but I began to feel sure of myself and plunged ahead. 'Tell me,' I said after the waitress brought his drink, 'do you study women for prospective affairs as carefully as surfers study the waves?'

Nat took a sip of his drink and shifted uncomfortably. 'You make me sound so cold, so calculating. Is that the impression I've made on you?'

'Not exactly,' I said truthfully. 'But you do sound . . .' I didn't know how to say it.

'What, Jenny? Finish what you started to say.'

'You . . . you sound sophisticated. Maybe experienced is a better word, as if you know what you want, as if you weigh the risks before deciding to take a chance so you'll come out of an affair with as little trauma as possible. Am I wrong? It's not a bad idea,' I replied with more bravado than I felt.

He looked directly at me, his eyes like deep blue magnets in the darkness. 'It isn't that I study the risks. When I'm attracted to a woman, I don't go in for heavy mental calculations. Sometimes a woman may be special for one reason or another. You're one of those women.'

'Why?' I asked, not knowing whether I should be flattered or insulted.

'You're vulnerable, for one thing. You're new at being alone, and I could tell without asking that you've never had an affair.'

303

'Then why did you ask?'

'I wondered how you'd reply.'

I began to perspire in earnest, and the black upholstery felt sticky. 'I didn't know it was that obvious,' I said.

'It wouldn't have been if I hadn't observed you at that bar where we first met for lunch. I can't recall seeing anyone who was more out of her element than you were.'

I remembered and laughed. 'Well, he wasn't particularly appealing,' I said, 'and he wouldn't accept a tactful refusal.'

'That's another thing,' said Nat. 'You're a lady. You play by the rules, so you didn't want to hurt his feelings. You seem to have an ingrained sense of propriety. But you're living in a place where there are no rules, at least none that I've been able to discern.'

'Every place has rules,' I said.

'Every place but California,' replied Nat, 'and the rest of the country will follow California's lead, if it hasn't already.'

'Lead in what?'

'The self,' said Nat. 'When I first arrived in California, I knew immediately that there was something uniquely different going on, but I couldn't figure out what it was. In the newspaper business, it is crucial to have a feel for the place in which you're working, and a feel for the place means an understanding of the people. It took me a while to catch on, because it was so simple that I just couldn't see it until everything clicked – self-improvement, self-enrichment, self-fulfillment, personal space, games of philosophical hopscotch – people concentrating on themselves. And when existence begins and ends with the self, rules are dispensed with because they are no longer necessary.'

'And you, does your existence begin and end with Nat Witton?'

Nat flinched. 'There is a spark of narcissism in everyone, and there is no better place in the world to fan it than here.

I suppose I've gone native, but you seem to be pulling me back for some reason.'

'Is that good or bad?' I wanted to know.

'We'll have to find out,' he said.

After we left the bar, Nat asked me if I wanted him to stop off at his apartment to pick up John O'Hara's books, but I knew what he was really asking.

It would be easy to tell you that I flatly refused, or that I hesitated and then refused, or that I vacillated and half-refused, keeping my options open. But that wouldn't be the truth, and the purpose of my writing to you has been to tell the truth, to look life straight in the eye without blinking. Perhaps I have blinked a few times, but only in relation to the past. You know everything that has happened to me since you died; nothing has been withheld, not even Charlie.

I told Nat that I would like him to stop for the books.

It wasn't the same as it was with you. I didn't expect it to be the same. We had years together, good years when we were young and in love and time meant memorizing each other's bodies. I could tell how close you were by feeling the tension in the muscles of your back with a finger tip, and you made love to me until my entire body sang and vibrated with gladness. Even during that nightmarish last year when we rarely spoke, our bodies still talked to each other. It was hard sex then, hungry sex without affection or laughter, but it was release. There were nights when I almost felt that I was trespassing, that I was violating you because I could reach across the bed knowing exactly where to touch, how to excite you beyond your anger, beyond your silence, beyond yourself. And you also knew and did the same with me.

Nat is an experienced lover, although I wasn't aware of it at first. Now that I think about it, his experience doesn't surprise me. Nat Witton is attractive, and there are thousands of unattached women in California who I imagine would be happy to oblige him. He was cautious with me in the beginning, careful as if it were my first time.

His consideration bordered on tenderness, and when he sensed that I had relaxed, he made love to me skillfully, matching his responses with mine. I didn't realize what he had done until we made love again last night. My nervousness was gone, and Nat became more aggressive. I didn't need much encouragement before I, too, became freer.

It has begun, Richard. Nat Witton and I are beginning to know each other.

There are other ways in which we are beginning to know each other. All of us. Nat took me and the children to Newport Beach yesterday. 'My friend is away for the weekend,' Nat said, 'so we can have the place to ourselves.'

It was a glorious beach day: the sun was brilliant, the ocean a calm palette of blues. When Nat saw that Catherine couldn't swim, he played with her until he had her floating. She was so pleased with herself that she became overconfident, took in a headful of salty water, and emerged sputtering and wailing. Nat picked her up, comforted her, then put her back in and had her floating again before she had time to develop a fear of the water. By the day's end, Catherine was gazing at Nat adoringly, and when I tucked her into bed last night, she said sleepily: 'I like Nat. Could he be my daddy for a while since I don't have a real one?'

My heart lurched. 'You had a real daddy, Catherine,' I answered, 'but he died. Let's just think of Nat as our friend for now.'

Matthew wore an expression of skepticism on his face during our ride to the beach. He sat in the back seat of the car looking first at me, then at Nat, then back at me again as if he were a stranger in a foreign country who didn't know what the customs were or what local etiquette demanded. Nat accepted Matthew's uneasiness as being normal behavior for an eight-year-old boy without mentioning it. He was casually friendly rather than assertively friendly, giving Matthew room either to accept or to reject him. Matthew was still withdrawn at the day's end, but he wasn't glaring at Nat the way he had at Craig Howard. I consider that a good sign.

We had an early dinner, which Nat cooked. He had brought steaks with him, and we stopped at a supermarket on the way to the beach for lettuce, vegetables, milk, and soft drinks. When we were ready to eat, he disappeared and returned with a bottle of chilled red wine. It was the perfect touch for a perfect day.

I began to think that Nat Witton was perfect, too. Not only did he cook the steaks and prepare the salad, but he even helped me clear the table. When he picked up a towel to dry a large serving platter I had washed, he must have noticed my surprise. 'Didn't your husband help you with the dishes?' he asked.

'No,' I replied flatly, deliberately discouraging him from questioning me further.

Nat didn't speak of you again until late last night after we made love. I was able to get a sitter, and we went back to his apartment. The day's combination of sun, salt air, and sex had made me irresistibly drowsy, and I was close to falling asleep on Nat's shoulder when he asked: 'How long were you married?'

'Eight years,' I answered sleepily.

'That's a long time,' he said, 'most of your adult life. Why don't you ever mention your late husband? He couldn't have been that bad, even if he didn't dry dishes.'

I became suddenly awake, on guard. 'Richard wasn't bad,' I said defensively. 'I wouldn't have married him if he were.'

'I know that,' he replied placatingly. 'Really, I didn't mean to upset you. It's just that I do know some things about him, and the fact that you never mention him doesn't make sense.'

I sat upright in bed. 'What do you know?' I demanded.

'First, he was good looking. You told me that yourself,

remember? Second, he was intelligent. I can't imagine you married to a man who wasn't intelligent, so he must have been bright. And third, he was successful. You live well, on a scale far beyond what Social Security and your part-time salary at Briarhill could possibly provide. With all of that going for him, I would think he would merit an occasional mention.'

'Very good,' I said sarcastically. 'You win first prize for the best detective work of the year. Congratulations.'

I was furious and started to get out of bed. Nat grabbed my arm. 'I deserved that,' he said, rubbing the muscles that had knotted on the back of my neck. 'I apologize. Sometimes my curiosity gets in the way of my good sense. I know you didn't want me to ask; you've drawn a curtain around your past. If you don't want to tell me, you don't have to, and I won't speak of him again. But we have started something, so you can't completely fault me for asking. Maybe you just need time.'

'There will never be enough time. There can't be when . . .' I couldn't say it.

'When what?'

'When a man commits suicide,' I exploded. 'Now do you understand? My husband killed himself. He was handsome, he was bright, and he died of asphyxiation from carbon monoxide. Have I left anything out? Would you like to know the make, model number, and year of the car he used? Would that satisfy your damned curiosity?'

'I'm sorry, truly sorry. I shouldn't have asked,' Nat said quietly. 'Perhaps I should have known or at least made a fairly accurate guess without putting you through this.'

'How could you have known? And what right did you have to put me through this?'

'Most people usually mention how their loved ones died, especially when they died young. The only hesitation I have ever noticed is with cancer; the disease is so feared that most people don't like naming it. But suicide is something else – death by choice, which makes it the hardest to accept.'

I didn't have to be reminded or want to be reminded; nor did I want to continue our conversation. I looked pointedly at the clock on Nat's nightstand. 'It's ten o'clock,' I said, 'and I promised the sitter I'd be back before eleven.'

'We have time. You asked me what right I had to put you through reliving your husband's death. I didn't have the right, not yet anyway, but I wanted the right. Let me earn it. Let's see what will come of this. Unless I'm mistaken, until a few minutes ago, you were as attracted to me as I am to you.'

'Attraction has nothing to do with it,' I said. 'I'm mad as hell.'

'Then let's make use of that heat,' he said persuasively.

We were making love again before I found the strength to resist.

Nat Witton is charming. He is intelligent, attractive, and a proficient lover. But he is not perfect, and I am sure I will discover other things about him, in addition to his compulsive curiosity, that are irritating. And he will discover things about me that are less than desirable. It is to be expected. We aren't children, and at this point in our lives, neither one of us can hope to find a fairy tale happy ending in the other. What I am trying to say, Richard, is that I am being realistic. I am not expecting the world in the person of one man as I did with you. This is a different beginning. I am beginning to live again, and I am starting with Nat Witton.

Crazy as it may seem, you were in bed with us that first night, too. Nat wasn't aware of you, but I knew you were there. You lived in the responses of my flesh as in a dream, your maleness in another man's body, a body so foreign yet strangely familiar that my flesh had to adjust and readjust, as if I were programmed to respond to only one man and every fiber in my body was conditioned to his touch. I know there is a logical explanation for what I felt, that it wasn't you but rather the habits of our years together that made me feel it was you. Perhaps it is so, but you were there.

I initiated a change at Briarhill today. It won't be written up in geriatric journals as being of significance, but it does mean something to me. I suggested that all second floor residents be taken to group activities, that they be automatically included in the socials, the organized games, the sing-alongs, the craft demonstrations, and so on. Most of the programs I plan are attended only by first floor residents who are mobile and in touch with the world. The others, the second floor residents, are usually absent from group activities unless they specifically ask to attend, and they rarely ask. When the elevator takes them up to the second floor, they seem to drift away mentally as well as physically. Their need for custodial care places them on an island between the viable first floor and the third floor, the death floor, and they know it.

Simon resisted my idea at first. 'This is a private home,' he said. 'The residents have always been given a choice as to whether they want to attend activities or stay in their rooms. Aren't you taking their options away from them?'

'No,' I replied, 'I don't think so. When residents move to the second floor, they seem to give up. They begin to wait for death, for that final trip to the third floor, and they quietly resign from group activities. I want them to keep in touch with life. I'm not suggesting that they be forced to participate, only that they are given the opportunity to stay tuned to what is going on around them. There is no reason why residents needing custodial care can't listen to a speaker or watch a movie. Even if they sleep through an entire program, they won't be alone.'

Simon agreed that it was worth a try. Then, looking at me shrewdly, he said: 'Tell me, Jenny, was Mrs Fry behind your idea? Her death affected you more than you let on.'

'I'm not sure,' I replied honestly.

It occurred to me later that, if it hadn't been for the

children, I would have been a perfect candidate for the second floor. You have helped, too. Through this journal, I have been able to keep in touch. It has been a form of discipline, and if I have failed to unearth the truth, I have kept my mind intact, which, under the circumstances, has been no small feat.

I believe that I am finally ready to stop writing, Richard. I am back on the first floor.

It has been almost two weeks since I last wrote to you. I was so happy then, so sure I could survive on my own. Things haven't worked out as well as I had hoped.

The problem is Matthew. He resents Nat Witton. No, it is more than resentment: Matthew believes Nat is trying to take your place, and he is fighting a private war that is tearing him up inside. It has affected his speech to the extent that he is barely able to talk, even when he uses his tricks – pressing on his forehead and closing his eyes to postpone a block.

Nat cannot be blamed for what has happened; he has done everything possible to meet Matthew on Matthew's terms. If it is anyone's fault, I suppose it is mine for welcoming Nat into our lives. He is my choice, not Matthew's. I feel guilty that Matthew is suffering, but I also feel that I am entitled to some happiness of my own. I like Nat almost as much as Matthew resents him. If I am forced to choose, I shall naturally pick Matthew. He is my son, and his happiness and well-being come first. Still, I can't help but think that it would be nice if I didn't have to choose, although I have my doubts after what occurred tonight.

Until a few hours ago, I misunderstood the reason for Matthew's behavior. I was worried about his withdrawal and speech regression, but Nat didn't seem to feel that I had cause for concern. When he came over last Saturday night to take me out, Matthew marched upstairs, deliberately ignoring Nat's greeting. I started to go after him, but

Nat stopped me. 'Leave him alone,' Nat said, holding my arm.

'But he was rude. He's obviously upset.'

'I've been here twice this week. He probably thinks that I'm trying to take you away from him or that I'm usurping his position,' Nat explained. 'Don't worry. Matthew's reaction to me is normal. He'll get over it.'

'It might help if I talked to him,' I said, reluctant to leave.

'If you confront him, he'll be embarrassed, and that will make it worse. Matthew needs room; he'll come around when he's ready,' Nat assured me.

I wanted to believe Nat. Besides, what he said made sense. I recalled Matthew's hostile behavior toward Craig Howard and realized that I overlooked his rudeness because I subconsciously agreed with him. 'You're probably right,' I said with relief.

We had planned to spend Sunday together, all four of us, but I called Nat after breakfast to cancel our plans. 'Why?' he asked.

'When I told the children that we were going out, Matthew left the table. He didn't finish his breakfast.'

'He'll survive.'

'You don't understand,' I said. 'Matthew always eats breakfast. It's his favorite meal. I don't think we should force the issue.'

Nat agreed, though I could tell from the tone of his voice that he was disappointed. I stayed home with the children until they were in bed for the night, then left to see Nat and was back by eleven to relieve the sitter.

On Tuesday morning, I overheard Matthew talking to himself while he was getting dressed for school. He didn't block, not once. His speech was so miraculously fluent that I called Nat at work to tell him. He was as excited as I was. 'I knew Matthew would come around,' Nat said. 'Can we celebrate? If you invite me over for dinner, I'll bring champagne.'

Matthew stopped speaking the moment he saw Nat. 'I

thought you said he'd gotten over it,' Nat whispered while we were in the kitchen.

'It doesn't make sense,' I whispered back. 'His speech was perfect this morning when he was talking to himself, but he was blocking when he came home from school. Maybe he's doing this for spite. I'm going to discuss it with him now.'

'No, leave him alone,' Nat advised. 'The champagne will keep.'

Matthew didn't utter a word during dinner, but Catherine more than made up for his silence. She chatted nonstop through the meal, happy that she didn't have to share our attention with her brother. Under normal circumstances, I would have encouraged her to eat more and talk less, but Tuesday night her monologue was welcome. Without it, the dinner would have been deadly.

On Thursday, Matthew's speech therapist asked to speak to me privately after his lesson was over. 'Last week's session didn't go well, and today's was worse,' she said. 'Matthew's blocking as severely as he did when you first brought him to me. He had been making steady progress; now he's tensing so badly that he's having one hard block after another. He's upset about something. Do you know what it is?'

I hesitated. Mrs Armatage is a formidable-looking woman, unusually tall, with stern features and a brusque, clinical manner. From what I have observed, she seems to have unlimited patience with children and none with their parents.

'I can't help Matthew if you are unwilling to cooperate,' she said, studying me disapprovingly.

'I . . . I've started to date. I'm seeing a man, and I think Matthew resents him,' I confessed. 'He's nice, really he is . . .'

'You don't have to explain,' Mrs Armatage interrupted. 'Matthew's difficulty is understandable now. Any change in authority figures – any change in relationships – will cause problems in a child like Matthew. It's the rule rather than the exception for nonfluent children, especially for those whose speech was affected by the loss of a parent, as Matthew's was.'

'Should I stop dating?' I asked anxiously.

The glacial Mrs Armatage smiled. 'No, I don't think that's necessary,' she said.

'I overheard Matthew talking to himself the other morning, and he didn't block at all. Could he be doing this deliberately to make me stop seeing my friend?'

Her smile vanished. 'Absolutely not,' she replied firmly. 'Nonfluent children can sing and talk to themselves without blocking. I thought you knew that.' Then she left me abruptly to take her next appointment.

When I spoke to Nat later, I told him about my conversation with Mrs Armatage. 'I was beginning to have doubts,' he admitted. 'I'm glad that my instincts were right. Can you meet me tomorrow after work? There's a place near the newspaper that has a terrific fish fry on Fridays. It's run by New Yorkers; they have the best batter-fried fish in L.A.'

'Let's eat here,' I suggested, wanting to avoid Friday rush-hour traffic on the freeways.

'I'd really like that fish,' he said.

'You could stop on the way over and order it to take out,' I said, trying to sound casual. I didn't want Nat to know about my fear of the freeways.

'All right,' he agreed reluctantly.

Matthew was watching television when Nat walked in. 'Hi, Matthew,' he said, carefully handing me a large brown paper bag that contained our dinner.

Matthew stared at the television screen, silent.

'Matthew, would you please get Catherine?' I asked, forcing myself to overlook his rudeness. 'She's at Lisa's.'

Nat and I went into the kitchen. I started to unwrap the fish, listening for a sound of movement coming from the living room; there was nothing but the noise of a commercial for aspirin. 'Matthew,' I called, competing

314

with the testimony of a woman who had just gotten rid of her headache, 'I want you to turn off the television and get Catherine.'

Nat made drinks while I put the fish in the oven to warm. 'It looks delicious,' I said with a forced smile. The television seemed to grow louder, although I knew Matthew hadn't moved to touch it.

'Relax,' Nat said, raising his glass.

We stayed in the kitchen for approximately five minutes, though it seemed like hours, both of us waiting for Matthew to move. Nat tried to talk to me, but I couldn't concentrate on what he was saying. When the television newscaster intoned: '*There was an accident on Sunset Boulevard late this afternoon that claimed the life . . .*' I put my drink on the counter and started toward the living room. Nat put his hand on my shoulder. 'I'll get Catherine,' he offered. 'Just point me in the direction of Lisa's.'

'No, Matthew will get Catherine,' I said.

'You're pushing, Jenny.'

'Matthew was asked to do something. Twice. He was asked nicely. I've tried to ignore his rudeness, but I won't ignore disobedience.'

'Let me try,' Nat said.

He walked into the living room ahead of me. Matthew sat motionless in front of the television. I knew that he was tense; his head was bent slightly forward, as if he were listening for the sound of an encroaching enemy. 'Matthew,' Nat said pleasantly, 'dinner is ready. It should be delicious. Aren't you hungry?'

Matthew's jaw tightened.

'I'm starving. So is your mother. We'd like to eat,' Nat continued, approaching Matthew cautiously.

Matthew's eyes stayed fixed on the television screen.

'I'd appreciate it if you'd get Catherine,' Nat said.

Matthew remained motionless. Nat stepped in front of the television. 'Son,' he started to say.

Matthew sprung to his feet. 'I-I-I-I-I-I-I'm n-n-n-not

'y-y-y-y-y-y-your s-s-s-s-s-son,' he stammered, the veins in his head and neck bulging.

'I'm sorry. It's only a figure of speech . . . an expression,' Nat said, stepping back.

'Nat was just trying to get your attention,' I explained, shaken by the intensity of Matthew's reply. 'You were asked to do something.'

'H-H-H-H-H-H-H-He's n-n-n-n-not m-m-m-m-m-my f-f-f-f-f-f-father. H-H-H-H-H-H-H-He c-c-c-c-c-can't t-t-t-t-t-tell m-m-m-m-me wha-wha-wha-wha-what t-t-t-t-to d-d-d-d-d-do. I-I-I-I-I-I-I-I w-w-w-w-w-w-w-won't l-l-l-l-l-l-l-l-let . . .' Matthew couldn't finish. He stood in front of us trembling, his face crimson with effort, then turned abruptly and ran upstairs to his room.

'Whew,' Nat said. 'That was a mistake. I shouldn't have interfered.'

'It was my fault,' I replied, feeling weak. 'Now what do we do?'

'Get Catherine and eat dinner, I guess,' he answered, putting a comforting arm around me.

After Nat left, I went upstairs to talk to Matthew. The lights were on in his bedroom, and toys were strewn all over the floor. Matthew was lying on his bed fully dressed, sleeping fitfully. I tried to awaken him gently, but his eyes opened instantly, as if he had been startled out of a bad dream. 'I brought you a glass of milk,' I said.

He drank the milk in noisy gulps.

'Would you like more?' I asked, taking the glass.

He shook his head.

'A sandwich?'

Again, he shook his head.

'Nat didn't mean to upset you,' I said, removing a pile of comic books so I could sit down beside him. 'He wants to be your friend. He likes you.'

'I-I-I-I-I-I-I d-d-d-d-don't c-c-c-c-c-c-care.'

'Doesn't it bother you that you're hurting his feelings?' I asked, appealing to Matthew's sense of fairness.

'N-N-N-N-N-N-No,' he stammered painfully.

'He wants you to like him,' I said, trying a positive approach.

'I-I-I-I-I-I c-c-c-c-can't l-l-l-l-l-l-like h-h-h-h-him and-and-and h-h-h-h-h-he c-c-c-c-can't m-m-m-m-make m-m-m-m-m-m-me.'

'Why?' I demanded, unable to contain my growing frustration.

'D-D-D-D-D-D-D-Daddy w-w-w-w-w-would th-th-th-th-think I-I-I-I-I-I st-st-st-st-st-stopped l-l-l-l-l-l-loving h-h-h-h-h-him.'

'But Daddy's dead,' I blurted, grabbing him by the shoulders. 'Don't you understand? Daddy's dead. He's dead.'

Matthew just looked at me, his jaw set, his eyes dark and determined.

He is sleeping restlessly now. When I checked on him an hour ago, his covers were off and his pillow was on the floor. I rearranged his bed, careful not to disturb him. As I was leaving the room, Matthew said plaintively, 'I can't like Nat. I can't.' I turned quickly and saw him thrashing in his sleep. I stayed for a few minutes, covered him again, then left.

What am I going to do? I know Matthew would accept Nat if he allowed himself to like him, but he won't; he is determined to preserve your place, no matter what the cost. It is almost as if he doesn't believe you are dead, that he thinks you will magically return to us and things will be as they were before. I cannot fight Matthew's loyalty or his impossible hope. Tonight, when he told me he couldn't like Nat, his face mirrored yours that day on the beach in Florida when you refused to consider buying The Golden Steer. Your son looked exactly like you, Richard, and I had the same failure reasoning with him as I had with you.

I admit that I was obsessed with The Golden Steer after we returned from Orlando with Anson, particularly the one hundred thousand dollar promoter's fee, but it appeared to be an ideal solution to our problems. 'You

317

could even take fifteen percent rather than ten percent for putting the deal together,' I said the next day after we went for a swim. 'Think of it – one hundred fifty thousand dollars on a ten-thousand-dollar investment! We wouldn't have to move.'

'It isn't as simple as it sounds,' you replied, frowning. 'In the first place, I would have to find investors. Ideally, there should be no more than twenty-five to keep it private, which would mean that each investor, if the shares were priced at ten thousand dollars per unit, would have to buy a minimum of five units. A super salesman would have difficulty selling a fifty-thousand-dollar-a-shot investment, and I've never sold a thing in my life.

'Second, we don't have the ten thousand to invest. You saw the figures. Before we left for Florida we had under two thousand in cash, and that included both our savings and our checking accounts. I've been stalling some outstanding bills, but I'll have to pay them when we return. It will wipe us out.'

I knew by the familiar expression on your face, the tight way you held your mouth and the distant look in your eyes, that you had begun calculating how much we would have left to the dollar. 'Why would the number of investors have to be kept down to twenty-five?' I asked, trying to pull the plug on your mental adding machine.

'An investment like The Golden Steer would have to be kept small,' you replied, still adding and subtracting figures.

'Why?'

'Because,' you said, totaling up, 'a limited number of investors keeps the offering private. Charlie did some work on a limited partnership last year. The group that put the offering together wanted to keep it private so they wouldn't have to file with the SEC; an offering doesn't have to be registered if it goes through with under twenty-five people. Charlie wouldn't have mentioned it if the deal hadn't fallen apart. They couldn't get enough investors, and Charlie is still trying to collect the remainder of his fee. He tried to feed the accounting work to me and was relieved later that they went to another firm. Otherwise, I could have been stuck, too.'

'Maybe they didn't go to the right people or didn't know how to sell,' I suggested.

'One of the men who put the deal together is in real estate. He has the reputation of being a hard sell, and he must be successful because his firm grosses more in business properties than any other firm in the city.'

'Maybe that was his problem,' I said. 'I don't think a fifty-thousand-dollar investment can be sold the same way a business property can. People who have fifty thousand dollars to invest wouldn't want to be pushed.'

You adjusted your chaise, leaned back, and closed your eyes. 'I told you, Jenny, I don't know anything about selling.'

'You've sold yourself,' I argued. 'I don't know how many times I heard you intimate that you could save a prospective client hundreds on his tax returns, and it's almost always worked.'

'That's different.'

'Why?'

'Because I was selling my skill, my expertise. I know what I can do. It's a matter of confidence,' you replied with irritation.

'Then why can't you project the same aura of confidence in The Golden Steer? It wouldn't be difficult.'

'I don't have confidence in The Golden Steer. I don't know a damn thing about it, and I don't have ten thousand dollars to invest,' you snapped. 'Drop it. We came to Florida for a vacation, remember? If you keep talking, your tongue will get sunburned.'

You swung your legs over the side of the chaise and sat up to face me, blocking the sun. I looked at you, at the set of your jaw and the dark determination in your eyes, like Matthew's tonight, and knew that my arguments were useless. I dropped it. But I didn't forget it, Richard; neither did Anson. He mentioned The Golden Steer each time he saw us. However, he was careful not to refer to the motel within Aunt Maggie's hearing, and when he did say something, it was always in the form of a tactful suggestion. Anson said just enough to keep my interest buoyed.

The day before we left, Aunt Maggie gave me an unusual diamond pendant. 'It isn't valuable,' she said, 'although it won't be long before it's considered an antique. The diamonds are mostly chips, but it's my most cherished piece of jewelry. My first husband gave it to me as a wedding gift. He was the great love of my life, so the pendant has always been special. A reminder, I think, of my youth and foolishness. I would be pleased if you would accept it and give it to Catherine when she's grown. Perhaps she'll pass it on to her daughter one day, if she's lucky enough to have one.'

I thanked Maggie and promised to follow her wishes.

'I never told this to a soul, but I divorced my first husband because we were childless. I wanted a baby desperately and couldn't conceive. He refused to adopt. He said that it was God's will and that if we were meant to raise a child, we'd have one of our own. We argued bitterly. It wasn't until after we were divorced that I realized I still loved him, but it was too late. A matter of pride, you know. I married my second husband to forget my first, which is a poor excuse for a marriage. That divorce was inevitable. I wasn't happy with a man again until I met Walter. By then, I was too old to bear a child.

'My first husband eventually remarried. I kept track of him through mutual friends, always waiting for and half dreading the news that his new wife would be pregnant. The marriage was childless, but I never knew the reason. One could not ask.

'I have waited to make my will. I'm not a wealthy woman – this house is my major asset – but I'm comfortable enough. I had toyed with the idea of leaving you and Linda the bulk of my estate, but I don't know where Linda is, and I doubt that she'd be interested anyway. Linda is a headstrong, independent girl, much like I was at that age. Money isn't important to her, a reaction to living with your mother, I suppose.' Maggie chuckled. 'Forgive me, Jenny, but your mother does put an over importance on material things.'

I nodded my agreement, thinking that it was a mild remark for Maggie to make about Mother, considering all the unkind barbs Mother had directed toward Maggie over the years.

'I can see that you and Richard are comfortable,' Maggie continued. 'You have lovely clothes and jewelry and an expensive car. You don't seem to want for a thing, so I have decided to leave my money to a research foundation that specializes in infertility problems. You see, two questions have always haunted me. Was it me or my first husband who had the problem? And could we have been helped? Infertility problems weren't talked about back then, and there was no place to go for answers. I would die comforted knowing that my money will be used to help young women like myself. If just one woman can be spared the disappointment that marred years of my life, I'll consider the money well spent. That is, if you don't object.'

'Of course I don't object,' I said, swallowing. 'It's a wonderful idea and a fine legacy.'

How could I object, Richard? On what grounds? Maggie had already given me more than I had given her and far more than I had deserved – happy childhood memories, special gifts on my birthdays and Christmas, generous hospitality for the two of us in Florida. Maggie had done everything possible to ensure our good time. And how could I tell her that we weren't as affluent as we appeared to be? Linda had Maggie's temperament, but I had her pride. To admit that we couldn't afford to live in our house would have been impossible. Also, Maggie looked so tanned and fit that day. Her imminent death seemed to be the remotest of possibilities as we sat under the Florida sun.

I showed you the pendant that evening while we were dressing for dinner, but I didn't repeat Maggie's conversation. At the time, I felt that it would be betraying a confidence. I didn't think Maggie would have wanted you to know about her private disappointments; she had kept them to herself for too many years to have them shared as if they were quaint relics from the past. I tried to explain this to you after Maggie's funeral six days later, but you didn't understand. You didn't understand because you didn't want to understand. It was much easier and more to your purpose to blame me. I suppose you thought we were even then, your stock market losses balanced against my greater loss of Maggie's estate. It galls me to remember how you accused me of acting irresponsibly. 'You're all impulse and no thought,' you said.

You are wrong, Richard. And if you were alive today, you would still be wrong. I don't want to be reminded of the mistakes I've made, but signing a waiver to release my claim to Maggie's estate was not one of them. It was her money, and she had every right to spend it where she damn well pleased, in life *and* in death. Contrary to what you believed at the time, Maggie was not our fairy godmother. She was simply a lovely lady we once had the pleasure of knowing. Amen.

I promised myself that I wouldn't write to you again. Ever. I was so unstrung after that last session six weeks ago that I wanted to ask Deirdre if she had any tranquilizers left, but I was too embarrassed to call. It was then that I vowed that nothing – absolutely nothing – could happen that would make me want to communicate with you.

Something has happened, a crisis of sorts. It's nothing major (the children and I are fine), but it was so aggravating that I can't stop thinking about it. Perhaps if I tell you, I'll be able to stop mulling over what I should have said and done, which serves no purpose except to rekindle my anger. I am now at the point where I have replayed the whole business so often that I feel as if I have been strapped into a seat in a movie theater and condemned to watch the same reel of film endlessly, catching overlooked details with each viewing until every frame has been painfully memorized.

It all started on Monday while I was driving to work. The car began to shake violently, and there was a loud pounding noise – chuck, chuck, chuck – that wouldn't stop. I was in a center lane of traffic and tried to pull the car over on to the shoulder, but it would barely move, even with the gas pedal pressed to the floor. The car gave its last gasp sitting on an angle, straddling two lanes. Brakes screeched, horns from cars behind me started blasting, and for a moment I panicked, sure that I was going to be annihilated. I could actually see the headlines when I closed my eyes and braced myself for the impact:

TWENTY CAR PILEUP ON FREEWAY:
FIRST CAR AND BODY BEYOND IDENTIFICA-
TION.

When I realized that the other cars had managed to stop and that I was not going to die, I tried to start the car. Nothing happened. I tried again. Nothing. The damned car sat as if all of its moving parts had been welded together. By that time, the noise of blaring horns from other cars I had blocked was deafening. Not knowing what else to do, I started to open the car door to get out and wave traffic around me, but a green sports car that had managed to maneuver itself out of the line of stopped vehicles almost sheared the door off. Then I tried to get out through the passenger side and had one foot on the pavement when I saw another car coming straight at me. Quickly, I jumped back in, slammed the door shut, and prayed. It missed my car by an inch, if that much. I felt the car sway slightly, and I began to shake.

There was nothing to do but sit in the car and wait, so I waited. A policeman had to come eventually. I knew that a number of the motorists pounding on their horns had CB radios; their antennas glistened like needles in my rearview mirror. If they would only take their hands off their horns and call, I thought. But they were too busy venting their anger at the delay I caused to make a call on my behalf.

I waited for fifteen minutes for a policeman, and it was a minor miracle that I wasn't killed before he arrived. No one stopped with an offer of help, which didn't surprise me, because I wouldn't have stopped, either. People on the West Coast wear the same jackets of fear that cover Easterners: a stalled car could be a trick, a ploy for robbery or an excuse for violence. But the cars circling around me at full speed were terrifying, some of them coming so close that I could actually feel the heat from their engines. My wait was a front-row seat in hell.

The policeman, a beefy, sandy-haired fellow of about forty who walked with an unmistakable swagger, tried to start the car after I told him what had happened. I was insulted. 'I know how to start a car,' I said. 'I didn't stop here intentionally.'

He looked at me with disgust. 'Oh, you're one of those,' he sneered, getting out of the car. As he spoke, he rubbed the handle of his gun with his thumb and forefinger.

'One of what?' I asked, bewildered.

'A libber. One of those broads who thinks she has balls. Since you're such an independent cookie, let's see you get your car off the road.' He pointed toward the shoulder with his free arm; his thumb and forefinger were still on his gun, rubbing absentmindedly.

'Sure,' I replied, furious. 'I'll get it off the road the same way you'll get it off the road.'

'How's that?' he asked caustically. The thumb on his gun started to move faster.

'I'll call a tow truck. Can I use your radio?'

'Don't touch that radio,' he ordered, now grasping the

handle of his gun firmly. 'It's for official business, and no one can use it but an officer of the law.'

'You don't have to pull your gun on me,' I said, looking pointedly at his hand. 'I haven't touched your radio or broken the law.'

He glanced down. 'Just a natural reflex,' he said, flustered. He jerked his hand away from the gun as if it had been scorched and hurried to make the call.

A tow truck came within minutes. I waited inside my car while the policeman directed traffic around me with exaggerated motions, not once looking in my direction. If I hadn't been so upset, I probably would have sat there laughing at the ludicrousness of our conversation. It was funny, but I wasn't laughing. The car was dead, I was late for work, and the temperature outside was already at least eighty degrees; the smog level was high, and the air in the car was stifling. At that moment, there was nothing to laugh about.

It just occurred to me that the policeman incident would have made a perfect Eagles' Landing anecdote, a cocktail story or one to accompany after-dinner drinks like a choice piece of cheese. I can see you telling it now, pausing at the right places, duplicating the man's swagger while fingering an imaginary gun at your hip, directing traffic with a drink in your hand, capturing the policeman better than he could have played himself. And I can hear the responses to your performance, the appreciative laughter, the remarks I heard so often: 'Richard can really tell a story' or 'No one can tell a story like Weaver.' And I can see you relax and finish your drink with satisfaction, having paid your evening's dues.

But there is more. You shouldn't have killed yourself, Richard. You lost a full year's supply of anecdotes.

I told the tow truck operator, a wiry man with deep creases around his eyes and mouth, that I wanted the car taken to Ripley Oldsmobile. 'That'll be thirty-five dollars,' he said. 'Cash, if you have it. If not, I'll take a major credit card.'

325

Fortunately, I had the money and handed it to him.

'Sorry I had to ask for payment in advance,' he said, putting the money into a pocket of his overalls, 'but I've been stuck too many times. I can't spend my time chasing after people. I've gotta family to feed.'

When we were on our way, the tow truck operator became talkative. 'I miss home on days like this,' he said, wiping perspiration from his forehead with a grease-stained handkerchief. 'We had some hot ones, but out here it's murder. The air stinks along with the heat. It's like breathing in poison.'

I asked him where he was from.

'Blasdell, New York,' he said. 'You probably never heard of it. It's a small town outside of Buffalo, not far from Niagara Falls. Sure do miss it. We had a lotta snow, but the air was clean. Cleaner than here, anyway.'

'Then why don't you go back?' I asked.

He looked at me as if I had said something absurd; his shirt was soaked with perspiration, and he was breathing with difficulty. 'I couldn't do that,' he said, shaking his head. 'Never.'

'Why not?'

'If you go back, it means you failed, that you couldn't cut it. "So you're back, Tony," people would say. "Weren't there any more pots of gold in California?" I heard it too many times. The only way I could go back is rich. Then people don't ask. When you're rich, you can do what you damn well please. Money shuts people up. Ain't no way I'm gonna get rich towing cars,' he wheezed. 'The smog'll get me long before that day comes.'

'Maybe you'll be able to go back when you retire,' I suggested.

'Hell, no. It wouldn't make sense. There won't be a familiar face in Blasdell by that time, if I make retirement. Everyone'll be down in Florida or Arizona congratulating themselves on escaping the snow. A few might even come out here. Boy, will they be surprised when they get a whiff of this air,' he chortled bitterly.

As we drove the remaining blocks to Ripley Oldsmobile in a silence broken by the man's shallow wheezing, I began to wonder about how many transplanted people there are in California who are unhappy and want to return home but are afraid to do so for fear of being labeled failures. Probably thousands. Then I thought about myself fleeing Eagles' Landing and never wanting to return, and I realized that failure, like success, can be measured in degrees; for both the tow truck operator and myself, California is not so much a choice as it is a lesser hell.

The garage at Ripley Oldsmobile was impenetrable. There were two people waiting inside with their cars, and a tow truck was blocking the entrance. My tow truck operator groaned. 'Jeesuz,' he wheezed. 'I can't sit here all day.'

I told him that I would talk to the service manager to see if he couldn't get the car in quickly. 'You stay here,' he ordered. 'I'll talk to him.'

After he disappeared, I glanced at my watch. It was ten o'clock, and I was already an hour late for work. I jumped out of the truck, ran around the building to the front entrance, dashed into the showroom, told a salesman that I was a customer, and asked if I could please use one of their telephones. I was dialing before he had a chance to give me permission.

I asked the switchboard operator at Briarhill to connect me with Ellen. 'Where are you, Jenny?' she wanted to know. 'Everyone is in an uproar here. Briarhill is being investigated today, or didn't you remember? Jim and Simon are with the men now, and Jim is stomping up and down the halls like a bear with rabies.'

I had forgotten. Last Thursday Simon had received notification that Briarhill was going to be investigated on Monday. Rumors had circulated that it was the Fry brothers' revenge. Since they weren't suing, they had one of their friends, a bureaucrat who works for the state of California, order the investigation.

I told Ellen that my car had died on the freeway. 'I'll get there as soon as I can,' I said.

'I don't envy you,' she replied. 'Try to see Simon first.'

I returned to the garage and saw that my car had been deposited on a wide strip of concrete alongside the building; the tow-truck operator had left. I found the service manager and asked him how long it would take to fix the car. 'It will be a while before we can find space for it inside the garage,' he said. 'Then we'll have to find out what's wrong. I can't tell you anything now.'

I told him that I was late for work and asked if I could borrow a car.

'All of our loaners are out,' he replied.

'I must have a car,' I insisted, trying to retain his attention. While we were talking, he had been writing on a form attached to a large clipboard.

'There is nothing I can do for you. Look, why don't you sign this work order,' he said, handing me a pen and the clipboard. He had marked an 'X' on the bottom of the form.

'Why should I sign it?' I asked.

'We can't work on your car without your permission. This is just a formality,' he explained.

I recalled signing a form at Ripley's once before and without thinking, signed again.

It was almost eleven o'clock when I arrived at Briarhill, and I saw Simon, starched and erect in his wheelchair, through the glass doors. He was talking to two men in the main lobby who I assumed were the investigators. I hesitated, thinking that it might be wise to avoid them and use a different entrance. But then I decided that avoiding them was foolish. Anyone could have car trouble, and slinking around the building could be interpreted as an admission that my tardiness was intentional. I also thought of you, Richard. 'Be assertive,' you used to say. 'Take the first step. Then others have to adjust themselves to your action.'

It was good advice. I should know. You followed it down to your last breath, and I've spent the past two years of my life adjusting.

I walked through the glass doors into the main lobby and greeted Simon, explaining my tardiness with more self-confidence than I felt. Simon accepted my excuse with aplomb and introduced me to the men. 'I would be happy to brief you on our recreational program,' I said crisply, extending my hand. 'We're quite proud of it.'

I thought I saw a flicker of admiration register in Simon's eyes. It was the high point of my week.

I met Jim Gentile before lunch. He had been conducting a tour through the kitchen and pounced on me as soon as the man he was escorting left to meet the other inspectors. 'Where the hell were you? We're being investigated, and you can't even manage to haul your ass in here on time,' he bellowed.

'She was detained,' said a voice behind me.

We both turned to stare at Simon, who had glided silently behind us. 'Go to your office and stay there, with the door closed, until I call for you,' said Simon icily, pointing an arthritic finger at Jim.

'But she . . .' Jim protested.

'GO,' Simon ordered.

Jim left, blotchy-faced.

I called Ripley Oldsmobile before I left Briarhill, and the service manager told me that they had just started working on my car. 'We won't know anything for a while,' he said.

He hung up before I had the opportunity to ask him for the loan of a car.

I took a cab home and called at four o'clock to find out if my car was ready. 'No, Mrs Weaver,' said the service manager, 'but we've taken it apart. Your valve stem broke off and embedded itself in the piston. The piston is busted.'

I didn't know what he was talking about and asked naively if he could replace the piston.

'No,' he said, laughing at my ignorance. 'When the piston broke, it caused the block to crack. You need a new engine. Now do you understand?'

I didn't understand.

'You have a cracked block,' he said exasperatedly. 'Once a block is cracked, that's it. You need a new engine and a new head.'

I asked him how much a new engine would cost.

'Roughly $1,481 plus tax for a new engine and a new head. Now that's only an estimate,' he warned. 'We don't stock blocks and heads. We have to get them from the factory. I can give you an accurate estimate at the time of repair, which will be in three or four weeks.'

I was too flabbergasted to reply.

'Are you there, Mrs Weaver?' he asked.

'I can't wait three or four weeks,' I managed to say, 'unless you can loan me a car.'

'We can't keep a loaner out for that long,' he replied. 'We have to keep loaners available for customers who need them for a few hours, maybe a day or two at the most. If it were me, I wouldn't sink my money in a car as old as yours anyway. Why don't you trade it in on a later model? I've already told the general manager, Mr Tucker, about your car. It might be a good idea to come in tonight with your husband to discuss it with him.'

'I'll be there,' I said, unwittingly springing the Ripley trap.

We had an early dinner, just the three of us, before the sitter arrived. Nat plays baseball on Monday nights with a group of newspapermen, so I knew he wouldn't be available to go to Ripley's with me. Even if he had eaten dinner with us, I don't think I would have asked him to come. He would have had to offer to take me.

It may seem strange to you, knowing that I sleep with Nat, that I would wait for his offer of help. I'm sure he would have offered, but that is the way it is with affairs, at least with this affair. There is a definite language in my involvement with him, an intimacy that is not too intimate, with the exception of sex. Although it was never clearly stated, I have become sufficiently familiar with the language of affairs to realize that the word *depend* is taboo, as are the words *need*, *rely*, and, most important, *commitment*. I have learned that sophisticated affairs are for independent people who choose to be together, as Nat and I have chosen to be together, and independent people don't bring their problems to bed with them.

I would like to believe that our relationship is based on more than physical attraction, but I am not sure that it is. Nat has respected my desire for privacy concerning my past, which is an effort for him considering his intense curiosity. He has also had remarkable patience with Matthew, whose speech has improved dramatically since I wrote you six weeks ago. Matthew is still blocking, but he is improving daily. Nat has consistently given Matthew warmth without pressure; I don't think Matthew will be able to resist Nat's offer of friendship much longer. Still, with all the kindness and patience he has shown toward us, Nat has never alluded to a more permanent understanding. It has become increasingly clear that he is the navigator of our relationship, and he has set an obstacle-free, no-strings course for us.

I don't know how long our affair will last, or if it will last. Nat isn't the type to allow a relationship to drag on interminably, one of those five-year courtships climaxing in nothing, and he does have an eye for women. That much I have observed since I began seeing him, and the responses he receives from women to his inquisitive glances are unreservedly inviting. One of these days he may accept an invitation. There would be nothing I could do to prevent it, for we are theoretically free. There are no pledges, no claims, no symbolic pieces of jewelry, no whispered promises of faithfulness in our relationship. I know Nat is fond of me, at times almost more than fond, but fondness isn't love any more than sex is. Neither one of us has uttered the word love. We are very careful.

What worries me is not that my relationship with Nat

may end, for I am a big girl and could adjust (I adjusted to your death, didn't I?), but what effect our break-up would have on the children. Nat has made a difference in their lives; his presence has added a dimension that I am responsible for. He has dinner with us several times a week, and the four of us usually spend one day of the weekend together. They have been happy days with easy laughter, light-years away from the empty weekends we struggled through after your death. I had almost become accustomed to my new-found happiness when Catherine rippled the untroubled water of my acceptance with an innocent remark. 'I'm glad Nat is with us now. He's such fun. Maybe he can stay with us all of the time instead of just sometimes,' she said after we had spent an afternoon together at Knott's Berry Farm.

Her remark did more than unsettle me. I actually became frightened when I realized what the termination of our affair would mean. Nat is honestly fond of the children, but it is only because of me that he is with Matthew and Catherine. If Nat and I stop seeing each other, he will stop seeing them, too. In other words, he may vanish from their lives as abruptly as he entered. Matthew and Catherine have already suffered the loss of a father. Nat isn't as important to them as you were, but they will feel his absence and have to adjust to it. They were younger when you died, less aware and more resilient, and Matthew still hasn't recovered.

I try not to think about Nat and the children, but I do, and after the fight Nat and I had over what happened to me at Ripley Oldsmobile, I have been thinking about it more often.

The general manager was on a dinner break when I arrived at Ripley's. Since he was aware of the condition of my car, I decided to wait for him rather than discuss my problem with a salesman. It was probably another mistake. If I had dealt with any one of the half-dozen salesmen who seemed eager to wait on me, I would have had a fighting chance. Against Hadley Tucker, there was no contest.

Hadley Tucker strolled into the showroom with a toothpick dangling from a corner of his mouth. I thought he was a customer, for he looked around nonchalantly with his hands in his pants pockets, jingling loose change. He was dressed in black slacks and a maroon sport jacket with gold buttons, and his appearance would have been forgettable had it not been for his pomaded black hair and a slickly waxed, full mustache that curled at the ends. Apparently Mr Tucker hasn't heard of the dry look. The commercial must be on during his business hours.

A salesman walked up to him. The men spoke briefly, glancing in my direction, and Mr Tucker approached me, his right hand extended. 'Mrs Weaver,' he said, transferring the toothpick to the opposite corner of his mouth with a quick roll of his tongue. 'I'm Hadley Tucker. Call me Hal. Pleased to meet you. Why don't we talk in my office.'

We shook hands, and I followed him to one of the cubicles off the showroom floor. After we were seated, he said, 'Too bad about your wagon, the engine going like that. I'd kind of hoped your husband would come in with you tonight. It's a pretty complicated business when an engine goes.'

Then I made what in retrospect was another mistake. 'I'm a widow,' I replied.

'Oh, a widow so young,' he said consolingly, suspending the toothpick in the center of his lower lip. It hung there miraculously while he continued. 'Please accept my apology. Life is just full of tragedies these days. Well, I'll have to try my best to help you under the circumstances.'

He spoke to me as if you had taken your last breath within the hour.

'Now about your car. As the service manager told you, the block is cracked, which means that you'll need a new engine and a new head. If it was a fairly new car, it might make sense to put a new engine in, but your car is almost five years old.'

'Four years old,' I interrupted.

Hadley Tucker shifted the toothpick back to a corner of his mouth and smiled. 'Five years,' he corrected me. 'The new models will be coming out soon. Cars depreciate faster than most people realize. Anyway, with a car the age of yours, I would recommend investing in another vehicle. Trust me, Mrs Weaver. It's good advice.'

'I hadn't planned on buying a car,' I said.

'Hmmmm,' he muttered through pursed lips. 'Let me put it down for you in black and white so you can see why you should take my advice.'

He scribbled some figures on a pad and presented them to me.

$1,481.00
144.00
───────
$1,625.00 plus tax

'The first figure is for your new engine,' he said. 'The second figure will take care of a tune-up, touch-ups, and an oil change. And that doesn't include the tax you'll have to pay. You're talking a lot of money.'

It was a lot of money. I had recently spent almost five hundred dollars on the car. This latest disaster would bring the total to well over two thousand dollars.

While I was mentally adding repair bills, Hadley Tucker studied me shrewdly. 'I see from your expression that you agree with me, Mrs Weaver. I'll honestly do everything in my power to get you out of this mess with the best possible deal,' he said reassuringly. 'Now tell me, would you consider buying another Custom Cruiser Wagon? We have some beauties in stock.'

I asked him how much a new station wagon would cost. He picked up his pad, tore off a sheet of paper, and rapidly jotted figures down. The toothpick in his mouth jerked constantly while he was writing.

'This is it,' he said when he was finished. 'A new station

wagon equipped like yours goes for $8,450. I'll take your car off your hands for $7,350. It's a terrific deal for a new air-conditioned wagon. A terrific deal. If the owner saw it, he'd have me certified crazy.'

I couldn't believe it. 'That's ridiculous Mr Tucker,' I said. 'Aren't you allowing me anything for my car?'

'I sure am. I'm allowing you eleven hundred bucks. And call me Hal. We don't go formal around here,' he said.

'But my car is worth more than that.'

'If your car was in good shape, I could allow $2,850, but your car isn't in good shape. It needs a new engine, remember?' He smiled so brightly that his mustache curls rose an inch.

'But I've already spent close to five hundred dollars on the car,' I protested. 'It has a new battery, alternator, and exhaust system.'

'None of that means a thing if the car doesn't run. An exhaust system is no good without an engine,' he said, leaning back in his chair. 'Now if you don't have that kind of money to spend, considering how you're a widow and all, you can trade down into a used car. I happen to know of a cream puff that we have on the lot right now. It's a beauty.'

I was becoming suspicious of Hal Tucker. 'I suppose you're going to tell me that it was driven by an old lady only on Sundays,' I said.

'Now don't get angry, Mrs Weaver. Buying a car with Hal Tucker should be a pleasant experience, and those old car dealer jokes hurt. I'm trying to help you,' he said, sincerity oozing out of his pores. 'As a matter of fact, the car I have in mind is a one-owner – it belonged to a schoolteacher. You can't do better than a one-owner, schoolteacher's car. For all I know, it might have been sold while I was on my dinner break. If you're interested, I'll go check it out. Like I said, it's a real cream puff.'

At that point, I realized Hadley Tucker had the upper hand. He could deal with me on his terms, and unless I fought back, I would become the Ripley sucker-of-the-week.

'No, thank you,' I said, lighting a cigarette. I inhaled deeply and winced when the smoke burned my throat. 'I don't want a used car. It seems to me that if the car is as good as you say it is, the owner wouldn't sell it, especially not a schoolteacher. Schoolteachers can't afford to trade in perfectly good cars.'

Tucker chewed on his toothpick. 'Your smoking concerns me, Mrs Weaver. It isn't good for your health. Where I come from in Nebraska, the people are giving up cigarettes. Why, it has almost become bad manners to smoke.'

I took another puff of the cigarette, then put it out. 'Where I come from in the East, Mr Tucker, it has *always* been bad manners to put a toothpick in one's mouth in public.'

He smiled, a slow challenging smile, and removed the toothpick. 'It's going to be a pleasure dealing with you,' he said, expertly flipping the toothpick into a wastebasket. 'I like a customer who has her wits about her. Now tell me, would you consider trading down from a big wagon? I could get you into a four-door Cutlass much more reasonably.'

'How much more reasonably?' I wanted to know.

He tore another sheet off his pad and jotted down some figures. 'You could have a Cutlass with a V-8 engine and steel belt radials for six thousand dollars.'

'How much are you allowing me for my car?'

'Five hundred dollars.'

'Five hundred dollars!' I exploded. 'You just allowed me eleven hundred toward a station wagon.'

'That's true,' he said slowly. 'But we make more on a bigger car.'

'But I just put four hundred fifty-five dollars into the car. That means I'm only getting a forty-five dollar allowance. I could get more from a junk dealer. My father deals in scrap metal, and I know that my car is worth more than forty-five dollars.'

Hadley Tucker had me, and he knew it. 'Look, Mrs Weaver,' he said, 'with that five hundred dollar allowance, we're absorbing your three hundred sixty-five dollar repair bill.'

'What repair bill? You didn't repair my car.'

'Oh, but we took it apart,' he said coolly. 'The men had to take off the head and the air conditioning. It costs money to dismantle a car – labor. You have to pay to find out what's wrong. Why don't you look at it this way: you're really getting an allowance of close to nine hundred dollars because we're absorbing the repair bill. That's a helluva deal.'

I desperately wanted a cigarette but controlled the impulse to light up. I wouldn't give Hadley Tucker the satisfaction. Then I had an idea. 'How much would a new Cutlass cost without trading in my car?' I asked.

'A clean deal?'

'A clean deal.'

Tucker didn't need his pad and pen to answer me. 'Four hundred dollars off retail,' he said quickly.

'But doesn't that mean you're only giving me one hundred dollars for my wagon?'

'No. We'd have to charge you for the work we did. You still have a repair bill of three hundred sixty-five dollars.'

I knew I could get more than thirty-five dollars for my car and looked at my watch. It was close to eight o'clock. 'I have to leave,' I said, standing up. 'I'll call you and let you know what I've decided.'

'Now just a minute,' he said, rising out of his chair. 'We still have a problem here. Your car is in one of our stalls, and stall rental is forty dollars per day.'

'What?' I shrieked.

'You're tying up a work area worth five dollars per hour.'

'No one told me that when I had the car towed in.'

'We worked on the car. Now it's just sitting in an

expensive space,' he said. His voice was no longer friendly. 'If you're considering going to another dealer, you'll have to pay us your repair bill plus the cost of putting the car back together, which will be an additional charge of two hundred forty-eight dollars. That's not to fix it, understand. It's just to put it back together. Right now, everything is in pieces. No dealer could tow it away in that condition.'

He had articulated my thoughts. 'I have to call home,' I said shakily, 'and I'd like to think about this deal you've offered me.'

'You're welcome to use my phone,' he said.

I refused. 'I'll call from a pay phone.'

'Don't be gone too long,' he warned. 'It's a helluva deal, and I can't hold it past closing time.'

I left the showroom and walked to a drugstore two blocks away where I found a pay booth and called home. Then I grabbed a telephone book and started calling other Oldsmobile dealers. Not one of them would give me a price over the telephone. In desperation, I explained what had happened to me at Ripley's to the fourth dealer I called. The owner had answered, and he was understanding. 'I could send someone out to pick you up,' he said, 'but there isn't much I can do about your car. You'll have to settle the matter with Ripley. We had a customer once before that that happened to, and Ripley jacked the service bill up when we came to tow the car away. They wouldn't release the car without an additional seventy-five dollars. We had already written the deal and had a deposit, but it fell through.'

'Why didn't you report them?' I asked, fighting tears.

'We complained, but it didn't make a difference. All they care about in Detroit is getting cars sold, and Ripley sells a lot of cars. We don't sell the way he does because we value our reputation. We want people to come back. At Ripley's, they have one-shot deals. Now don't quote me,' he added. 'I shouldn't have told you what I did, but there's something in your voice ... I feel for you, but there's nothing I can do to help.'

I thanked him and walked back to Ripley's. It was close to nine o'clock, and the few remaining customers in the showroom were in salesmen's offices. Hadley Tucker was in his office, also. I entered without knocking.

'What have you decided, Mrs Weaver?' he asked. His manner was smooth, but his eyes were eager, black and shiny like cheap plastic buttons.

'I am going to buy a Cutlass and leave my car here,' I said coldly.

'I thought you would make that decision. It makes good sense, and you strike me as being a woman of good sense. In fact, I was so sure that I wrote up the deal.'

If I had been a man, I would have slugged him until his pomaded hair was standing on end.

I read the contract and saw that an additional one hundred twenty-five dollars had been added to the price I had been quoted. 'What is this for?' I asked, pointing to the charge.

'Dealer preparation,' he replied. 'I haven't had time to add the sales tax and charges for the license transfer, but that won't take long. Now all you have to do is pick the car you want. We have six identically equipped automobiles in stock that you can choose from. The only thing we have to do now is discuss the financing.'

'There won't be any discussion, Mr Tucker,' I said. 'Show me the cars.'

'We have to talk about payment,' he insisted.

'I'll pay cash, and you'll give me a car to drive until my car is ready,' I said.

'My pleasure,' said Hadley Tucker.

I selected a burgundy Cutlass, probably because the color reflected my mood, signed the contract, and drove home in a loaner. The children were already in bed, and the sitter told me that Nat had called, but I didn't call him back. I paid her and made myself a drink. And another drink. Then I went to bed mad as hell and woke up furious in the morning.

The car was supposed to be ready late Tuesday afternoon. Early that morning, I called the Better Business Bureau to report Ripley Oldsmobile, and a sympathetic woman listened to my story. 'Did you sign the purchasing contract?' she asked.

I told her that I had signed.

'Then there is nothing we can do but send you a form on which you can formally file your complaint. We have a thick file on Ripley Oldsmobile, but unless people call us before they sign a contract, we can't help them. All we can do in any case is suggest that they go to another dealer, that is, if they haven't signed. Unfortunately, most people don't call until the damage has been done.'

'You mean you can't do anything?' I asked, beside myself.

'If you mean put them out of business, no, we can't. All we can do is make recommendations. In your case, I would also suggest writing to the Attorney General's office to tell them what happened. Possibly the state of California can pursue the matter for you.'

I wrote the Attorney General's office during my lunch break but tore the letter up when I reread it. I realized that I sounded like a fool.

The car was ready late in the afternoon as promised. I handed Hadley Tucker a certified check, and he gave me the keys. 'I'll need the spare set from your car,' he said.

I wasn't going to make it easy for him. 'You'll need to have a spare set made,' I replied, 'unless you intend to junk the car.'

'Oh, no, the car can be repaired,' he said. 'It will be costly, but it can be done.'

'Then do it. And I want you to know, Mr Tucker, that you will hear from me again.'

'I hope you come back to buy another car. We like to keep our customers satisfied.'

'Well, I'm not satisfied,' I said, my voice rising. The

customers in the showroom turned to look in my direction. 'You ripped me off, and you'll get the publicity you deserve.'

I turned and quickly walked over to a young couple who were looking at a car. 'Don't buy a car here,' I warned them. 'They're crooked. Check with the Better Business Bureau. I didn't find out until it was too late.'

Hadley Tucker came up behind me. 'The lady is distraught,' he explained, taking my arm. 'She's a recent widow, you know.'

'Let go of me,' I ordered. 'I am not a recent widow, and I am not distraught. I was telling the truth. Let them use your telephone right now to call the Better Business Bureau to check you out.'

The couple didn't call. Instead, they backed away from us and out of the showroom, bug-eyed.

Tucker grabbed me again, this time by the elbow. 'Don't touch me,' I said through my teeth.

He stepped back and followed close at my heels. As we walked past the cubicles the salesmen use as offices, I saw that a salesman was handing an elderly, well-dressed gentleman a purchase contract. Before Hadley Tucker could stop me, I dashed into the cubicle. 'Don't sign that,' I said to the old man. 'Call the Better Business Bureau first, or go to another dealer. This outfit is crooked.'

The salesman and his customer stared at me dumbfounded.

'Ignore her,' said Tucker, stepping into the cubicle. 'She's a highly nervous woman. A widow, you know.'

'I'm not nervous. I was cheated, and I don't want you to be cheated. Go to another dealer,' I shouted.

Hadley Tucker had to practically carry me to get me out of the building.

I wasn't a lady, Richard. I made a scene, a public spectacle of myself for the first time in my life. It felt good, surprisingly good, and I'm not ashamed. You aren't here, so my behavior can't embarrass you. Besides, I'll never see those people again. I'm not rationalizing. California isn't

Eagles' Landing. There is anonymity here, and if I'm going to be treated like a native, I might as well act like one.

Wednesday morning was a repeat of Tuesday morning: I jumped out of bed angry, snapped at the children, and choked on my breakfast. I was so furious that I cleaned the bathrooms, scrubbed the kitchen floor, and took a shower in a quarter of the time it normally takes and did a better job than usual. The chrome, tile, and floors glistened with my anger. I was still livid when I left to run my errands, and on the way to the supermarket, I spotted a novelty store that had a large display of bumper stickers in the window with a sign that said: 'If we don't have what you want, we'll make it for you.' I pulled the car over, parked, and went inside.

The store had a fabulous array of bumper stickers in a rainbow of colors:

BEE NICE: EAT YOUR HONEY

A GOOD LOVER
stays on top of things

PROTECT OUR WILD LIFE—
THROW A PARTY

HONK IF YOU'RE HORNY
YOUR HAIRDRESSER
DOES IT BEST

I'M POLISH

THANK GOD

FIREMEN MAKE THE HOTTEST LOVERS

MAFIA STAFF CAR
[suggested for black or burgundy Lincolns]

I studied the bumper stickers until a slender young man

with an auburn beard came over to wait on me. I told him that I wanted to have a custom bumper sticker printed.

'How many?' he asked.

'Just one,' I replied, 'with a bright yellow background and black letters. Those seem to stand out the most. And I want the largest bumper sticker you have in stock.'

He returned with a yellow, oversize sticker and handed me a pencil and paper. 'Print what you want the sticker to say,' he said.

In large block letters, I printed:

I WAS RIPPED OFF
AT RIPLEY OLDSMOBILE

I handed him the paper.

'Hey, that's something else,' he said with admiration. Then he frowned. 'I don't think I can fit Oldsmobile on.'

I took the paper back and crossed off MOBILE. 'Will that do?' I asked.

'It's great,' he said. 'I'll really take care with this one. I might even make a copy leaving off Ripley Oldsmobile. There are a lot of people out there who would like to get even. This bumper sticker could be a hot seller.'

He did an excellent printing job. After I paid him, I returned to my car and carefully put the bumper sticker in place:

I WAS RIPPED OFF
AT RIPLEY OLDS

The acid taste in my mouth wasn't quite as strong.

Nat and I had our fight Wednesday evening. He had come over for dinner, and I told him what had happened to me at Ripley's when the children went out to play. 'I want you to expose them,' I said. 'Do a series of public-service articles for consumers and start off with Ripley Oldsmobile.'

'I can't do that,' he said. 'I'm sorry for what happened to you, but I can't authorize that kind of article.'

'Sure you can,' I said. 'Aren't you an editor, and don't editors make assignments?'

'I'm a city editor – an employee, not the publisher. I don't own the paper. Ripley spends enough in three months of advertising to cover my salary for a year. It's a matter of money: Ripley is worth more to the paper than I am. Also, we could be inviting a lawsuit. I just can't do it.'

'You're afraid to do it,' I said.

'It's not so much a matter of fear as it is a matter of practicality. Don't you understand?'

I was too angry to understand.

'It could have happened to me, Jenny,' he said soothingly.

'It wouldn't have happened to you,' I replied bitterly. 'You're a man. And if it did happen to you, you'd expose them.'

Nat exploded. It was the first time I had seen him lose his temper. 'That's ridiculous,' he said, his eyes turning into crystals of blue ice. 'What makes you think that women have an exclusive on getting ripped off? They aren't the only easy prey in the world. I doubt that there is a man alive who hasn't been ripped off at one time or another, but men don't walk around crying about it.'

I shook with frustration. 'I'm not crying. I'm fighting back, and you could help me fight back.'

'You seem to be managing quite well on your own. You lost Ripley a possible sale, and you're giving him rotten publicity with that bumper sticker. Isn't that enough? What do you want me to do, go to Ripley's, grab Tucker and string him up by his balls? Would that make you happy?'

'That's not a bad idea,' I said. 'But that isn't what I want. You know what I want.'

'You want the impossible. Well, I can't give you the impossible,' he said wearily.

'It isn't that you can't,' I retorted. 'It's that you don't want to. You won't even try.'

'No, I won't try, but not because I don't care. I care, but there are some things that I simply cannot do, and I am realistic enough to recognize them. I can't fill the role that you've set up for me.'

'What role?' I demanded.

'I can't be your avenging warrior, a knight on a white horse who will fight your battle and save your honor. You want a hero, but you drew a peasant without a horse, armor, or a shield. I'm sorry, Jenny. I may be a peasant, but I'm not a stupid peasant. I won't walk into an obvious slaughter with a smile on my face, and I won't let you push me into one. And that's final.'

We stood in the center of the living room staring at each other, but I wasn't seeing Nat Witton. I was staring at you, Richard Weaver. Then I started to hiccup.

'Are you all right?' Nat asked, putting his hands on my shoulders.

'I ... hic ... don't know,' I said truthfully. 'I really ... hic ... don't know.'

My hiccups wouldn't stop. I excused them, explaining that I occasionally get attacks of the hiccups when I am upset. Nat wanted to stay, but I made it clear that I would prefer it if he left. I haven't seen him since. He called the next day as if nothing had happened and mentioned plans we had made previously to go to a play Saturday night. We usually spend Friday evenings together, also, but when he telephoned late this afternoon, I suggested that we not see each other tonight. I told him that it had been an awful week and that I wanted to go to bed early. 'I know you'll understand,' I said, giving him no choice.

'Sure,' he replied, 'I understand.'

Nat's voice betrayed him. I know him well enough to recognize the slightest change in his inflection. He was hurt, but his recovery was quick. 'I'll call you in the morning,' he said.

I'm going to be uncomfortable with Nat. I was

impossible Wednesday night, completely intransigent, and I didn't apologize. But I'm not avoiding him solely because he saw me at my worst. I need room. I need to put space between us. So much has happened in such a brief period of time that I haven't stepped back to gain perspective.

And there was also that moment at the end of our fight when I saw you. I've been avoiding it, but I'll have to think about that, too.

I spent part of my lunch break in the solarium with Mr Gallisdorf today, and I told him what had happened to me at Ripley Oldsmobile. He shook his head in dismay and patted my arm sympathetically with his good right hand until I told him about the scene I made in the showroom with the other customers. Suddenly, he brightened. And when I described having the bumper sticker made, the dignified Mr Gallisdorf slapped his leg and laughed uproariously. His reaction astounded me. 'Why are you laughing?' I asked.

'It's wonderful, just wonderful,' he said, wiping tears of laughter from his eyes. 'I venture to say that even Frederick Jackson Turner would have approved.'

'Who?' I asked, taken aback.

'Frederick Jackson Turner, the frontier historian I told you about,' replied Mr Gallisdorf, catching his breath.

I was crushed and looked at Mr Gallisdorf painfully, sure that he had just entered the netherworld of senility.

'Oh, Jenny,' he said, 'don't you understand what you did? You fought back the only way you could, and more important, you fought back within the context of your time. Using their showroom to lose sales for them was a fine start, but the bumper sticker was a masterpiece, a stroke of genius. As I recall, Ripley was one of the first dealers in the area to put his decal on the trunk of every car he sold to get free publicity. I bought a car there for my wife years ago, and they slapped a sticker on, over my protests, which I wasn't able to remove later without destroying the paint.

'Now do you see what you've done? You've used one

of their methods against them. Mark my words: they'll be screaming their heads off about that sticker within a week, and there won't be a thing they can do about it.

'You know,' he continued, 'I've been concerned about you. I've had this feeling for some time now that you weren't adjusting too well to California. There were moments when I sensed that you regretted coming here, that you couldn't seem to find a comfortable place for yourself. I'm fond of you, and it bothered me that I couldn't figure out a way to help you settle in. I went so far as to curse this wheelchair, something I hadn't done in a long time, until I realized one day that I couldn't help you even if I had a whole body instead of half a body. There are some adjustments people have to make for themselves; no one can help them, not even those with the kindest thoughts or best intentions.

'Well, I can see that I don't have to be concerned any more. You are on your way. It has been a rather traumatic start, but now I'm sure that you'll make it. You have wonderful spirit, and I'm grateful to that awful fellow at Ripley's for bringing it out. He may have cheated you financially, but in the end, he did you a favor by pushing you to the point where you felt compelled to fight back. You were fortunate. You got a good jolt to get you going again, and I'm glad.'

If I'm so fortunate, Richard, why don't I feel fortunate?

Mr Gallisdorf thinks that I am on my way, that I am finally adjusting to California, but I am not too sure. I am not even sure that I like California or that it is worth the effort of adjustment. However, there is one thing of which I am sure: adjusting has more to do with you than I realized. The day I stop writing to you will be the day that I have finally adjusted.

Richard, I hope you don't hear from me again.

But thank you for listening.

I have to make a decision: Simon Gentile offered me Jim's job today. I knew Simon was upset over Jim's performance with the state investigators (Briarhill passed in spite of his ineptitude), but I hadn't realized the extent of Simon's dissatisfaction until he met me at the door this morning. 'I'd like you to go directly to my suite,' he said, his face expressionless except for his shrewd brown eyes, which were glittering behind his steel-rimmed glasses.

'Is anything wrong?' I asked, noting that everything about him, from his freshly pressed charcoal gray suit and polished shoes to his crisp manner, meant business.

'Nothing that can't be corrected,' he replied, spinning his wheelchair around.

I followed Simon to his quarters, wondering nervously if I had offended a resident or overlooked a detail in planning that was important. I hadn't paid as much attention to my job as I had when I was originally hired. To be truthful, my duties had become repetitious, and my handling of them increasingly mechanical. There are only so many activities that can be programmed for the elderly, and when those activities are repeated with slight variations, day after day, week after week, the effect can be numbing. I knew it wouldn't be long before planning programs became as automatic as a reflex, which worried me. If I have learned nothing else from working at Briarhill, I have come to understand what it means to be old and institutionalized. I had seriously considered quitting next month, not only because I would have the summer free, but because I felt the residents deserved more than a human robot coordinating their final activities. Still, I was uneasy when I faced Simon in his elegant living room. It is one thing to contemplate resigning and quite another to be fired. I did not want to be fired.

'I'll get directly to the point,' said Simon. 'I want to hire someone to replace you in recreation so that I can ease you into Jim's job.'

'Where will Jim be?' I asked, surprised.

'Gone. I've decided to set him up in the sporting goods

business. It's the best investment I can make,' he said candidly. 'The merchandise will be worth something whether he makes a go of the business or not, and I'll have him out of here. He signed an agreement over the weekend stating that he would not interfere with the running of Briarhill during my lifetime or after my death. The proviso states that, should he set a foot in Briarhill's door without a specific invitation, he will lose the business and all but minimal claims to my estate.'

'Isn't that rather harsh?' I asked, thinking that even if Jim was an idiot, he was still Simon's son.

'No, it's realistic, and I am a realist,' Simon replied firmly. It was clear that he didn't want to discuss Jim. I noticed a slight tremor pass through his body before he continued, which Simon ignored. 'I've been watching you since you started working at Briarhill. Your capabilities far exceed the requirements of your job. You were a little green in the beginning, but that was because you were new and unsure of yourself. I never had doubts about you, not for a minute, although I believe Jim hired you for your looks rather than your brains. Whatever his reasons, he didn't get what he bargained for, but I did: I found the right person to assist me.'

'Thank you,' I said, flattered.

'Rubbish,' said Simon. 'I didn't ask you in here to sweet-talk you. That's not my way. I'm a practical man, and I'm making you an offer. You'll have to work full time and take evening courses in hospital administration, which Briarhill will pay for. Your schedule will be demanding, but you must think of it as an opportunity – you could be running this place on your own one day. Are you interested?'

'I don't know. It's so sudden.'

'Your new job will mean a substantial raise in salary,' he said coaxingly. 'Maybe that will persuade you.'

I wasn't sure.

'Why the hesitation?' Simon asked. 'I was positive that you'd jump at the chance.'

'I don't know if I can handle it,' I replied, stalling.

Simon grabbed the rubber tires of his wheelchair impatiently. 'That's an excuse and we both know it,' he said sternly. 'You've been handling matters out of Jim's office for months. What's really on your mind?'

'My children,' I said truthfully, thinking about the problems Matthew had adjusting to Nat. 'I would be working full time, and they only have one parent.'

'So?' questioned Simon.

'What if one of them becomes ill? What about my son's speech therapy? My daughter's dancing lessons? Who will take them to their activities? Who will be there when they come home from school?'

'You'll make arrangements. Your children aren't babies, and you'll be doing them a favor,' said Simon emphatically.

'How will I be doing them a favor?'

'They won't grow up like my son or John Gallisdorf's daughter. My late wife did everything for that boy. Everything. And he grew into a totally incompetent man,' said Simon bitterly.

I ignored Simon's remark about his wife and son and instead concentrated on Mr Gallisdorf's having a daughter. I couldn't believe it. 'You said that Mr Gallisdorf has a daughter. Are you sure?' I asked, stunned.

'Of course I'm sure,' replied Simon. 'John pretends that his marriage was childless, but he and his wife had one child, a girl, and she was the center of John's universe. She stayed close to home until she went away to college in San Francisco. During her first year there, she met a boy and became pregnant. It wasn't surprising. As I recall, she was the most naive, sheltered child I had ever met, a real daddy's girl. I watched her grow up; she was Jim's age, but socially she was a baby.

'Anyway, it was before the time of abortions, although John could have obtained one for her and offered to do so. But she refused. She said she loved the boy and wanted to marry him. There was the catch – the boy was Chinese.

John couldn't accept the boy or the idea that his grandchild would be of mixed blood. They argued bitterly. My wife told me about it; she and John's wife were close friends. John disowned the girl. He told her that, as far as he was concerned, she no longer existed, that she had never existed. To my knowledge, he has neither seen nor mentioned her in over twenty years.'

I was shocked. 'He lied to me,' I whispered to myself.

Simon's sharp brown eyes softened with understanding. 'Be kind, Jenny,' he said gently. 'Don't hold it against him. John Gallisdorf didn't deliberately deceive you. He has spent all of these years deceiving himself without having the luxury of one moment of grieving aloud. He may appear to be a delicate old man, and he is, but he has a mind as strong as a vise. She doesn't exist for him; she never existed. That vise of a mind clamped her out of his thoughts forever. But he has suffered. When he lost her, he also lost a portion of his life that he'll never be able to reclaim.

'I trust that you will keep what I have told you in confidence. I know that you are fond of John Gallisdorf. If your attitude toward him changed, he would sense it, and it could prove to be too much for him.'

Simon cleared his throat and became his usual business-like self. 'Are you willing to take the job? I'm game, if you are,' he said.

'I'm not sure,' I answered, confused. Simon's offer and what he had told me about Mr Gallisdorf were too much to sort out at once. 'I don't know if I want to make nursing home administration a career. It's depressing.'

Simon nodded. 'You're thinking of Mrs Fry again, I imagine. Don't fool yourself. There are thousands of Mrs Frys,' he said. 'No matter where you go, you'll find them. And worse. Leaving Briarhill won't make them disappear.'

When he mentioned Mrs Fry, the confusion in my head became chaos. What had been flashing through my mind was not Mrs Fry or Mr Gallisdorf or any of the other individuals whose horror stories continue daily within

Briarhill's walls, but images of the institution itself: the maze of gleaming corridors that lead to lonely rooms, vinyl-upholstered furniture against which human flesh cannot breathe, pill trays crowded with medication in neat paper cups, professional cleaning crews spreading clouds of disinfectant – all immaculate and impersonal, as chilling as the vacant stares of residents who no longer see their surroundings, not because they are blind, but because they no longer care.

I was about to refuse Simon's offer when he spoke. 'I have to admit that I'm disappointed,' he said, as if reading my thoughts. 'I was positive that you would accept the challenge, even welcome it. Maybe I expected too much from you, although I'm usually not far off when it comes to judging character. I guess I made a mistake this time. I thought you were a fighter, like me.'

'I didn't say no,' I replied hastily. 'I just need time to think it over.'

'How much time?' Simon asked. His eyes were glittering again, dancing as they had when he had met me at the door.

'I'll let you know in the morning,' I promised.

Simon knew what he was doing when he told me that he had misjudged my character. It was the perfect remark, the only one he could have made that would force me to reconsider. He is as perspicacious as he is practical, a man who knows what he wants and how to get it. I doubt that anyone has ever been canny enough to outwit Simon Gentile. It is flattering to be chosen as his assistant, but I have no illusions about either Simon or the job. He will retain full control of Briarhill as long as he is breathing; he will be aware of every detail, from the daily quantity of towels used to the exact state of each resident's health, both mental and physical. I'll be responsible directly to him, and it is likely that I'll serve more as a buffer between Simon and the residents than as a person in my own right. I don't object to the idea of taking orders from someone as astute as Simon; it is doubtful that I'll ever be offered a better learning experience. But learning at Briarhill isn't an enticing prospect. Still, I could find myself in worse places. My degree in psychology has prepared me for nothing except perhaps a career in sales, which appeals to me even less than a career in geriatrics. (You should certainly be able to understand that, Richard.) In other words, my options are limited. I probably wouldn't have been hired for my present position in recreation if Jim Gentile hadn't had ideas for employing me in private recreation of his own. If it hadn't been for Simon's intervention, Jim would have fired me when I refused to cooperate with him. It was an unpleasant experience that could happen again.

However, I shouldn't accept Simon's offer in order to avoid men like Jim; nor should I take the job because it is my only option at the moment. My acceptance should be based on positive reasons. The last major decision I made was to come to California, and it was more negative than positive, a reaction rather than a choice. But I can think of a positive reason other than learning from Simon: changes could be initiated at Briarhill that would make the place less institutional. Simon has strong opinions, but he is reasonable as long as he isn't crossed. I am positive that he could be persuaded to soften some of Briarhill's policies in time.

So far I have two negative reasons and two positive reasons, and I still haven't considered the children. They will definitely be a negative reason, especially Matthew. His speech therapist told me that any change in authority figures or important relationships will cause him difficulties. I don't want to risk upsetting him, not after he has just overcome his problems with Nat.

If I knew why Matthew has finally accepted Nat, perhaps I could risk taking the job, but I don't. I can think of nothing specific that either Nat or I did to cause Matthew's change in attitude. We continued to treat him as we had before, with as much understanding as possible, ignoring his recalcitrance until it seemed to disappear on its own. It could be that Matthew came around simply because Nat didn't go away. Whatever the reason, Matthew and Nat are friends now, and for that I am glad. Nat borrowed a boat on Saturday and took us sailing. Matthew stayed at his side the entire time, anxious to help him. It was a lovely afternoon, as bright and balmy as the weather, with none of the undercurrents that had marred our outings in the past.

Simon would argue that I am being overprotective. He believes that I would be doing the children a favor by working full time, for he blames Jim's failures on his wife's overprotectiveness. Maybe I am overprotective, but Jim Gentile didn't lose his father unexpectedly as Matthew did; nor was he uprooted by a move across the country; nor was he expected to accept a stranger, a man who threatened his memory of his father. Now that I think about it, Simon's judgment of his wife doesn't seem fair. He absolves himself of any responsibility for Jim's shortcomings, instead accusing a dead woman who can't defend herself. Hard as I try, I can't picture Simon watching in silence while his wife botched the job of parenting their only child. He must have contributed his share, perhaps more than his share knowing Simon, whether he admits it or not.

But I can't shield Matthew forever. Life demands adjustments, and Matthew will have to learn to make them eventually. He might as well start now, while he is young, so that he isn't forced to grow up suddenly after years of living under my protection, which is what happened to me when you died.

There goes another argument.

When I told Simon that I was concerned about the children's activities, he argued that I could make arrangements for them. I suppose he is right. Matthew's speech therapy can be rescheduled, and it might be possible to switch Catherine's dancing lessons to Saturdays. But I want to be at home when they get off the school bus, and there is no way I can manage that if I am working full time.

If you were here, you would probably tell me that I am

suffering from a case of delayed guilt because I left them with Ginny for weeks at a time when we lived in Eagles' Landing. I won't disagree. To be honest, I have an excellent babysitter, a teenager who is intelligent and reliable (and sober!). Matthew and Catherine adore her; they have great fun together. And I am sure she would be willing to take care of them. Just last week she mentioned that she was looking for an after-school job and asked me if I knew of one.

I can't decide. I don't want to look for a new job, but if I quit, I'll have the summer free.

My raise in salary will cancel most of our Social Security benefits.

If I accept Simon's offer, I'll have no time for myself. But if I refuse, I'll have too much time, and Mrs Feltcher will be at my door every day.

Then there is Mr Gallisdorf. I have avoided thinking about him. It is too painful. If I leave Briarhill, I'll have a perfect excuse for not seeing him again. But that wouldn't be fair. Until today, I honestly cared for Mr Gallisdorf. I still do, although I am deeply disappointed in him.

The pros and cons are almost evenly balanced. I thought that writing to you would help, but it hasn't. I'm no closer to a decision than I was when I started two hours ago. If anything, I may be even more confused. And my hand is beginning to feel stiff.

I shouldn't complain. At least I'm writing about something positive. I hesitate to say this for fear of breaking what seems to be a magic spell, but I think my life is finally turning around. It is taking a new direction, leaving the despair and loneliness that were my constant companions in the shadows of the past. Even my trouble with Ripley Oldsmobile has brought me unexpected satisfaction. I must tell you what happened.

The bumper sticker had been on the car for less than a week when I received a call from Hadley Tucker. 'Mrs Weaver,' he said, oily-voiced. 'This is Hal Tucker. I understand that you had a bumper sticker printed.'

I interrupted him before he could say another word. 'Yes, I did, and when it wears out, I'll have another one printed. Good-bye, Mr Tucker, and don't call me again.'

I slammed the receiver down as hard as I could without breaking it.

A few days later, I received a call from Martin Ripley, the owner of Ripley Oldsmobile. He wasn't as easy to dismiss as Hadley Tucker, for after he introduced himself, he immediately told me that I would be hearing from his lawyer if I were unwilling to work things out. I listened to him for several minutes and understood that working things out, according to Mr Ripley, meant removing the bumper sticker. But I began to understand something else. As he was speaking, I realized that I had Martin Ripley exactly where I wanted him.

'Will you remove the sticker?' he asked after he had repeated, for the fourth or fifth time, that I had willingly signed a purchase contract to buy the car.

'No,' I replied.

Martin Ripley raised his voice. 'If you don't cooperate, Mrs Weaver, I'll start litigation to force you to remove that sticker. I'll also sue you for damage to our reputation.'

'What reputation?' I sneered. 'I'm sure that I'm not the first person you've cheated. Your Mr Tucker is an expert rip-off artist. If you sue me, you may walk into the courtroom to find it filled with dissatisfied customers. I'll see to it that the lawsuit is publicized if I have to pay for the ads myself.'

'You weren't cheated,' he answered sharply.

'I was cheated, Mr Ripley,' I said. 'If you had stolen my car off the street, you couldn't have been more dishonest.'

'You'll have to hire a lawyer,' he warned.

'So will you,' I retorted, 'but at least I'll be getting something for my money.'

'What?' Martin Ripley shouted.

'I'll find out how much you receive for my station wagon when you sell it.'

'I won't sell it,' he replied heatedly.

There was silence on both ends of the line. I was grinning, and I had the feeling that Martin Ripley was silently cursing, for I knew that he had planned to repair and sell my car.

I was the first to speak. 'Good-bye, Mr Ripley,' I said, replacing the receiver with satisfaction.

Martin Ripley's lawyer called early last week. I adamantly refused to remove the sticker and told him that I did not want to be bothered again. 'Ripley Oldsmobile is harassing me,' I said, 'and harassment is against the law.'

'Your bumper sticker is against the law,' he replied.

'What law?' I asked, suddenly nervous.

'I have no intention of discussing the law with you,' he replied, hanging up.

I knew then that I was safe.

The bumper sticker has drawn a surprising amount of attention. Drivers stopped next to me in traffic frequently comment about it through their open windows, and I have lost count of the number of former Ripley customers who have congratulated me for performing a public service. But the comments I appreciate most come from strangers who pull up next to me and ask if the bumper sticker is true. I tell them that it is and warn them not to shop at Ripley's. They drive off thanking me. It has been more than satisfying. I have discovered the joy of getting even, and it sure beats crying in the privacy of your room.

I still haven't made a decision, Richard, but I believe I understand why I wrote to you tonight. I wanted you to decide for me, as you did in the past. It isn't necessary now. I can trust myself, and I'll know what to do in the morning.

I had an experience late this afternoon that makes my evening at Ripley Oldsmobile look almost pleasurable in comparison. It is now one thirty in the morning, and I am still so upset that I cannot sleep. I feel sick, as if bacteria

357

from spoiled food are multiplying by the thousands inside me. My skin is clammy, and my hands are so cold that it is difficult to hold a pen, but I must try. The nausea seems to get worse when I lie down, and I spent the past hour in the living room, moving from chair to sofa to chair. I don't know what else to do.

It happened after I left Briarhill. I was driving home in rush-hour traffic when I noticed a green Cadillac a car length behind me. It was Jim Gentile. As soon as he sensed that I was aware of him, he hunched over the wheel of his car, gunned the motor, and braked within inches of my bumper. I looked into the rearview mirror and saw a malevolent smirk on his face, a nasty expression that could not be interpreted as teasing, and decided to pass the car in front of me in an attempt to lose him. I waited for an opening and made my move, but it didn't work. Jim pulled out immediately after I did, ignoring oncoming traffic. He drove like a man with no sense of peril, as if he were either crazy or drunk, and cut off a red Datsun in the left lane. Fortunately the driver was a young man with quick reflexes; he swerved and slammed on his brakes, narrowly avoiding an accident. I switched back to the right-hand lane, and again, Jim followed me, driving like a maniac. Brakes squealed and horns sounded, but he ignored them and kept his car directly behind mine, not more than a foot away. Nervous, I put my lights on, hoping he would think I was braking, but when he caught on to what I was doing, he inched his car even closer. If I hadn't been frightened, I would have probably done something sensible, like pull into a gas station to ask for directions to the nearest police station, then lead him there. But I was so anxious to get out of the car that I drove directly to Sherwood Village, Jim's Cadillac a bumper away.

I parked in my assigned space behind our building and debated what to do as Jim pulled in further down the lot. There was no one around, but I reasoned that he wouldn't harm me in broad daylight. He's a bully, I thought, but he's all bellow and no bite. Besides, I wasn't sure that he had followed me from Briarhill. He could have spotted my bumper sticker and decided to intimidate me as some kind of bizarre joke or perhaps to prove himself macho, a cowboy in a Cadillac. Whatever his purpose, I was angry. His reckless driving could have caused an accident. Jim Gentile had no right to endanger my life or the lives of others.

Jim was out of his car first. I watched him walk toward me, swaying slightly. He looked like a walrus who had just lost his tusks, weak-chinned and ponderously fleshed, stuffed into a brown polyester leisure suit. I stepped out of my car, locked the door, and confronted him. 'Why did you follow me?' I demanded. 'You could have gotten us killed.'

'So you don't like being pushed,' he said, grinning maliciously. His pale eyes were red-rimmed and bloodshot, and there was a strong odor of whiskey on his breath.

'You're drunk,' I accused. 'I should have driven to a police station. You would have been arrested on the spot. I could call them right now and have you picked up.'

'Don't threaten me,' he said, grabbing my arm.

'Let go,' I ordered, trying to pull myself free.

He tightened his grip. 'Stop, you're hurting me,' I cried, hoping someone would hear us.

'Good,' he said. He smiled again, but his eyes were small and mean. 'You planned it from the beginning, didn't you? Buttering up my father so that you could have my job.'

'I don't know what you're talking about,' I said.

'Of course you do, you bitch. You were sitting at my desk on Tuesday. You didn't even have the decency to wait a week to let the office get dusty.'

Then, as if to prove himself right, he twisted my arm. The pain was exquisite. 'Please, stop,' I pleaded. 'I didn't want your job. When your father offered it to me on Monday, I almost quit.'

'Bullshit,' he said, spitting the word in my face. The stench of his breath made me gag.

'I'll have you arrested for assault,' I said desperately.

'You can't push me around like you push my father around,' he bragged, twisting harder. 'You must have pushed your husband around, too. That's probably why the poor guy's dead. I'll bet you pushed him right into his grave.'

I gasped, unable to reply.

'Hah, I'm right,' he said, gloating with satisfaction.

A car turned into the parking lot on the opposite side of the driveway. 'Look,' I cried, weak with relief. He loosened his grip, startled. I wrenched my arm free and ran toward the back door of our townhouse, Jim lumbering close behind.

The screen door was locked from the inside, which meant that the babysitter was out with the children, probably at the Village Green. I wheeled and raced around the building, wondering whether I should risk the time it would take to unlock the front door or instead go straight to Mrs Feltcher's. Jim was panting after me, calling out, 'Schemer, manipulator,' but he was a safe distance behind, moving in a stumbling, inebriated gait, so I decided to head for our front door. I clutched my keys, so intent on reaching my destination that I didn't see Matthew coming in our direction. Quickly, I unlocked the door, stepped inside, and slammed it shut as Jim started up the steps. 'Bitch, ball breaker,' I heard him shout through the closed door. 'Did you use a gun on your husband or did you just push until you crushed the life out of him?'

I leaned against the bolted door, unable to catch my breath. My forearm was red and sore where he had held it, but I wasn't harmed physically. Yet I felt as if I had been assaulted, beaten to the point where I couldn't fight back. When the door knob turned, I jumped with fright. 'M-Mom,' a voice called, 'the door's l-locked.'

It was Matthew. I stiffened with apprehension, afraid that Gentile had grabbed him. 'Is anyone out there with you?' I called back.

'N-No, the man is gone,' he replied.

I dashed to the living room window, saw that Matthew was alone, then ran to the door and unbolted it. As I pulled him inside, I glimpsed Jim's Cadillac speeding down the driveway. 'Where's Catherine?' I asked frantically.

'Sh-She wanted to stay on the swings. L-Liz said I could l-leave 'cause you'd be home. Wha-What's a ball breaker?'

I stared at Matthew, sick with the understanding that he had overheard Jim. 'It's . . . it's nothing,' I said, trying to sound casual. 'It's just a nasty expression. Forget it.'

But Matthew wasn't willing to forget. 'Wh-Who was that man? D-D-Did he know D-Daddy?'

'He's a man who used to work at Briarhill. He didn't know Daddy.'

Matthew frowned. 'Th-Then why did he talk about him?'

'He wanted to upset me.'

'B-B-But he said you p-pushed Daddy. I-I-I heard.'

Sickness rose in my throat, and I ran to the bathroom with my hand over my mouth. Matthew followed me and stood in the doorway while I vomited, watching solemnly. I retched until I tasted bile.

'A-A-Are you okay?' he asked, pale with concern.

It was a while before I could answer him. 'I'm fine,' I managed to say.

I'm not fine, Richard. I still feel sick, although I have told myself, over and over again, that Jim Gentile's parting words were nothing more than a retaliatory insult, a loser's attempt to get even. But that isn't true. With the unerring accuracy of a lucky fool, Gentile made the one accusation that could devastate me. And what is worse is that Matthew heard and believed him. *B-B-B-but he said you p-pushed Daddy.*

Yes, I pushed you. But you pushed me first, and you pushed hard. What did you expect when you cornered me with insults in that lawyer's library? Not only did you ignore my grief, but you turned everything around; you set the burden of our failure squarely upon my shoulders for keeping a promise. That wasn't fair. I had to fight back. I had to push as hard as you did. But there was a difference between us. You knew what you were doing; I didn't. I realize that my lack of awareness doesn't excuse what happened, but at least my intention was honorable.

I remember how stunned we were when Anson's call came within hours after we arrived in Eagles' Landing. 'I'm sorry,' he said, 'Maggie had a massive coronary yesterday. She went quickly, which was a blessing. I hope I'm that lucky.'

You were with the children, and I called you aside to relate Anson's message. Then I ran upstairs, closed our bedroom door, and cried. Later, I found you sitting in the living room, staring out the window into the frigid winter night.

We flew back to Florida early in the morning the day of the funeral; my parents had left for Florida the day before. Anson met us at the airport dressed in a somber navy blue suit. 'The service will be at two o'clock. Jenny's parents are at the funeral parlor now. Then they're meeting with Maggie's attorney,' he said, glancing at his watch. 'You have plenty of time for lunch. I can take you to Maggie's first if you'd like to freshen up. Did you bring any luggage?'

'Just a change of clothes,' you replied, indicating that all we brought with us was contained in the garment bag you had slung over your shoulder. 'We're planning to catch a flight out this evening if we can get one.'

'That's good to know,' said Anson. 'I'll inform Maggie's attorney. It appears there are some papers Jenny will have to sign.'

Anson left us to call Maggie's lawyer, and we went to the reservation desk to confirm our flight back. There was no problem. The airline had managed to find us seats on fully booked flights when we explained the necessity of our trip. I made a remark about the flight and seat availability after my original call from Eagles' Landing. 'There is supposed to be an energy crisis,' I said, 'yet the airlines are operating and seats are available.'

'There is an energy crisis,' you argued. 'If we didn't have to get to Florida for Maggie's funeral, the airline wouldn't have booked us. We'd be on the bottom of a waiting list hundreds of names long.'

'Sure,' I said sarcastically.

We had lunch with Anson before the funeral. 'I was in Orlando when Maggie's housekeeper called to tell me that she had passed on. I had had this awful premonition. In fact, I wouldn't have gone to Orlando if it hadn't been absolutely necessary. The feeling was so strong that I left the telephone number of the place where I'd be staying. I had never done that before, but I was concerned about Maggie. She became suddenly busy after you left. She met with her attorney and had a will drawn. Then she went to the bank, checked on her safety deposit box, and talked to her insurance agent. When I asked her why she was doing those things, she just laughed and said that she had procrastinated long enough. But when she mentioned that she was going to take an evening to balance her checking account, I was sure that something was wrong. It was a job Maggie detested. I urged her to see the doctor. "Why?" she said. "I feel fine."'

Anson shook his head sadly. 'She knew. I'm positive that she knew. Maggie was a wonderful woman. She died as she deserved, without suffering.'

My parents left for the airport after the funeral. I was concerned for my father, who appeared drawn and unusually quiet. He seemed to have aged, not that my mother noticed. She was wearing her martyr expression, which meant that she would give him a rough time on the way home, irrespective of the flight conditions.

Anson drove us to the offices of Maggie's attorney. 'Would you like me to wait?' he asked.

You thanked him and told him no, that we would probably go directly to the airport and that he had already extended himself too much on our behalf. 'It was the least

I could do,' he said. 'Here, take my card. You never know. Something may come up, and you'll want to call me.'

Maggie's attorney, a man of such indistinct features that I can't recall anything about him except his horn-rimmed glasses, wasted no time. 'Mrs Weaver,' he said in a legal monotone, 'I won't have the exact figures of your aunt's estate until it is completely settled, of course, but I would estimate that it will be somewhere between three and four hundred thousand dollars. The selling price of her house will determine the final figure, that and the sale of her furnishings. For a woman of your aunt's means, she was surprisingly conservative. To my knowledge, there is little in the way of jewelry or other valuables.

'It is my understanding that she spoke to you before she engaged me to draw her will, which was fortunate considering the untimeliness of her death. I must ask you to sign this waiver, as your father did, releasing all claims to her estate so that it may be disposed of as she wished. Ordinarily I would wait until the figures were final before having you sign, but there is the problem of distance, and your aunt was quite definite in expressing her desire to have the estate settled as quickly as possible. She made a remark about not getting bogged down in technicalities.'

'That sounds like Aunt Maggie,' I mumbled, fighting tears.

I had sensed your astonishment while the lawyer was speaking, but I was unprepared when you said: 'My wife has no intention of signing the waiver.'

The attorney pushed his horn-rimmed glasses on to his forehead and stared at you. 'I understood . . .' he started to say.

'You understood correctly,' I interrupted. 'Please give me the waiver.'

The attorney started to hand me the waiver, but you intercepted it. 'My wife and I have a private matter to discuss,' you said. 'Is there a place where we can talk?'

'Certainly,' said the attorney, adjusting his glasses. 'The library. It's the second door on the left.'

You took my elbow and steered me to the library. 'Are you out of your mind?' you asked in a muffled scream when the door was closed behind us.

I tried to explain it to you, Richard. I told you about my promise to Maggie and how much it meant to her, but you refused to understand. Instead, you accused me of being all impulse and no thought. 'That's not true,' I said in a *sotto* yell. 'Maggie wanted her money to be left to research, and that's where it will go. She didn't die to save us. We'll have to do it ourselves.'

'Since you've just blown four hundred thousand dollars, how do you intend to do it?' you *sotto*-yelled back.

I didn't know how I was going to do it. At that moment, all I could think of was my promise to Maggie. 'I'll ... I'll ... I'll sell shares in The Golden Steer,' I said desperately, hating you.

'Sure you will,' you replied with a sneer. 'Tell me about it, Jenny. You've never worked a day in your life, and you're going to sell a million dollars' worth of shares in a Florida motel.'

You walked away from me and leaned against the bookcases. Then you crossed your arms and looked at me with such disgust, or was it contempt, that I said: 'You're damned right I will. All you have to do is come up with ten thousand dollars and sign your name. I'll have every share sold a month before the money is due.'

The air in the library, which had a musty, leathery smell, had become so close with the heat of our argument that I opened the door. You charged past me and disappeared down the corridor. I struggled to regain my composure, then returned to the lawyer's office alone. 'Where is Mr Weaver?' he asked, peering at me through his glasses.

'Outside,' I said, embarrassed.

'If there is some disagreement...'

'No,' I said, interrupting him. 'I'm ready to sign.'

He took a black ballpoint pen from an imitation marble stand on his desk and indicated where he wanted my

365

signature. I wrote my name without hesitation, sure that I had done the right thing.

You weren't there when I left the building, so I went back inside hoping I had missed you. Actually, I was afraid that you had abandoned me. You found me sitting in the lobby frantically counting the money in my wallet; there wasn't enough to buy a bus ticket out of Florida. 'I was angry, and I still am,' you said, sitting down beside me while I was concentrating on counting my loose change. 'But I'm not a bastard. I wouldn't have left you here.'

'Where were you?' I asked, dropping the change into my purse. I was both relieved to see you and furious that you had left me and come back in time to witness my panic.

'Across the street calling Anson,' you said. 'I told him that I was definitely interested in buying The Golden Steer.'

'That's the best news I've heard in weeks. We'll be out of trouble in no time.'

'Don't be too sure,' you admonished me.

'But I am sure,' I said, feeling as I had in the lawyer's office when I signed the waiver. 'I'm more than sure. I'm positive.'

I was positive, Richard. I sincerely believed The Golden Steer would give us a chance to save ourselves, and I was willing to do anything I could to help. As I told you before, my intentions were honorable. I had no inkling of the disaster that lay ahead.

You didn't tell me where you obtained the ten thousand dollars plus the additional money we needed to tide us over, and I didn't ask. Instead, I busied myself with plans for selling the units and choosing a name for the corporation. You liked my suggestion that we call it Bestmark, and I can recall how pleased I was when I saw the title page of the prospectus:

CONFIDENTIAL REPORT
ON
BESTMARK ASSOCIATES, LTD
A REAL ESTATE LIMITED PARTNERSHIP

I felt as if I had accomplished something.

But my real accomplishment was the selling of the units. While you were working with Charlie setting up the corporation and limited partnership, I was setting up Eagles' Landing. I promoted Bestmark with the finesse of a seasoned politician and the psychology of a P.T. Barnum. It was a no-fail combination, and I outdid myself. To this day, I don't know how I managed to carry it off. I said everything I wanted to say by saying nothing. I fed our Eagles' Landing friends begrudging innuendoes as if I were reluctantly parting with tins of Beluga caviar, always handing them containers that were impossible to open. I whetted their appetites and kept them starving until you were ready. Then I delivered them to you, one by one, as anxious to buy shares in The Golden Steer as people who have been waiting in line for hours are eager to buy tickets to a sell-out show.

I began promoting the Bestmark Partnership the morning after I returned from Florida. I called Molly Springer to offer her a ride to the art gallery; it was our day to volunteer. On our way there, I casually mentioned that you were still in Florida and that I didn't know when you'd be coming back. 'Something has happened, Molly,' I said confidentially.

Molly, who was always lethargic in the morning, perked up. 'Is it serious?' she asked.

'Exciting is the word,' I replied, keeping my voice deliberately low, although there was no one else in the car.

'What is it?' she asked, now fully awake an hour before usual.

'Oh, Molly, I wish I could tell you, but I can't. I promised Richard that I wouldn't say a word.'

Her normally pale skin flushed. 'I'm your closest friend. You simply must tell me,' she urged, pink-cheeked.

I concentrated on my driving, deliberately stalling and chewing my lower lip for effect until I was certain that Molly was beside herself with curiosity. 'A promise is a promise. Besides, if I tell you, you'll tell Ike. Richard wants this kept quiet until the investment goes through.' Then I gasped. 'Damn, I've said too much already.'

Her generous mouth quivered with excitement. 'What investment? You have to tell me. You must,' she insisted, sounding more like an eager child than a sophisticated suburban matron.

'I wish I could,' I said with such sincerity that I surprised myself. 'But I promised Richard. Also, I'm afraid.'

'Of what?' Molly asked anxiously.

'It's almost too good to be true. If I say anything, I might be jinxing it,' I said. 'And if that happened, I'd never forgive myself. Promise me that you won't mention a word of this to anyone, not even to Ike.'

Molly promised me that she wouldn't breathe a word of what she didn't know, and with the emphasis I placed on not telling Ike, I was positive that she would call him before the day was over.

I repeated my conversation with Molly, adding minor changes and variations, until everyone we knew in Eagles' Landing was buzzing about Richard Weaver's investment. To make sure they didn't forget, I allowed myself carefully planned slips of the tongue, instantly followed by regret for saying more than I should, even though I managed to say nothing at all. I was promoting an illusion around you, and you were perfect for the part. In adulthood as in your youth, you had the unmistakable aura of a winner.

Richard, I just realized something. If you had been a lesser man, my promotion would have failed. I was a brief success because you were exceptional, and that success killed you. Somehow it doesn't seem fair.

We saw less of each other after you signed the purchase agreement to buy The Golden Steer than we had before. You cautioned me to spend as little money as possible and stayed downtown. When you weren't with Charlie, you were with a member of the brokerage house that was handling the offering or the firm that was putting the prospectus together. In between, you were screening hotel management firms and traveling to Florida. It wasn't until you showed me the finished prospectus the night before our party that I saw the name The Landing Corporation. 'What is this?' I asked, pointing to the unfamiliar title. 'And why is the offering for one and a half million dollars? I thought Anson told us we would need a million dollars.'

'The Landing Corporation belongs to us – we're the general partner in Bestmark. And as for Anson,' you replied bitterly, 'he said a lot of things, but they weren't necessarily true. I warned you that Anson was slick. He lured us in with nice round numbers, but when it came to working the figures out, a million wasn't enough. The million couldn't possibly cover the hundred-thousand-dollar promoter's fee he used as bait; nor did it allow for the broker's expenses and the cost of printing the prospectus. We'll have to sell one hundred fifty units at ten thousand dollars a unit to pull this off.'

I groaned at the thought of selling additional shares, then brightened. 'Does that mean you'll make a bigger promoter's fee?'

'Yes, but we're not going to see too much of it.'

'Why?' I asked, upset and confused.

'I've had to borrow a substantial amount of money. We have debts of close to one hundred thousand dollars that will have to be paid.'

It didn't seem possible. 'From this?' I asked, despising Anson.

'From living. I owe my client over seventy-five thousand dollars. He's been floating us for over a year, but he wants his money back, all of it including interest, by September. I promised he would have it.'

'And if the units aren't sold?' I asked nervously.

'If the units aren't sold, we'll be completely wiped out,' you said coldly. 'Completely. It doesn't look as bright as

369

it did in Florida, does it, Jenny? Your party had better be a success.'

'It will be,' I replied with shaken confidence.

Somehow I had the feeling that the information you had given me was incomplete. 'Why didn't you tell me that this was a break-even deal? You could have explained. It doesn't make sense to work this hard if we're going to end up where we started.'

'If it's successful, we'll be all right,' you said, avoiding my eyes.

'What do you mean "we'll be all right"?' I demanded.

'We'll own twenty percent of the shares,' you admitted.

'And?' I prodded, sure that you were holding back.

'And we'll get a management fee for running the partnership,' you said grudgingly, walking out of the room before I could ask another question.

You wanted to deflate me, didn't you, Richard? What you did to me that night was inexcusable. If I hadn't pried the facts out of you, I would have believed that there was nothing for us in the Bestmark Partnership but the promoter's fee. Why did you do it? Were you still punishing me for signing away Maggie's estate? I have lived with soul-blackening guilt for two years, which I'll have to accept, but I won't accept the blame for the deep silence between us dating from that evening. You can carry that yourself, wherever you are.

The party was a success, worth every bit of the twelve hundred dollars I spent. Even you agreed, for you paid the country club without a comment or complaint. You also admired the invitations that had COME CELEBRATE WITH US printed in block letters on the cover. No one knew exactly why we were celebrating, although they must have guessed that it was your mysterious investment, and neither one of us told. 'Richard and I just want you to have a good time,' I said obliquely when anyone asked. 'When the Weavers have good fortune, everyone shares.'

I watched every man at the party and noted with

satisfaction that each one sought you out for a private chat during the course of the evening. I had delivered as I had promised. All you had to do was refer them to the brokerage firm that was handling the Bestmark Limited Partnership. As the broker told me later when I called him: 'They were the easiest sales I've ever had. I couldn't believe it. Every customer who inquired about Bestmark was prepared to buy. We've never known anything quite like it for this type of offering. There was only one customer who hesitated.'

'Was it Bruce Lynch?' I asked.

'I'm not permitted to say,' he replied.

It was Bruce Lynch, Richard. I knew it was without having to be told. Bruce didn't want to be left out of the pack, so he went to his daddy to ask for the money. It wouldn't have surprised me if old man Lynch had Bruce sign his false ball as collateral. When Bestmark collapsed, I felt sorry for every investor with the exception of Bruce. There seemed to be a perverse justice in the loss of Lynch money. The Lynch males – father, son, and grandson – were deserving bastards.

Just thinking about the Lynches and your behavior the night before our party has made me feel better. Anger must have been the antidote I needed to stop this sickness. I still feel weak, but the nausea is gone. I should be able to sleep now.

Well, Richard, here I am again and with good reason: Mother was here for a week. I doubt that even you, in your present condition, could escape unscathed after spending a week of togetherness with my mother in California. It may take me a month to recover.

The visit was off to a poor start before she packed her bags and purchased her ticket. She called on a Sunday evening almost two weeks ago to inform me that she would be arriving on the following Friday at six o'clock. 'We can go out to dinner from the airport,' she said. 'I won't eat on the plane. They serve paste.'

But I barely heard her. The thought of battling Friday rush-hour traffic on the freeway to get to the airport blocked everything else out of my mind. Since my experience with Jim Gentile, I am more terrified than ever of the freeways, and Friday between five and seven is the worst time of the week. 'That's a bad time,' I said, thinking aloud.

'Are you telling me that I'm not welcome?' She sounded miffed.

'Of course I want you to come,' I said as convincingly as I could. 'It's just that the freeway traffic is impossible at that hour. Couldn't you catch an earlier plane or a later one?'

'No,' she replied. 'I have an early hair appointment, and I'll have to rush as it is.'

'Couldn't you have your hair done on Thursday?'

'You know I like having my hair done on Friday, Jennifer. I *always* have my hair done on Friday. If I could manage to have my hair done on Friday before going to Europe, then I can certainly have it done on Friday before going to California.'

Mother was never one to win points for flexibility.

It occurred to me that she hadn't mentioned my father. 'Will Dad be coming?' I asked.

'Not with me,' she replied.

Then she gave me her flight number, had me repeat it, cautioned me three times to call the airport to check on her time of arrival, repeated her flight number again, and hung up. It was not one of our better conversations.

Nat had been upstairs saying good night to the children while I was on the telephone. I hadn't heard him come downstairs, and when I put the receiver down, I cursed, long and hard.

'Whew,' he said, coming up behind me. 'I didn't know you had such a firm grasp of the language. That must have been quite a call.'

'It was my mother,' I replied, 'and she has always been able to inspire me.'

'Oh,' he said, playing hurt while studying me with the inquisitive look that I have become accustomed to. 'I thought I inspired you, but you never gave me a tribute like that.'

'Would you want one?' I asked, puzzled.

Nat became thoughtful. 'With feeling,' he said finally, 'yes, I think I would.'

I asked him why, for his response didn't make sense to me. I was sure Nat Witton enjoyed life too much to be a hidden masochist.

'Because the only time I've ever seen you moved enough to curse was that night in bed when we first started seeing each other, and I asked about your husband. When you cursed, and it was mild, he was the inspiration, not me. I was the irritation. You cared for him sufficiently to loosen the normally tight reins you hold on your language. Apparently your mother has the same effect on you. I can't seem to touch you in the same places they can. Even that night we fought about Hadley Tucker and Ripley Oldsmobile, you didn't curse. You were mad as hell, furious with me and hiccuping like crazy, but you didn't curse.'

'If I had cursed, would you have gone after Ripley?' I asked.

'No,' he replied, 'I meant what I said. I'm no hero, and I know better than to let anyone push me into becoming one. There are enough everyday traumas to handle in life without deliberately courting disasters.'

Then Nat became uncharacteristically contemplative. He held my face in his hands and looked at me so intently that I felt as if I were becoming submerged in blankets of blue. 'But if you had cursed,' he said softly, 'I would have been tempted. Sorely tempted. And if you had cursed the way you did tonight after talking to your mother, I might have come close to succumbing. Do you know what I'm trying to say?'

I wasn't sure. Either Nat was telling me that our affair

had progressed as far as it could go, that it had peaked, or that he wanted something more from me, an openness or commitment. But he hadn't hinted at any kind of commitment. Our relationship had remained essentially the same, free of future promises and utterances of love. I felt vulnerable, as if I had to protect myself, so I said: 'I don't understand.'

'I think you do, but you're afraid. We've been close for four months, and there are still some areas, certain parts of Jennifer Weaver, that I haven't been able to reach. I've tried, Jenny. God knows, I've tried. I've waited patiently for you to open up, to let me know you the way I want to know you, but you won't let me. You've drawn a damned line somewhere, and you won't allow me to cross it.'

'I thought that affairs, by their very nature, are terminal,' I said defensively. 'Didn't you tell me so yourself? And I'm the one who is taking the risks in this affair, not you, so don't congratulate yourself for your patience.'

'Whatever gave you the idea that you are taking all the risks?' he demanded. 'What makes your feelings more important than mine?'

'I didn't say that my feelings are more important than yours. My concern is for Matthew and Catherine,' I explained. 'I'm an adult playing an adult game, but I'm playing with a handicap – my children. They're crazy about you, and each time you are with them, they become more attached to you. Haven't you noticed how Matthew's speech has improved? I don't recall him blocking more than twice today.'

'I did notice,' he admitted.

'I don't know how much of his improvement can be credited to you, but I'm certain that some of it is your doing. And I'm also certain that his speech will suffer if and when we stop seeing each other. I'm not telling you this to lay guilt on you. On the contrary, you've been marvelous with the children. But you are right: I am afraid.

When you and I stop seeing each other, they will stop seeing you, too. How will I explain it to them? What will I say: "Mommy and Nat don't want to sleep together anymore" or "The affair peaked" or "Affairs are a temporary thing, and Mommy will eventually find another man to replace Nat?"

'They are children; they can't be expected to accept adult explanations. So if I am protecting myself, it is for them. Matthew and Catherine will need every bit of stability I can provide once you are gone, and if I am an emotional wreck, there will be no one to help them.'

'I can see your point,' Nat said, 'but I don't agree completely. Right now, I think you're hiding behind the children. You're using them as an excuse, a rationalization. I've thought about the children, too, but I've hesitated to mention them.'

'Why?'

'As I said before, I've been waiting for you to open up. Have you told your mother about us?' he asked.

'No,' I replied.

'You haven't?' He looked at me in disbelief.

I shrugged. 'There didn't seem to be anything to tell.'

Nat raised his voice. 'Nothing to tell after all of this time?'

'Not to my mother. I could have told her that I was seeing you, but she would have wanted to know *exactly* how I was seeing you, so I decided that it would be best left unmentioned. My mother believes sex belongs only in marriage.'

The muscles on the sides of Nat's jaw began to work ryhthmically. I had never seen him so tense. 'Does this mean that I am supposed to disappear for a week?' he asked. 'What if I called or dropped in after work? How would you explain me? Would you tell her that the local papers give personal service? You're really unbelievable. How could you not warn me? And is that all our relationship is – sex? A roll in the hay on a regular basis?'

I didn't know how to answer him and felt nervous and confused. My mother was three thousand miles away, but her announced visit had already taken its hold on my life.

'Well, Jenny?' His jaw muscles were working furiously.

'You didn't give me a chance to warn you,' I said. 'She just called, remember?'

'But what about us?' he demanded.

'I don't know about us. I've been following the rules – your rules, dammit, not mine. Of course I like the sex. So do you. But when you told me about affairs, you warned me that they can end as quickly as they begin. I've never had an affair before. You know I haven't. So when you gave me your capsulized course in affairs, I took what you said seriously. I suppose I've been steeling myself for the end of our affair from its very onset, waiting for a sign from you that it was over so I could slip out of your life making as few waves as possible. Is it over now?' I asked, breathless after my outburst. 'Is that what you're trying to tell me?'

The muscles in his jaw slackened. 'You mean that you've waited all this time for our affair to end so you could walk out of it a heroine? This is incredible.'

'Not a heroine. I just didn't want to look like a fool or feel like a fool. It is a matter of pride. No one wants to be dumped, and from the manner in which you spoke, I believed that you would want out first.'

Nat leaned against the kitchen wall with his head slightly bent. He was quiet. 'I didn't realize that you were so literal,' he said finally. 'Look, maybe your mother's visit is a good thing. We won't see each other the week she is here. I don't know if it will make a difference in our relationship, but it will be a breather that I think we both need. I would like to meet her, though.'

'Of course,' I said, not attempting to hide the edge of sarcasm cutting through my voice, 'your curiosity.'

He grinned. 'Yes, my curiosity. And thank you,' he added.

'For what?'

'You swore at me. Granted, it was only a small dammit, but it was mine, and I'll claim it.'

I saw Nat twice during the past week, one time planned and once unexpectedly. But more about that later. I don't believe that I could cope with telling you about the unexpected time right now.

My job at Briarhill was the next problem I had to confront. I dreaded asking Simon for a week off after holding my new position for five weeks, but I had no choice. The children would be in camp all day, and I couldn't leave Mother fending for herself in Sherwood Village. Even if I had wanted to, and I was tempted, she wouldn't have allowed it. Simon agreed to my taking a week's vacation under the condition that I come in if he thought it was absolutely necessary. I agreed. By the fourth day of her visit, I was praying for Simon's call to rescue me.

He didn't call.

I left for the airport with the children as soon as the camp bus brought them home, and spent the next hour in traffic. By the time we arrived at the airport, we had minutes to park the car and dash to the gate to meet Mother's plane. The children were bickering in their dirty camp clothes, and I had the start of a tension headache. We were, in short, a motley group; we looked like California left-overs.

We were too late to see the plane land, but we did watch Mother disembark. She walked carefully down the metal steps as if they were missing a tread or would collapse before she reached the ground.

'I can't find Grandma,' Catherine said.

'She's the lady in the brown outfit with the fresh hairdo,' I replied.

'Is she afraid of the stairs?' Catherine asked with her

usual perception. 'She isn't looking up like everyone else. See how she's hanging on to the railing.'

'No,' I said, concerned that Catherine might ask Mother if she were afraid of stairs. 'It's windy outside.'

'But it isn't windy,' Catherine protested. 'Her hairdo isn't blowing.'

'Yes, it is windy,' I said, pulling her away from the window. 'Grandma's hair isn't blowing because the hairdresser sprayed it to stay in place.'

The first thing Catherine said to Mother was: 'Can I touch your hair, Grandma? Mommy says you had it sprayed.'

Mother took one look at Catherine's dirty hands, wrinkled her nose with distaste, then glared at me and took off with the three of us following close behind to search for her luggage. It was not an auspicious beginning.

I don't know if it was because I hadn't seen her in better than a year, but I found myself looking at my mother as if she were an acquaintance, someone whose features were familiar yet slightly out of focus. She has aged, Richard. She still colors her hair a honey blonde, but her natural color must be completely gray, for the artificial color has lost its vibrancy, as if it is no longer in competition with her true brown hair. Her makeup was applied as skillfully as always, but it could not hide the sad pouches under her eyes, the lack of tension in the skin on her neck, or the lines extending from her nostrils that parenthesized her mouth. When I asked for the ticket to claim her baggage, I was shocked to see faint liver spots on the backs of her manicured hands.

Then I looked at her clothes. Mother was a walking promotion, a mobile display of initials and logos. There were Anne Klein lions embroidered across the toes of her beige espadrilles, Yves St Laurent's signature on her brown print scarf, Givenchy G's woven into the fabric of her blouse, Pierre Cardin's logo stamped all over the fabric on her canvas and leather handbag, Bill Blass's initials, back to back, on her blazer buttons, and Oscar de la Renta's initials on the temples of her metal sunglasses. I almost laughed, not because the ensemble was mismatched, for it was impeccably coordinated (to Mother's credit), but because the meaning of the symbols suddenly hit me. My mother had paid a premium to wear initials other than her own; she had purchased the identity of designers to tell the world that she had money, that she had taste, that she had class.

I have grown in California. The thought would never have occurred to me in Eagles' Landing, probably because I bought signatures, too. They were important there. I dressed in status clothes to make the statement that you were doing well. I wasn't unique. Every gathering we attended was a mass of initials, a garden of logos, a designer's wet dream.

Richard, the true promoters of our time aren't advertising men, nor are they real-estate developers like the one who carved Eagles' Landing out of a swamp, nor are they successful Simon Gentiles. The most accomplished con men of our age are clothing designers who have promoted their signatures into fortunes, for they have harnessed that old nag insecurity, and made her run like a thoroughbred.

I stood next to my mother and vowed that I would never again wear initials other than my own.

If Mother had been offended with the unkempt appearance of her grandchildren, her displeasure was mild compared with her reaction to my new car. She took one glance at the bumper sticker, and her mouth fell open. I tried to ignore her open mouth while I stuffed her suitcases into the trunk, hoping that she would climb into the car without a comment, but I should have known better. Mother always has a comment. This time, she had a mouthful. 'How awful,' she said with disgust, as if the sticker read GONORRHEA IS GOOD FOR YOUR HEALTH. 'How positively awful. A bumper sticker, Jennifer. Really. One does not put a bumper sticker on one's car. Ever. What has happened to you? Have you lost your senses?'

'No, but I did lose money,' I replied, inadvertently punning. 'Ripley made a killing on me, and I'm going to keep the sticker on my car until it wears off.'

Mother was appalled. 'You have been taught that, if you have a business dispute or any kind of dispute, it must be settled in a dignified fashion, not in this disgusting manner. What has become of your breeding? What has happened to you since you moved to this, this . . . place?'

'A lot,' I said.

'Well,' she exclaimed, 'I simply cannot drive in a car with a sticker attached to it like an unsightly blemish. You'll have to remove it. Now.'

Matthew and Catherine had been listening to us with interest, and when Mother ordered me to remove the bumper sticker, they could no longer contain themselves.

'A-Are you g-going to take it off, Mom?' Matthew asked.

'Do you have to obey?' Catherine chimed in.

I was close to exploding and told them to get into the car.

'We don't wanna get into the car,' whined Catherine.

I opened the car door and pushed them inside over their protests. Then I turned to face my mother. 'If we are going to have a pleasant visit together,' I said, struggling for control (I wanted to throttle her), 'both of us will have to overlook some things. This is my car. I paid for it, and I want the bumper sticker to remain. I'm sorry if the sticker offends you, but it would do more than offend me if I had to remove it.'

Mother turned away from me as if I had struck her. 'You could be a little more understanding,' she said in a trembling voice. 'I didn't come three thousand miles to receive *this* kind of treatment.'

Guilt. Mother had brought her old knife to California and was expertly spreading guilt like soft butter on the bread of my conscience. At first, I reacted as I had always reacted, with knots in my stomach and forbidden, threatening anger pressing against the base of my skull. But standing in the parking lot, I saw her, really saw her, and realized that it wouldn't be long before she would be a candidate for a place like Briarhill. I softened. 'Yes,' I agreed, 'we could both be a little more understanding. I'll tell you what happened to me at Ripley Oldsmobile later. I have dinner prepared, so we don't have to eat out.'

She got into the car reluctantly, glancing pointedly toward the bumper sticker. I suppressed another threatening surge of anger and tried to be civil during our long drive home.

I don't know what to tell you about Mother's visit. I'm sure you wouldn't be interested in a mini-sightseeing tour of California. Come to think of it, neither was Mother. The only specific request she made was to visit Rodeo Drive. 'I've read about Rodeo Drive,' she said. 'It's supposed to have the most luxurious, beautifully stocked stores in the world. I don't want to miss it.'

We went to Rodeo Drive on Monday after the children left for camp, and I had the distinct feeling that she was relieved to see them disappear behind the bus doors. It isn't that she doesn't love Matthew and Catherine, for I know that she is fond of them in her way, but she certainly isn't a doting grandmother. Once the children were cleaned up, she commented on how much they had grown and how well they looked. 'They are handsome,' she said after they were in bed, 'particularly Matthew. He could be a model or do television commercials if he didn't have that little speech problem.'

Again, I suppressed the urge to throttle her. It was difficult, but I realized that Mother's remark had nothing to do with her feeling for Matthew, so I decided to ignore it. She is proud of the children. Unfortunately, pride in one's grandchildren isn't the same as taking honest pleasure in them, and Mother didn't seem to take pleasure in Matthew and Catherine. It was almost as if she didn't know how to enjoy them.

Perhaps I'm being unfair. Mother does love the children. But her love for them, which has taken the form of calm acceptance, as if grandchildren are nothing more or less than part of the natural progression of life, contrasted sharply with Mrs Feltcher's effusiveness.

Mother and Mrs Feltcher met on Sunday as we were leaving for Disneyland. (I had made comprehensive plans for the weekend, hoping to divert the children's attention so they wouldn't miss or mention Nat.) The Feltchers were returning from church, and when Mrs Feltcher spotted us in the parking lot, she bounced over and greeted the children with her usual ebullience. I wasn't included in the greeting, for Mrs Feltcher strongly disapproves of my working full time and warned me when I started that my decision would be harmful to all of us. 'Your place is with your children,' she said. When I pointed out that the children are in school most of the day, she told me that it made no difference. 'It is important for the children to know that you are at home waiting for them,' she replied with righteous insistence.

I hadn't asked for her opinion, and the tone of her voice was so irritating that I lost my temper. 'If I stay home waiting for them until they are grown,' I said defensively, 'I'll wake up one morning to an empty house and empty time.'

My remark injured Mrs Feltcher, and she left in a huff. She has avoided me ever since.

Mother's presence forced a greeting from Mrs Feltcher. I introduced them, Mother behind sunglasses in her casual skirt and blouse, her blond hair protected from the sun by a designer scarf, and Mrs Feltcher in her matronly Sunday go-to-church dress and veil. Although there probably isn't more than a five-year difference in their ages, the two women appeared to be generations apart, worlds apart. Mother appraised Mrs Feltcher coolly, as if she were an antique, and was taken aback by her enthusiastic praise of

Matthew and Catherine. 'You are so fortunate to have such wonderful grandchildren,' said Mrs Feltcher heartily. 'I don't know how you can stay away from them. If they were mine, I'd want to see them every day.'

'Abrasive woman,' Mother commented as we drove off. 'Definitely not one of our kind.'

Mrs Feltcher came over later in the week to give Mother some of her homemade potholders. The gesture was kind, but I knew that Mrs Feltcher's primary motivation was curiosity, for I have stubbornly managed to evade her prying questions since we have lived here. Mother accepted the potholders graciously, although I could tell from the expression on her face that she thought they were tacky. Mrs Feltcher, however, was oblivious to Mother's reaction. She accepted her thanks, settled into a chair, and started to talk. And to question.

It wasn't necessary to give Mother a high sign. After approximately ten minutes of Mrs Feltcher's company, Mother put her hand on her forehead and said, 'Please excuse me, Mrs Feltcher. I seem to have developed a headache. It's probably due to the change in time, but I must lie down. I know you'll understand. And thank you again for the potholders.'

She vanished before Mrs Feltcher could advise her on the best remedies for headaches.

Mrs Feltcher was clearly disappointed. 'I did want to get to know your mother,' she said. 'There are a number of things I would have liked to chat with her about.' She stayed to tell me what remedies to use should Mother's headache fail to disappear and continued talking until I excused myself to prepare dinner.

After she left, I thought about curiosity, the Mrs Feltcher variety and Nat's. There is a difference. Nat's curiosity is generally impersonal, with the exception of his curiosity about me. He likes to know simply for the sake of knowing. It is an almost pure curiosity, untouched by malice or a desire to gossip. Mrs Feltcher's curiosity, on the other hand, is the prying variety, details collected about other people's lives to fill voids in her own life. She is not malicious, but she is forever trying to open private doors to gain entry where she is not wanted. Once the difference became clear to me, I no longer felt guilty that I had shut Mrs Feltcher out.

Nat called late Monday afternoon. 'Are you enjoying your mother's visit?' he asked. 'I've missed you.'

Mother was in the room, so I responded in an impersonal tone of voice, friendly but not too friendly. Nat caught on and asked me if it were possible to talk on an extension. I told him that it wasn't, recalling how Mother had never paid attention to Linda's or my calls unless we wanted privacy. Then she became interested and wasn't above 'accidentally' picking up the receiver in another room. Nat seemed to understand that, too.

'I'd like to stop by tomorrow night,' he said, 'that is, if you can figure out a way to explain my presence.'

There was unmistakable irritation in his voice. I could almost see his jaw muscles working and felt a sudden surge of anger toward my mother for sitting in the room, for coming to California, for intimidating me. But as quickly as the anger came, there came the realization that it wasn't completely Mother's fault. The blame was as much mine as hers, for I had let her presence intimidate me; I had allowed it to happen because it had always happened. The possibility that there was another way had never occurred to me.

'Thank you. I'd love to go to the movies,' I said as warmly as I could.

'You've got to be kidding,' he replied.

'My mother is visiting,' I said, smiling at his surprise. 'I'm sure she won't mind babysitting. See you tomorrow night.'

When Mother heard me mention her visit, she looked up. 'Who was that?' she asked, closing the Gucci purse she had purchased on Rodeo Drive.

'Nat Witton,' I said nonchalantly. 'He asked me to go

to the movies with him tomorrow night. I hope you won't mind babysitting.'

Then the questions started. Mother wanted to know who Nat was, where I had met him, and how long I had been seeing him. I told her as little as possible. 'You'll meet him tomorrow night,' I said, sure that Nat would win her with his easy charm.

'You know, Jennifer,' she said, shifting uncomfortably in her chair, 'when a woman your age sees men, it isn't the same as a teenage girl dating. Men have . . .'

'Have what?' I asked, playing dumb.

'Expectations,' she managed to say. 'Adult men have . . . urges, and they aren't shy about them.'

The color in Mother's cheeks was unnaturally high, and she started to fidget, first with her hair, then smoothing out nonexistent wrinkles in her skirt. When she started twisting the buttons on her blouse, I decided to end her suffering. 'Don't worry,' I said. 'I can take care of myself. I was a married lady, remember?'

She was relieved at once, as if she had just removed an excruciatingly tight girdle. 'I'm glad you understand,' she said, sighing. 'These conversations can be so difficult. But I'm happy that we had this little talk.'

Then: 'Is it too early for a drink?'

Mother drank three martinis before dinner, rationalizing, I am sure, that she had earned everyone of them.

Nat's meeting with Mother was a success, as I knew it would be; she was practically purring at him by the time we left. There were only two awkward moments, the first occurring when the children saw Nat. Catherine ran up to him excitedly with her arms outstretched, expecting to be picked up and hugged. Nat's eyes met mine, which were open wide with alarm, so he tousled Catherine's hair and diverted her with questions about camp. Fortunately, Catherine had had an exciting day and started to chatter without missing her usual greeting.

The other awkward moment occurred when Mother asked Nat about his background. (You know how Mother insists upon placing everyone she meets in their proper social slot. She did it with you, and you never forgave her for it. 'Who in the hell does she think she is?' you exploded. 'She doesn't have pedigree papers.') She and Nat were chatting pleasantly, for each was curious about the other, until Nat mentioned that he was from Pennsylvania. 'Bucks County, I assume?' she asked. 'I have some close friends who live there.'

Mother's remark about close friends didn't disguise the implication of her question – the words 'Bucks County' hit Nat like twin bullets. He immediately understood what she meant: if one was anyone from Pennsylvania, one came from Bucks County. 'You may not believe this,' he said, 'but there are Pennsylvanians who do not consider Bucks the crowned county of the state.'

I held my breath waiting for Mother's reaction. She raised her eyebrows slightly as if expecting to sneeze, then recouped gracefully. 'I am afraid I'm guilty of believing everything my friends say,' she apologized. 'I'll have to inform them that their county isn't the only one in Pennsylvania.'

The next day she told me that she found Nat charming, even if he didn't come from Bucks County. 'One must be overlooking,' she said.

Nat's review on Mother was mixed. 'Now I can understand why you wrote me a thank-you note instead of calling,' he commented as we walked to his car. 'It must have been an involuntary action, like breathing. Your mother is an attractive woman, but I have a feeling that there is a tough core under that immaculate exterior. How was it growing up in her house?'

'It wasn't easy,' I said, feeling the weight of an encyclopedia of words from my childhood and adolescence that I dared not utter in rebellion. 'I was always in training.'

Nat looked at me quizzically. 'Training for what?'

'To be a lady,' I replied, getting into the car, 'which

requires a great deal more than a full box of stationery for writing thank-you notes.'

We went to Nat's apartment instead of going to the movies.

You may not believe this, but Mother checked on me the following morning. She actually asked me to tell her about the movie we saw. Her question was embarrassingly obvious, for we both knew that she wasn't inquiring to make idle conversation. Mother has never been interested in films. I was tempted to tell her that we went to a movie called *The Affair*, then changed my mind and mentioned a film Nat and I had seen several weeks ago, briefly outlining the plot for her benefit. I could have told her that it was none of her business, but that would have been a deliberate challenge, which I decided against. It was nine o'clock in the morning. The day had already promised to be long, and I didn't want to stretch it further with a confrontation.

Mother also met Deirdre. I hadn't seen Deirdre or spoken with her in nearly three weeks, so she wasn't aware of Mother's visit. She popped in unexpectedly after supper on Wednesday, probably to keep me current on the progress of her lawsuit against Ken Jamison.

I don't believe I told you that Deirdre is trying to get complete custody of Kerry. The weekend after my ordeal with Jim Gentile, Ken picked Kerry up late Sunday morning and had an accident on the freeway. Apparently he had taken a heavy dose of drugs before collecting Kerry, for he was weaving back and forth between freeway lanes and misjudged his exit, overturning his pickup truck. Kerry's left arm and collarbone were broken, and he was severely bruised. The only injury Ken suffered was a broken nose; the police said Ken wasn't badly hurt because his body was completely relaxed from the drugs he had taken. They charged him with driving while under the influence (of drugs), reckless endangerment, and a slew of traffic violations.

Deirdre came racing through my back door after she

received a call informing her of the accident. She stood in the kitchen, screaming and crying unintelligibly. I panicked, fearing that she had been raped again. Fortunately Nat was there, and he calmed her down sufficiently to extract broken pieces of information from her. Once we understood, I drove Deirdre, still weeping hysterically, to the hospital, and Nat took Matthew and Catherine on the Sunday picnic we had planned. Steve was with Herb for the weekend, which helped.

After Deirdre saw Kerry and spoke with the doctors who were taking care of him, she dried her tears, assured that he would survive. I suggested that we go to the cafeteria for coffee and noticed her face hardening as we walked down the cold hospital corridor. 'This is it,' she said emphatically when we arrived at the cafeteria door. 'Ken has relinquished his last claim to Kerry. There will be no more fatherhood shit. Never again. I am going to go to the Legal Aid Foundation tomorrow to find a lawyer. By the time I'm finished with Ken Jamison, the only chance he'll ever have of seeing Kerry is if he happens to pass him on a busy street twenty years from now, and I'll start praying today that Kerry is looking in the other direction. I'll even move if it's necessary, but Ken will never see Kerry again.

'And Kerry will be told the truth. Everything, even the rape. I'll wait until he's older to tell him about that, but I'll tell him. Kerry is not going to grow into manhood fed on illusions. He will know about his father so that he can be free of him.'

I agreed with Deirdre's decision to go to Legal Aid to keep Ken away from Kerry and herself, but I questioned whether she should tell Kerry the truth. 'It could be a mistake,' I said. 'You could keep them permanently separated without telling Kerry everything. Think of how it could hurt him – the drugs, the rape. Kerry is a child. Those are hard facts to cope with, even for adults. How far back will you go? Will you tell him about Ken's prostitution and your syphilis? Once you start talking, you may not be able to stop. And if that happens, will you be telling Kerry because he has a right to know or because you want to get even with Ken? No matter what you say to Kerry, Ken will still be his father. You can't change history. Some things should be forgotten; they bring nothing but pain, and nothing can be learned from them.'

'No, dammit, you're wrong,' said Deirdre, slamming her cup on to the saucer. 'If I don't tell him the truth, he'll think Ken abandoned him. He'll feel that he failed, or that I failed, but never that Ken failed.

'I may not be able to rewrite history, but I've lived with it every day since I married Ken Jamison. Kerry is a part of that history; he's lived with it, too. But he has lived in ignorance, and that must be changed. Unless he is told, Kerry won't be able to grow up feeling right about himself. No truth is worth that price.'

Deirdre could see from the expression on my face that I disagreed. 'There are many ways to tell the truth, Jenny. You can bludgeon someone with it, as my mother bludgeoned me with sin, or you can ease them into it. It's all in your approach. It will be as hard for me to tell Kerry as it will be for him to know, maybe harder, but he will know. And if I can tell him the way I want to tell him, he will understand.'

We finished our coffee in silence, each lost in her own private history.

Deirdre's visit was brief. She didn't say anything about her lawsuit, but she did mention her attorney several times. His name is Michael Flaherty, and he has taken more than a professional interest in Deirdre; they have been seeing each other frequently. After she left, Mother commented on Deirdre's attractiveness. 'She's stunning,' Mother said. 'Such long legs. She really looks like a native Californian.'

'Deirdre is from Gary, Indiana. The only native Californian I've met since I've lived here is Jim Gentile, and he resembles a checkered blimp,' I replied, shuddering.

When Mother started asking about Deirdre's background – where she went to school, who her people were, what her ex-husband did for a living – I knew why Deirdre had kept her visit short. Mother's manner, the way she has of speaking, dressing, and carrying herself, must have alerted Deirdre like a flashing red warning light to stay away. I was both saddened and embarrassed, not for Deirdre, but for Mother.

As usual, it was Catherine who first noticed that all wasn't well with Mother. When I put her to bed Sunday night, she asked why Grandma was sad. 'Why do you think Grandma is sad?' I inquired, tucking her in.

'Whenever Grandma thinks no one is looking, her face falls down,' said Catherine, pulling her cheeks downward with both hands until her lower eyelids were exposed to give a visual explanation.

'Grandma isn't used to a lot of walking,' I explained, 'and we walked miles at Disneyland today. She was probably tired and didn't want to say anything to spoil our good time.'

'But her face fell down yesterday, too,' insisted Catherine. 'We didn't go to Disneyland yesterday.'

'Grandma was tired from her trip and the time difference yesterday,' I said, kissing her good night. 'Don't worry about it.'

By Tuesday, I was beginning to worry. I didn't see Mother's face fall down as Catherine described it, but there were other signs. Mother shopped with quiet desperation on Rodeo Drive, as if she absolutely had to purchase something – anything – but there was no spirit of enjoyment in her shopping. We went from one thickly carpeted store to another, examining outrageously expensive clothing, jewelry, and leather goods until the one-of-a-kind items seemed to be all-of-a-kind. Mother bought her purse before lunch, but I noticed that she appeared to be happier with her luncheon cocktail than she was with her purchase.

That was another thing that bothered me: Mother's drinking. To my knowledge, she was strictly a social drinker, nothing more. I know she has always enjoyed her liquor and has had the habit of a pre-dinner cocktail for as long as I can remember, but on Tuesday it became apparent that a pre-dinner cocktail wasn't sufficient to carry Mother until dinner the next day. Before we sat down for lunch in the kitchen, Mother suggested that we have a drink. 'With tuna fish sandwiches?' I asked, surprised.

'Why not?' she replied. 'Is there a rule against a drink before a tuna fish sandwich? We haven't seen each other for a year. It would be pleasant to have a cocktail together.'

I told her that I wasn't interested in a drink but I would be happy to sit with her if she wanted one. 'You're busy,' she said, watching me fold the children's camp clothes that I had just taken out of the dryer. 'I'll help myself. Call me when lunch is ready.'

She mixed herself a martini that was so generous it almost filled a highball glass. Then she went into the living room to drink it alone.

I waited to call her to lunch, folding the clothes slowly to give myself a chance to think about Mother's problem, for it was obvious that she did have a problem. I went back to our shopping expedition on Rodeo Drive, where I had first noticed Mother's insistence on a midday drink, and came up with nothing. There was the difference in our reactions to Rodeo Drive's opulence, but I attributed that to my change in attitude, not Mother's. I have changed, Richard. Material things once mattered to me, more than I care to admit, but that is no longer true. My compulsive shopping ended with your death. I don't know if it was due to the tranquilizers I was taking or to the abrupt dissolution of our marriage, but I became indifferent to the possessions that had been so important to me. Now I am embarrassed by my former materialism, and ashamed.

When I couldn't find an explanation for Mother's drinking, I became frightened for her. She's an alcoholic, I thought. Why, after so many years?

Catherine unearthed the answer, although she did it inadvertently. When the children had originally asked why my father hadn't come to visit, Mother told them that he was busy working. We had all accepted her explanation until we were eating dinner Wednesday night and Catherine innocently asked: 'Grandma, why can't Grandpa take a vacation? My friend Lisa's grandpa takes vacations.'

'It's his busy season,' replied Mother in a less than encouraging voice.

But Catherine wasn't put off. 'Why don't you tell us about Grandpa, then?' she persisted.

I happened to glance at Mother and saw her deliberately spill her coffee. 'Excuse me,' she said, rising. 'I'll have to clean this up.'

I waited until the children were in bed before mentioning my father, wondering how I could broach the subject tactfully, for it was finally clear to me that business hadn't kept him away. There had been clues, of course: Mother's frequent, noncommunicative long-distance calls, her remark that she wouldn't be traveling with my father, her avoidance of discussing him. But I had been so involved with my own life that I hadn't realized how long it had been since I had spoken with my father; at least three or four months had elapsed since we last talked.

'Would you like a drink?' I asked Mother guiltily after the children were asleep, hoping it would sit comfortably on the three-martini foundation she had had before dinner. I knew she wouldn't refuse and made her a double, plus one for myself.

I handed her the drink and started to talk, attempting to subtly weave my father into a conversation, but it didn't work. Mother held her drink and our conversation exactly where she wanted it, and it appeared that my father was not to be included. When I saw that her glass was almost empty, I knew I had to say something quickly. Taking a lesson from Catherine, I decided to be open and direct. 'Are you and Dad having problems?' I asked.

It wasn't until after she replied that I realized it was the first personal question I had ever asked my mother.

Mother drained her glass. I could see that she was upset, but she hid it well. 'There are certain questions one does not ask, Jennifer,' she said, speaking to me as if I were an impossible, ill-mannered child. 'Now if you will excuse me, I am going to bed.'

'Wait,' I said, stepping in front of her. 'I didn't mean to offend you. It's just that I can see you are troubled. If it isn't Dad, then what is bothering you?'

She made herself another double, this time without excuses. 'Linda,' she replied after the glass was safely in her hand. 'I'm going to see Linda after I leave on Friday.'

'Where is she?' I asked excitedly.

'Linda is living in Arizona. She has a son. However, she doesn't have a husband,' she said distastefully. 'She tried to contact you, also.'

'Why didn't you give her my address? Do you know how long it has been since I've seen Linda or heard from her?'

'You don't have to remind me,' she replied, working on her drink. 'I put a lot of effort into you and your sister, and the results haven't been what I would call rewarding.'

I wanted to shake her inviolate shoulders. Mother had stood like a wedge between Linda and me throughout childhood, and she was still keeping us apart. 'What right do you have to decide if and when we can communicate with each other?' I shouted. 'Linda is my sister.'

'Every right. You are both my daughters,' she said, as if we were matching figurines she had purchased to display on her mantelpiece. 'And stop shouting.'

Somehow I managed to control myself. 'I want Linda's address and telephone number,' I said levelly. 'Now.'

'Can't it wait until the morning?' Mother asked. 'I'm not going to run away.'

I am not sure if it was something in the timbre of her voice, a note of relief, which told me that Linda wasn't the source of her drinking problem, or if it was because she sat down to finish her half-filled glass rather than openly take it upstairs, but I knew then that Mother had used Linda as a diversionary tactic. I was not going to be so easily sidestepped, however. 'How is Dad?' I asked, trying again. 'You haven't talked about him since you arrived.'

'Haven't I?' she replied, still in control though her speech was slightly sodden.

'No, you haven't,' I said. 'Why didn't he come with you? And why doesn't he pick up an extension when you call? He has ignored us for months.'

Mother finished her drink and set the empty glass on the table next to her, placing a coaster under it with elaborate care. 'You aren't the only one he has ignored,' she said, fussing with the glass and coaster. 'I might as well tell you: your father and I are no longer together. He left me three and a half months ago.'

'Do you know where he is?' I asked incredulously.

'Must we continue with this ... this inquisition?' she asked in an anguished voice, instinctively twisting her diamond wedding bands.

'I'd like to know where he is,' I said.

'No, you wouldn't,' she replied in a voice that was a mixture of alcohol, anger, and hurt.

I was tempted to drop the conversation, to suggest that we have a cup of coffee or go to bed, for she looked pathetic. She was pathetic, an aging woman twisting her wedding rings in misery, but I pressed on. 'Do you know where he is, Mother?' I asked softly.

'Of course I know. He's living with someone. The insult of it. The insult,' she repeated with breathless indignation. 'A sixty-two-year-old man and a forty-five-year-old woman. It wouldn't have been so bad if she had been younger, a girl in her twenties, but the woman is forty-five.'

'What difference does the woman's age make?' I asked,

finding it difficult to imagine my father with a woman other than my mother.

'When a man your father's age runs around with young girls, it can be laughed off. Oh, it hurts, but people will attribute it to a last fling, to a final spree before dotage. But when a man picks a mature woman, he's saying something else. He's telling the world that . . . that . . .' She could not finish.

'That what?' I asked, puzzled.

'That he isn't getting what he wants at home,' she answered painfully. 'That his wife is inadequate.'

I had always known that sex was a difficult subject for my mother, but had assumed her difficulty was one of articulation. Apparently it extended far beyond words.

'I had always endured that part of marriage,' she said. 'I accommodated your father thinking that it would eventually end, that his desires would diminish as he grew older. Instead, they seemed to grow stronger. There were times when I actually suffered. And for what? To have him advertise that he is an animal? What he has done is as indecent as exposing himself, and me, in public.'

As she spoke, I became increasingly uncomfortable. It is difficult to think of one's parents as sexual beings. To conceptualize them mating, one with lust and the other with disgusted resignation, borders on irreverence. I was repelled by the image.

'Are you listening to me, Jennifer?' I heard my mother ask. 'I'm talking to you.'

'Yes,' I replied, disconcerted.

'I came to California hoping to persuade you to come back with me,' she said, swallowing audibly. 'But I can see now that it would be useless for me to ask. You have started a life for yourself here, and you have a fine job. There is also that man, Nat. You wouldn't be interested in returning.' There was a disheartening wistfulness in her voice, as well as a slight whine.

'I'll call Dad if you think it will help. I don't have to see him to talk to him.'

'Don't you dare call him,' she ordered. 'I didn't want you to come home to fight my battle for me. I have hired a lawyer to do that. Your father won't get his divorce easily, and when he does, he'll pay for it.'

'Then why did you want me to come back?'

She grasped the arms of her chair and pushed herself into a standing position. 'It's so lonely, so unbearably lonely,' said my mother, walking stiff-backed toward the stairs to bed.

I wanted to rush after her, to hold her and comfort her, but I couldn't. There had never been physical affection between us, touching of any kind, and it was too late to begin. I watched her start up the stairs, knowing what would happen once her door was closed for the night: she would weep. Alone. And I was helpless. I could do nothing for her. The rules were the rules.

I turned off the lights and carried our glasses into the kitchen. Then I waited until I was sure she was safely behind her bedroom door, painfully aware that privacy was the only comfort I could offer my mother. While I waited, I listened to the night sounds, the hum of the refrigerator and occasional, unexpected creaks in the walls, and the soft sobs coming from my throat, filling the darkness.

Thursday was the last full day of Mother's visit. Neither of us mentioned my father, and we carefully avoided any reference to what had happened the previous night. But the revelations of the evening lingered in our consciousness with the tenacity of stale cigar smoke that has permeated upholstered furniture; a single word, like a touch, could release its fumes to engulf us. The result was an overcheerfulness on Mother's part and an overbrightness on mine. The day was deadly.

Mother had expressed an interest in Mexican food earlier in the week, so I suggested that we go out for dinner, and made a reservation for us at the restaurant where Nat had taken me on our first date. When the children came home exhausted after a full day at camp and balked at the idea of eating out, I fixed them a light supper and called a sitter. Surprisingly, Mother seemed disappointed that they weren't coming with us, and she sat with them while they ate.

Perhaps she didn't want to be alone with me.

During dinner we concentrated pointedly on our food. I wanted to talk to her, to tell her that I understood, that I cared, that I was willing to help her in any possible way, but I said nothing. I could not violate her pride. It would have been unforgivable. I know my mother too well. We are not friends, nor have we ever been friends, but we do share an awareness of each other, an awful knowing that only a mother and daughter can share. And it was the awful knowing that silenced me.

As we were leaving the restaurant, Mother said: 'Look in the far corner. Isn't that Nat Witton?'

'Yes, that's Nat,' I said, struggling to keep my voice expressionless.

The room was dimly lit, but not too dark to see Nat. He was with a woman, a stunning blonde, and they were talking animatedly.

But my mother knew exactly how I felt. 'Let's leave directly,' she said quietly. 'I don't believe you'll want to stop to say hello.'

That is what I mean, Richard, by the awful knowing.

On our way home, Mother said: 'I realize this isn't the proper time, but there is a matter which I feel compelled to discuss with you. I regret that we saw your friend, but I'll be leaving tomorrow, and it cannot be put off. Do you remember Claudia Hauser?'

I remembered Claudia Hauser vividly. She was a rather plain-looking girl with curly brown hair and a tendency toward plumpness. She had pudgy fingers and moved her hands constantly when she talked, unashamed of her fingernails, which were bitten to the quick. Claudia and I had attended the same grammar school, and it was through Claudia that I learned my first bitter lessons in human manipulation and cruelty. My early years of grammar school are a blur, but my memory can focus to precision sharpness on the sixth grade. A clique of girls had formed. The group was undefined at first, with stray girls entering and exiting, but it solidified by the time Claudia and I reached the seventh grade. We were both part of the group.

There were ten of us, and all but Claudia had come from comfortable homes. It had seemed natural to us that Claudia had less, because her mother was a widow who worked as a clerk in a better dress shop to support herself and her daughter. We never referred to Claudia's circumstances, for we were in the process of learning to be ladies. And Claudia had always seemed to enjoy her fatherlessness. With her stubby fingers flying, she told us how handsome her father was, how deeply in love her parents had been, and how tragic it was that he had had a fatal heart attack when he was such a young man. We listened to Claudia talk about her father endlessly, sighing pubescent sighs. None of us had a father as romantic as Claudia's. Our fathers belched and fell asleep reading the evening paper. The ghost of Claudia's father was infinitely more attractive.

The group was close, as girls are at that age; we did everything together in exaggerated friendship. But soon there was trouble. By the middle of our year in seventh grade, each girl in the group became insecure. One by one, girls would be temporarily excluded. No one knew precisely how it happened, and no one seemed to ask. Very simply, one girl would be shut out. She would be cruelly ignored; her telephone wouldn't ring, and we would snicker at her in the halls. I acted with the rest of the girls, although I didn't know why. None of them had done me harm. Yet when the time came, I could not separate myself from the others' cruelty. I was one of them.

My turn came in the spring, and it was hell. I told no one. I walked to and from school alone. I ate lunch alone. I spent Saturday afternoons alone. I stared at my shoes and choked back tears of bewilderment. I didn't know what I had done and couldn't ask. One did not ask.

The torture lasted for two weeks. Then, magically, I was part of the group again. But I was uncomfortable. I could relate to one or two girls at a time, but I couldn't seem to breathe in the group. I was suffocating and was grateful when school ended.

No one seemed to notice that Claudia Hauser was the only girl who had not been excluded.

Eighth grade was a repetition of seventh grade: the group reunited and the cruelty started, a victim at a time. In November it became apparent that it was to be Marietta Emery's turn. Marietta was a pale, quiet girl who would have been pretty if her face hadn't been dominated by oversized, protruding hazel eyes. When Marietta had been excluded the year before, she had become hysterical, and Mrs Emery had called my mother. When Mother asked me why the girls were being cruel to Marietta, I couldn't answer. I honestly didn't know. This time, however, Mrs Emery didn't call. She had figured things out for herself.

When Marietta was eventually encouraged to re-enter the group, she hesitated instead of rushing back with gratitude. 'I'll be friends with you as individuals,' she said, 'but I don't want to be part of the group again.'

I understood, and I knew the others understood. We agreed to be her friends, all but Claudia. 'Marietta Emery is a jerk,' said Claudia. 'She's nothing but a big cry-baby.'

I'm ashamed to say that not one of us argued with Claudia.

One by one, Marietta invited us to her house after school. Her mother served milk and cookies, then Marietta took each girl to her room for a serving of the truth. 'Claudia Hauser's father committed suicide,' said Marietta Emery in whispered confidence. 'He hung himself with his belt. He didn't have a heart attack like Claudia says he did, and her parents weren't happy. They were going to get a divorce.'

I can still recall my shock. 'Are you sure?' I asked.

'Yes,' said Marietta, her eyes bulging triumphantly. 'You can talk to my mother. She knew Claudia's father. He wasn't even handsome. My mother says he was just ordinary looking, maybe a little fat, that's all. My mother says Claudia's mean because she's insecure; she doesn't have as many things as the rest of us. That's why she needs to hurt people.'

It wasn't long before everyone knew about Claudia's father, and I can recall the knowing looks we gave each other when Claudia became poetic about her handsome daddy who had had a heart attack. 'Oh, yes,' we said in unison, envisioning him swinging by his belt.

'Jennifer, do you remember Claudia Hauser?' my mother repeated.

'Yes,' I said.

'I want you to tell the children how Richard died. They need to know, and I don't want them to find out the way Claudia Hauser found out about her father,' said Mother emphatically.

'I wasn't sure if Claudia knew,' I replied, starting to perspire.

'Claudia didn't know until she was in college. You were away at school at the time, so you probably didn't hear how she found out. While on a double date, Claudia made an unkind remark to a girl who went to grammar school with you. The girl was embarrassed, and in anger she referred to Claudia's father swinging by his belt. Claudia had a nervous breakdown afterward and lost her scholarship.'

Then: 'I can't understand why the girl mentioned him swinging by his belt. Actually, he hung himself with a rope.'

I concentrated on my driving.

'How Claudia's father killed himself isn't important,' Mother continued. 'What is important is that you must tell the children. I won't have my grandchildren growing up in ignorance.'

400

'I'll tell them when they're older,' I said. 'We live in California; no one knows us here. The circumstances are different from Claudia's. Matthew and Catherine have the advantage of distance.'

'Now, Jennifer. You'll tell them now. Matthew needs to know. The boy is troubled. We didn't talk much, but when we did, he practically begged me to tell him. Catherine is different. She just wants stories about Richard. But the time will come when she will want to know, too. The truth travels, and three thousand miles is a relatively short distance.'

'Give me time, Mother,' I pleaded.

'I'll give you until Christmas,' she said. 'If you haven't told them by then, I'll tell them myself.'

'It's easy for you to give ultimatums,' I retorted angrily. 'You have no idea of how difficult it is for me to even articulate Richard's name.'

My mother's voice came out of the darkness. 'You are my daughter, Jennifer. Please give me credit for some understanding. I can feel your pain, but what must be done, must be done.'

We went home, and Mother packed her bags. She boarded her plane this morning and left me holding the truth.

I told the children, Richard. It wasn't as hard as I had imagined it would be. I'm not saying that it was easy, because it wasn't. It was difficult. And painful. But that doesn't matter now. What is important is that the children know and understand, so you can rest and I can live, both of us in peace.

Mother's ultimatum, backed by her threat to give the children the truth as a bonus Christmas present, didn't force me to tell Matthew and Catherine. This is the last weekend in August; Christmas is four months away, still too distant for even department stores to begin promoting Christ's birthday into their most lucrative yearly enterprise, although I did see a premature Christmas tree in a store window last week.

Nor was the change in my relationship with Nat the impetus behind my telling the children. There are times when they miss him, particularly on weekends, but that could also be because I no longer feel obligated to provide them with two days of entertainment; one treat per weekend is sufficient. When I explained that I wanted to rest after working a full week, I was surprised to find that the children understood. Now we plan our weekend treat as a family, and the three of us seem to enjoy it more. The days of my searching through newspapers, frantically looking for places to take them to keep them occupied, are gone. This morning we took a long bicycle ride together and came home content.

How can I tell you about Nat when I don't know what to tell myself about him? I suppose the logical place to begin would be where I left off, after my mother's visit seven weeks ago.

Nat came over after work on the Friday Mother left. I had spent the afternoon writing to you and was in worse shape than I had been when she departed (after going to the hairdresser, of course). It was the first time that writing hadn't helped. When the doorbell rang late in the day, I jumped up from my desk and dashed downstairs, thinking that the children were home from camp. I opened the door and saw Nat.

'I'm early,' he said, walking in. 'The city room was unusually quiet today.' He bent down to kiss me. I turned away and started walking toward the kitchen.

'You must be cooking something special if you can't take time out for recreation,' he quipped. 'What's for dinner?'

'Nothing,' I said.

Nat followed me into the kitchen. 'Didn't your mother leave?' he whispered. 'Is that the reason for the chill in here?'

'She left at noon,' I said flatly.

Nat looked around. The counters were clean, the oven was off, and there wasn't a pot, pan, or particle of food in sight. Then his eyes, which had narrowed into deep blue hyphens, rested on me. 'What's wrong, Jenny?' he asked. 'If you're tired of cooking, you could have said something. Your behavior isn't what I could call subtle. Why are you so cold? We haven't seen each other since Tuesday.'

Actually, I was tired of cooking. Preparing meals for him had been a lark at first because Nat is an appreciative eater, unlike the children who sometimes suffer through the main course to get to dessert. And cooking for four is easier than cooking for three, especially when the fourth is an adult with a healthy appetite who helps with the dishes. But what had begun as a lark became a chore when I started working a full week. There wasn't enough time to prepare the dinners Nat had become accustomed to, and rather than tell him that it was becoming a strain, I began cooking at night for the next day. 'The way to a man's heart,' I had thought grimly and more than once while washing out pots before going to bed.

The chill Nat felt, however, had nothing to do with cooking. 'We saw each other last night, at least I saw you. Did you enjoy your dinner?' I inquired frostily.

'Last night?' Nat frowned.

'Last night at Esteban's,' I said. 'My mother and I ate dinner there.'

The furrows in his forehead disappeared the instant he understood.

I don't know if I expected an explanation or an apology, or if I was afraid of receiving neither. I was also unsure of how I felt. Seeing Nat with another woman had slashed my pride, but when we stood facing each other, it occurred to me that my hurt could possibly be nothing more than a surface wound, like a cut on the lip or forehead that bleeds with such profusion that there is shocked surprise at its insignificance once the blood is wiped away.

Nat started to explain. 'Victoria works for one of the wire services. It was innocent, believe me. I've known her for years, and there is nothing between us. She was transferred to LA last month, and I happened to bump into her yesterday. I was at loose ends and invited her to dinner. Nothing happened.'

But my pride has never been insignificant, not to me, and a wound was a wound. I had to protect myself. Or was it resurrect myself? Besides, I wasn't sure that I believed him. 'You don't owe me an explanation,' I said with composure. 'I was hurt, but that's my problem, not yours. I'll recover. Maybe you were right. We do need time away from each other, but I think we need more than a week. Let's separate for a while.'

'You saw me with another woman, so you're punishing me,' Nat snapped. 'I told you, Jenny, I was eating dinner with her, not fucking her for chrissake. You're being unreasonable.'

'You're turning this around,' I said, 'making me feel guilty for being angry.'

'You're damned right, I am. I would have told you if you had given me the opportunity, but you couldn't wait. Instead, you dumped it on me like a pail of ice water when I walked in the door,' he accused, raising his voice.

He was right; I did dump it on him. But I had lived with it for an unhappy twenty-four hours. 'How would you have felt if the situation were reversed?' I retorted. 'If you had seen me with another man, would you have greeted me with smiles the next day? Or would it have bothered you?'

The tendons in Nat's cheeks started working, but he didn't reply. 'Well, would it have bothered you?' I repeated. 'Are you saying that we are both free? As I recall, you didn't cover a situation like this when you briefed me on affairs.'

'I was bored, and eating alone didn't appeal to me,' he said, shrugging. 'So when I ran into Victoria, I invited her out to dinner. It was harmless, nothing more than a pleasant way to spend the evening, but you're blowing it into a major transgression.'

'I'm not interested in what happened,' I said, which wasn't completely true. 'I'd rather have you answer my questions.'

'What questions?' he asked evasively.

I angrily repeated the questions, fully aware that he had heard them from the first. I also knew that I was forcing the situation, that I was pushing Nat beyond where he was willing to go. Strangely, it didn't bother me as much as I would have anticipated had there been time for anticipation. I had already been hurt, and I knew every possible reply he could make, including the worst. It was then that I realized I didn't love Nat, not as I had once loved you. If I had loved him with that total, all-consuming intensity, I never would have taken the risk.

Nat didn't reply, so I answered his silence by walking into the living room. I sat down on the sofa and lit a cigarette. 'It's over,' I muttered, inhaling deeply. 'First Mother's visit, now this. It's been a banner week.'

Nat came into the living room and sat next to me. When he put his arm around me, I removed his hand from my shoulder and edged my body away from his. 'You don't have to say anything, Nat,' I said, turning to face him. 'And the fact that you haven't tells me everything I want to know. Silence is an excellent communicator. Please go now. The children will be home from camp soon, and if you leave after they arrive, I'll have a lot of unwelcome explaining to do.'

'I haven't answered because I'm unsure of my reply,' Nat said. His jaw muscles were no longer working, and his eyes were almost believable, a clear, honest blue. 'Silence can be misinterpreted, especially when it's the silence of hesitation.'

'Not really,' I replied. 'I'm an expert on silence. Every silence, even the silence of hesitation, makes a statement.'

'How do you know? What makes you an expert?' he asked caustically.

I thought for a moment and decided to give Nat a lesson

in silence. He had given me one in affairs, so I couldn't let him leave empty-handed. 'During our last year together, Richard and I had a marriage of silence. Did you know that once one has become a student of silence, every silence can be read as clearly as one of your newspapers? There is the silence of anger, the silence of fear, the silence of disappointment, the silence of hope, and the silence of desperation, which is the silence I dread most. Every human emotion has its own silence, unique and unmistakable as yours was. And is.'

Then: 'The kindest thing you could do now would be to leave.'

'But I'm not Richard,' said Nat, rising. 'Isn't every man entitled to his own silence?'

I didn't answer. Nat walked to the front door and opened it. 'I'll call you after I have worked this out,' he said, closing the door behind him.

To their delight, I took the children to McDonald's for dinner. It was an apropos finale to a dreadful week.

The weekend was a disaster. For lack of something better to do, I took the children skateboarding on Saturday, and they were both injured: Matthew twisted his ankle, and Catherine landed on her hip, bruising it badly. Nor was I able to explain Nat's absence to either child's satisfaction. I didn't want to tell them that Nat and I were no longer seeing each other (or was it myself that I didn't want to tell?), so I told them Nat was busy with one of his friends for the weekend, mentally picturing the blond Victoria. I was convinced, but they weren't.

By Sunday, I was lonelier than I had been in months, and the full, mocking face of the California sun made me feel gray and cold inside, like the bark on a maple in late November. I felt a desperate need to talk to someone and walked over to Deirdre's. She and her lawyer friend, Michael Flaherty, were having a late breakfast before taking Kerry out for the day. Although they were cordial and invited me to join them, I refused and left, feeling that I had intruded. Then I tried writing to you and couldn't;

I felt too abandoned to talk to a ghost. And all through the long weekend Nat's words played in my head, 'I'll call you after I have worked this out,' like a tape recorder repeating a single, endless message.

He didn't call.

I was glad when Monday came, for it meant Briarhill and a chance to immerse myself in work. But no matter what I did or how hard I tried to concentrate on my job, my mind was with Mother and Nat and my failure with both of them. Simon noticed my preoccupation while we were checking the following week's menu and food order. 'You're not yourself, Jenny,' he commented. 'Is something troubling you?'

If he had been looking at me when he spoke, I might have opened up. But Simon was poring over the food order to estimate its cost, which is one of his weekly games – to see how close he can come to the final figure after the order has been purchased and billed – so I told him that I was adjusting to work after a week of vacation. I don't believe he even heard me. 'I know I've hit it on the nose this week,' he chuckled with satisfaction, jotting the figure down.

I have observed that certain compensations come with age. One's pleasures may not be as strenuous, but neither are one's risks. For an instant, I envied Simon his harmless fun.

Two weeks elapsed before Nat called, and when I picked up the receiver and heard his voice, tentative yet friendly, as if it had been two days since we had last spoken, I was beyond caring. 'I'd like to talk with you,' he said. 'Could I come over tonight?'

'No,' I replied. 'It would be impossible.'

'Tomorrow night, then?'

'I'm afraid not,' I said.

I don't know whether Nat had expected me to purr in gratitude at his suggestion that we get together or if he had anticipated my wrath for taking so long to call, but he certainly wasn't prepared for my unresponsiveness. 'I realize that it has been a few weeks,' he said, sounding defensive, 'but I have done some thinking, serious thinking, and we have to talk.'

'I can't,' I said.

'Why not?' he demanded.

Nat's annoyance reached me. 'I'm having a problem with Matthew, and until it's settled, I can't cope with anything else. Or anyone else.'

'Let me help,' Nat offered. 'Matthew and I are buddies. We have a good rapport now. Besides, I miss the kids. I'd like to see them.'

'No,' I said. 'Your presence would only confuse them. And me. You can't walk in and out of our lives whenever you happen to feel like it. I'll call you.'

'When?' Nat wanted to know.

'When I have worked this out,' I said, inadvertently echoing Nat's parting words to me two weeks before.

'Stop playing games, Jenny. I know what you're doing – you're paying me back for not calling.'

'Frankly, I haven't thought of you in days,' I said truthfully, aware but not caring that I was cutting Nat Witton to the core. 'Do you still want me to call?'

Nat cleared his throat. 'I need you,' he said with difficulty.

'Not as much as Matthew needs me,' I replied.

The trouble with Matthew started the Friday following Mother's departure. As usual, the children went out to play after dinner, Catherine with her friend, Lisa, and Matthew on his ten-speed bicycle. I was reading the entertainment section of the evening paper, searching for activities to divert the children on what promised to be another dreary weekend, when Matthew came running into the living room, white-faced. 'M-M-M-M-My b-b-b-b-bike,' he stammered, panting.

I waited for him to tell me more, but he stared at me inarticulately, his mouth open and his jaw locked. Fearing that he had fallen, I walked over to him and quickly checked for signs of blood or bruises. There were none. 'Did you fall?' I asked, puzzled.

He shook his head negatively.

'Then what is wrong?' I demanded impatiently. I was tired and in no mood to play guessing games.

'Th-Th-Th-Th-Th-The g-g-g-g-gears,' he managed to say. 'Th-Th-Th-Th-They're b-b-b-broken.'

In retrospect, I don't know whether it was my dislike of the bicycle, my weariness, or Matthew's speech regression that sparked my irritation, but I didn't even bother to ask him how it had happened. 'That bicycle was a mistake,' I said. 'It's much too complicated, and you were warned that there could be trouble with the gears if you were careless.'

Matthew started to cry and pleaded with me, between sobs, to take the bicycle in to be repaired. 'Th-Th-Th-The store is st-st-st-still o-o-open,' he begged. 'P-P-P-Please, M-M-M-Mom.'

I refused, rebelling at the thought of packing both children and the bicycle into the car at seven thirty in the evening.

Matthew became hysterical. 'Th-Th-Th-Th-Then I-I'll g-g-get another b-b-b-b-bike,' he screamed. 'I-I-I-I-I have the m-m-m-m-money, and I-I-I-I'll g-g-g-g-get it m-m-m-m-myself.'

'No, you won't,' I yelled back. 'That money will stay where it is – in the bank.'

Matthew's body stiffened. He stopped crying and glared at me with open resentment – hatred, really, the pure, undisguised hatred of childhood. I recognized it instantly, but it was too late. What had been said, had been said. As I once tried to explain to you, Richard, I can't always handle the children. It is hard being alone with them, bearing the full responsibility for their welfare when I have difficulty coping with my own life. There are times when our frustrations, theirs and mine, meet head-on and explode in our faces. This was one of those times. And because my authority is greater than theirs, I must carry the guilt. But their burden is worse, for they will forever bear the scars.

I was about to apologize when Matthew, in tongue-locked rage, picked up the ashtray I had been using and threw it, narrowly missing my head. The ashtray ricocheted off the wall behind me, wildly scattering its contents. We looked at each other in mute shock. Then, before I recovered, he turned and ran out of the room. I stood in place for a long time, long after I heard the back door slam, covered with ashes.

When it became dark and Matthew hadn't returned, my concern grew into panic. 'I wonder where Matthew is,' I said casually to Catherine, trying to conceal my apprehensiveness. 'Did you see him while you were playing outside?'

'Lisa and I played inside with her new doll house,' Catherine replied matter-of-factly. 'Don't you remember? I told you that Lisa got a new doll house. Can I have a snack?'

I poured her a glass of milk and put a package of her favorite cookies on the kitchen table. 'I'm going out to look for Matthew while you have your snack,' I said, hoping that the food would keep her busy. 'I'll be back soon.'

I must have traipsed through every corner of Sherwood Village, quadrangle after identical quadrangle, searching and calling Matthew's name softly in the darkness until I began to shake with alarm and could no longer modulate my voice. When I heard myself screaming his name, 'Matthew, Matthew,' and saw draperies move, emitting triangles of light in protest to my shouts, I headed toward Deirdre's.

Deirdre wasn't home, and the babysitter, under strict orders, refused to let me in. I finally managed to persuade her to let me speak to Kerry through the locked, half-screen back door.

Kerry didn't know where Matthew was. 'He went home after Robbie O'Connor broke his bike,' Kerry said excitedly. 'We were playing and the big kids came and Robbie took Matthew's bike. He raced it with another kid on someone else's bike and broke the gears. Matthew and I wanted to catch them to get the bike back, but the big boys made us stay where we were. They said they'd beat us up. We couldn't get Matthew's bike until after they left. Robbie dumped the bike on the grass after the race; he didn't even use the kickstand.'

Kerry waited for my response. I nodded with understanding, filled with regret for what I had done to Matthew. Instead of giving him the comfort and help he needed, I had shown him nothing but inflexible irritation.

He continued. 'Matthew didn't cry. He just ran home,' said Kerry with admiration. 'Can you get the bike fixed?'

I ignored Kerry's question and thanked him. Then I ran home to call the police, sure that Matthew had run away.

The minutes between Deirdre's townhouse and ours were a nightmare. Images of Matthew wandering lost among strangers in a strange place flashed across my eyes. Matthew walking aimlessly among California junkies. Matthew pasted on one of the endless freeways that snake about the city. Matthew lying mutilated on a perimeter hill where he wouldn't be discovered for days. Matthew being picked up and abused by one of the thousands of sickies who live here, who are always on the prowl, always looking for kicks. Hysteria rose in my throat. I ran as fast as I could, afraid that I was already too late.

Catherine was standing at the door in tears waiting for me. She started to speak, but I rushed past her to the telephone. She followed me, whining. 'Can't you be quiet?' I yelled, picking up the receiver.

She stopped crying. 'Matthew won't talk to me. He shut his door in my face and told me to go downstairs and leave him alone. I don't like being downstairs in the night all by myself,' she complained. 'Matthew's mean.'

I put the receiver down. 'Where is Matthew now?' I asked, praying that I had heard her correctly.

'In his room,' Catherine said in a tone that let me know how abused she felt.

I ran upstairs and knocked on his door. There was no response. 'May I come in?' I asked, twisting the doorknob. Still no response. I tried to open the door but couldn't budge it: Matthew had barricaded himself in his room.

It was impossible to elicit a word from Matthew. His door remained closed to my apologies, my cajoling, and, finally, my threats. When I started to shriek at his closed door, I decided to put Catherine to bed and go to bed myself. I spent a restless night and dragged myself out of bed exhausted in the morning.

Usually the children forget unpleasantness within a day, often within hours if I am able to divert their attention, but Matthew did not forget or forgive. He ignored my repeated offers to take his bicycle in to be repaired. The day was overcast, yet he refused to go out to lunch or to the movies with Catherine and me, so we stayed home. And his refusals were silent. Matthew wouldn't speak. Not a word. Not to anyone, even Catherine.

Sunday was a darker repetition of Saturday; time didn't spring Matthew's locked tongue. We saw him only at meals, and he wouldn't eat if I sat at the table. I tried to pretend that nothing had happened and ate after the children were finished, because Catherine was becoming increasingly agitated. 'Please talk, Matthew, please,' she begged at lunch.

Matthew pushed his plate aside and stalked upstairs to his room. The sound of his door slamming reduced Catherine to tears. 'I don't like it when Matthew won't talk,' she said, crying.

'Neither do I,' I replied, comforting her. I was close to tears myself.

When Matthew again rejected Catherine while they were eating dinner, I could no longer control myself and grabbed him as he was starting up the stairs. 'If you won't speak, you will at least look at me,' I ordered, gripping him by the shoulders. He turned his face defiantly sideward.

To my horror, I slapped him hard across the cheek, something I had vowed I would never do. My mother struck me in the face when I was a child, and it was the worst violation to my person I had ever experienced. I never forgot or forgave her. Now I had done it to my son.

'I'm sorry,' I said, feeling him flinch under my one-handed grip. His lower lip trembled, and a tear oozed out of his closed eyelid and worked its way down the red handprint I had left on his face. 'I'm sorry,' I repeated. 'Really, I am. I didn't mean to hit you. I only wanted you to look at me so I could talk to you.'

He wriggled out of my grasp, climbed the stairs, then stopped and turned to face me when he reached the top. His eyes were so dark they were almost charcoal, and the words he spoke were coated with ice. 'You're not sorry,' he said. 'You won't be sorry until I'm dead. Like Daddy.'

There was no hesitation in his speech, not a trace of a stammer or hint of a block. Matthew's message was clear, and before I could reply, he disappeared behind his bedroom door.

Matthew's silence continued; neither Catherine nor I were able to communicate with him. I took his bicycle in to be repaired on Monday during my lunch hour and offered to pay extra if it could be fixed immediately. The bicycle was ready late Tuesday afternoon, and I gladly drove in rush-hour freeway traffic to get to the store before going home, sure that I could bring an end to Matthew's silence.

The camp bus pulled up as I was turning into Sherwood Village. I stopped in the driveway, got out of the car, and waved the children over, but only Catherine responded. She came running to greet me while Matthew trudged up the walk, his eyes focused on the pavement. 'Your bicycle is fixed,' I called to him. 'Come help me get it out of the trunk.'

Matthew's head didn't turn. He continued walking and

opened the door with the key I had given him months ago. I didn't know whether to cry or curse as I struggled with the unwieldy bicycle while Catherine watched helplessly.

On Thursday, the director of the children's camp called me at work. 'This is Clifford Gates,' he said, introducing himself. 'I try not to disturb parents at their places of business unless it's absolutely necessary, but I must talk to you about Matthew.'

'Has he been hurt?' I asked anxiously.

'No, it's nothing like that,' he replied. 'Until this week Matthew was a model camper – cooperative, willing to participate in camp activities, well-liked by his peers. For some reason, his attitude has changed drastically. Matthew has become a disruptive element in his group, and his behavior is beginning to affect the entire boy's unit. He refuses to join the others in activities, will not communicate with anyone, and has already had two fistfights this morning. His counselors have tried to talk to the boy and so have I, but we can't seem to reach him.'

Clifford Gates paused, waiting for my response, but I couldn't speak. There was a tightness in my chest, and my limbs felt heavy, as if my blood had stopped circulating and was pooling in my arms and legs. 'Are you there, Mrs Weaver?' he asked.

'Yes,' I replied, lightheaded.

'I reviewed Matthew's camp application before calling you to see if we overlooked any mention of erratic behavior, but you didn't seem to indicate that Matthew had a problem aside from his speech. To be honest, I wasn't surprised. It has been my experience that most parents don't like to talk about their children's problems, especially not write them on printed forms, which is why we insist that a separate, detailed evaluation by the child's physician accompany each application. In Matthew's case, the pediatrician's report concurred with yours, not that it means anything. Doctors today are too busy to know their patients very well, and most of them sign forms that are completed by their secretaries. Tell me, has Matthew had a history of antisocial behavior?'

'No,' I replied. Several days of silence didn't add up to a history.

'We can't help Matthew unless you are honest with us,' he said impatiently.

'I have never received a complaint about Matthew's behavior,' I told him. 'If anything, he has been introspective rather than aggressive.'

'What you're saying doesn't make sense in the light of Matthew's behavior this past week. He has been looking for fights. The slightest provocation starts the boy's fists flying,' the director said coldly. 'You aren't leveling with me, Mrs Weaver, so you give me no choice but to dismiss your son from camp.'

'Wait,' I said, panicking. 'Matthew did have a bad experience last weekend. A boy broke the gears on his bicycle, and he was terribly upset. It will probably take him a while to forget what happened.'

'Was he injured in any way?' the director asked.

'No,' I replied.

'Did you have the bicycle repaired?'

'Yes, but Matthew won't touch it,' I said truthfully.

'Your son has a problem,' he said in a kindlier tone of voice. 'I'm not a psychologist, but it is my guess that the unfortunate incident with his bicycle is not the underlying cause of Matthew's radical change in behavior. Something is disturbing the boy. I have been working with children for sixteen years, and I have observed that almost anything can trigger children with emotional problems – a disliked food, a cross word, the loss of a turn at play – the most insignificant of circumstances can act like a lit fuse. I would strongly recommend that you seek professional help for Matthew.'

'Then you don't want him to return to camp?' I forced myself to ask.

'Not until I am assured that he can relate with the other children in an acceptable manner,' said Clifford Gates.

I quickly called the pediatrician to ask him for the name of a child psychologist, but his office was closed. I left a message with his answering service for him to call me at home, acidly noting that California wasn't different from Eagles' Landing, where the doctors didn't work on Thursdays. You joked about that, remember? 'It's against the rules to get sick on Thursday,' you used to say when conversations turned to the physicians' day off. 'Thursdays are reserved for dying. It's written in fine print in the Hippocratic Oath.' You always said that in a large group, and you enjoyed watching the doctors of Eagles' Landing squirm uncomfortably as they tried to laugh with everyone else. Only I was aware of the resentment you concealed under a facetious grin. Only I knew how you envied them for their effortless streams of patients when you had to cultivate each one of your clients. Only I knew how you despised them for their exorbitant fees, backed by government guarantees of payment, when you had to justify your bills. And only I knew how you hated them for their wealth and ease of survival in Eagles' Landing when you worked as hard or harder and couldn't quite make it. 'Damn them,' you seethed in private. 'They're secular gods sitting on six-figure thrones.'

Richard, you committed suicide on a Thursday. Until this moment, it didn't seem possible to me that the day you chose was anything but a fluke, a free evening in a busy week. Now I wonder.

I debated whether to tell Simon that I wouldn't be in on Friday or to wait until the morning to call. I decided to wait. My week's vacation was too recent to ask for another day off, and I was certain that Simon wouldn't be sympathetic toward my problem with Matthew. He has been crediting his late wife with Jim's ineptitude more frequently now that Jim is in the sporting-goods store. Apparently the business isn't doing well. Simon has tried to talk to me about it, but I change the subject whenever he mentions Jim.

The pediatrician returned my call after dinner and

recommended a child psychiatrist rather than a psychologist for Matthew. When I disagreed, fearing that a psychiatrist would mean months of analysis before Matthew's problem surfaced so it could be treated, the pediatrician replied: 'If Matthew needs treatment for an emotional problem, and from what you say he does, you can't expect a one-visit cure. These things take time. And as far as a psychologist is concerned, I wouldn't take my child to one. I would want a psychiatrist with a sound medical background, nothing less, and I can't recommend less for my patients. I'm sending you to a man who is top in his field. I'll talk to him in the morning and set up an appointment sometime next week if he has an opening. My secretary will call you after the arrangements have been made.'

'But it can't wait until next week,' I protested. 'Matthew needs help now.'

'You have to be patient. Whatever is bothering Matthew has been disturbing him for a long time, and a few days aren't going to make a difference. Remember, we're talking about a child, not an adult in a crisis with a bottle of sleeping pills in one hand and a gun in the other.'

Or the keys to a Mercedes in an oak-paneled garage, I thought bitterly as I put the receiver down.

We never did get to the psychiatrist's office.

I wasn't aware of Catherine while I was speaking to the pediatrician, but when I returned to the living room, I realized that she had been listening to my half of the conversation. 'Where is Matthew going?' she asked.

'To a special doctor,' I replied casually.

'Why? Matthew's not sick.'

'Matthew hasn't been behaving at camp,' I said, trying to keep my explanation brief, 'and he won't talk to us. The doctor will find out why.'

'But I know why,' said Catherine.

'Why?' I asked, nearly jumping off the sofa.

'Because,' she said simply, 'Matthew's mad.'

For a wild moment, I thought Catherine meant mad as

in crazy, that she was telling me Matthew was insane. But then I looked at her and saw a child, a literal child to whom mad meant mad. 'How do you know Matthew is mad?' I asked gently so as not to betray the urgency of my question.

'Matthew doesn't like to talk when he's mad because his words get stuck,' said Catherine succinctly. Then she frowned. 'But you said it wasn't my fault, Mommy. I didn't make Matthew mad, did I?'

I hugged Catherine and assured her that she hadn't made Matthew mad, but she wasn't satisfied. 'How will the doctor know what's making Matthew mad?' she questioned. 'Does he have special medicine? Will Matthew get a shot?' The idea of a shot made her grimace and clutch her arm.

'He'll probably talk to Matthew until Matthew tells him,' I replied.

'Is that all?' She sighed disappointedly. 'Why can't we talk to Matthew so he doesn't have to go to the doctor?'

I have never felt so utterly stupid as I did then. Neither Catherine nor I had attempted to talk to Matthew after I had slapped him on Sunday. Instead, we had respected his silence, waiting for him to communicate with us. When he ignored his repaired bicycle on Tuesday, I had assumed that he still wasn't ready to talk and told Catherine, who was as upset with Matthew's lack of interest as I was, that we should leave him alone.

If a doctor can talk to Matthew, I thought, a complete stranger paid for his time, then so can we.

My decision wasn't based on the idea of playing psychiatrist. It was simply the realization that I had given up, that I had allowed Matthew to cut our lines of communication without attempting to mend them, a task which would require more effort on my part than repairing a bicycle. 'Let's start talking to Matthew,' I said.

'But Matthew doesn't want to talk to us,' Catherine argued. 'He goes away.'

'He can't go away forever,' I answered. 'We'll start at breakfast.'

I got up earlier than usual on Friday and called Simon to tell him that I wouldn't be coming in to work. Then I made the children breakfast and sat down to eat with them for the first time in a week. When Matthew saw that I had no intention of leaving in spite of his repeated glares in my direction, he moved his dishes to the far end of the table. But he stayed, as I knew he would, for Matthew is always hungry in the morning. Most important, I talked to both children generally so Matthew wouldn't feel that I was pressuring him.

When the ordeal of breakfast was over, the children started toward the door for the camp bus. I called Matthew back: 'You won't be going to camp today, Matthew. I'll explain why when Catherine leaves.'

Matthew looked at me, startled, but he didn't run upstairs. Instead, he waited for my explanation. 'It seems that you have been having some trouble at camp,' I said carefully. 'The camp director called me and suggested that you take a few days off. I'll stay home with you today.'

Matthew's face reddened.

'When he told me that you have been having fights at camp, I didn't believe him at first,' I continued. 'You've never liked to fight. Is there a reason?'

Matthew shuffled his feet.

'Did someone say something to upset you?' I persisted, trying to lay the blame elsewhere so Matthew wouldn't feel threatened.

Silence.

'I want to help you,' I offered.

Silence.

'I can't help you if you won't talk to me,' I said, pushing as hard as I dared.

Silence.

'Why won't you talk to me, Matthew? Why?'

'W-W-W-W-Why should I-I-I-I-I talk to y-y-you?'

'Because I'm your mother and I love you,' I replied earnestly, relieved that he had finally spoken.

'Y-Y-Y-You don't t-t-talk to to m-m-m-me,' he accused.

'But I do,' I said.

'N-N-No,' Matthew said, starting up the stairs. 'If-If-If-If you t-t-t-t-talked to m-m-m-m-me, you'd t-t-t-t-tell me how D-D-D-D-Daddy died.'

I stayed downstairs alone all morning and cleaned the kitchen cupboards to keep myself occupied, but I wasn't distracted. Nothing, not even the radio which I turned on to blasting, could keep Matthew's words from ringing in my ears.

At lunch, I tried again. I talked nervously, hoping to draw Matthew out, but he sat at the far end of the table and picked at his food. 'Talk to me, Matthew,' I pleaded in desperation. 'We can't live like this.'

Matthew looked up, and his eyes – your eyes, green-flecked in anger – met mine. 'W-W-W-When you t-t-talk to m-m-me,' he said.

I knew what he meant. 'How Daddy died isn't important. He's dead, and nothing I can say will bring him back. What is important is that we are alive. We live together, and it is wrong to shut each other out.'

'It-It-It-It is important,' shouted Matthew. 'N-N-N-Not knowing h-h-how Daddy died m-m-m-makes me feel dumb. S-S-Sometimes kids ask. Th-Th-They look at m-m-m-me like I'm weird when I-I-I-I say I don't know. And-And-And I want to know, n-n-n-not just because of the k-k-kids. H-H-H-He was my d-d-dad. M-M-M-M-Mine. I-I-I-I-I won't t-t-talk to you any-anymore until you t-t-tell.' With that, Matthew threw his fork on the table and ran to his room. What followed next were sounds: his door slamming, the thump of objects thrown against his wall, and finally sobs, great sobs that rushed down the stairwell into the kitchen. Then there was silence.

The silence was frightening, a terrifying mix of rage and

heartbreak, frustration and loss. I went upstairs several times, knocked on Matthew's door and tried to talk to him, but there was no response. Nothing. Only the silence. Nat Witton's call asking to see me after our two-week separation was the one interruption in the long afternoon.

And the silence grew, feeding on itself, until it blocked the flow of time. I sat stiffly in the sun-drenched living room as if in a tomb, reliving our last year in Eagles' Landing, remembering the awful silences that enshrouded us, layer upon layer, until we were wrapped so tightly in our own suffering that we could no longer reach out to each other.

The first silence was anger, mostly mine for what you did to me the night before our party. We rarely spoke after that evening. You didn't apologize the next day, or in the days following when all of the shares were sold. Soon I was almost glad that you didn't apologize, because it justified my feeling of having been wronged. When you finally approached me in bed several weeks later and tried to romance me as you had in the past, I was unable to forgive you. There were nights when we came together out of need, out of lust, but without love. From that time until your death, sex and silence were our only communication. The love we once felt for each other was supplanted by a hate so vibrant that its very intensity was frightening. Still, we stayed together. I don't know why, unless it was because neither one of us had anywhere to go. It was as if we had stretched our lives as far as they could reach so that we had no choice but to wait together to see what would happen.

After The Golden Steer was officially open, the silence became anxious. We were waiting to see how it would do. I never asked. It wasn't necessary. Your nervousness and heavy drinking told me that The Golden Steer was slow in starting. Then, during the winter months, there was the silence of hope. The Golden Steer was booked to capacity.

You spent more time with the children and cut down on your liquor.

But the silence of hope soon gave way to the silence of fear. The high season was short-lived. There were reports in the newspapers that Disney World had closed its gates early due to capacity crowds during the Christmas season, complete with photographs of the disappointed faces of vacationers. Advance bookings at The Golden Steer fell. You lost weight. You took your suits to the tailor to be altered and bought shirts a collar size smaller.

When the silence of fear grew into one of desperation, I became frantic. I switched off the radio and television every time I heard a plea to conserve energy and tried to ignore the profusion of articles I saw everywhere that discussed the continued energy crisis, but it didn't help. Soon there wasn't a part of the newspaper that was safe to read. The travel page reported that hotels in Florida were hurting because thousands of condominiums were owned and rented by out-of-state people. *Vacationers in Florida are staying in private lodgings*, it said. Even the real-estate page forecast doom. Condominiums had been overbuilt in Florida; there were more apartments than there were buyers for them. I began to have severe stomach pains and went to see Barney Leadman. After X-rays were taken, he told me that I had a small ulcer and prescribed medication and a bland diet. I drank milk, ate cheese, and gained ten pounds, which upset me more than the ulcer. I felt unattractive and became self-conscious and withdrawn. You didn't seem to notice.

The year was almost over when I overheard you speaking to someone on a long-distance call. You had discovered that the hotel management firm you had hired under Anson's urging had been falsifying payrolls. You flew to Florida the next morning and returned with deep circles under your eyes. The silence of desperation became one of despair. There was no hope. I knew it then, and blamed myself. I lay awake nights dreaming of schemes to salvage the mess, but they always seemed stupid in the morning, so I said nothing.

On the weekend before you died, you spent Saturday and Sunday in your study working on a projected yearly report for the Bestmark Limited Partnership. All of the figures weren't in, but you knew what they would be. You emerged with a stoicism so deep that you appeared to be more of a shadow than a man. The silence had turned into itself; I could no longer read it. On Thursday you were dead.

I stayed in the living room reliving the nightmare of our last year together until Catherine returned from camp. The day had been brutally hot and her hair was damp, either from swimming or perspiration. 'Look at what I made for Matthew,' she said, proudly showing me a frozen-orange-juice can she had covered with beige yarn. 'I worked on it all week, every day in arts and crafts. Lisa finished her pencil holder in two days, but the yarn got hard 'cause she put too much glue on it. I only used a little glue, and I washed my hands first so the yarn wouldn't get dirty. I was very careful so Matthew would like it and stop being mad.'

'I'm sure he'll like it,' I said, trying to sound enthusiastic. 'It matches his carpet.'

'Can I give it to him now?' she asked excitedly. Without waiting for my reply, she raced up the stairs.

'Catherine,' I called, afraid that Matthew would reject her again.

I was too late. By the time I reached her, she was standing dejectedly in the hall. 'Matthew won't open his door,' she said. 'He won't let me give him his present.' Her lower lip quivered. She looked at me helplessly, then dropped the pencil holder and ran to her room, crying.

I picked up her gift and turned it around in my hands. She had taken a single strand of thick beige yarn and had painstakingly wound and butted it together to cover the can. I imagined her working on it, driven with her perfectionism, believing with a child's naive and unquestioning hope that her efforts would somehow put an end to the despair that was gripping us as tightly as the yarn was fixed to the pencil holder. The sound of her sobbing drifted into the hall. I stood in front of Matthew's door, thinking about the burden I had inadvertently allowed my daughter to carry, and the silence of the afternoon came crashing down on me. 'Open your door, Matthew,' I called, unable to fight it any longer. 'I want to talk to you about Daddy.'

Catherine came running out of her room. I dried her tears, then took her hand in mine; it was warm and trusting, but her face was pale with apprehension. 'It's all right,' I assured her as we watched Matthew's door open.

We sat on the floor, the three of us, in Matthew's bedroom. 'I want you to listen to me carefully,' I cautioned, 'and I'll try to explain how and why Daddy died.'

I had mentally rehearsed what I was going to tell them. I planned to say that you had had a big problem which you had tried very hard to solve. Then I was going to explain how you became sad when you couldn't solve the problem. I wasn't quite sure how I was going to connect your sadness with your suicide, but I thought I might say something like: 'Daddy felt so sad that he didn't realize what he was doing when he started the car without opening the garage door.' It wouldn't have been the unexpurgated truth, but it would have given you an honorable death. To Matthew and Catherine, you would have been a daddy who grew sad and died rather than a daddy who chose death as an escape.

But Matthew interrupted me almost immediately. 'D-D-D-D-Did you know that D-D-Daddy had a p-p-problem?' he asked.

His unexpected question disconcerted me, and like a child who stumbles in the beginning of a memorized speech, I was unable to recover. My uneasiness grew while the children waited expectantly for my reply. I began to

424

wonder how much Matthew actually knew. He was five years old when the real trouble started, too young, I reasoned, to be fully aware of what was happening. But then I remembered how quiet Matthew had become during that period, how he seemed to materialize out of nowhere when we least expected him, how we would turn and see him looking at us with solemn gray eyes, the gray eyes that were looking at me waiting for my answer. 'Yes,' I said with effort, 'I knew that Daddy had a problem.'

'What was the problem?' asked Catherine.

'Money,' I said reluctantly. 'The problem was that we didn't have enough money to live in our house anymore.'

'Were we poor like people on television?' she asked. 'The Waltons are poor.'

'No, not exactly,' I replied.

Matthew frowned. 'Th-Th-Th-Then why didn't w-w-we move? If-If-If we moved, I-I-I-I wouldn't have had to p-p-play with Adam Lynch. A-A-A-Adam was mean.'

'Yes, he was,' I agreed. 'I didn't like him either, but you don't move simply because you don't like someone; you just learn to avoid them. Besides, Daddy and I had worked very hard. It didn't seem right to give up, especially when there was a chance that we didn't have to move.'

The children inched closer, listening intently. 'Daddy and I found a business that we thought would help us make enough money to stay in our house,' I said. 'We felt that it was worth a try, and Daddy worked very hard putting it together.'

'How do you put a business together?' Catherine wanted to know.

'Y-Y-You buy a st-st-st-store and put things in it,' said Matthew impatiently.

'Sometimes,' I interrupted, 'not always. This wasn't that kind of business. Uncle Charlie helped Daddy set up a corporation to buy a motel. Then Daddy sold shares in the motel to people who wanted to invest in it.'

'What are shares?' the children asked in unison.

I instantly regretted mentioning shares. 'A share,' I said, struggling, 'is, is . . . a piece of paper which shows that you have bought an interest in something, that you own part of it.'

My explanation was inadequate, but I could see from the expression on Matthew's face that he understood. Then he asked the one question that I had hoped would remain unuttered. 'D-D-Did you help him s-sell the shares?'

'Yes,' I answered painfully, 'I helped him.'

'W-W-Who bought the s-shares?'

'People we knew in Eagles' Landing.'

'That's good,' said Catherine.

'No, it wasn't good,' I replied, suddenly sure of myself. 'Because Daddy knew the people, he wanted to make sure that their investment was safe. He began working very hard. He took trips to Florida to check on the motel and spent a lot of time with Uncle Charlie and other men trying to make it a success. It was as if Daddy had two jobs, his regular work and the motel.

'Daddy became very tired. He was working too hard. Also, the business wasn't going well. There weren't as many customers for the motel as Daddy had hoped there would be, so he worked even harder. But it didn't help. No matter how hard he tried, Daddy couldn't make the motel a success.

'Daddy began to worry. He became very sad and one night he went into the garage and started his car without opening the garage door. The fumes from the car had no place to go, so they stayed inside and killed him.'

The children sat quietly. I began to wonder if they had comprehended what I had told them when Matthew asked: 'D-D-Did Daddy know the g-garage door was c-c-closed?'

'He might have,' I answered gently, unable to tell him outright that you knew. 'Please understand. Daddy was tired. He was tired and worried and sad. Also, and most important, he was a proud man. The success of the business meant a great deal to him because his friends had

426

invested in it. They trusted your father, and he deserved that trust. It is harder for some people to live with problems than it is for others. It was hard for your father.'

'Does that mean some grownups have to die when they have a big problem?' asked Catherine.

I looked at the trusting faces of our children and realized with alarm that Matthew or Catherine could possibly contemplate suicide one day. Their lives could become difficult and strained as yours was, and in a moment of despair, they could choose death as a way out. I thought for a long time before I answered, and when I did, I selected each word with care. It seemed then, as it has since, that the well-being of our children was in jeopardy and that my response could either help or harm them.

'Human beings cannot live without having problems,' I said, 'and both of you will have problems. Some of your problems will be so small that you will hardly notice them. Other problems will be so great that you will think they are impossible to solve. And they may be impossible. Not every problem can be solved, but that isn't important. What is important is that you will be alive, and life is what matters. Every day you live is a promise. It means that you will have another chance, and that chance is what life is all about. So hang on to each day no matter what happens to you. Don't let go of your chances because you can never get them back.'

It was after seven o'clock when I went downstairs to prepare supper. The children were quiet while they ate, but they didn't appear to be disturbed. I began to wonder what they had imagined about your death and concluded with remorse that their thoughts must have been dreadful, for their acceptance of your suicide was almost easy, as if they had feared a truth far worse than what I had told them. They've suffered needlessly because of my cowardice, I thought. I promised myself that I would make it up to them, and by the time I turned off my bedroom light, I was convinced that the shadow of your suicide had finally passed over us.

I don't know how long Matthew was in my room before I became aware of him. He was sitting on the floor beside my bed when I awakened. A shaft of light from the hall illuminated his face, which was swollen from crying, and he was shivering in his thin cotton pajamas. 'What is it, Matthew?' I asked, glancing at the clock on my nightstand. It was one fifteen.

'D-D-D-D-Daddy,' he said through chattering teeth.

I got out of bed and touched his forehead and arms. His skin was ice cold. 'Get under the covers,' I said. Then I put my bathrobe on and sat next to him. 'What about Daddy?' I asked.

'D-D-D-Did you know that D-Daddy was sad?'

'Yes,' I admitted.

'Wh-Wh-Wh-Why did you l-l-let him st-st-start the car? Wh-Wh-Why didn't you t-t-turn it off?'

'I was sleeping.'

'Wh-Wh-Why?'

'It was after midnight.'

'Wh-Wh-Why wasn't D-D-D-Daddy sleeping, too?'

'Sometimes Daddy worked late.'

Matthew sat upright in bed. 'B-B-B-But you *knew* h-h-he was sad,' he stammered.

Although his statement was accusatory, his voice was pleading. I sensed that he wanted an explanation from me and didn't know how to reply. 'People can be sad,' I said, fumbling for an answer, 'without other people knowing how sad they really are.'

Matthew started to cry. 'I-I-I-I knew D-D-Daddy was sad,' he sobbed.

'How did you know?' I asked, putting my arms around him.

'S-S-S-Sometimes he didn't h-h-h-hear me when I-I-I-I was t-talking to him. S-S-S-Sometimes he d-d-didn't even know I-I was there.'

My heart lurched with the sudden understanding that

428

Matthew was blaming himself for your death. By withholding a portion of the truth, I had told him a lie; I had led him to believe that your death could have been an accident.

'Daddy knew the garage door was closed,' I whispered. 'He knew that it was closed when he started the car.'

'D-D-D-D-Did h-h-h-he w-w-w-want to-to d-d-die?'

'Yes,' I said, crying, 'he wanted to die.'

We clung to each other and wept.

Later, when I walked him back to his bedroom, Matthew asked: 'D-D-Did Daddy know about chances?'

'I think he forgot about them because he was so sad,' I replied anxiously. 'But he wouldn't want you to forget. Before he died, he made sure that I would be able to take care of you and Catherine. Maybe he was giving his chances to us.'

'I-I-I loved D-Daddy,' said Matthew, looking up at me with brimming eyes.

'I loved him, too,' I whispered, hugging my son.

I meant what I said to Matthew. I do believe that you gave us another chance, but unlike Harry Grubman, I don't expect the chance to come by running away. There is no point in living someone else's life, even if that life has been self-created. Harry will always be uneasy when he sees a face from the past; his life will be like a watercolor painting obscured under a cloudy glass. That's not for me. I'm no saint, but I can live with what I am.

Everyone has another chance, even my father at sixty-two. He was here several weeks ago on business and brought his wife-to-be along. We argued when he called because I didn't want to invite her for dinner. I said that it would confuse Matthew and Catherine, reminding him that Mother had just visited. 'You can't hide life from your children,' he replied angrily.

I relented and invited her. It was an uneasy evening. I didn't forewarn the children; my father had insisted upon giving them a slice of life, so he could be the one to section it for them. We had started eating our main course when

Catherine, who had been puzzled by the self-conscious woman, Eunice, asked her: 'You're not our aunt, are you?'

Eunice's olive skin flushed. 'No, I'm not,' she said quietly.

'Then why did you come to California with Grandpa?' Catherine pressed.

I almost felt sorry for Eunice. She covered her mouth with her napkin, and my father shot me a look for help. I excused myself and went into the kitchen. 'I think we need more sauce for the chicken,' I said, deciding that my father could handle the situation since he created it.

Apparently he informed the children that he and Eunice would be getting married. Later, Catherine wanted to know what her grandma would be if my father married another grandma. Sad, I thought, but I said: 'Grandma will always be your grandmother. Some things never change, and that is one of them.'

My father is happy. When I met him for lunch the next day, he talked about his plans animatedly. 'I'm a lucky man,' he said. 'I still have some time left to enjoy myself. Eunice is a wonderful woman, kind and thoughtful. You were gracious, but you didn't give her a chance. She was nothing more than a guest in your home, and she knew it.'

I had disappointed him. Eunice was pleasant enough in an ordinary way – she's a small-boned, dark-complexioned woman who has two teenage sons – but I couldn't welcome her. Nor did I excuse myself. My father had disappointed me so many times, especially after your death, that I didn't feel an apology was in order. I think he sensed this, for he said in that stumbling way he has: 'I wish you well, Jenny, and I hope that you will wish me well. I know I haven't always been the father you wanted me to be. I guess I was too busy or too preoccupied. *I was busy*, you know.' He winced, embarrassed by his rationalization, then continued with effort. 'Maybe I just didn't have it in me. But you are my daughter, and we can give that much to each other ... best wishes.'

I wanted to weep. I was sitting in a restaurant in California with my father, and he was telling me that all we could give each other at that point in our lives was best wishes, a Hallmark special. Perhaps he was right, but I was overwhelmed with regret. He was still my father, and I hardly knew him. Now I would never know him. We would have a greeting card relationship. It is one pain that Catherine will be spared.

Linda is coming to visit us tomorrow with her son. He is two years old, and his name is Richard. 'I named him Richard,' she said, 'because your Richard was so perfect. I used to dream about him when I was growing up. Oh, how I envied you, Jenny. You were pretty and popular and you had Richard. I wouldn't be surprised if half of my old friends from high school named their sons Richard, too. I was shocked when Mother told me that he had died.'

I know Linda even less than I know my father. We are sisters, but we were never friends. She isn't an unwed mother, as Mother had intimated. Linda was married to an architect. She divorced him before their son was born and is doing graduate work in anthropology on a fellowship. 'School was the thing I always did best,' she said. 'And as for anthropology, I suppose it was inevitable. Growing up in a home like ours, it was natural for me to gravitate toward the study of human relationships. You, more than anyone, should be able to understand that.'

I have been looking forward to seeing Linda, at times almost anxious. We grew up in the same house and know less about each other than people who work side by side in an office. I am anxious because I want us to be friends, to honestly like and care for each other as Deirdre and I do. That's a lot to expect from a stranger, even if she is your sister.

I get upset every time I think about Deirdre. She's getting married again, and I have this apprehensive feeling that she's making a mistake. 'Why?' I asked when she told me that she was going to marry her lawyer, Michael Flaherty. 'You were doing so well. You made the dean's list in school, and you have a court order against Ken. Your life has straightened out.'

'I'm not like you,' she said. 'I can't live alone anymore. For weeks after the rape, I would wake up crying in the middle of the night. It still happens sometimes. I needed someone, and I need someone now. So do the boys. They must have a single male figure to unite them or they'll grow up hating each other. Kerry resents Steve even more now that he knows he won't see Ken. I can't leave them alone together for more than two minutes. Mike is good with the boys, and Kerry doesn't pick on Steve when he's around.'

'But that isn't a reason to marry him,' I argued. 'You can get help for Kerry without marrying it.'

'I told you, Jenny, I'm not like you. I used to wonder how you managed to live alone, needing no one. I couldn't understand it then, and I still can't. Nor could I fathom how you managed to live unaided. If you were into a philosophy or belonged to a self-help group or something like that, it would have made sense, but you didn't even belong to the Automobile Association. You're a feminist in your thinking, but you're not what I would call a liberated woman, either. You're not that sure of yourself. If you were, you wouldn't allow your boss to run you around like an errand girl.

'What I'm trying to say, I guess, is that you are one of those women who have enough inner strength to be a loner, a single survivor. I just wasn't born with your strength. I need someone to talk to, not only about the big things, but about the little incidents that occur during the course of a day. Half the fun of living is being able to share your life with someone else. I've been living a half-life, and it has been hell for me.'

I felt ashamed, then. But how could I tell Deirdre that the strength she admired wasn't strength at all, that my very survival had depended upon a pen and paper, notes to a dead husband in the night? Yes, I was a survivor, but not the survivor Deirdre thought I was.

I told Deirdre that Nat Witton had asked me to marry him. Ordinarily I wouldn't have said anything. Discussing Nat's proposal with Deirdre was a betrayal of his trust – no one, man or woman, would want a private rejection known to an outsider – but I had hoped to persuade Deirdre to reconsider or at least postpone her decision for a while.

'Then you don't love him,' Deirdre concluded after I told her.

'I didn't say that. I suppose I do love Nat in a way. If I didn't, I wouldn't be seeing him again. Too much has happened. But that isn't the point. Nat and I don't want the same things. He wants a child.'

'Is that so terrible? Most men want to have their own children, and Matthew and Catherine are crazy about him.'

'I don't want to have another child. I'm going to be thirty-three next week. Having another child would mean postponing my life for six years. I certainly wouldn't want to have a baby within the first year of our marriage, and I don't want to wait until I'm forty before starting again.'

'Starting what?' Deirdre wanted to know. 'If the marriage works out, you won't have to start anything. You can fill your time with activities that please you. It wouldn't be a bad life, yet you make it sound awful.'

'For me, it would be awful. I wouldn't be happy. I need something of my own. I once lived through my husband's life. I made it my life, which was a great mistake, and when he died, it was as if I were still married to him. Even in California where he wasn't known, people would ask about him, about who he was and what he did.'

'But that's normal,' Deirdre argued. 'People will always be curious.'

'Yes,' I agreed, 'but if I marry Nat and it doesn't work out, there will be more questions and explanations. I could handle that, but I don't think I could handle the problems a third child would bring. I would have to begin again, and it would be harder. I would be older and responsible for three children instead of two. It's difficult not being able to share your days with someone, but for me, it's harder being a single parent. Think about it, Deirdre. What if you have a child with Michael Flaherty? You'll have three children by three separate fathers. What will you do if the marriage doesn't work?'

'It will have to work,' Deirdre said determinedly. 'I'll make it work. This one has a chance. We have common backgrounds. We're from large Irish families, and we're both lapsed Catholics. His father was a steelworker, too – Bethlehem, in Lackawanna, New York. Also, he's been divorced, so he understands the problems I've had. He wants to protect me, and I want that protection.'

Then, as if her argument weren't convincing enough, Deirdre added: 'Mike and I are into TM now. Our marriage can't fail. It's practically guaranteed.'

Well, I tried.

I don't really know how I feel about Nat. He is a point of confusion in my life. I don't love him, not as I once loved you, but I don't expect a love like that again. Nor would I want it. I couldn't live with a relationship as intense as ours was. I have grown up, Richard. I need more than a romance.

When I told Deirdre about Nat, I didn't tell her everything. Nat was aloof when I finally returned his call. His ego, which is as large as his frame, was bruised, but he was more interested in me than he had been before. I think I was the first woman in a long time who hadn't come running when Nat Witton called. Perhaps that is why he proposed; I still can't be sure.

'I'm tired of fooling around,' Nat said when we met later. 'I want to settle down and have a family. You know how I feel about Matthew and Catherine, and I'd like to have a child of my own. I'm forty-three, and it's time.'

'And I'm a convenient choice? You make it sound as if

434

I happened to arrive at a propitious moment in your life, as if I'm the millionth customer to walk through a door, which entitles me to a prize.'

'No,' he said earnestly, 'that's not it at all. I haven't enjoyed a woman since you. I guess sex has become too much of a sport, even for me. The variety that was once exciting has become meaningless. When I found myself thinking about you in other women's beds, I knew for certain that I was in love with you.'

'Did you go to bed with your friend, Victoria?' I asked, not quite believing him.

'It was a mistake,' he admitted uncomfortably. 'But I didn't go to bed with her the night you saw us together. I told you the truth.'

'When did you . . .'

'A few hours after you asked me to leave,' he interrupted. 'I was angry and went to Victoria's thinking that I'd justify your suspicion. It was stupid. She sensed it was an effort for me after we started. Victoria's sharp. It nearly destroyed our friendship.'

'Why did she agree to sex in the first place, if all you were to each other were friends?'

'Why not?' he shrugged, as if inviting a woman to bed weren't different from inviting her to dinner.

On a hunch, I asked Nat if he had been with anyone else while we were seeing each other. 'Once,' he said, 'while your mother was here. I had nothing else to do. Try to understand. I've lived this way for years. It's hard to change, but I'm ready.'

Nat is ready, but I am not. I don't trust him, not yet anyway, and we haven't built anything together except in bed. We haven't tried to develop common interests or make friends with other couples. A great share of the blame is mine because I've held back, and I don't have any friends my age, except Deirdre. But Nat does, and it bothered me that he never introduced me to his friends, as if I were someone he wanted to hide. When I told him, he explained. 'I knew you were probably wondering why. I wasn't ashamed of you. My feelings were and are quite the opposite. It was just that I have a ... a reputation, I guess you'd say. I didn't want you to hear a remark that would make you feel that you were nothing more than another one of Nat Witton's women. I knew you'd run, and you were too important to me.'

Nat's reputation is deserved. I don't know if his sexual prowess is the result of years of experience with a parade of women or if it is a natural ability, like that of a gifted athlete, but if there were an Olympics for lovers, Nat Witton would be a sure gold medal winner. He understands the female body almost as well as he understands his own; with Nat, sex is poetry. I was lucky to have had my first affair with him and will have no regrets, regardless of the outcome.

Nat was hurt and defensive when I didn't jump at his proposal. 'I don't want to pressure you, but this could be one of the best chances you'll ever have. You're a woman with young children; that turns a lot of men off. And you're in your thirties. You're still desirable, but you're not getting any younger.' Then he smiled apologetically to take some of the sting out of his words and added: 'I'm not a bad catch.'

I bristled. 'Getting married isn't the same as fishing,' I said. 'I wouldn't want to marry a man simply because he was a good catch. A large fish can spoil as easily as a small one can. I would never marry you if I sensed that you thought you were doing me a favor. I don't need to be rescued. And as for my chances, who knows what they will be? The most important thing I can do now is take my time so that neither one of us makes a mistake.'

I could marry Nat. I could have another child, too, although I don't want one. But there is another reason why I want to wait. If I marry him, it will mean living in California, and I don't belong here. I can't seem to relate with people who have one foot someplace else – in a new life or a new relationship or a new philosophy. In California, the self changes daily. It is enriched and re-enriched like Wonder Bread. I don't understand what the people here are looking for. Perhaps I'm missing something, but after all I have been through, I have learned that nothing happens beyond what actually happens, that there are no deeper truths beyond the truth, that there is no self beyond the self.

I tried to explain this to Nat, but the very things that disturb me about California attract him. 'There is something new happening every day,' he said. 'It fascinates me. And I'm happy with my job. It would be difficult to find another one as exciting. There is no place like California.'

He's right. There is no place like California. Even Mother would agree. When she discovered that the ladies' rooms have disposable paper toilet seat covers, she was overjoyed. 'California is the only place I've found with sanitary public facilities,' she exclaimed ecstatically. 'It's a splendid idea.'

I can't live in a place simply because it has clean toilet seats.

I have come to realize that much of life is simply a matter of timing, that the decisions we make are frequently governed more by chance than by forethought. We once believed unquestioningly that we were meant for each other because the timing of our lives was perfectly synchronized. It was our first and greatest mistake. If Nat had asked me to marry him before Mother's visit, I would have responded with an unequivocal yes. Marrying him would have assured me a new life; it would have eliminated the oppressive loneliness of the past two years and most, if not all, of the children's how-and-why-did-Daddy-die questions. They would have been too busy with their new daddy to dwell upon their dead daddy. I would have been safe.

I'm not opting for safety anymore. For the first time in my life, I feel confident and responsible. I'm no longer afraid to make decisions and have been toying with the idea of moving to Boston. Like Mrs Feltcher, I have begun to miss the seasons, especially the winter I used to despise. There is something about the cold that clears the mind and sharpens the senses; it gives one the will to be strong, to endure and survive the wait for spring. I don't know why I'm thinking of Boston, unless it is because I'm familiar with the streets from my college days. With my sense of direction, I'll need all the help I can get. And there will be some compensation in a move to Boston. I may be losing paper toilet seat covers, but I'll be escaping from the freeways. Squatting over a dirty toilet inhibits one's plumbing, but the alternative, possible death in a chain-reaction freeway accident, is far worse.

I won't move until Matthew and Catherine have finished another year of school, and I won't move at all unless I am positive that it will be permanent. I want to have roots again, Richard. I want to belong to a place, to be able to identify with it, and I want the children to know that sense of belonging. Nat thinks we can find it here. He's persuasive, and he's courting me earnestly. We see each other several times a week. However, the children aren't included, at my insistence. I wouldn't want to marry Nat because he became too important to them; nor would I want him to marry me out of a feeling of obligation. Nat says he plans to wear me down with patience. We'll see.

I am starting school in September as I promised Simon I would. There were two courses scheduled at convenient times: *Death and Dying* and *Topics in Gerontology: Images of Aging*. I enrolled in *Topics in Gerontology*, for I have had a private course in death and could not take another.

I am also learning about dying, not textbook dying, but the real letting go of life, one string at a time. Mr Gallisdorf has had another stroke. He can no longer hold his history books or clip his mustache or sit erect in his wheelchair. An aide wheels him into the solarium every day, where he sits in the sun, listing toward his weak side like a sailboat bowing in obedience to a strong wind. I sit with him as often as I can, sometimes reading aloud, other times just

438

holding his hand. Occasionally, we talk. 'Try to live a life you can acknowledge, Jenny,' he said haltingly on one of his stronger days. 'I hope it doesn't happen to you, but the time may come when you will find yourself living in your skull as I am. There isn't as much room in there as you may think. The past has a way of taking up space whether you want it to or not. It can get damned uncomfortable if your memories are painful, for there is no place for the pain to go. It just settles in and eats away at what is left of you.'

I squeezed his hand. Then Mr Gallisdorf and I turned our faces upward toward the noonday sun, both of us crying silently.

That night I began writing to you for the last time. It has taken me better than a week to finish. There were moments when I simply stared into space, remembering how it was with us. Other times I couldn't see the paper through my tears. I rocked with the pain of guilt and loss and put my pen down, thinking that it was insane to continue, but still I pressed on. Somehow it seemed necessary, although I didn't understand why until now. You saved me three times, Richard: as a teenager, in Eagles' Landing, and again in California. You gave me the best and worst days I have ever known. You were owed a final acknowledgment.

A selection of bestsellers from SPHERE

FICTION

CHAMELEON	William Diehl	£2.25 ☐
THE CAMBODIA FILE	J. Anderson &	
	B. Pronzini	£2.25 ☐
TRANCE	Derek Lambert	£1.75 ☐
THE STONE FLOWER	Alan Scholefield	£1.95 ☐
TWIN CONNECTIONS	Justine Valenti	£1.75 ☐

FILM & TV TIE-INS

E.T. THE EXTRA-TERRESTRIAL	William Kotzwinkle	£1.50 ☐
THE IRISH R.M.	E. E. Somerville & M. Ross	£1.95 ☐
THE GENTLE TOUCH	Terence Feely	£1.50 ☐
THE PROFESSIONALS:		
OPERATION SUSIE &	Ken Blake	£1.25 ☐
YOU'LL BE ALL RIGHT	Ken Blake	£1.25 ☐

NON-FICTION

THE NUCLEAR BARONS	P. Pringle & J. Spigelman	£3.50 ☐
THE HEALTH & FITNESS		
HANDBOOK	Ed. Miriam Polunin	£5.95 ☐
NELLA LAST'S WAR	Nella Last	£1.95 ☐
ONE CHILD	Torey L. Hayden	£1.75 ☐

All Sphere books are available at your local bookshop or newsagent, or can be ordered direct from the publisher. Just tick the titles you want and fill in the form below.

Name _____

Address _____

_____

Write to Sphere Books, Cash Sales Department, P.O. Box 11, Falmouth, Cornwall TR10 9EN

Please enclose a cheque or postal order to the value of the cover price plus:

UK: 45p for the first book, 20p for the second book and 14p for each additional book ordered to a maximum charge of £1.63.

OVERSEAS: 75p for the first book plus 21p per copy for each additional book.

BFPO & EIRE: 45p for the first book, 20p for the second book plus 14p per copy for the next 7 books, thereafter 8p per book.

Sphere Books reserve the right to show new retail prices on covers which may differ from those previously advertised in the text or elsewhere, and to increase postal rates in accordance with the PO.